EXPANDING PROFESSIONAL SERVICES
A Manager's Guide
to a Diversified Business

EXPANDING PROFESSIONAL SERVICES
A Manager's Guide
to a Diversified Business

Larry E. Kuhlken

BUSINESS ONE IRWIN
Homewood, Illinois 60430

This publication is designed to provide accurate and authoritative information in regard to the subject matter covered. It is sold with the understanding that neither the author nor the publisher is engaged in rendering legal, accounting, or other professional service. If legal advice or other expert assistance is required, the services of a competent professional person should be sought.

From a Declaration of Principles jointly adopted by a Committee of the American Bar Association and a Committee of Publishers.

Sponsoring editor: Cynthia A. Zigmund
Project editor: Jane Lightell
Production manager: Ann Cassady
Designer: Larry J. Cope
Compositor: The Wheetley Company, Inc.
Typeface: 10/12 Times Roman
Printer: Book Press, Inc.

Library of Congress Cataloging-in-Publication Data

Kuhlken, Larry E.
   Expanding professional services: a manager's guide to a
diversified business / Larry E. Kuhlken.
      p. cm.
   Includes index.
   ISBN 1-55623-784 -7
   1. Professions—marketing. 2. Consultants—Marketing. 3. Service
Industries—Management. I. Title
HD8038.A1K84 1993
658.8—dc20

92–23793

Printed in the United States of America
1 2 3 4 5 6 7 8 9 0 BP 9 8 7 6 5 4 3 2

This book is dedicated to Jeanine,
Julie, and David.

Preface

This book describes the business and financial management of a large professional services office. It is written for the office manager in a major firm and, of course, all who aspire to that responsibility. Although I use illustrations from computer technology consulting, readers of the book agree that the techniques presented apply to all people services businesses, including law, management consulting, architecture, and engineering.

Expanding Professional Services takes the local office manager's view and is written specifically for:

- All managers who face the challenge of expanding services while maintaining profits.

- Project managers who need to understand the financial attributes of their engagements.

- Planners and strategists within professional services firms (and the parent companies of these firms), who want a wider understanding of the field operations of their business.

The book contains both basic and advanced material on each of the business management facets of professional services. Those of you with experience will find the book to be a useful reference and may find techniques that you may not have considered. The person less experienced in management will find the book to be a comprehensive source on topics related to professional services business management.

I offer the business principles and procedures in this book as a formula for success to those firms that have grown beyond their core services. Growth has brought complexity and increased cost to professional services. Business practices that are successful for a profitable, hourly rate business become inadequate, when rock climbing through fixed-price and systems integration engagements. The book focuses on knowing how and when to vary the cost of the measurement process in balance with higher risk and equal rewards.

Expanding Professional Services is complementary to the many works that focus on consulting methods, project management practices, and professional services marketing. The book assumes that readers are generally knowledgeable in those subjects and wish to expand their horizons in the profit management responsibilities of the business. I made a studious endeavor to avoid rehashing the basics of professional services marketing that is well documented in numerous texts, four of which are referenced.

Expanding Professional Services begins with the basic management principles that span all management actions in the professional services business.

- Maximize placement of consultants.
- Maximize client satisfaction.
- Manage each engagement for follow-on.
- Hire people who are marketable.
- Manage for profit today.
- Manage marketing as an investment.

These six principles are examined in terms of the controls and measurements needed to grow revenue and maintain profitability. The book addresses each measurement process as a layered presentation from simple to complex, focusing first on those elements that are essential and proceeding on to those demanded by complexity and high risk. Each chapter introduces the basics, then proceeds to more advanced techniques that can be introduced into the management of a professional services office.

The book stresses the importance of managing communication. The products of the consulting process are ideas and know-how. A firm cannot afford the cost and embarrassment of their loss or duplication. A full chapter is devoted to the challenge of channeling information among highly creative and loosely managed professionals. The techniques presented are proven and provide a balance between strangling administrivia (as perceived by the consultant) and uncontrolled loose cannons (as perceived by the manager).

I examine the management principles of professional services in terms of five measurements.

- Revenue, including market segmentation and territory compensation.
- Utilization, including labor distribution and availability tracking.
- Profit, including expense control.
- Backlog, including sales tracking.
- Productivity, including engagement profitability.

I expect experienced managers who practice all of these today to debate technique, and invite you to tune your measurement process where it makes sense. To those who practice less than all of these techniques, I offer a package that is proven and can prevent complexity from diverting order into chaos.

Examples of techniques that the experienced manager may find helpful are:

- Methods to combine revenue per year with utilization to assess resource performance on fixed-price engagements.

- Matching resource and vendor cost against revenue contribution to compute engagement profitability.

- Alternatives for sharing revenue across offices for borrowed resouces.

- Computing backlog on systems integration and other combined consultant and vendor delivered services.

Because the book presents each of the five professional services measurements from simple to complex, project managers, new consulting services managers, and experienced consultants contemplating management can learn to practice each at a pace that is consistent with the size and complexity of their current engagements. Project managers, in particular, can learn better to judge the effect of satisfying a client on overall profitabiltiy.

Guidance to those less experienced in the full range of professional services business measurements includes:

- Information needed to measure revenue contribution of each consultant as an elemement of performance evaluation.

- Computation of the relative cost of consultants and subcontractors in deciding which to use.

- A description of the data, business processes, and information systems that support the management of a professional services office.

- Simple approaches to forecasting revenue and expense based on current performance and backlog.

I draw on 20 years of direct experience in marketing and managing consulting and systems integration services. Through interviews and close working relationships, I have added the views of many others in the business. Thus, the business management techniques in this book are derived from the experiences of managers on the front line. These techniques evolved by trial and error as complex professional services emerged within major corporate enterprises. The principles and processes described in the book have survived a multitude of organization strategies and corporate cultures. The practitioners among current field executives are as varied as the core businesses of the enterprises to which they reprort.

Expanding Professional Services presents techniques you can use today; and it contains others that you will defer until they are demended by complexity. This is a book that should be kept in a readily available place by the manager who knows that the professional services business has only one constant— change.

Larry E. Kuhlken

Acknowledgments

I thank all those who helped bring this book into being. To my editor Cindy Zigmund. To Ray Herndon of the *Los Angeles Times*, for the advice and assistance of a pro. To Marty Berkman of Berkman Associates, Jim Ehinger of Jennings, Strouss & Salmon, Brian Griffin of IBM, Gary Van Der Linden of Ernst & Young (and Cap Gemini America), and Ed Zebrowski of Ernst & Young for reading the book and providing their valuable feedback. To Alec Vlahos for the names. To all who invented the business this book is about: Don, Russ, Mike, Cathie, Al, Ed, John, Jon, Joe, Beatrice, Dick, August, Bil, Dave, Mark, Dale, Duane, Dallas, Gale, and Bob. To David for help with the figures. And most especially to Jeanine, who gave both her time and devotion to this project.

Contents

Chapter 1

Professional Services: Growing Out of Control

There seems to be little doubt that the professional services business is booming. Overall, annual revenues are in the tens of billions and compound growth rates are over 20 percent, even taking into account the recession periods that have opened the last three decades. Most of this phenomenal growth comes from all kinds of businesses choosing to expand well beyond their core businesses of the 1970s and earlier, and move into widely diverse offerings of people for fee. The challenge for many of these businesses, however, has been to increase profit at a pace with revenue.

The professional services industry is unique in the variety of individual enterprises that makes up its firms. It is comprised of thousands of business units, encompassing every legal entity and ranging from staffs of one person to thousands of people. The common denominator is that these units provide professional people who assist businesses, governments, and institutions for fees ranging from $200 per day to more than $2,000 per day.

The diversity of this industry reflects the variety of professional skills that the age of technology has created. Professional services, as a business, is very simple in concept: someone (a client) decides that it is less risky and/or more profitable to use an outsider rather than an insider for a purpose requiring a professional skill. To meet this demand, someone forms an enterprise to make this skill available to clients, and a fee is charged based on what the market will bear. There are now dozens of professional skills and thousands of these enterprises.

The common designation for these enterprises is **firm**, which we will use throughout the book, regardless of legal structure. Our focus will be on the management tasks needed to consistently make profit for a professional services office and the overall firm. Most firms are small, do only one kind of service, offer one kind of contract, and perform very basic business administration. At the other end are a few very large firms, with very large offices and diversity, where substantial time, tools, and knowledge are applied to administration. The practical balance between the cost and benefits of business administration and its effect on profits is the subject of this book.

SIZE: ONLY ONE PART OF GROWTH

The business and financial management needed for professional services is directly related to how a firm has chosen to grow. As will be discussed throughout this book, doing a lot of the same thing with more and more people does not necessarily strain a management system. Doing different things, regardless of the number of people, is the ground from which complexity grows.

Every office in every firm must practice basic financial management tasks of billing clients, paying bills, payroll, and tax reporting. Upon adding a few more employees, the office begins to trouble itself with controlling the utilization of its people resources. As soon as one of these offices chooses to diversify into mixed terms and conditions in its contracts (i.e., per hour and fixed price) and to offer multiple services (i.e., consulting and classroom education), the amount of time and energy needed to stay in control starts to grow rapidly. When control is lost, making profit becomes equivalent to buying a lottery ticket.

Firms in the professional services industry tend to fall into three broad categories.

- Small sole proprietorships, partnerships, and corporations of up to 20 people that do not intend being big national or international players in their marketplace. They are content to stay in their skill niche or geography and, as a group, represent well over 90 percent of the firms. They are the backbone of the industry.

- Partnerships and corporations of all sizes that have or plan to have a major presence nationally or beyond and offer a variety of client services. These are the small firms that aspire to greatness, and those consulting, engineering, accounting, architecture, law, and other professional people services businesses that have a major presence in their market.

- Operating units of national and international corporations that provide independent people services in addition to their core products. By their very nature these firms plan to grow their people services business at least as rapidly as their product businesses. These are predominantly insurance, financial services, aerospace, computer equipment, computer software, and telecommunications companies.

People who start any of these professional services businesses are entrepreneurs and visionaries, particularly those who found a market for their own unique professional skills or convinced a major corporation to try a new business. They typically started with a small group of clients with a common business problem. Their initial success got them more clients, so they hired more people with like skills.

All these people have learned that on a small scale, the professional services business requires little investment, has a low operating overhead, and can be very profitable. At some point every successful business reaches a decision point: stop growing, continue to grow cautiously doing the same things, or try to grow exponentially. The decision is precipitated by internal pressures to have more and more of this wonderful profit and the welcome discovery that the market for professional skills just seems to go on forever.

The vast majority of firms can grow but don't, because they see growth as a threat to their freedom as entrepreneurs (and rightly so). Most remain in the first category and are blessed with a fairly simple business to administer (despite the determined efforts on the part of governments to make business taxation equivalent to nuclear science).

Some decide to grow by carefully opening offices in other cities and being very narrow in the variety of services offered. Their success comes from filling a strong niche with consistently good people and avoiding price competition. Growth is slow, but many of the firms in the second category have arrived nationally and internationally through 50 years of steady growth in a niche. Most have preserved simplicity in their business operations by organizing as a confederation of separate small businesses, each doing much the same thing in the same way under the same logo. Business management and administration in the offices of these firms is a model for the basic financial measurements of the professional services business.

The other major professional services firms in the second category and all of the large units that make up the corporate spin-off group were not nearly as patient as the slow growth group. These started with plans of 500 or more people as their minimum goal and expected very quickly to exceed $100 million in revenues. The survivors are well on their way. For the most part, they have chosen a broad line of service offerings and contractual terms and conditions in order to be in a variety of markets. Their success has drawn many of the more traditional firms into the same arena. From this has emerged a group of 20 to 30 very large firms that have set the example for any firm considering an expansion into the big time.

In an article titled "The Ever-Bigger Boom in Consulting," Anne B. Fisher discusses how the traditional management consulting firms of McKinsey & Co. and Booz, Allen & Hamilton (along with others in more than 24 big-name firms) are dealing with the competition from Andersen Consulting (nee Arthur Andersen) and IBM.[1] At that time, these firms were faced with moving into the very complex service of systems integration—a marketplace that continues to grow at better than 30 percent per year.

Systems integration means multimillion dollar engagement opportunities. It also means very high risk. As we will discuss later, systems integration is a complex service involving multiple parties and financial relationships. The client expects to pay the professional services firm a high price to accept the risks. It is up to the professional services firm to take advantage of the opportunity and execute the work in a manner that brings the desired profits. Too often this is not the case, and large firms are finding that one of the consequences of expanded services is a dilution of profits.

The successful firms, though, have achieved growth in both revenues and profits. They have been successful because they have learned to change their business controls to meet the complexity of their service offerings. Although the need for this seems self-evident, many businesses avoid the added administration necessary to control the added complexity. This comes from a conscious effort to avoid increased overhead and an unconscious desire to preserve existing practices and avoid change. Many of these firms have literally grown out of control and into bankruptcy.

Every professional services office manages its people, delivers its services, sells to its clients, and administers business controls. The trick is to balance the amount of time and paperwork that each requires based on the changing degree of complexity in client engagements. The successful firm can vary its levels of administration and its overhead depending on its current business diversity.

EVOLUTION OF DIVERSITY

There are many ways to define the different services in the professional services. Each list reflects its author's view of market discrimination, logical groupings of skills, and geography. The distinct services discussed in this book and shown in Figure 1-1 are designed to characterize progressively more diverse and complex contract terms, contract conditions, and work products. This definition of services will be used to illustrate the demand each level of business mix has on correspondingly more complex controls and measurements.

Each of these three groupings of services has unique administrative and accounting needs. All of the business controls for the basic people services are

---

[1]Anne B. Fisher, "The Ever-Bigger Boom in Consulting," *Fortune*, April 24, 1989, p. 113.

FIGURE 1-1
Services Offered by Professional Services Firms

> **Professional Services**
>
> *Basic People Services*
> Consulting
> Education
>
> *Complex People Services*
> Custom development
> Product installation
>
> *People and Nonlabor Services*
> Product support
> Systems integration

also necessary for complex people services; so are the complex people services controls needed when moving to the people and nonlabor services mix. The additional controls that come with nonlabor services are bureaucratic and unjustifiably expensive, if applied to basic people services.

An office of a major firm will see wide swings in the relative mix of these six services. These swings come about as client demands change and projects begin and end. It is important to understand how to layer these controls in such a way that they can be added or subtracted as the business mix for an office changes.

The six services came into existence in the order in which they are listed. They evolved through a market demand fueled by increasing technology and a desire to further utilize already available professional people. Their history describes the market they have come to satisfy and gives a clue as to how their control might be layered. Following this history lesson we will look at how the national professional services firm is now structured to offer all six services in their infinite diversity.

Every business has a vocabulary that can be ambiguous when used outside of its industry. As a general rule, consultants work very hard to avoid jargon, simply because their business is to be intimately involved in everyone else's business. Even so, some definitions are necessary, and terms used extensively will be defined at their first occurrence.

IN THE BEGINNING: CONSULTING AND EDUCATION

Consultants have existed since humans organized. There has always been a market for valuable ideas and advice. It is not surprising that the 20th century growth in the number and variety of business enterprises has also brought growth in the number of consultants. An excellent essay on the definition and history of consulting was written by Joseph W. Wilkinson titled, "What Is Management Consulting?" Wilkinson traces consulting as a business from its origins at the beginning of this century. By the late 1960s, it had grown to hundreds of firms and had become a separately recognized American industry segment, offering assistance in personnel, marketing, finance, procurement, research and development, packaging, administration, and litigation support.[2]

Early on, consulting firms saw the need for segmenting their consulting and education services into separate financial groupings. Client training was a common use of consultant skill and an engagement usually ended with a class. When the same classes were performed repeatedly, it became mutually beneficial to both parties for the charge to be a fixed price per class. In addition, pricing for education had to consider the recovery of unique expenses such as proprietary materials and teaching facilities, which commanded their own profitability requirements. Because income was different and costs were also different, it was a short step to keeping separate books.

Since the education business competed with the consulting business for the same people resources, while at the same time complementing mainstream consulting services by demonstrating professional expertise, firms had to find new ways to ensure that both businesses prospered. Prosperity meant that available people were used to the maximum, with a minimum of confusion among multiple assignments. This led to utilization management and a professional skills inventory as a fundamental management practice.

Utilization views people as income-producing inventory and measures the percentage of their available time that derives revenue. "Utilized" consultants are those that are devoted to income-producing activities to the maximum of their personal and professional availability. We will see in Chapter 5 that a number of activities get in the way of maximizing utilization, including vacations, education, sickness, administration, and marketing.

Utilization management includes the inventory of professional skills for each consultant. Management uses a combination of utilization reporting and skills inventory in determining assignments and decisions regarding hiring and training.

Software: The Professional Services Explosion

An intense demand for computer software caused the consulting business to undergo a dramatic change in the early 1970s. When things settled, significant

---

[2]Joseph W. Wilkinson, "What Is Management Consulting?" in *Handbook of Management Consulting Services*, eds. Sam W. Barcus, III, and Joseph W. Wilkinson (New York: McGraw-Hill, Inc., 1986).

additions had been made to the services offered by many traditional consulting firms, and a large set of new services providers had emerged. These new offerings included custom development (particularly software), systems product support services, and systems facility management. These new services brought major diversity in contracting and relationships and the business and financial administration of firms had to take on a whole new scope.

The change was triggered by a combination of technology and the sudden availability of large numbers of professionals. The technology was in computers and, more importantly, computer software. The people came from the withdrawal of funds from America's space program. In the next 15 years, the simple combination of consulting and education services offered at daily rates or low-risk firm fixed price was to explode into a vast array of packaged services and complex relationships. The result was consulting's transformation into the professional services industry.

The process began with the emergence of the business computer as an accepted part of an organization's operating assets. In the late 1960s the computer came out of the financial closet. Banks and insurance companies had already discovered that computers not only saved money, but were competitive weapons. Manufacturing companies observed the incredible leaps in technology during the Apollo space project and saw great opportunities in productivity. The travel industries woke up to the competitive advantages that had been grabbed up by American Airlines, Holiday Inn, and others who pioneered on-line reservations.

More and more, consultants found themselves dealing with the issues of investment, timing, and process for computerization of a client. Consulting firms became students of the selection process for computers and a number of firms became specialists in the planning and organizing needed for computerization.

Additionally, programming was the new skill in great demand and application programming, in particular, was not yet taught in universities. For a variety of reasons (some of which are historically valid, while most are not), business and government enterprises chose to build their own unique applications, rather than share between themselves. This institutional desire to reinvent wheels served to create an even greater demand for programmers. A measure of the demand for programming consultants is reflected in the sixfold increase in the average daily rate for these professionals in the years from 1970 to 1978. Firms quickly added this skill to their inventory.

In 1970, the U.S. government decided to get out of the space business. At its end, some key American businesses found themselves with an excess of professionals in a wide variety of job descriptions. When the space funding torrent slowed to a trickle, these companies decided to see if services offered to NASA could be marketed to commercial clients. Most notable were IBM, McDonnell

Douglas, Boeing, and Martin Marrieta. These companies saw the explosion of application software demand as an opportunity to make profitable use of the people resources no longer paid for by the government.

IBM, for example, put 500 consultants into a nationwide unit and turned them loose on its commercial computer customers. Ten years later this combined custom software and computer system consulting business was one of the most profitable in the IBM Corporation. McDonnell Douglas formed its McAuto subsidiary and built or bought specialized software and consulting services in such diverse application areas as manufacturing and hospitals. Boeing Computer Services became a major player in the remote computing service business, which combines on-site consultants with leased computing.

The government had by now institutionalized the practice of contracting for intellectual work products. Up to that point, typical products of a government contract were physical, such as equipment, buildings, roads, and bridges. Paper deliverables were merely ancillary descriptions of how to fix and how to use. By the end of the 1960s, a large portion of work product (cynics might say the largest) delivered under government contracts was on paper. Hidden behind all this paper were reels of electronic media. Companies learned that producing these stacks of paper and computer tape was a large, lucrative business, but it required project management process and discipline no less formidable than those previously needed to build buildings and ships.

No longer could a single contract cover the extensive terms, conditions, charges, relationships, and work products of these multiphase projects. The term now used for the total relationship between a firm and a client became **engagement**. It involved multiple legal agreements (**contracts**) over an extended period. An engagement became a relationship with a specific business end objective, limited only by time and ultimate expenditure. The same cynics as mentioned previously would say that the true extent of engagements with the government can only be viewed in hindsight.

Concurrent with the new entrants came a decision by traditional auditing and accounting firms to expand into the custom development business. The accounting consulting business was a well-established segment among the major consulting firms. A subset of these firms, most notably Arthur Andersen, came to realize that a vast percentage of their recommendations for improvement in business controls involved recommendations for computerization and, of course, software acquisition or development. It was a small step for these same professionals to suggest that the accounting firm was a qualified resource for the design and implementation of these business improvements.

The remaining accounting firms saw what was happening and jumped in. Within five years, all accounting firms had entered the computer consulting marketplace, or had consciously decided to stay out. By 1980, Arthur Andersen (now Andersen Consulting) had established itself as the largest generalized consulting firm in American business.

A price paid by all who took on custom development was the inadequacy of administration and controls that had existed for basic people services. This business required highly disciplined project controls and new approaches in backlog management, revenue and cost productivity analysis, complex new rate structures, and a conversion of utilization from daily to hourly. Many found these changes to be very agonizing. The new entrants started from scratch or attempted to adapt their existing manufacturing and distribution systems and procedures.

Nonlabor Services: Software Product Support

By the late 1970s, the demand for programmers and the corresponding cost in salaries and consultant fees forced businesses to reconsider the luxury of building their own unique software applications. Preprogrammed software was becoming generally available. Most of these packages could be delivered, customized, and installed in less than a year.

The new professional services firms quickly aligned themselves with software packages that needed substantial customizing. Most packages could be implemented for a service fee of a few thousand dollars and these became the bread and butter of a number of firms. Some, notably the Hogan Systems retail banking software, offered an experienced firm such as Andersen and, later IBM, the opportunity to perform over $1 million in installation services for large clients.

By 1976, the courts had resolved that software was intellectual property covered by copyright laws. The new professional services firms were particularly experienced in the ownership and transfer of rights for intellectual property. These firms recognized that they could increase their markets by being the only source of customizing services for high demand software. Quickly, firms began to acquire the rights to popular software components. A common method was to retain the rights of custom software written for one client and then to market the software and customization to others. The wider the industry scope of the firm, the wider the variety of software being offered.

Now these traditionally people firms were seeing large blocks of income and corresponding cost from nonlabor components. In effect, these firms found themselves needing to control these two income streams separately to ensure each brought its corresponding share of the profits.

Of course, everything comes around that goes around. A sizable number of new software businesses emerged during this period. Many of these formed professional services units in support of their product. As the margins from the software began to deteriorate, the consulting often grew to be a predominant source of profits. Many of these were bought out by other growing firms that also obtained rights to the software in the process. Some of these now count in the top 30 professional services firms.

Systems Integration

It was inevitable that the growth in computer technologies would bring hundreds of vendors into the business. The number of combinations of hardware, software, communication networks, and support services facing a business enterprise are staggering. The probability that all components chosen come from a single vendor are slim to none.

The effort to bring multivendor system components together into a cohesive set of controllable processes has become a high-risk proposition for most businesses and governments. The professional services firms with substantial experience in custom software development, product installation, and software product support services were perfectly positioned to step in with an offer to share the risk for a sizable fee.

Typically, the professional services firm is under contract to design the total system, implement software jointly with the client and coordinate the delivery, installation, and testing of multiple equipment and software components. The personnel involved are those of the client and firm, supplemented by subcontractors and vendor personnel. In many cases the services firm contracts for a number of related services including the planning and reorganizing of a client's business processes resulting from the new systems. Extensive custom education programs are often a by-product of a systems integration engagement.

A firm that had already mastered the administration of both labor and nonlabor generated revenue saw those controls put to good use when it took on systems integration. A typical systems integration set of contracts will often have an equal amount of people versus vendor and product income and expense. The profitability expectations of the two are vastly different, however, and must be treated separately when analyzing financial success or failure.

Obviously, a firm must be prepared to embrace a wide range of skills and disciplines to be competent to offer systems integration. A typical project involves the following skills.

1. *Business/administrative process strategy and design.* The client typically requires significant change to its information, decision, and process controls. The systems integrator provides the consulting work products of methods analysis, strategic plan, process design, and systems requirements.

2. *Systems and procedures design and test strategy.* The integration process itself requires substantial technical design for interfaces to be customized and unique software to be developed. The client requires process description for its

user and management personnel to participate in design approval and acceptance planning. The systems integrator typically provides external systems documentation, often using software engineering tools.

3. *Project management.* The key responsibility of the systems integrator is coordinating the combined efforts of all vendors and the client. In addition to the intellectual effort to lead the multiple parties, the firm typically provides a wide variety of management planning, tracking, and assessment work products.

4. *Packaged software.* The systems integrator customizes and installs systems and application software, either directly through its own personnel or through the subcontracted efforts of other vendors.

5. *Customized software.* The systems integrator develops, tests, and installs software built specifically for this client using firm, client, and subcontractor personnel.

6. *Computer equipment and networks.* The systems integrator installs and tests vendor-supplied computer systems.

7. *Facility construction.* The systems integrator coordinates the teardown, construction, and occupancy of physical facilities customized to support the new computing and workstation environment. This often includes the moving of equipment and people from other locations.

8. *Education.* The systems integrator coordinates the delivery of training to educate the project personnel in the processes and technologies to be designed and implemented. Additionally the client management and user staff are educated in preparation for assuming ownership and control at project completion.

9. *Technical support.* The systems integrator often contracts for time and materials assistance to the client following the implementation of each phase of the project. This may include acting as a prime contractor to the various vendor personnel.

According to the June 3, 1991, issue of *CSN Top 50*, all major mainframe computer, aerospace, and telephone companies now offer systems integration services. They are joined by four accounting firms and Booz, Allen & Hamilton of the major management consulting firms. In addition GM/EDS and a number of others have come to the business through computer software and related services. The top three, IBM, Andersen Consulting, and EDS each have over 5,000 people assigned worldwide. It is a major part of their professional services capacity.

PROFESSIONAL SERVICES IN THE 90s

The high growth companies of the professional services industry have sorted into a few very large firms that offer systems integration and custom development, but not consulting; a smaller group of very large firms that offer only management consulting and education; and an even smaller group of large firms that offer everything. The full-service firms are just that—they offer any of the consulting and technology assistance services of the specialty and sole proprietorships, and they offer a wide range of software, systems integration, software support services, and education.

For the full-service firm, the days of daily rate or low-risk fixed price as the only relationship with a client are long gone. Contracts have become complex instruments of estimated or guaranteed numbers of hours at tiered rates per hour depending on the intended skill levels of the people to be assigned. In some cases these are expressed and billed as separate rates for each person on an effort, while on others the tier of rates is consolidated into a single weighted rate for all consultants and subcontractors that work the effort.

As we will see later, the full-service firms have learned that their management systems had to change as their businesses expanded. In the past they measured the growth and profitability of one or three independent service offerings with no more than one or two price options. Now they have typically eight to ten services that can be offered independently or in combinations with multiple pricing options for each.

The surviving firms have learned another valuable lesson during their evolution and growth. Complexity and its trade-offs cannot be managed from headquarters. The day of the entrepreneur is not gone from professional services and, in fact, is a critical success factor to making profit when complexity creates so many choices.

The successful firms are those that are willing and so structured to delegate maximum authority and accountability to their field executives. As we will see in later chapters, the first instincts and priorities are to the people and clients. The degree of control and the risks to be taken are determined daily from being in touch at the field office level. Qualified field executives who are empowered to hire, negotiate terms and conditions, and regulate levels of business administration will be the profit makers in the full-service firm.

Structure of a National Firm

The structural character of a national professional services firm is the reflection of its evolution and the relationship it has with its parent corporation. There are some consistencies worth commenting on, and they will help in understanding the business processes of field offices that will be discussed in later chapters.

The organization strategy that has existed from the earliest days of consulting is to place consultants as physically close to their clients as is practical. The typical pre-1970 firm was organized very similar to personal service legal and accounting firms with one or more partners, associates, paraprofessionals, and administrative staff. If it was a national firm, the headquarters office contained one or more senior partners who had overall executive and financial responsibility for the business, similar to any other CEO and CFO responsibility. In general, though, the senior partners left the local partners to themselves.

As the business diversified and as the new corporate spin-off players entered the professional services marketplace, all firms began to struggle with the difficult problem of critical mass. The critical mass problem is simply this:

> If a firm has more than one line of service and specializes in more than one industry sector, what is the mass of consultants needed locally to meet the demand of the diverse clients in that geography, while ensuring that all consultants are utilized to their optimal potential?

One solution is to establish performance or competency centers staffed by consultants specialized in a set of methods, technical skills, and/or the business needs of a specific client set. When the skill is needed, it is flown to the client and is on temporary travel assignment until completion of the engagement. The competency center staff that is not utilized by clients works together to extend their personal knowledge through cooperative education or they expand their influence in the marketplace by developing procedures, software, and marketing materials.

The down side of this approach has been twofold. First there is considerable wear and tear on the consultants and their families. Youth helps, but knowledge and experience tend to come with age, and older professionals tend to need more time for personal commitments. The second difficulty with this approach is that it shifts responsibility for understanding the future needs of clients from the local consultants and their management to the central competency centers. Only the locals understand the unique requirements of their clients, and the longer the communication channel to the solution providers, the less likely that all client needs will be anticipated.

The alternative organization strategy is groups of cross-trained professionals in all geographic offices. Each consultant is a specialist in at least two skills (usually a combination of method, technical, and client industry) and is trained in many more. The national firm assumes a responsibility for delivery of professional education to its consultants on a massive scale to maximize the probability that a local office can meet enough of the needs of its client set.

Predictably, the typical professional services firm of today is a combination of these two approaches. Figure 1-2 shows the structure of a hypothetical full-service firm. With the exception of those firms that have chosen to specialize in a narrow offering of software services, most major firms have field offices in large cities, and to the degree possible, all have commutable geography. These offices contain a critical mass of consultants (enough to meet most local client needs for skill and specialty, while not so many that any sit idle for lack of work). The offices are managed by a field executive who is a member of the management or partner structure of the firm. We will explore the local organization choices for these offices in Chapter 10.

In addition, firms have performance or competency centers that contain a critical mass of consultants who specialize in combinations of methods and client industry knowledge. Typically, there is one center for each specialty, although economics may dictate that more than one competency group be housed in the same location under an overall site management structure. The strategy is to bring work to the center when the client environment supports it. Otherwise, these consultants travel to the work in "tiger teams" to perform specific duties in support of the local consultant organization. The local office keeps in touch with its clients and provides a channel through the tiger teams to communicate and test national strategy.

As can be expected, there are a variety of ways to manage the effectiveness and, ultimately, the profitability of this complex structure. This book recommends that the accountability for growth and profit be delegated to the local office. This makes each field executive operate as a profit center—making decisions that best serve the client set, as opposed to meeting national goals based on performance center objectives. Under this structure the performance centers are cost centers with overall revenue growth measurements that determine their viability.

The Project

Before leaving the subject of local organization, we need to look at the unavoidable freight train of the consulting business—the project. A project becomes an organizational entity separate from either an office or a center, when its size causes it to take on semipermanence. This happens when the combination of local consultants and competency center personnel are combined in sufficient quantities to require its own field executive level manager and, thus, is separated from the measurement system of the local office (or center). Typically, it involves more than 50 consultants and a duration of more than a year (although it is foolish to imply any standards in this area).

Projects are considered a necessary evil by any field executive whose battle scarred experience includes trying to organize or disband one of these temporary monsters. A project provides increased and concentrated revenue, and, if priced and performed correctly, will be very profitable. It also very often takes

FIGURE 1-2
Structure of a Full-Service Firm

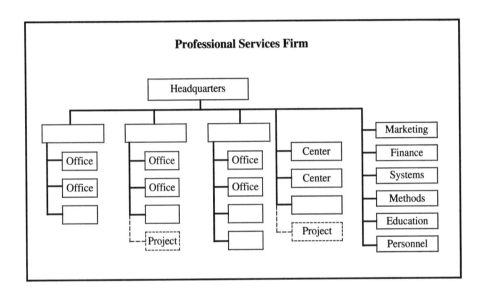

the office and supporting competency centers to below critical mass, making it a challenge to keep all other client business stable.

When the project ends, the office is suddenly flooded with too many people. A surprise ending of a project can be a financial disaster. The negative effects of projects are minimized by good project management and disciplined backlog and utilization forecasting.

The first lesson learned by any firm that has survived the 70s and 80s is the totally necessary requirement for solid project management. Every successful firm has made project management methods and disciplines the primary skill of all experienced consultants. It is not unusual for some elements of project management to be included in every year of the consultant's annual training requirement.

Poor project management almost guarantees that multiparty, multiphase consulting efforts will miss cost, time frame and quality objectives. If the firm has assumed the financial risk for any of these, the probability is high that its costs will exceed budget. Well-executed project management should ensure that at least 85 percent of a firm's complex engagements meet each of its expectations. The remaining 15 percent can then be covered by the premiums charged for risk taking.

The National Headquarters

Today's national (international) professional services firm is in a continuous struggle with the costly growth of headquarters staff. A law of bureaucracies is that staff breeds staff. Since this book views the business from the local organization's point of view, comments regarding this staff may be sprinkled with the common cynicisms of a field executive's view of the "help" provided by headquarters.

There are some key functions that appropriately reside in a headquarters and which cost will be legitimately apportioned to the costs of the local units. These are as follows.

1. *Business plan and finance.* Although professional services is a low assets, minimum capital business, it requires very careful cash flow management. A carefully constructed and monitored business plan is the best protection against a cash shortage and a function best performed across the business. A key element of this is pricing guidelines.

2. *Business systems and administration.* Economies of scale in expenditures toward equipment and business application software dictate the need to consolidate computer support and to standardize administrative practices across a multilocation business.

3. *Quality assurance and methods development.* The success or failure of a professional services firm rests in its reputation and its ability to provide creditable client references. Satisfied clients are the product of high quality and unique services that reduce the client's business risk. The dissemination and auditing of the practices that are the foundation of a firm's success are best managed centrally to ensure consistency and effective feedback.

4. *Compensation and personnel.* The incentive and personnel practices of a people firm are particularly complex and sensitive. The continuous sharing of resources across the business demands a consistency and evenhandedness best managed from headquarters.

5. *Education.* Economies of scale alone dictate that the professional development classroom training needs of the firm be provided as a service across the business. A more pervasive reason is the coordination needed to lock education strategy to methods strategy and to nurture the expansion of locally generated subject matter when it has national application.

6. *Marketing and advertising.* A professional services firm typically relies heavily on its field organization to sell its reputation and image and, thus, identify the opportunities that lead to proposals of its services. To be effective,

though, there needs to be a national strategy for marketing that includes training, incentives, advertising, materials, and competitive analysis. When the firm is a division or subsidiary of a parent, the headquarters marketing staff performs much of the coordination to promote lead generation from other products and services offered by the parent.

7. *National services.* It is not unusual for the headquarters of a firm to sell services to its local units. These services are overhead to the entire business until the sum of the cost of its specific services are completely charged out. Often, the amount of cost charged directly to offices and then to clients is disappointingly less than the final cost incurred. This causes unpleasant debates at year end regarding adjustments to apportionments. Examples are:

- **Computer programming:** An efficient resource base of programmers with needed machine support for contract coding and unit testing of software designed by field teams.

- **Technical writing:** A resource base of experienced writers and editors to proof and rewrite documents to be delivered to clients.

- **Publishing/graphics:** A resource of advanced technology in the development of graphic materials and the large-scale printing of documentation.

Throughout the top levels of the business are the executives. The number and the distribution of executives between a central executive headquarters and regional management centers varies with every firm. Typically, there are at least two levels above the field executive and they each have their own immediate staff. Where regional executives are in place, they may have an empowered set of the headquarters functions, such as quality assurance and personnel.

Guiding Financial Principles

The manager new to professional services will be faced with management approaches in the full-service professional services firm that are very different from those of product businesses. The professional services office today is a result of learning and evolution and is run through a set of processes and controls that are unique. Mostly, it is a practical set of administrative disciplines that keep complexity under control.

The number of firms that have fallen by the wayside during the growth of the professional services industry is a testament to excellent consulting and ineffective management. The financial strategy of the successful firms is guided by four principles.

1. **Marketplace segmentation is a necessary control of professional services growth.** Each service offered by a firm has its own market demand and, therefore, its own margin opportunity. It is essential to know whether revenue growth and actual margins for a segment are meeting expectations.

2. **Profitability is directly proportional to people resource utilization.** Consultants are inventory. Their availability must be carefully apportioned to revenue earning, nonrevenue earning, and personal enhancement time. It is essential to maximize their revenue earning performance while maintaining their growth in value.

3. **Adequate margins are maintained when effective cost rates by people resources are understood.** Professional services profits come from delivering the maximum number of hours of work for the highest difference in revenue per hour and cost per hour. This is accomplished most effectively by selecting the cheapest person resource that can accomplish needed quality for the least risk.

4. **The profitability of a professional services firm is the accumulated profitability of its offices.** Each office should be measured as a profit center and have the authority to select and price the services that satisfy the needs of its local clients. Accountability is the highest motivator for careful business controls, disciplined project management, and the ability to say no to a client.

The firms that have made the successful migration to systems integration and other complex services understand these principles. They have put in place the means to stay in control despite all the odds against it.

GROWING OUT OF CONTROL

This first chapter described the growth and complexity in today's expanded professional services business. The following list contains points that will be important throughout the book.

- Choose growth wisely. Growing without diversity is slow, but it can be very profitable; while diversified growth will be rapid and profitable when business management is given its due attention.

- To achieve rapid growth, firms expand their offerings and their markets. An industry-wide example is that of adding custom development, product support, and systems integration to traditional consulting and education.

- Diversity creates complexity. Complexity increases the variety of business controls.

- National firms depend upon the profitability of their individual offices, are very lean at their headquarters, and empower their office executives with considerable authority and accountability.

- The financial principles that guide a national firm are a recognition of market segmentation, emphasis on people utilization, attention to cost rates, and a roll up of profit.

To feed growth, the major firms must continue to find qualified executives to manage their field offices. Many candidates have little understanding or experience in professional services. These new managers are often faced with revenue growth and profit objectives that seem impossible. Their previous education and experience hardly prepares them for the perplexing array of complex service offerings and multiparty client agreements that typify modern professional services.

The purpose of this book is to provide an understanding of the basics in business management to current and future professional services office executives. The book is written for those who wish to expand a small office; for that individual in the large corporation who sees professional services as an opportunity for new revenue and profit; and for all who are in the business now. The processes, methods, and techniques in this book are proven and practical. They are designed for growth with less pain.

Chapter 2

Managing Professional Services

C orporate America can be a lonely place for the entrepreneur. Although many major business enterprises are run at the top by successful entrepreneurs, few corporations are willing to delegate enough authority to satisfy the appetite of its emerging entrepreneurs. Professional services has come to be a welcome exception to the corporate norm. In fact, the enterprise that withholds empowerment to its professional services offices smothers their freedom to adapt to the rapidly changing client demands that fuel growth.

A professional services unit can be an entrepreneur's dream come true. Its business has few of the components that dictate the pace of business processes and require complicated bureaucracy. There is no waiting for assets to be acquired or products to be shipped. There is no waiting for financing. Even corporate agonizing over hiring or staff relocations is shortened when there are clients ready to pay money for people added to employee ranks.

It is not, though, a business that can be run by the seat of one's pants. In return for reasonable authority to acquire and relocate employees as needed, to structure and price services to local competition, to purchase complementary services from vendors, and to innovate consulting methods that satisfy unique client demands, the professional services field executive must implement and pay careful attention to a minimum level of business control and administration.

This chapter serves to introduce the topic of business control and administration. It is followed by a series of detailed chapters on the controls necessary for effective client relations and for each of the five measurements of a professional services business: revenue, utilization, profit, backlog, and productivity. This introductory chapter examines why minimum controls are needed. It also stresses the importance and provides examples of the computer applications necessary to the controlled operation of a professional services office.

FUNDAMENTAL OPERATING STRATEGIES

The successful manager of professional services is by definition a good manager of people. The ideas, energy, and leadership of its employees are the product line of the professional services business. These same employees are also its inventory, and they represent the majority of the cost of operating the business. It should be no surprise then that people management is the most important responsibility of a professional services manager.

Time needed for the various hiring, communication, motivation, recognition, and evaluation responsibilities of people management takes precedence over any other demands placed on the manager. When an office provides quality management to its people, it is able to consistently employ the kind of professionals that deliver quality to its clients. On the other hand, top consulting professionals are so in demand that they little tolerate an environment where management cannot provide the personal and professional support they need.

Although people management is the number one responsibility of managers, it is not all they have to do. They also have a business to run. When an office is small, managers have time beyond their people responsibilities to do a number of consulting, marketing, and new offering development activities and still have time to get the bills out and manage the books. As the business grows, so does administration. When an office begins to approach the level of 25 consultants, the management staff begins to see business management and administration growing to be a sizable demand on their time. Keeping the business process and profits under control becomes a higher and higher priority. If left to grow unchecked, administration of the business will take management's attention away from those they can least afford to ignore—the people.

The first step in keeping business administration from growing into a monster is to execute the basics. During the 90-year evolution of the professional services business, successful managers have learned to be guided by six fundamental strategies in day-to-day business operations. These strategies, as listed in Figure 2-1, are the common sense advice given by the veteran to the rookie, who wants to know what it takes to be successful in running the business. Ignoring any one of these strategies exacts a payment in administrative time and energy that is not worth it.

The first two strategies, to maximize placement of consultants into revenue-bearing assignments and to satisfy clients, are the highest priorities for any services manager after people management. The remaining four are of equal importance, but do not consume the day-to-day attention of all managers to the degree of the first two.

Figure 2-1
Fundamental Operating Strategies of Professional Services

Fundamental Operating Strategies

- Maximize placement of consultants
- Maximize client satisfaction
- Manage each engagement for follow-on
- Hire people who are marketable
- Manage profit today
- Manage marketing as an investment

Maximize Placement of Consultants

Maximizing the placement of consultants begins with simple economics. The wage, benefit, and overhead costs of a consultant employee are an ongoing expense that must be covered by income. When everyone is assigned on a correctly priced engagement, sufficient revenue will be earned to make a profit. Rarely does a professional services management staff get to live in such a fantasy world for very long. Within a staff of 25 or more consultants, at least 6 will be on vacation, out ill, in class, or between assignments at any one time. The office needs its highly skilled people to address the pressing needs of estimating new opportunities, developing new service offerings and methods, and simply attending important employee meetings about the company and the business. The challenge for the manager is to resist as many of these distractions from earning revenue as possible.

Chapter 5 is a detailed discussion of consultant utilization and describes typical distributions of an employee's available work time. The illustrations provided in the chapter quantify the various examples of work and personal activities that make up a consultant's available work year. A surprisingly large number of activities do not bring in immediate revenue. This conflict between getting revenue now, the personal needs of the employee, and the desire to spend consultant time to invest in the future becomes increasingly complex as an office grows and diversifies.

Managers have a very narrow margin for error in profitably managing consultant availability. Let's assume that with 25 consultants and corresponding management, marketing, and business controls staff, an office can make a desirable profit if all consultants spend 75 percent of their available year bringing in undiscounted revenue (they charge full rate for all of their time). Assuming the consultants actually work 105 percent of a 2,080 hour year (professionals work voluntary overtime), management can allow 546 hours or approximately

68 days of a consultant's year to be spent on all activities other than full rate billing.

These are mature, professional employees, so they will use 34 of these days for personal time to include holidays, vacation, illness, and personal emergencies. To keep them at the highly skilled level for which their clients will pay full rate, they will need four weeks of classroom and self-study education (including attending conventions and reading professional society communications). This leaves 14 days or 112 hours that can be allocated to other than the above.

Good people management will demand some of this for employee communications. Business controls will need a few of these hours to be devoted to paperwork. Another 50 to 60 hours just disappeared. Marketing will need some of what is left for technical support in estimating new offers and demonstrating skills to prospective clients.

To maintain 75 percent billed utilization and 5 percent overtime, this office has nothing left for emergencies. The bane of the professional services business is "on the bench" time, that time between engagements when the consultant has literally nothing to do. In the exercise above, bench time can only be accommodated by increasing the work year through more overtime, decreasing the other nonbilling time allocations, or raising rates to get higher revenue from lower utilization.

The best approach is to reduce bench time through careful planning and tracking of consultant assignments and performance. Although it may seem impossible at times, it really is a matter of good communication among the management and marketing staff.

With regular attention and the use of good administration tools, managers can work with their consultants and with marketing to anticipate gaps in assignments. When known well in advance (at least before the consultant shows up in your office unexpectedly on Monday morning), activities can be prescheduled into the gaps. The gaps first can accommodate reschedulable personal, employee communication, and education time. After necessary personal needs, gaps can be filled from a planned backlog of marketing and business investment work.

Utilization planning and tracking involves the time and actions of all managers and marketing. It requires computer support to be done efficiently and effectively. In the example, the problem was greatly simplified. The actual billed utilization for consultants varies from 55 percent to 85 percent, depending on the experience of the person and the corresponding price a client will pay per hour. Additionally, utilization expected on fixed price engagements is vastly different than that on hourly or daily engagements.

The office that does the best job of planning and tracking consultant time will maximize the time spent billing to clients and will reduce bench time. Regardless of business mix, this office is in the best position to weather the unexpected or to invest in new markets. Consultant time is inevitably wasted when decisions are delayed through poor preparation for the unexpected. Wasted hours (and its corresponding expense) cannot be recovered without loss of profit, driving employees to unreasonable overtime, or increasing rates beyond what the market might bear.

Maximize Client Satisfaction

A dissatisfied client has two recourses—demand money or demand the work product they expected for no additional payment. In our litigious society, a dissatisfied client poses a steadily growing threat to the future of a business, even when a firm has protected itself against consequential damages and has acted in good faith and with ethical behavior during the engagement. The major price to be paid during client dissatisfaction is the hours of management time needed to negotiate an agreeable extrication from the pit into which the engagement has fallen. Inevitably, other priorities are ignored.

On the other hand, a satisfied client lets the firm get the job done. This client demands a minimum of extra attention. This client is willing to let the firm choose methods and resources and is likely to agree to more work when time is taken to sell it correctly. The satisfied client is the one that has been conditioned at each step of the engagement to expect the events and work products as they actually happen, regardless of any prior conflicting perceptions.

The client's first priority is to get the work finished. The client has engaged the firm because of a real business need and the satisfaction of that need will provide a very real benefit. Usually, the client can ill afford to quit when it becomes dissatisfied. It has made commitments to employees and customers. It has financed the activity and the funds spent so far need to be recovered. Most likely the firm is faced with a request to expend considerable hours with no revenue.

Client dissatisfaction is most often a result of failure on the part of management and consultants to communicate end results that a client should expect. As we have discussed, the work product of the professional services firm is an intellectual one. It consists of paper and magnetic media and its effectiveness is measured by the client in very intangible ways. The methods and procedures of the major firms are designed to carefully lead participants through a learning and conditioning process as unknowns are encountered and directions change accordingly. These methods depend upon a satisfaction measurement process that tests client expectations each step of the way to ensure that the client is in agreement with the winding path that is being taken.

Inevitably, the process breaks down. Rarely is the methodology incorrect or executed incorrectly, although the client might view it that way. The breakdown usually occurs in the communication process. The consistently profitable firms are those that can minimize both the occurrence of these breakdowns and the magnitude of the resulting concessions. This is done very simply by understanding the client's satisfaction level every day and getting formal confirmation of satisfaction on a regular basis.

As a general rule, clients choose professional services firms because of their methods and their track record, rather than the price of their offering. At the outset, the client's expectation of what steps will occur and what output will pour forth is based heavily on the images created by the firm's presentations and documents, and on a faith that the firm knows what it is doing. It is up to the consultants and their managers to navigate the client's expectation through the many twists and turns that the intellectual process will take.

Again, the means to a successful client satisfaction strategy is solid planning and tracking by both the consultants and management. In addition, it requires good communications and the effective training of consultants in the proven methods that have sustained the firm's reputation. Every engagement is unique. Every engagement requires innovation and judgment. The client is paying a premium over the cost of attempting the effort on its own to get the added value of the firm's intellectual contribution. The client will be satisfied, if the firm appears to do what it has led the client into believing ought to be done.

In Chapter 3, we will cover client relations in more detail. Measuring client satisfaction is a combination of formal and informal communications that are planned into the structure and schedule of the engagement. The methods and procedures of the firm are usually extensive and specific on what actions to take when client dissatisfaction is discovered. The objective is to discover the dissatisfaction before it is too late to minimize the cost of its correction. Services managers must establish communications early in an engagement and test these communications at least monthly throughout. It can then be up to the consultants to do the quality job for which they are paid.

The debate over concessions and the amount of pro bono work (work for no pay) will most likely be decided by whether the client provided ongoing support, whether qualified people and vendors were assigned, whether the methods and procedures were executed as advertised, and whether the client received value. Each of these can be determined long before the end of the effort. Each of these involves normal good news and bad news, neither of which should be ignored nor allowed to occur unnoticed. The strongest end game for the firm is when its consultants clearly followed proven practices, and management obtained confirmation from the client for actions and decisions at each crucial point along the way.

Manage Each Engagement for Follow-on

Keeping clients satisfied leads to the third fundamental operating strategy of professional services—actively market additional and follow-on business to every current client. As we have discussed before and will quantify in Chapter 6, marketing resources are often an expensive luxury in a tight margin consulting business. One full-time marketer per 20 consultants may be the best that one can afford. On the other hand, a consultant who is doing an impressive job for a client is a walking advertisement of the firm's capability and credibility.

Consultants and their immediate managers can sell additional service offerings to their current clients in three ways.

- They can expand the work in which they are currently involved, particularly by selling the next logical phase of the work (i.e., operating procedures after strategy development, software programming after software design, hot line support after systems integration).

- They can show interest in other functions in the client's business, looking for those that also need attention (i.e., analyze field office procedures in addition to a current engagement of installing new home office systems and procedures).

- They can identify additional client organizations that would benefit from other service offerings from the office or the firm in general (i.e., sell education to a client training unit, sell software support to a client technical support service, sell strategic planning to a client corporate planning committee).

As any marketer knows, half the battle in a selling effort is to find an inside salesperson to carry your message through a client decision structure. The ability to develop inside salespeople goes up exponentially, when consultants are on-site. By cultivating their immediate client counterparts, skillful consultants can learn the complete organizational structure of the client, where its problems reside, who makes decisions, and whether the firm has the expertise. This takes little time and is often part of the analytical and leadership professionalism that clients expect of consultants.

Managers play an important role in supporting any unobtrusive selling done by consultants. Managers have the follow-up responsibility for uncovered opportunities. Consultants believe, and rightly so, that much of their credibility comes from the client's perception of objectivity on their part. The consultants are neither part of the client's organization nor a part of the firm's organization. Many consultants feel that open selling bursts the bubble of objectivity that surrounds them.

Managers must take the time to debrief consultants on their selling activities and to assist them in developing the next steps in the selling process. The manager provides the bridge between marketing efforts by their consultants and others (including themselves) who can make formal offers of additional services and can close the new business.

Getting follow-on business is built into the methodologies of professional services firms, particularly those majors that provide a wide spectrum of offerings. As we discussed before, consulting methods are designed to address unknowns and involve the client in deciding among alternatives. The number of unknowns and possible alternatives decreases as the discovery and analytical process moves toward a final, single business solution. By design, service offerings create business solutions in discrete phases to allow the firm to make contractual commitments even knowing that some unknowns will be faced. Service offerings also allow the client to determine whether the business case justifies the next step. Each phase has one or more logical follow-on phase and the major firms are prepared to offer and perform engagements that encompass the entire series. Examples of starter engagements that can lead through follow-on to greatly extended engagements are:

- **Develop a strategic plan** to be followed by one or more specific project/program plans.

- **Document requirements** to be followed by a design and/or implementation effort.

- **Develop/install a prototype** to be followed by implementation of multiples.

- **Teach an introductory class in a series** to be followed by further classes taught multiple times.

Selling the starter service requires the best marketing talent the firm can assemble. Unless the client decides to open the next phase to competition, selling the follow-on simply requires good execution of the starter service and attention to the steps needed to convince the client to continue. Typically, those consultants and managers involved in the engagement are the most effective in seeing that the firm gets the follow-on.

Should the client use the starter system work product to solicit competitive bids, the firm enters the competition with the highest odds of winning (assuming they managed client expectation and satisfaction during the starter service). Competitive follow-on becomes very expensive, though. Top marketing talent is needed, along with key managers and consultants from the starter service, who are off-contract until the decision is made. It becomes a high stakes contest where the office needs to win or choose not to play.

Hire People Who Are Marketable

The next fundamental operating strategy addresses how to expand a professional services business in new territories. A new territory is a city where the firm has no current clients, professional skill or service offering that the firm has not previously provided locally, or a new alliance with a vendor to provide product services.

Clients let firms in the door based upon the credibility of a firm. In most cases, though, clients actually buy the people of the firm that they have met. Even with systems integration, where capability to deliver includes competent equipment, software, network, and vendor partners, it is the person of the project manager that often convinces a client that a firm has the talent to get the job done.

To demonstrate this credibility, the professional services business needs at least one person on board, before any can be sold. Rational accounting would dictate that one have committed revenue before committing to the people cost. Unfortunately, this is not a workable strategy when selling people who address abstracts such as solving business problems or supplying business assistance. The client wants to see an example of such a person before buying.

It is imprudent to incur people cost when no market exists. Some marketing to new territories has to occur to create latent demand. The issue becomes one of marketing productivity. With marketing expense such a dire commodity in the professional services business, a reasonably high sell rate for engagements versus opportunities marketed must be achievable. Without people to demonstrate, the sell rate is often infinitesimal.

Firms choose a number of ways to implement a strategy of demonstrating people to make the sale. The most obvious is hiring or transferring proven professionals into the territory. Once a critical mass is in place, existing or new staff can be trained using these role models and mentors. This is only prudent when the latent demand for such people and their expertise is very strong.

A common practice is to transfer proven professionals from other locations onto temporary assignments that will end either with their living in the new location or returning to their previous location. Obviously, this approach presumes that the firm is large enough to have people available for relocation. A questionable practice is to hire on contingency and lay off, if the business doesn't materialize.

Competency centers within the major firms are a very successful approach to demonstrating credibility in new markets. Competency center personnel can be flown in at any point in the selling effort. Often the center has tiger teams that work temporarily on-site at the client location to get an effort started and transfer their skill. A combination of local tiger team and remote competency center people is accepted by most clients as a reasonable balance between work done where it can be observed firsthand and work done by the best expertise available.

One market where the demonstration of people may not be required for getting business is government, both national and local. Governments are often required to buy services at arm's length, which precludes them from getting to know their potential vendors personally. For this reason, firms that can win engagements by referencing other government work can fund building and training a staff after the source of revenue is committed. The investment in marketing to win these highly competitive opportunities can be prohibitive and is often less profitable than hiring good people, demonstrating them to clients, and putting them to work.

Professional services is an entrepreneur's business. The decision to acquire professionals on a payroll before committed revenue to cover their cost is not one made by the timid. The timing requires just the right level of interest among one or more clients so that at least one buys the person and the service. Bringing in people too soon quickly destroys profits. Bringing people in too late or not at all means missing out on growth opportunity.

Manage Profit Today

It may seem obvious, but the manager of a professional services office should strive to be profitable every day. This is not a business where money is made through financing investment and building equity. Hiring people ahead is the only investment required in the business and that should be recovered from profits within a few weeks. Even setting up a new office can be done on a shoestring, since most of the initial personnel are to be assigned to client premises and only need a file cabinet to keep their company private materials. Once a few people are billing, overhead in facilities and administrative personnel can grow against the incremental revenue for each new consultant added to the staff. (At this point it would be well to give consultants a desk they can call home away from the client.) On the other hand, the professional services business has few ways to make up near term loss with future revenues, short of increasing rates. As will be seen in Chapter 6, most cost is labor and it does not decrease that much as a percentage of revenue as revenue increases. Only in rare cases can repetitions of a service pay high margin dividends when repeated for multiple clients (i.e., an education class).

The temptations to postpone profit are many. We have already discussed a number of built-in personal reasons that take consultants off billing for short periods. Added to these are very real needs to staff marketing and planning activities that only require a morning here and an afternoon there.

The pressure of competition also acts as a temptation to forego immediate profits. An office will believe beyond doubt that it should come down 15 percent on its normal margin to get people off the bench, rather than making the tough decisions to reduce the consultant staff or quickly retrain consultants in expertise and services that are selling for a better margin. Profit is much easier to maintain in those offices that have a variety of offered services and can shift resources when demand changes.

Simply increasing revenue will not ensure profitability, although low-margin business does get people off the bench. The astute executive assumes that today's margins will be tomorrow's margins (particularly when clients learn they can get low rates) and takes immediate action to improve today's margins if they are not adequate. This often requires dramatic shifts of marketing approach and people.

Manage Marketing As an Investment

The last fundamental operating strategy, and one that again leads from the previous one, is to manage marketing as an investment, rather than simply as a necessary expense.

Expense is justified when it generates revenue in sufficient quantities to cover the expense plus profit. Investment is justified when an expense will return revenue at rates of return that are substantially greater than normal operating margins. Effective management of client satisfaction leads to follow-on business that sustains the current consultant population. Marketing is an investment expense directed to opportunities outside of the current client base to grow the business base and, as a by-product, replace client attrition.

The marketing investment worth pursuing is the winnable one with the highest net profit for the lowest marketing expense. Conversely, a professional services office avoids moderately probable prospects that require massive effort and will generate little profit. Managing marketing as an investment involves this conscious evaluation of every marketing opportunity in terms of its probability of success and its ratio of marketing effort to expected profit.

Evaluating ongoing marketing efforts is 90 percent discipline and 10 percent form. The form requires keeping a minimum of information about current prospects and having the experience to evaluate the size of a marketing effort and the probability of its success. The discipline requires that each marketing effort be reviewed on a regular basis to determine, even subjectively, whether

Figure 2–2
Professional Services Business Operations

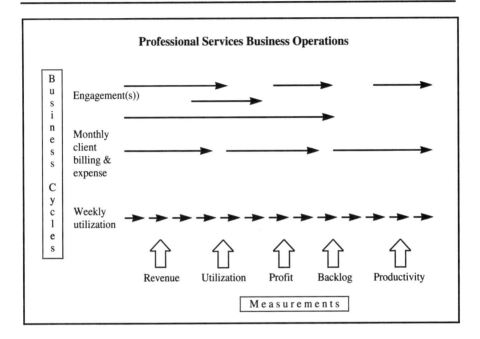

the remaining effort is consistent with the forecasted profit and current odds. Management must be prepared to reduce marketing resources and put them to billing, when marketing investment is not needed.

PROFESSIONAL SERVICES BUSINESS OPERATIONS

In order to control any business, one must understand its basic rhythms and cycles. A business has production and administration process cycles that have repeating beginnings and endings. In addition, there are control processes that cross all cycles to test whether the business is healthy and meeting objectives. Professional services business operation has five measurement and control processes that cross three repeating performance and administrative cycles as illustrated in Figure 2-2.

The three production and administration business process cycles of professional services are listed below and are expanded to more detail later in this chapter.

- **Engagement cycle:** The period from the first marketing call on a client through the establishment of the engagement which continues for weeks, months, or years through the postmortem of the last contract.
- **Monthly client billing and expense cycle:** The monthly issuing of invoices, crediting of the corresponding revenue, summarizing of incurred and accrued expenses, and computation of profit.
- **Utilization cycle:** The weekly recording of labor distribution, assessment of resource level, assignment of labor resource, and labor resource utilization analysis.

Five Measurement and Control Processes

Each of these business cycles is controlled by a combination of five measurement processes. Each of the measurement processes are themselves quarterly, monthly, or weekly. They test business health. These regular measurements provide a common mechanism to keep the three business cycles in synchronous rhythm. In addition, the measurements act to keep management focused on the fundamental operating strategies discussed in the earlier part of this chapter. Chapters 4 through 8 are each dedicated to one of these measurements. The following overview serves to introduce each and describe its relationship to the six operating strategies.

1. *Revenue* (Chapter 4). Revenue measurements track earned, billed, and credited revenue per month in each of the types of businesses offered by that office against the corresponding revenue plan.

Segmentation of revenue into types of businesses measures growth in markets such as consulting, education, product support services, systems integration, and any other service or offering segments that are meaningful and practical for marketplace analysis. Revenue measurements support paying incentives for revenue performance by such segments as marketing territory and consultant office. As we will see, territories are the clustering of clients into geographic, industry, and a variety of other groupings that represent logical approaches to preventing overlapped client coverage.

Revenue forecasting is the basis of any business plan and its tracking is the first test of whether any of the operating strategies are working. Revenue tracking is the easiest of all measurements to manage administratively, especially when relatively straightforward computerized business systems are in place (to be discussed later).

2. *Utilization* (Chapter 5). The people utilization measurement determines whether optimum revenue is being generated by the current inventory of people resources. It includes the planning and tracking of how labor is distributed

among client, business investment, and personal activities. It includes tracking and forecasting of people assignments and availability. It includes an inventory of skills and experiences that define the placement potential of each person and, coupled with utilization tracking, aids in the placement of under-utilized resources. Utilization, tracked against a plan, is an early signal of profitability and aids in understanding the cost and revenue effects of such diverse business issues as hiring, seasonality, employee communication meetings, and education.

Utilization is measured in hours, and is tracked for all people who have contributed or will contribute to revenue generation. Utilization measures the efforts of temporary employees, contract personnel, and indirect personnel that bill in special situations. As will be seen later, productivity measurements depend upon data from utilization measurements.

Measuring utilization and taking immediate actions to optimize utilization are basic to the operating strategies of maximizing placement of consultants, determining whether people are marketable and determining when to market. Careful tracking of utilization measures the reserve capacity of an office and triggers short term investment actions, such as education in skills for new markets, new offerings, and increased client marketing. Conversely, low utilization may trigger such extraordinary actions as increased overtime or people reductions.

3. *Profit* (Chapter 6). Profit is the difference between credited revenue and actual plus accrued (committed) expense per month against plan. The plan for each month is based on the needed margin to meet overall net before tax requirements after subtracting apportionments from the parent corporation (if any).

Measuring profit includes the tracking of actual and anticipated expenses. These are accumulated in a chart of accounts appropriate to a professional services business and are each measured against a budget. Within the account, expenses specific to an engagement or group of like engagements are separated for profit analysis of individual engagements (i.e., cost of classroom resources for multiple clients and classes). Profit measurement includes management of the computerized monthly general ledger, income and expense statement preparation, and the necessary procurement process and purchasing/accounts payable system for systems integration.

Measuring profit is essential to all operating strategies, but is obviously the underlying test for managing profit today. Combined with revenue and utilization measurements, current profit tracking allows an office to react quickly to fix problems or seize opportunities. An office that is on track in revenue and utilization but not profit should examine its pricing. An office that is on track in all three areas can consider reducing utilization to explore new markets. An office that is behind in both revenue and profit against plan in May can take actions to be back on track by year end.

4. *Sales and backlog* (Chapter 7). Backlog measures the amount of unbilled revenue of current engagements and the high potential revenue in the marketing forecast. When added to the revenue to date, the backlog measurement determines whether additional sales are needed to meet the year-end revenue plan. Backlog drives decisions to vary the level of marketing investment. Backlog also measures the effectiveness of historical changes in marketing investment when compared with a corresponding history of marketing resource levels. Historical analysis is particularly helpful in determining how long it takes to increase revenue after an increase in marketing resource.

Backlog and utilization measurements taken together will trigger the timing of increased marketing. A major drop in backlog next month, coupled with deteriorating utilization signals an immediate need to get more new business. A backlog shortfall three months from now coupled with no deterioration in a fully utilized resource base usually means marketing resources are sufficient.

5. *Productivity* (Chapter 8). The productivity measurement tracks the revenue and cost rates per resource hour for each type of person and each type of contract (service). Detection of differences between actual productivity rates and planned productivity rates trigger actions to change pricing. Actual productivity rates by labor resource are used to compute engagement profitability when coupled with segmentation of expense and revenue generated by nonlabor elements specific to an engagement.

Productivity computations are a monthly by-product of income and expense reporting. The revenue and cost per person are computed for each person resource category (i.e., consultant employees, contractors, etc.). The computed revenue and cost rates per hour are used to evaluate trends for the year and against the previous year. The values are plotted to observe the effect of programs to improve productivity or activities, such as hiring, that reduce productivity. In addition, productivity rates are used to quantify the relative contribution to profit for each significant engagement each month, as well as the accumulated profitability of an engagement since its inception.

The need for rigorous productivity measurements is minimal in a simple daily rate consulting business. It serves only to reset pricing assumptions as costs per hour change relative to revenue per hour. It is also useful in assessing the relative effects of tiered pricing and other programs to increase overall revenue per hour.

Once an office moves into multiple types of offerings with multiple types of contracts and corresponding pricing complexity, computing effective revenue and cost rates per resource becomes essential. Actual cost rate subtracted from

Figure 2–3
Engagement Cycle

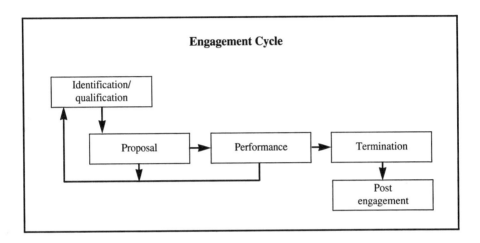

revenue rate determines relative contributions to profit (and loss) between re-sources, engagements, and types of businesses. This is key to obtaining the maximum leverage in choosing resource cost alternatives such as subcontractors. Furthermore, productivity analysis determines whether both labor and nonlabor generated revenue components of a systems integration engagement are holding up their profit ends of the deal.

Engagement Cycle

The engagement cycle, illustrated in Figure 2-3, traces the life of the relationship with a client for an engagement from the first marketing call to the final archiving of the engagement and contract files. The process is a recording of the communication within the firm and between the firm and the client to make visible the needs, expectations, and ongoing satisfaction of the client. It also protects the firm from unethical practices.

Identification and Qualification.   The cycle begins with the recording of a prospect generated by a marketing **lead** and/or contact with a client. The source of a marketing lead identifies a client that might need the firm's services. Leads come from consultants, from other businesses that have alliances with the firm, from other offices in the firm's parent company (i.e., Andersen's accounting offices, IBM's hardware marketing branches), from comarketing relationships (i.e., software houses), and from advertising and other promotions. The identification step collects the information needed to assess whether the firm is qualified to market to the client.

The effort to qualify the opportunity and submit an offering usually follows one of three paths.

• If the marketing lead is for an extension of existing services or a packaged service where the price and work products are unambiguous, the lead is given to a consultant, manager, or marketing assistance function. The minimum of offering material is prepared and presented to the client for signature.

• If the marketing lead is perceived to be for complex services that the firm is qualified to pursue, but will require further client qualification to determine the client's view of affordability and expected results, the lead is scheduled for assignment to an experienced marketing person. The effort required to pursue leads of this kind often takes weeks and months. The identification process will require a secondary qualification process that includes one or more visits with the client to confirm that the firm can make an offer that has a high probability of acceptance. A particular example of this type of lead is one that includes a request for a formal proposal. This lead requires a business case to evaluate marketing investment in the proposal against probable profit from the engagement.

• If the marketing lead is for a totally new service opportunity, where the office has no previous experience, a decision has to be made as to the worth to the firm. In some cases, a competency center may be available to investigate and report whether the firm should proceed further. In many cases, it requires a visit to the client by a senior member of the firm to understand the client's problem and reason for wanting the firm's involvement. If the profit potential appears high and the client is willing to share some risk, a significant marketing and people investment might be warranted. If the return looks low, the lead will require the best in marketing and executive talent for the office to politely back away. This is particularly true when the lead is from a very determined business alliance.

The qualification phase of the engagement cycle is a combination of file building, offer preparation, and weekly assessment. Every communication with the source of the lead and the client results in paper that must be stored for future use by the consultants and management who will be assigned if an engagement results. Much of the material is handwritten notes and copies collected in interviews and phone conversations, as well as formal correspondence. Some is computer output resulting from searches into historical records relating to the subjects of the engagement.

A regular status review, preferably weekly, assesses the priorities and assigns resources to marketing efforts. A key decision at these reviews is whether to continue an investment. The decision results in an assigned action to continue marketing or to convince supporters of the effort to allow a graceful retreat.

Proposal. At some point, the marketing activity will create and file materials that are formally presented to the client to develop interest, including the formal offer. The offer may be a letter and promotional material, a letter and a presentation, a formal proposal and contract, or any combination of these. For control purposes, a clear distinction is made between materials that the client is holding versus those that are for internal firm eyes only.

The formal offer may require multiple iterations in order to get final firm and client agreement. The formal offer contains materials that set expectations for work to be done, methods to be used, work products to be produced, and specific or implied benefits to be received. The offer additionally contains an agreement to be executed and the terms of the offer as to estimated schedule, completion criteria, and price. Price is either a fixed amount, an effort in hours or days times a set of rates plus estimated nonlabor expenses, or a combination of all of these.

A critical step in preparing the offer is the estimation of the effort. In a perfect world, these estimates would be developed by the lead consultant or project manager to be assigned. This rarely happens, because utilization measurements and current client commitments preclude releasing personnel to new assignments until the last minute. The major firms have sophisticated rules and guidelines for estimating. These are taught to all consultants early in their employment with the firm. This allows estimating to be done by the first qualified consultant who can break free. Marketing personnel are also trained in estimating and the best marketers are ones that develop rule of thumb techniques. These are used as rough planning estimates early in the process to qualify a client's affordability limits.

Actual pricing (converting the estimate to a dollar price) of the effort is often a closely guarded decision process. The office has responsibility for sizing work effort, choosing sources of personnel (consultants, contractors, other borrowed people as may be available from competency centers and the parent company), estimating vendor costs and travel expenses, and determining levels of management and methods. The office may not have the authority to apply pricing assumptions against all these components to determine the final terms to be offered to the client. Those firms with a long record of good local business controls and consistent profitability have delegated this responsibility to their field executives. Most other firms hold pricing as a power reserved for headquarters finance.

Engagement Performance.   The final step in the marketing process is obtaining a client signature or a letter of intent to proceed. Performance begins with the assignment of a date upon which consultants and managers will begin work. A record of this engagement is transferred to the computerized billing system and invoicing begins as agreed. The more sophisticated offices have been tracking the marketing effort all along in prospect management, consultant assignment, and consultant availability systems. Following signature, client communication management responsibility shifts from marketing to consulting services management.

The performance of the engagement follows a project plan laid out by the lead consultant, project leader, or project manager with concurrence from the client's designated coordinator (customer) of the effort. There may be formal phases, with renegotiation of price and terms. There will be at least a series of checkpoints to assess client satisfaction and to ensure that the work is on track. Even when the entire service is a one-day class or a two-day installation effort, a consultant or manager will be in contact with the client to assess satisfaction and the client's willingness to order additional services.

The practice of most firms is to deliver a status report to the client on a regular basis (preferably weekly) that is asynchronous to the phases and checkpoints of the effort. This report is usually prepared by the lead consultant and briefly summarizes the work done in the previous period, the work to be done in the next period, and the problems and issues that need client attention. If the effort is hourly or daily, the report gives the client an accounting of the hours or days for the period (week) for reconciliation against an invoice. When done on a weekly basis, this report is usually on one page and is brief and to the point.

Major engagements involving many people and/or vendors (projects) require a monthly progress report prepared by the project manager. These reports are often lengthy and are accompanied by an executive briefing delivered formally to a senior client executive.

Many firms perform formal reviews of their long-running engagements. These are often done by quality assurance personnel who perform these as an added value client service. Reviews are usually performed within 30 days of the beginning of an effort, every 2 to 3 months thereafter and within 30 days of termination. The results of these reviews are used by the firm's management to address significant client issues that may not have surfaced in day-to-day relations.

The central file of all information pertinent to each engagement is audited for completeness on a periodic basis. The file structure is usually defined through administrative guidelines to encourage consistency. This reduces the time needed to search the file of a long-running engagement for back records of such diversity as weekly labor sheets, periodic correspondence, or the post-mortem of a client meeting. This file is likely to be organized alphabetically by client name with subsections by contract, but may have intricate cross-indexing by territory and type of service up to and including computer managed indexing of document content.

Engagement Termination. A contract within an engagement ends when the completion criteria are met. This can be as simple as reaching the end of the last day of a class or as complex as running the last series of tests on a new business process that finally executes with no defects. Typically, the firm obtains an acknowledgment of completion from the client for all but the most uncomplicated contract completions. Obtaining an acknowledgment of completion can be a challenging assignment when client satisfaction has not been tested and addressed regularly throughout contract execution.

Periodic attention is needed in professional services offices to those contracts that have become dormant, but are still listed in the backlog. Usually, the client has chosen to withhold funds for one of many reasons, not the least of which is that the client simply does not agree that continued work is needed. It requires management discipline to terminate efforts that are truly dormant and to remove them from active engagement status with the uncomfortable negative sales credit that accompanies such action.

Postengagement Activities. Most firms have a wrap-up process for completed efforts. Where complicated estimation was required prior to offering the service, a postmortem analysis is completed to record actual expended effort for use in statistical evaluations of estimating guidelines. Where packaged services were delivered on behalf of software and other products, a feedback survey is often taken to bridge local experience to competency and central support centers. Student critiques are usually completed at the end of classes.

Many firms have a formal client satisfaction survey that is sent to all clients at least annually. These are general questions regarding a variety of service characteristics ranging from friendliness of firm personnel to fairness in negotiations. Since the questions are answerable across all types of services offered, the upward and downward trends in these surveys act as an indicator of overall quality between the many components of a major firm.

Figure 2–4
Monthly Client Billing and Expense Cycle

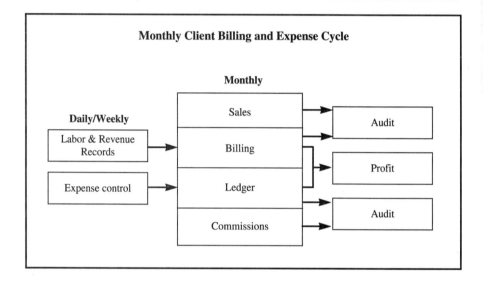

Monthly Client Billing and Expense Process

Figure 2-4 illustrates the steps in the monthly cycle for professional services. The monthly cycle contains the most basic of all business processes for a firm—that of sending invoices to its clients on at least a monthly basis. This is a computerized process that assesses the status of each client engagement and prints a computed bill, having determined that an invoice is appropriate for the period just completed. The invoice is recorded in a computerized accounts receivable awaiting payment. Upon receipt of the check, the payment is applied to the outstanding amount owed and the cash received is tracked into the bank for cash management purposes. If payment is not received, computerized dunning occurs until action is taken to begin a collections activity. In the event of default, the appropriate accounting transactions are made to write off the bad receivable and the amount is charged as an expense to the office that was credited with the revenue.

Some client engagements are not invoiced each month. In professional services, the agreement between the firm and the client determines under what circumstances a payment is due. Typically, a firm has four or five types of contracts, each having different payment clauses. It is not unusual for more than one of these to be in effect within a complex engagement involving multiple contracts.

Examples of charging options are the following.

- **Any time worked.** The client will receive an invoice at the end of any period (presumably a month) in which one or more consultants spent time on behalf of the client. The client is charged for at least one hour or one day, depending on whether it is an hourly or daily rate contract.

- **Scheduled payment due.** The client will receive an invoice at the end of a period based upon prior agreement of a schedule of payments. The payment schedule is all or part of a fixed price for a group of services delivered under a schedule consistent with the payment schedule.

- **Occurrence of anticipated event.** The client will receive an invoice triggered by the occurrence of a service event during the period, such as a class, installation of software, or a support service call.

- **Minimum service charge.** The client will receive an invoice for a minimum charge in lieu of actual services performed as a retainer for keeping resources available in the event of an emergency.

- **Any expense incurred.** The client will receive an invoice at the end of any period on which the firm incurs an expense other than labor on behalf of the client. This charge often occurs in conjunction with any of these other types of payments.

The monthly client billing process is divided into three periods—activities that precede billing, the billing cycle, and billing audit.

Activities That Precede Billing.   On a regular basis during the period preceding billing, labor and other expense charges are recorded against the client engagements to which they apply. A computerized system contains an inventory of client engagements, often broken down to the individual contracts. Labor is recorded and converted to its revenue equivalent based on rate per hour or day. Events are recorded with their corresponding billing triggers, such as number of students. Other expenses are recorded and converted to their revenue value for billing. Payment schedules and minimum charge amounts are modified in accordance with agreements with clients.

Typically, a trial billing is run at least once during the period to verify that each client will be billed correctly. This practice run is also used to track revenue buildup during the period for end of period forecasting purposes.

Billing Cycle. The billing cycle examines each engagement and contract to determine whether an invoice should be created. Separate invoices may be sent for each contract or they may be consolidated by engagement or client, depending on the capability of the system or the practices of administrative personnel that provide these custom client services. The decision to bill will be triggered by one of these criteria.

There are many styles of invoices across the industry. Some are very net with a summary line for each contract showing the amount due. Others print a detail line for every hour or day and every expense recovery line. Clients are usually ambivalent on the subject of invoice detail. Client satisfaction is more often determined by how prepared they are for the amount on the invoice. A major administrative challenge for billing is to ensure that the billing amounts match the reporting provided to the client by consultants and project managers.

The final step in the billing cycle is to post revenue. This can be very simple or very complex depending upon the variety of business segments and territories. Territory credits usually result in commissions and bonuses being computed (usually based on year-to-date attainment against a quota) and resulting payments recorded through the company payroll process.

Billing Audit. The billing audit step verifies every line item on invoices that have been sent to clients and commission/bonus amounts that have been sent to payroll. Invoice quality is a very high priority for those firms that value their client relations. If errors have been made, the firm plans to be the first to know and manually replace the invoice with a correct one (or at least advise the client of the error before they see it). Similarly, those firms that have a strong people culture will detect payroll errors in advance of the employee being aware and take the appropriate action.

If invoice and/or commission errors are detected, the appropriate corrections must be made to the client engagement files in anticipation of the next billing. The billing audit and resulting corrections are usually made within days after the billing cycle in order to have a clean start toward the next billing period.

Billing errors are an indication of control problems. The best protection against this time consuming and client irritating state of affairs is a good contract management computer system and a disciplined weekly billing preparation process.

Sales Crediting and Sales Commissions. Some firms have a further step in their monthly billing process for sales crediting and sales commissions. As we will see in the engagement life cycle, the anticipated value of a new contract and/or engagement is recorded for backlog measurement purposes. This value may change a number of times during the life of the engagement as the firm and client agree to additional work or termination of unjustified work. At the termination of the engagement, the expected value is reduced to the actual billing. The net change in value at each new, changed, or termination entry is called the sale value and territory incentives are often paid to stimulate backlog growth.

Where sales are measured or commissioned, sales activity is identified as part of the billing cycle and recorded for commissions computation. In this case the commissions process makes computations for both revenue and sales. Audit will additionally verify sales commission items.

Expense Control. The expense control process for professional services is very similar to any other business enterprise. Most expenses are immediate, thus requiring a minimum of expense accrual. The costs directly attributable to people comprise the largest amount of expense. In systems integration, costs specific to an engagement are a large item and must be related to their corresponding revenue. Another large category of expense is charges related to an office facility. Often these are controlled by the parent operating company and are charged to the office as internal expense.

The expense process is divided into daily expense control and monthly expense summary. Daily expense control is the timely processing of all nonrecurring transactions that pay vendor invoices, debit monies for resources obtained from other offices or the parent company, reimburse employees for expenses, and keep payroll records current. These expenses are usually processed through various computer systems unique to the transaction. An additional expense control process is necessary for those offices with revenue from other than labor (i.e., systems integration). Expenses that are committed and for which revenue will be billed should be accrued (manually or through a system) until the actual expense appears in the general ledger.

A computerized general ledger system is the typical expense summarization vehicle for a professional services office. Daily transactions and recurring expenses from payroll and internal rent (occupancy) are combined and posted by office. During the monthly expense closing, manual accounting may occur to allocate expenses incurred above the local level. Allocations are needed to allow local offices to compute net profit. Allocation formulas can be very elaborate. The primary purpose is to distribute regional and corporate expense in a proration as close to the distribution of actual revenue as possible.

Expense Audit and Profit Computation. The office expense summary step involves verifying the accuracy of all major expenses that appear in the ledger (particularly vendor payments and debit memos), making corrections as needed, assembling selected corrections and outstanding expenses recovered in current revenue into an accrual, and assembling the final result into an income and expense statement. If the creation of ledger expense categories and subledgers is flexible in the general ledger used, this is a reasonably quick and efficient step. Otherwise, it may involve extensive use of spreadsheets. Many offices develop lower level income and expense statements to measure the profit contribution from individual offerings or markets (i.e., education). This requires a further allocation of office overhead that is applied to the direct cost per hour of each resource type. These labor costs are combined with specific expenses to compute suboffice level profitability.

Year End. In professional services, the year-end cycle is rarely any different than a monthly cycle except with regard to computation of year-to-date accumulations. Most firms have some form of revenue accrual to reward last minute efforts toward year-end profit that missed input to billing. Clients often ask to receive a lump sum bill for the estimated remaining billing on a contract in order to use up budgeted funds.

Weekly Utilization Process

Figure 2-5 illustrates the third asynchronous process in professional services— that which provides day-to-day decision making on assignments of people resources. The purpose of the process is to reduce to a minimum the time to react to opportunities to place people in new revenue assignments or reassign people when revenue unexpectedly ceases. The secondary benefit of managing utilization and assignments with short reaction time is the ability to anticipate consultant off-contract periods and use that time productively for education, marketing, and office improvements.

The process is a combination of detailed labor claiming (the recording of how each hour in the work week was allocated) by all people, weekly maintenance of assignment calendars by management and administration, and computer support tools to make the information visible. The more consultants and contractors an office has, the more important it is to perform this cycle weekly. It is easy to decide where to place one available or soon to be available person out of a staff of 10. It is a major challenge for a group of managers and marketing personnel to optimize use of many available and potentially available people out of a staff of 50. The office that wastes the least amount of consultant hours in this process has the highest probability of consistent profits.

Weekly labor claiming is a time honored tradition in the professional services business. It is viewed as tedious but necessary by consultants. Some are

Figure 2–5
Weekly Utilization Cycle

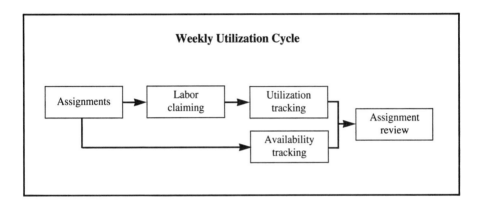

asked to keep a daily record, all are asked to record at least a weekly record. Some firms still use the day as the unit of measure for labor claiming, but most recognize the need for recording hours.

There are as many ways to record time as there are firms. The time that is recorded against specific contracts within engagements becomes input for the client billing process. Time that is recorded for holidays, vacations, illness, personal time, and so on becomes input for a company personnel or payroll process.

In a professional services firm, the total available time of a marketable person is additionally broken out for utilization tracking purposes. Utilization is the evaluation of how much of a person's time was billed, assigned without billing, personal (including both education and time off), and used in investment activities (marketing, new offerings, etc.).

Utilization is usually summarized in a report each week that shows the actual break out of the time of each resource for the previous week and some form of trend indication over the previous weeks and months. Additionally, a calendar of current assignments and future time commitments (vacations, classes, etc.) is built by managers, including potential needs for engagements and investments. Each manager maintains a list of skills and experiences for each person in a skills data base. Marketing uses the standard designations for these skills and experiences to describe resources needed for potential new opportunities.

These various alternatives of reporting create visibility of changing assignments and undesirable utilization. The reports are for relevant managers and representatives of marketing, who meet biweekly to develop an action plan that uses each potentially available person effectively.

COMPUTERIZING PROFESSIONAL SERVICES

The utilization business process requires business computer support, as do all the processes we have examined. No one system can satisfy all of the needs of these processes. It requires an overall set of business applications. By the same token, a business cannot manage three asynchronous administrative processes and five overlapping control systems without computerization. Inadequate computerization is a major inhibitor to growth in professional services and is a focus of national attention and investment in most firms.

It would be impossible to describe all of the computer applications that exist in the major firms today. What is provided in Figure 2-6 and the accompanying description is a hypothetical enterprise model for professional services. Each element of the model contains computer applications necessary to the processes described previously. The application descriptions relate the applications to their corresponding processes. The key operational systems that support the business processes we just reviewed are contract management for the engagement and monthly billing cycles and resource management for utilization and assignments.

• **Marketing.** The marketing systems in professional services manage the client and prospect data bases. The marketing systems contain descriptions and selectable standard terms for packaged services, as well as proposal text and standard statement of work guidelines for customized offerings. They often bridge to systems of the parent organization for access to client history and financial status and product and other service descriptions related to support service offerings.

• **Proposal management.** The proposal systems are sophisticated desktop publishing tools that draw standardized inserts from marketing data bases to be combined with original material generated by the professionals to create a unique set of documents for a client. Proposal systems require a complete range of text, chart graphics, presentation graphics, document management

Figure 2–6
Computer Applications for Professional Services

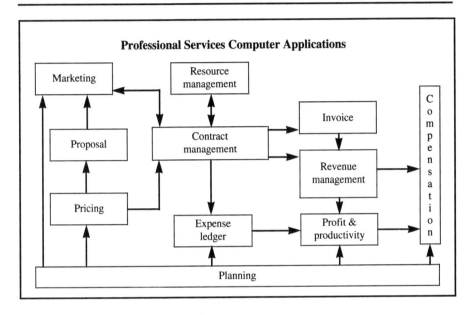

functions, along with formatting and color. Most firms use laser printing in local units. The text editors for proposal systems typically interface with templates created for standard offerings that require only input of client specific names, titles, estimates, schedules, and so on in order to produce a customized offering.

• **Pricing.** The pricing systems for professional services are analytical models that match input assumptions to computation algorithms supported by tables of pricing variables. These can be spreadsheets supported by data files that contain the variables. These can be more sophisticated models that query an input and then activate the appropriate computation model, building the price as it goes. For professional services offers that have standard rates and fixed prices, the marketing systems often contain a price quotation table.

• **Contract management.** The contract management systems are the heart of computer support to professional services. These systems manage the life cycle of an engagement, including the engagement data base. The contract management systems contain a record of all work and vendor resources applied to an engagement and trigger the billing based on each of the criteria discussed earlier. These systems record each historical event of an engagement and pass the information to revenue management systems. The contract management systems provide the trial billing, contract history, backlog, and current utilization reporting in the business cycle described earlier.

- **Resource management.** The resource systems manage and provide combined reporting from four data bases: historical distribution of people resource hours; inventory of people skills and experience; schedule of people resource assignments, personal commitments, and potential assignments; and resumes for marketable people to be used in client communications. Resource systems support the weekly scheduling of people. They support the planning of resources to be used on potential engagements and the effect their skill levels or capacity will have on pricing assumptions. The resource systems are used to assess hiring priorities and to develop and track education plans.

- **Invoicing.** The invoicing systems prepare and distribute client invoices, manage accounts receivable, manage collections and cash deposits, and bridge to revenue management and general ledger.

- **Revenue management.** The revenue management systems maintain and report revenue history for each of the business, service, and territory segments for which growth is being tracked. These systems give support to revenue sharing needed to measure and compensate the sharing of people across offices in a national firm. The revenue systems pass information to compensation systems for payment of individual revenue and sales incentives. Revenue management also bridges revenue to profit management and general ledger systems.

- **Expense management.** The expense management systems include payroll, personnel, purchasing, asset management, general ledger, outstanding expense logging, and any other financial systems designed to budget and capture expenses.

- **Profit management.** The profit management systems accept input from contract management, resource management, revenue management, and expense management to compute the income and expense statement for each level of the business and to compute the revenue and cost rates per hour that determine business line, service line, service offering, and engagement profitability. These systems prepare income and expense spreadsheets for the office level (and sometimes lower), which are rolled upward through successive organizational levels. Data for profit models by lines of business, types of service, specific service offerings, and engagements is exported to spreadsheets. The data contains actual revenue and cost rates by type of resource, actual expenses for nonperson resources, and the corresponding pricing assumptions from the pricing systems to compute and report profitability across various business segments.

- **Compensation.** The compensation systems receive input from revenue and profit management systems and decide whether incentives are due. Firms provide incentives for revenue against quota, expense against budget, sales or backlog against quota, or profit against quota. The compensation systems provide input to payroll and personnel systems to pay the individuals.

- **Planning.** The planning systems are tools to establish measurement objectives and quotas for each business segment and territory. Quotas and/or measurements can be assigned for revenue, expense, profit, utilization, backlog, sales, and productivity.

Most firms have a combination of newer systems specific to their professional services and older systems developed or purchased to support other functions in the parent corporation. Many firms have acquired standard software for common accounting functions such as accounts receivable, general ledger, and payroll. The prohibitive costs of business application software development have prevented even the majors from filling the enterprise model with professional services customized applications. The firms that evolved from a service-based business are not hampered by systems suited only to product distribution, but often do not have a base that can be expanded for the variety of services and resources involved in systems integration. Those that evolved from a product business base have the opposite problem (incomplete function for labor services).

PAPERWORK VERSUS CONTROL

Excessive paperwork and controls are the bane of the services entrepreneur. The level and complexity of controls described previously would be staggering to a manager of an exclusively daily rate consulting service. These controls would also appear to be overkill to those in per hour customized software. They would be viewed as absolutely essential to the systems integrator. The issue is not the complexity of the paperwork and controls, but rather the complexity of the underlying business.

In succeeding chapters, the administration and controls of professional services will be described at levels from simple to complex. In order to illustrate how controls take on the complexity of the business itself, we close this chapter with a summary of the measurements for a simple business.

The simplest services business is time and materials. Consultants are rented to clients to perform as a client directs for a fee per hour or per day, plus a direct reimbursement of any extraordinary expenses. At this level, the fundamental operating strategies continue to apply, but the five measurements are simple and require little time or sophistication.

- **Revenue** requires no segmentation. Managers may choose to periodically analyze revenue by client type or professional skill to determine where growth is occurring. Only per person per rate billing is needed and all clients are billed for every month that work is performed.

- **Utilization** requires weekly reporting and review, skills inventory, and availability scheduling.

- **Net profit and expense** does not involve vendors and complex facility expenses, nor does it require segmentation of expense by revenue segments. A relatively simple general ledger approach is sufficient.

- **Backlog** requires only computation of the remaining hours or days on the time and materials estimate. This can usually be done by hand.

- **Productivity** computations are very necessary to determine the actual revenue and cost rates for each price and skill level. These measurements are not complicated by fixed price prorations or engagement-specific costs such as vendors or classroom facilities.

The full-service professional services office doesn't have it so simple. As soon as any fixed price business is introduced, either as consulting offerings or through education offerings, the simplicity of the process disappears and the complexity of the control process starts. The degree of control is incremental by the number of separate billing and pricing choices offered to clients. All strategies, measurements, and processes listed above will apply in full force for the following business profile.

- A client base that includes both commercial and government institutions that both sole source and request proposals to acquire professional services.

- A set of services that include consulting under client direction, consulting under firm direction, classroom education, and/or product installation and support.

- Each of the services above available either by standard rate, customized rate, or fixed price depending on the risk and responsibility that the firm assumes from the client.

In the chapters that follow, we will see how each of the measurement areas becomes further complicated by the introduction of contractors as an alternative to employee consultants, vendors as part of a firm directed consulting, or systems integration effort and software product support services. The fundamentals remain the same as this complexity is added. The paperwork will increase, simply because the risk of losing control of profitability exceeds the higher margins that these elements bring.

Paperwork done efficiently does not smother entrepreneurship. Paperwork done in a panic to analyze deteriorating growth and margins is bureaucracy at its worst. The message is to bite the bullet and put the control systems in place.

MANAGING PROFESSIONAL SERVICES

The purpose of this chapter was to introduce professional services business management. The discussion focused on:

- The most successful entrepreneur is the one who implements sufficient levels of business control, thus producing the information needed to manage by instinct.

- A professional services office first maximizes the placement of its people, satisfies its clients, and gets follow-on business from those clients. From this base, the office can acquire people with ready credentials, strive for immediate profits, and invest in marketing for growth and diversity.

- The measurements of the professional services business are revenue (market), utilization (inventory), profit, backlog (forecasting), and productivity. These measurements are taken on a regular basis to counteract the unpredictability of the engagement cycle.

- Business computer systems and administration are the tools of business control. These must be comprehensive and reliable in those firms that aspire to diversified growth.

- Business controls can be layered from simple to complex. They are added as diversity increases and subtracted when diversity decreases or becomes routine.

The remainder of the book focuses on the details of managing a large people services office. It is important to keep a perspective of the overall process, while immersed in any part of the process. All processes and all measurements work together to form the whole. The successful professional services entrepreneur is a juggler who knows which ball is about to hit the floor.

Chapter 3

Communication: The Client Comes First

M uch is written on excellence in service to the customer. Quality service is never more essential than in professional services. The consultant and, by association, the firm join the client in a very close relationship—one where they must get close enough to think together. The relationship generates results that benefit the client and maintains the integrity, reputation, and financial health of the firm.

As mentioned before, the relationship between a professional services firm and a client is the realization of an abstract, intellectual end result. This creates innumerable difficulties. If the solution was easy to imagine and implement, the client wouldn't need a consultant. In many cases the client has tried and failed.

The consultants and client come together initially because of the firm's confidence in its methods and the client's faith in the firm's reputation. The firm and its consultants now must bring to the relationship a quality in communications that sees the problem through the minds of all parties and, using this collective brain power, create a solution.

Clients seek out professional services for three fairly broad reasons.

1. *Obtain leadership.* Successful efforts to improve a business or government require project management experience, methodologies, technical knowledge, analytical tools, objectivity, and perseverance that all together are difficult to muster in a client organization. Each of these involves the extensive training of individuals and subsequent application to gain practical experience. A client expends its training budget first in the methods and management of manufacturing, banking, insurance, and welfare administration.

A firm's ability to provide these abstract capabilities is very difficult for the client to validate. References and tangible pre-engagement analysis will be most of what convinces the client to retain the firm. During the engagement, the firm has the ongoing challenge of proving that it knows what it is doing in the face of raging debates over equally viable choices between solutions and alternative approaches. The client's continued credence in the firm's methods, people, and overall leadership will be the key to the success of this relationship.

2. *Supplement resources.* The oldest reason for retaining consultants is still around. Clients will spend short-term cash to avoid long-term expense associated with hiring, educating, paying, and nurturing professionals. Some clients even view this as a try and buy approach to acquiring employees with high priced professional and/or management talent.

This is a particularly tenuous relationship for the firm to maintain. It rarely survives serious disagreements in method or approach, and, as a consequence, the consultant keeps the peace by doing pretty much what the client wants. When the consultants bring a highly refined level of unique experiences and skills, the client will grudgingly keep them in place for the long haul. Otherwise, the client/consultant relationship terminates immediately upon the client determining that no intellectual added value is being realized, regardless of whether the need for supplemental resource has been satisfied or not.

3. *Off-load risk.* A very pervasive, but often subtle reason to retain a professional services firm is to share the risk of failure. Most client executives have seen a business improvement investment fail to achieve a tangible return against substantial unexpected time and cost, particularly one involving software development. The career conscious individual in business and government wants success first, and avoidance of the full responsibility for failure second. The experienced professional services firm can improve the probability for success and provide a partner in failure.

An investment to improve a business or government function can be a daunting undertaking. In many cases it is a bet-your-business and, particularly in the case of the politician and civil servant, bet-your-job proposition. Take for example the enterprise that has a deteriorating cash flow problem. In order to solve the problem, the enterprise needs to spend additional cash to analyze and develop solutions. If the solutions fail, the operation merely killed the patient sooner.

In this situation, the client is willing to pay a premium to get solutions that work the first time. A professional services firm that can demonstrate 85 percent and higher success rates for major ventures similar to those facing the client will be well worth the added expense. The relationship that is established for this reason is often the strongest, because there is a high degree of mutual need. The firm needs the utmost in cooperation from the client to perform at its best to meet the commitments of quality, effort, and schedule. The ethical client is prepared to make the relationship work to get the critical result.

The purpose of this chapter is to cover in detail the business administration and control practices needed to manage the relationship between a professional services firm and its clients. We begin with a discussion of the mechanisms of communication between a firm and a client. We go on to look at the form communication takes and its needed control. We look at using mechanisms, such as change control, to establish expectations and influence satisfaction. The latter part of the chapter is a detailed examination of specific information managed by the firm in its client relationship. The variety of this information increases as a firm moves from basic people services to complex people and nonlabor services.

CLIENT COMMUNICATIONS

Communication between a professional services office and its clients occurs at many levels and in many forms. Since our focus is on the control of the process, rather than its techniques, we will define each level and form of information in terms of its purpose, its media and storage characteristics, and the risk to the firm of its mismanagement.

Client Ownership

Once the first contact is made between the firm and a client, communication between the parties becomes a continuum. Only one office in the firm can "own" the ensuing communication process, and the assignment of this ownership is often a tangled and time consuming process in and of itself. The simplest test of client ownership is, "Which office has local access to the highest decision maker for the relevant services to be marketed?" There are no winners when two offices from the same firm end up in front of a client executive with competing offers.

The assignment of clients within the major firms is well established and steeped with tradition. The assignment of a client with a monolithic organization structure that tightly controls its operating locations from an all-powerful headquarters is generally easy—the office local to the headquarters or which specializes in that client industry is the communication and account owner. Offices near the operating locations may participate, but under the communication control of the headquarters owning office.

The assignment of a fragmented client enterprise is more challenging and is often an opportunity for senior executives of the firm to get together and share their thoughts. The logical (and sometimes actual) assignment is to bond with the authority structure of the client. Each operating unit of a client (division, marketing/distribution region, product/service provider) that makes all tactical decisions up to certain levels of funding is treated as an independent client and assigned to a firm's local or specialty office. In addition, the governing level of the client enterprise (corporate/subsidiary headquarters, central government body) is considered a client location itself and is assigned separately to an appropriate firm office. We will discuss various options for compensation and compensation sharing in Chapters 4 and 9. Very likely some form of sharing will be in place to encourage these offices to manage communication to benefit the client and avoid embarrassment.

Once ownership is established, all communication between the office and the client becomes part of a deliberate process.

- **The individual(s) who participate in any communication will be consciously assigned and coached.** This ensures that all parties, both client and firm, know who each are and know what mechanisms will be used to manage communication.

- **Needed communication will be planned and, if necessary, firm-assigned personnel will be rehearsed.** This emphasizes to all that the responsibility for coordinating communication lies with the firm. The client is owed a managed process for the collection and dissemination of information. Firm personnel, be they consultants or subcontractors, should represent the quality and professionalism the client expects.

- **The degrees of formality will not be left to chance.** Effective communication between firm and client requires clear channels and a variety of documentation levels. Someone has to be in charge and all must know who it is.

- **All communication will be reviewed regularly.** Communication needs reinforcement—something said once is rarely remembered. Repetition, both in face-to-face dialogue and through postmortems, is essential to the firm's responsibility to listen, consider, and advise.

Those who argue against the restrictions of controlled communication should remember that clients hire professional services firms for their composite brains, not the brain of any one individual. Keeping control over communications is simply a demonstration of the professionalism the client is buying. Clients will tell you, if their goal had been miscommunication and the loss of valuable needs, opinions, and ideas, they could have easily accomplished that on their own without the help of expensive consultants.

FIGURE 3–1
Levels of Communication and Information

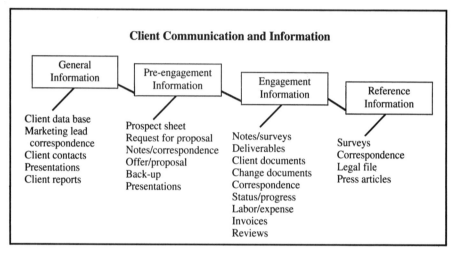

What Is Communicated

Later in this chapter, we will look at what and how information is stored in its various paper and electronic media. In general, all client information should end up in a data base from which it can be controlled and further used. In reality, there is rarely a single file, and the discussion that follows will identify common practices used to organize and store client and engagement records.

The office that owns a client will be concerned with managing four levels of communication and information as illustrated in Figure 3-1 and described here.

1. *Client general information.* This includes all data, correspondence, meeting notes, and marketing materials that are unspecific to any current or future engagements. Very often this involves communication with key executives on a variety of subjects. It always involves any communication between the firm and its sources of marketing leads. Most input to an electronic client record is generated from this level of communication.

2. *Pre-engagement information.* This includes all information collected and generated during the marketing and proposal process for an engagement. It could be as simple as notes from two or three meetings, a penciled plan, and an estimate and a letter with confirming agreement. On the other hand it could represent the results of months of meetings and interviews, prototype work products, sophisticated presentation materials, a massive proposal and assumptions document, a file of correspondence with the client and potential business partners, and pages of planning and estimating documentation.

3. *The engagement file.* This is a daily record of the communication that occurs during each phase, event, and contract of an engagement. It consists of the client confidential information collected as input to consultant analysis and usually kept at the client location. It consists of notes and analysis, which may or may not be client confidential. It includes all formal correspondence, progress reports, work products, labor records, expense records, invoices or other billing detail, audits and engagement reviews, and project management documentation, most of which is jointly owned by the client and the firm. It contains notes and reports of internal firm assessments of its performance, client satisfaction and financial reports on revenue, utilization, and productivity (engagement profitability).

4. *Client reference information.* This is correspondence, telephone and meeting notes, press materials, legal documentation, and survey results that relate to the client's attitude regarding the firm. This is usually a mixture of good news and bad news. The good news is public and private statements that a client has made and may be prepared to repeat regarding the competence and credibility of the firm and its people. The bad news is usually specific to an engagement and at best is an expression of dissatisfaction and at worst, a court proceeding.

The opinion of a client toward the firm is a perishable commodity. Its willingness to be referenced can change for a number of reasons, most of which have nothing to do with the relationship with the firm. The client needs to be contacted each time it is to be used as a reference. This file contains the continuing notes from those contacts.

BASIC COMMUNICATION CONTROLS

The secret to managing communication is to use points of contact, make records, and store the records where you can get at them. The high energy, entrepreneurial marketer and consultant considers none of these a very high priority. It requires continual diligence on the part of the office executive to ensure that these basic rules of communication management are part of the professional culture.

We will look at each of these practices in the context of the four levels of client information just discussed.

Points of Contact

Establishing a point of contact is simply assigning leadership to the process of communicating effectively. In some cases it is the assignment of a firm person to a corresponding client person who is an obvious point of information and decision in their organization. More often, though, it is a negotiated agreement between firm and client that will focus lines of communication within a large body of participants on both sides (i.e., a project administrator for the client and a project manager for the firm).

Points of contact are not intended to restrict the flow of information, although that is one of the results of its mismanagement. When put in place correctly and the leadership is effective, points of contact will allow free and spontaneous contact to occur at all levels. The freer the parties are to meet together, the more likely it is that the firm will learn what it needs to know with the least expense.

The responsibility of a communication point of contact is to act as a clearinghouse for communication traffic to and from the client. The most important element of this responsibility is to be aware of who and what subjects make up previous, current, and future discussions and what has been written. At a minimum, the point of contact should:

- Appoint and coach those representing the firm and point them toward their corresponding client contacts.
- Approve the objectives expected from each contact.
- Debrief all who have been in contact with the client.
- Prevent duplication.
- Collect and control all communication media.

Additionally, points of contact can find themselves with these greater responsibilities.

- Develop and disseminate the detailed plan for gathering information, developing marketing or engagement documents, and publishing materials and documents.
- Review and edit correspondence and documents.
- Prepare periodic status or progress reports of a protracted marketing or performance endeavor (usually a client version and a firm version).

The point of contact during a **general information** communication process with a client may start out as a senior marketing or management member of the office. As soon as ownership of the client is established, the ongoing point of contact for that client needs to be named for control purposes. The first contact this person makes will be to follow up the marketing lead that brought knowledge of the client to the office.

Often the member of the firm is acting alone during the initial contact pro-cess. The underlying purpose of these contacts is to qualify whether the client has a need that is within the capabilities of the firm to pursue and whether the client has the financial wherewithal to pay what may be required. Until the firm judges the client to be qualified in these two areas, further marketing invest-ment is not warranted.

Acting alone does not relieve the firm's point of contact from executing these basics. Each call to or on the client should have objectives. These should be reviewed with a second party (often the field executive for key client oppor-tunities). The notes from the call should be reviewed and edited by the individ-ual and a formal next action should be written down. The notes, resulting correspondence, and any gathered material should be placed in an accessible client file.

Often the general client contact involves delivering generic marketing mate-rials to a client. If these change very frequently, it might be well to have a note to that effect (or a copy of the materials) in the file to remind future firm per-sonnel of the need to update the client's perceptions created by these materials.

The point of contact in the **pre-engagement** and **engagement** contact with the client is the marketing representative, proposal manager, consulting services manager, project manager/director, or lead consultant who has development and delivery responsibility for the end products of the marketing or engage-ment efforts. The effort can be the work of one or two. It can involve the entire office.

The responsibilities are summed into the generic leadership role defined in dozens of publications as project management. Although the role of a project manager is substantially greater than that of communications point of contact, center post for communications is a fundamental part of project management duties.

The most difficult communication task of the proposal or performance manager is debriefing. When 10 or more people are in constant contact with a client, individual debriefings would require a 27-hour day for effective point of contact management. The more manageable approach is a weekly status re-view, where each individual recaps the communication of the previous period and the group plans its communication tactics for the next period. This allows the leader to both receive and disseminate at the same time, while members of the group learn from each other how to best interact with various levels of cli-ent personnel. Clients who argue that meetings of this type are a waste of con-sultant fee need to be reminded that they hired the firm for just such effective management of communication.

The point of contact for **client reference information** is again the individual in the firm who has overall marketing representation to the client. It seems that the less satisfied the client, the higher in the firm organization this point of contact gets assigned.

Making Communication Records

Recording communication is the hard part for busy consultants and marketers. They like to keep everything in their heads and some are able to retain incredible amounts of information. The issue is the dissemination of the information, rather than its archiving (although both are necessary).

Most records of communication are informal. These consist of notes taken during telephone conversations, meetings, and interviews. Informal records also include ideas, conclusions, and observations that are to be shared among the client and/or firm participants. Informal records should be stored and disseminated informally. Asking professional services people to convert notes into formal, typed documentation is time wasting and usually sterilizes the instinctual content of first-hand notes.

The most effective communication of informal records is in the regular status reviews discussed above. The natural tendency of review participants is to summarize their thoughts and comments from their detailed notes. The questions from their peers will clarify ambiguity and often cause the person to see their notes in a different light. In this way, all of the information is disseminated, not just one person's version of the important points. The point of contact for the group will record additional notes or prepare a status report that supplements the details of the individual notes collected from each person in the group.

Records of general client information. General contact between firm and client focuses on very narrow objectives. A client meeting may only be held to convince both parties to meet again. The bulk of the records from general communication are those prepared prior to meetings with the client. These include information that presents the firm's credentials and asks questions that get at the client's motivation to use the firm. The notes from this meeting will contain perceived reactions to the firm's presentation, answers to planned questions, impressions gathered from the later debriefing of the team, and any client data and documents that were gathered.

Meetings with a marketing lead source can generate a fair amount of material. The lead source likely has a lot of marketing materials, presentations, and assessments that relate to its products and services vis-a-vis this client. Some of this might even be useful to the professional services firm. All of it usually requires retention, simply because it may be needed later.

The most important piece of information to be gathered from the source of the marketing lead is an identification of key individuals in the client organization who will be key client contacts. The least credible alliance partner is the one that cannot lay out the decision structure of the client. Hours of purposeless telephone calls and meetings can be saved by knowing to whom, and in what order, the firm should make its approach. The notes on client organization and key contacts will be disseminated many times in the ensuing relationship and, because they change, will be a key management responsibility of each point of contact in the future.

Recordkeeping for pre-engagement activities. Typically, the general relationship with a client moves to the pre-engagement relationship when a prospect summary is prepared by the general point of contact, and assignment of a proposal manager is made. This can be a simple top sheet with notes on who to contact and a list of the key elements of the service, accompanied by copies of the relevant materials and notes. The prospect summary can be a more complex questionnaire-like document that assesses how far the client qualification process has proceeded. The materials provided may include a request for a proposal written by the client. Very often, the results of initial client contacts are summarized in a letter to the client and/or source of the marketing lead that confirms that the firm will proceed toward an offering, depending on the outcome of specific actions.

All of this material becomes part of the engagement file for the client. This file will build dramatically over time. The better the records supplied at the outset of pre-engagement, the more productive will be the effort to qualify the client and get an offer out. Clients are not very impressed when the firm's consultants go over old ground at $150 per hour, because information gathered earlier was not passed on.

There is one situation to look out for. When the individual who acted as point during the general contact with the client also performs the duties to prepare the offering, there is much less incentive to build a file. The formal hand off to someone else acts as a catalyst to get general client information documented and to separate the specific engagement starting materials. When everyone gets very busy, work on this prospect may get deferred and the undocumented knowledge will grow cold. Picking it up and trying to finish its qualification and offer will be like starting all over again.

Engagement records. Making records during engagement performance is a planned element of the firm's consulting methods. Generally, everything learned and concluded about a client is documented in a predefined work product. For its legal protection, all materials generated for or about the client is archived by the firm. This particularly includes the summarized notes of interviews, meetings, and telephone calls.

Clients often like to debate the subject of over- or under-documentation. In the eyes of a client, over-documentation is more volume and formality than it is willing to pay for. By the same token, under-documentation is less volume or less style than the client expected for the price it paid. Usually, over-documentation is a concern in per hour or per day engagements and the opposite is the issue when a fixed price is charged.

The best protection from losing these debates is to provide a clear outline of the work products to be produced as part of the offering and to have available examples of these documents and materials that have been declassified from previous engagements. Most firms take a hard line on this subject. After all, the client hired the firm because of its experience and track record in these endeavors.

An extensive list of typical engagement documents and electronic media is provided later in this chapter. Choices between media are also discussed. The modern client expects the modern professional services firm to be experts in documentation and desktop publishing technology. The major firms devote considerable attention to ensuring that engagement recordkeeping is a fine balance between cheap and impressive.

Postengagement recordkeeping.   Postengagement records are usually very formal. They document formal activities with the client: a survey was made of satisfaction, the client sent a letter or made a contact that was documented with a letter, or the client was contacted as a reference which was confirmed with a letter. Simple business courtesy dictates formal correspondence during this period of communication. It also makes the lawyers happier.

Because postengagement communication requires formal correspondence, it is often put off. If the client is unhappy, this can be a big mistake. If the client is happy, it means a lost opportunity, both with this client and others who would be influenced by a reference. Making sure that postengagement communication is timely and effective can have a large payback to a business that survives based on its reputation.

CHANGE CONTROL

No professional services effort is going to go precisely the way it was planned. This shouldn't be a surprise, since if the activity was easy and straightforward, the client wouldn't need an expensive consultant in the first place. Inevitably, however, the client is not going to readily accept the uncertainty and turmoil that change engenders. The successful firm is the one that manages change as an essential part of its communication discipline.

Education of the client in the process of managing change occurs from the very moment the detailed plan for the effort is presented. The plan description will include assumptions upon which the effort is based. The accuracy of these assumptions will be tested even within the first few hours after work begins. Inevitably, one or more of these will prove incorrect.

The following are changes to planning assumptions that are certain to occur early in the performance of an engagement.

- The number of people to be interviewed grows, or interviews are to occur in unanticipated locations.
- An interview is delayed beyond the schedule.
- A consultant or a contractor assignment is delayed.
- Client support (people, facilities, supplies) is delayed.
- Needed consultant or client training or materials are delayed.

These, of course, are the easy ones. Later in the effort, people will become unavailable, concepts will emerge that were not anticipated, the client business itself will change, and estimates will prove both too large and too small. It is the actions taken by the consultant leadership during the early hours of the effort that will set the tone and pattern for change management of the crucial, big ones near the end of the effort.

Given that the first priority is to keep the client satisfied, the natural instinct of a consultant might be to acknowledge one of these problems and reassure the client that it will have no effect on cost, schedule, or quality of the end products. This might even be true, but it ignores the opportunity to use change management as an expectation-setting vehicle with the client. Unless the effort is very short and very lucky, there will arrive a change in assumptions that cannot be absorbed into the cost and/or schedule without a compromise in end product. The sooner the pattern of negotiation on changes occurs, the more effective will be the expectation-setting process later on.

Too often, consulting leaders suppress the visibility of changes in order to stay on plan. They believe the client will be happier not knowing that schedule and cost are at risk. Inevitably, the first time a client becomes involved in the change assessment process is for a big one that cannot be accommodated. A working give and take on small changes can prepare the parties for tough decisions that need to be made on a large deviation from plan.

All project leaders and managers are trained in the mechanics of change control. These include techniques to sense when assumptions have become invalidated and the steps in assessing impact on cost, schedule, and work products. The training should include how to lead a client through assessing trade-offs and negotiating an agreement where scope, schedule, and cost will be affected.

The following is an example of how change negotiation on a day-by-day basis will build client expectation and reduce unpleasant surprises when work products begin to appear during the consulting effort.

> The plan for a consulting effort calls for a document to be produced at a ninth week checkpoint. An outline of the document was included with the proposal and listed five areas to be analyzed. The lead consultant's plan contains assumptions regarding the number of interviews, hours per interview and subsequent analysis, staffing of consultants, staffing of client support personnel, and the probable size and writing effort for the document.
>
> Two weeks into the effort, the client insists that two additional interviews will be required, while at the same time the lead consultant discovers that one of the consultants scheduled for the effort will be three days late due to delays in completing another assignment. Having assessed the impact of the two changes taken together, the lead consultant reports to the client that the schedule must be extended by four days and the expected cost might increase by the rate times 50 hours.
>
> Since one of the changes is firm initiated, the client refuses to agree to the cost increase, but indicates flexibility on the schedule increase due to the extra interviews. The lead consultant stands firm by pointing out that the schedule increase alone causes a cost increase in project leadership time and that the firm will not add more consultants to shorten the schedule.
>
> The lead consultant does offer an alternative that reduces some of the planned effort on the document to compensate for the 50 hours—the client staff can take responsibility for writing the glossary and for drawing and publishing process diagrams using rough notes from the consultants. The client agrees that this might be a solution and asks to see an example of the work his people would be doing.
>
> The consultant returns with examples of both notes and the process diagrams that the firm had intended to include in the document. The client is very surprised. These diagrams do not conform to their new standards recently published for such documentation, which may or may not have been communicated previously to the firm. To avoid considerable rework, the client insists that the new standard be used as the basis for this portion of the consultant's document.
>
> Since the change of diagram style is now known before any work on the process descriptions has started, the lead consultant agrees this can be absorbed into the new plan, assuming the client agrees to using his people on the document. An agreement is reached and documented and all *three* changes are absorbed with only a delay in schedule and no increase in consultant cost.

The moral to this story is that early change negotiation can uncover unknown unknowns—events that have no probability of occurring. Eventually, someone on that effort would have seen an example of the client or the firm's standard and mentioned the difference. A lot of luck would be needed, though, to avoid considerable wasted effort. The conversation probably included other areas of that document that the client had only considered in general terms, but now viewed in considerably more detail. The firm has used the change process to precondition the client to accept a work product that is many weeks away and has avoided unpleasant debates regarding rework after portions of the document have already been produced.

Obviously, these issues should be addressed during the offering stage of the consulting service, but no matter how thorough the proposal investigation, these types of changes will pop out of nowhere. The change management process, used to first address very small impact items that can be absorbed into the schedule, uncovers hidden stones and gets both parties ready to deal with the large items. It also prevents the accumulation of small items that often creates cost and schedule "creep" (20 delays of one day each is eventually a month). Most importantly though, the client who participates in this communication process is led step-by-step to each milestone and is not surprised by the end products. The client believes that the effort was managed well and that the products were the best that could be expected.

RETRIEVAL OF INFORMATION

Modern electronics have not been all good news to the control of information. To some extent we miss the days of all paper, because as long as any information was set down on paper, the paper could be placed in a file that could be stored in a very large room. Now information about a client is multimedia and likely to be stored in multiple locations and forms.

The concept surrounding storage and retrieval of client information is simple. General and postengagement information is stored in a client data base and pre-engagement, engagement, and specific postengagement information is stored in a series of engagement and contract data bases. These are various combinations of paper and electronic files that test the discipline, patience, and abilities of a professional services office staff.

Types of Information Media

Typically, the information about the client takes the following forms.

• **Electronically prepared correspondence.** These are letters, memoranda, notes, and reports that are processed and can be stored electronically. Office equipment for this purpose ranges from the simplest word processor with tape or disk storage to electronic mail networks. Electronic correspondence adds value to a business operation in two key functions: ease and efficiency of preparation, editing, and publishing; and ease and speed of distribution. We will focus primarily on its utility in distribution.

As a general rule, correspondence prepared electronically is stored in the medium of its distribution. A formal letter to a client is stored in hard copy, even though its image is available electronically. In this case a hard copy backup file is unnecessary because of the existence of the electronic version. By the same token, an electronic note or memo between members of the firm concerning a client will be stored electronically and its backup will be both electronic and hard copy.

The challenge here is indexing. The electronic storage media associated with word processing and electronic mail have default pockets into which to store letters, memos, notes, and so on when no specific designation is given. These can usually be retrieved by a knowledgeable user through default indexing by addressee and/or author. When all participants, though, are allowed to store client communications in default electronic files, the extraction of all of these to a single point of review can be a nightmare.

Three choices are available depending on the expected volume of communication and the expected longevity of the relationship. If the volume will be low, the simplest approach is to hard copy each piece of correspondence and store it in either or both the client or engagement physical files. This is likely to be the choice during the early general and pre-engagement periods of client relationships.

If the expectation is a long, single contract relationship with the client, a specific electronic log should be established on all word processors and in the electronic mail network to which any communication to the client is stored or routed. This requires direct and forceful action by someone to ensure that this discipline is put in place.

If the expectation is a long and multicontract relationship with the client, a combination of these approaches will be required. The points of contact for each current relationship will need to assume electronic communication storage control in addition to their other duties. Word processing storage should have a log for each client. The name of the point of contact needs to be associated with each item stored in the log, regardless of the author (e.g., a letter is signed by the field executive, but is actually prepared by the senior account marketer as part of pre-engagement activities). All electronic mail communication includes the point of contact at least by copy and is stored by that individual in a specific log for that client. This avoids having key communication between the firm and client mixed in with personal mail and notes. When the point of contact changes, the electronic client log can easily be shipped to the next person, either in hard copy or electronically.

Even though electronic distribution of correspondence is not a substitute for the sensible management of communication, it has become a major boon to the professional services business. Electronic tools increase communication and the flow of the information that is the essence of the consultant's added value to a client. This increase, when managed incorrectly, creates the opportunity to go out of control even sooner.

- **Informal notes and other hard copy materials.** Soon the capability will exist universally to scan and electronically store communications that originated via pencil and paper or paper copy distribution. When that is in place, the rules for electronically distributed communication will apply. For those who do not have the paperless office, an efficient filing system for paper is needed, short of keying everything that is recorded or received.

The point of contact has the pivotal responsibility for paper filing. As has been mentioned before, the paper goes either into a general client file or an engagement file (or sometimes both). The challenge here is when to file versus keeping the paper in a drawer or briefcase for easy use. The answer, of course, is when more than one person needs access. The signal should be when the point of contact is asked to make copies. As soon as that occurs, the entire file should be copied and/or stored for universal use.

- **Client documents.** Client documents fall into three categories: those that are public or represent external correspondence; those that are internal, but do not need to be returned following their use by the firm; and those that are provided on a limited exposure basis to members of the firm and are to be returned with any copies. Public documents and most correspondence from the client is stored and retrieved as with paper documents. (Or as electronic communication where the firm and client are on electronic mail together.)

Client internal documents, confidential correspondence, and confidential documents usually require special handling. Part of the contract agreement between the client and the firm must specifically address the identification of such materials. This usually includes some specific broad information categories, such as all accounting and financial documents. The agreement defines an identification mechanism for any materials that fall outside of broad categories, such as client generated correspondence or surveys and interviews conducted outside of the engagement.

Very often the client agrees that the firm can retain an archive of these documents with specific storage and access terms and conditions. This is particularly necessary when the documents become work products of the firm on behalf of the client, such as examples of reports to be included in the new system or lists of elements to be included in a new business process or data base. These should be logged as vital records and stored accordingly. The log becomes part of the engagement file. Confidential correspondence from the client always falls in this category.

If the firm cannot have the documents for archive, the documents should not leave the client premises and should be stored in a physical file maintained by the lead consultant or project manager. Copies made for individual consultants should be destroyed after use. Very often each consultant with a need to know will be asked to sign a nondisclosure agreement.

• **Client-related business management records (i.e., billing, backlog, profitability, status, etc.).** The best financial and measurement information system is one that produces reports on request, rather than pumping out reams of paper every time it runs. Unfortunately, this is rarely the case. Most businesses have four tree reports that contain everything for everyone in exquisite detail and get distributed to every business unit regularly. These arrive on paper and need to be broken down or manually summarized by engagement. Giant strides are being taken to improve the distribution of reports away from hard copy, but for the foreseeable future, computer printouts will remain a formidable part of communications.

Computer related documents usually fall into three rough categories: reports that provide summary and/or detail of overall business activity, such as billing, backlog, and contract changes; machine-produced documents that are broken down by client or engagement per page(s) such as invoices, purchase orders to client specific vendors, client status reports, and client profiles; and various forms of input documents that exist in their original handwritten or typewritten form, as well as in a recapped form on a machine-produced audit trail.

Most offices continue to see the traditional binders of computer printout for reports of overall business category and machine-produced audit trails. Even with electronic document distribution, there is usually one printed version in a binder for all to see. These are filed by week or month in separate binders for each report each year. The logical replacement for this will be the ability to locally store an electronic version of the report for call up, selective review, and selective printing at workstations.

All client specific output should be stored in the appropriate engagement physical file and cross-filed in a file specific to the type of document (i.e., purchase orders, invoices). The most efficient approach is to be provided with an electronic transaction log of these documents that is stored in a general file, with the specific document stored in the client or engagement file.

• **Marketing, client presentation, client training, and project management materials.** These materials present a special problem of storage and retrieval. They are usually graphic and spreadsheet output that requires special printing. They are often a combination of locally and nationally produced materials that are subject to version changes. The challenge is to be able to reconstruct the sequence in which a client saw various versions of the materials (and the expectation set at the time).

The simple approach is to store the complete hard copy package used with the client or engagement. Each package is dated to allow reconstruction of the sequence. This requires exceptional discipline and lots of file space. There are a variety of more complex approaches that either try to reduce the paper storage problem where general materials are typically disseminated to the bulk of clients, or try to make use of electronically retrievable versions of these materials, rather than their hard copy storage. The increased function in desktop publishing to allow insertion of graphics into electronic communication will ultimately reduce the problem to the one similar to electronic mail. It can't occur, though, until local printing equipment can reproduce nationally developed glossies from electronic distribution.

There is great embarrassment when a client (or separate parts of the client organization) has seen conflicting versions of marketing, training, and management materials. These may have the greatest effect on client expectation, simply because they are the most graphic. It is absolutely essential to be able to reproduce the order of delivery and audience of these materials.

Consultants and marketers will cooperate with communication disciplines, if they see them as a means to get information they need and if they fit into their normal work and movement patterns. These same people are also notorious pack rats and are often using old versions of information. An easy and effective way to build reliance on central information sources is to encourage the destruction of copies soon after their distribution.

Client Data Base

Very early in a client relationship, information about the client begins to be necessary. It starts with names, titles, and telephone numbers and goes on to addresses, organization structures, tax exemptions, and marketing territory classifications.

It is never too early to start collecting and disseminating the information. Nothing is more frustrating than for a busy marketer or field executive to have to call around for the address of a client an hour before a meeting. Nothing is more embarrassing than to arrive at the wrong building and be late for a meeting. At a minimum, these things waste valuable time. At worst, it can mean the loss of credibility and business.

The information to be collected and stored about a client falls into some logical categories. Much of this can and ought to be maintained in a computerized client data base. Some does not lend itself to computerization and will require paper files. Information in both forms is summarized in Figure 3-2. Information collected that is unique to an engagement becomes part of the engagement file, to be discussed later.

Client information that needs to be available to a professional services office includes the following.

Figure 3-2
Information in a Client Data Base and Client File

Client Data		
Item	**Paper?**	**Electronic?**
Client business names		✓
Key contacts	✓	✓
Addresses		✓
Marketing lead sources		✓
Territory assignments		✓
Organization structure	✓	
Financial condition	✓	✓
Taxation characteristics		✓
Discount characteristics		✓
Market characteristics/industry		✓
History		
Engagements		✓
Billing		✓
People used	✓	✓
Satisfaction surveys	✓	✓

- **Client business names.** It may seem trivial, but one of the earliest requirements and one of the most important pieces of information is the set of names that the client is known by. At a minimum, it will be the chartered name and the name of the local unit. It may also include an abbreviation and various trade and business names. Typically three levels of names and their corresponding abbreviated names will satisfy the various needs of correspondence, invoicing, proposal customization, contracts, and marketing materials that will be personalized for this client. The highest level is **enterprise** which is the parent corporation or government. The next level is **client** which is the organization that will own the contract and pay the bills. The third level is the **customer** or **establishment** where the work will be performed.
- **Key contacts.** There are at least two key people at each of the client and customer levels of a client organization. One is the individual who acts as point of contact for the client/firm relationship, and the other is the decision maker who controls the funds at the client level and approves performance at the customer level. There may also be the same pair of contacts at the enterprise level where a national agreement is in effect. There is likely one additional contact in the client level organization who approves invoices for payment (purchasing agent). For every name there is a telephone number.
- **Addresses.** Generally, there is an address for invoices and one for where the work is to be performed. Additionally, there may be addresses for each of the key contacts for contracts and correspondence, where different. It is ex-

tremely important to get zip codes for every address. Performance location and invoicing location zip codes will directly affect taxation decisions.

• **Marketing lead sources.** The detail needed about the source of a client marketing lead depends on whether the supplier of the lead will be a participant in the client relationship and whether compensation is provided for leads. If the answer to both of these questions is no, then the name of the business entity, person, correspondence address, and telephone number will likely be sufficient for acknowledgments and lead source analysis. If either of the answers is yes, then additional information will be necessary for payment addresses and coding to link up with corresponding computer systems, for the physical location address of the key contact for the lead for meetings, and for lead source classification information to trigger their compensation.

• **Marketing territory and marketplace classifications.** As discussed earlier, every client is owned by an office and the client data base identifies this owning office and any upper-level organizations (regions, areas) that participate in this ownership. In addition, the office probably has established territories within its ownership for marketing and engagement performance measurement purposes. These territories may be determined by geography, by the business or government purpose of the client, by a source of prospect leads, or by the service to be performed. The only sure bet on the future of territory assignments is that they will change. The person or team with account responsibility and their management will be measured on the success of the business with the client and compensated accordingly.

• **Organizational information.** Detailed descriptions of the organizational hierarchy of a client are also necessary for two reasons: to determine key decision makers who will participate in the marketing and performance checkpoints; and to determine how many people will need to be surveyed, interviewed, and won over during the performance of the consulting effort. The first reason is the basis for much of the marketing and performance strategy, while the second is fundamental to the estimates of effort that become a basis for the price.

Organizational information is awkward to maintain and distribute. It does not lend itself to computerization without sophisticated graphics capability at everyone's immediate fingertips, and it changes frequently. Responsibility for maintaining at least hand-drawn charts falls to the lead marketer prior to contract execution and to the consulting services manager and the corresponding lead consultant during execution. Engagement reviews often begin with a reexamination of the current client organization charts to see that they are accurate and assess whether communication tactics should change.

• **Client financial condition.** The information collected regarding the financial status of a client has a variety of uses and takes a variety of forms. Much of the information is client confidential and has restricted distribution designated by disclosure agreements, law, and all-important business ethics. Some is from public record. Some are the confidential opinions expressed by various members of the firm, which should be restricted to only those with a need to know. Typically, client financial information is collected and stored in three ways.

- Public data such as annual reports, government records, and articles that are maintained as part of the marketing and performance files for the client in general.
- Information collected in the performance of an engagement as described earlier.
- Data maintained by the firm regarding the credit and investment risk of the client. Both are internally confidential to the firm and likely have separate places of storage, although they may have been generated by the same financial analysis staff. The former guides the local office in deciding how much resource to expend on behalf of a client before obtaining at least partial payment.

Partitioning of client financial information is a serious control issue for a professional services firm. An accusation of leaking insider information can be devastating to the reputation of the firm.

- **Taxation characteristics.** Very few American tax jurisdictions charge a sales tax on service, but many charge tax on publications, software, and equipment. The client will get preferential tax treatment in some jurisdictions depending on whether it meets appropriate institutional criteria (education, health, federal or state, etc.). Usually, the taxation characteristics of a client are coded to activate the appropriate computations and accountings during billing.
- **Discounting characteristics.** Many clients have national agreements with the firm that establish volume discounts or other preferential pricing for local engagements. Discounting can easily be forgotten when not communicated properly, causing considerable embarrassment later.
- **Marketplace characteristics.** An important element of information about a client is the services market of which it is a part. The full-service firm will go for a growth in revenue from trucking clients, if economic observers signal an increase in noncapital spending within the trucking industry. A firm that concentrated only in a specific client set such as banks had to quickly expand to other markets in 1990. The range of complexity in marketplace definition used by firms for their clients can be illustrated by the following two examples.

- An industry classification for each of the client and the client parent enterprise, if any. The classification system uses U.S. government published standards for a high-level breakdown (major categories, such as manufacturing, insurance, state and local government, health, etc.). The coding has a second level of classification designed by the firm to designate subcategories (automobile manufacturing, life/health insurance, city government, private hospital, etc.). The dozen or so high-level classifications lend themselves to pie charts showing marketplace penetration, while the second level can be used to show the growth of a targeted business area such as retail banks.

- An affinity classification that designates the client's potential and past record regarding lines of services offered by the firm. The variety of affinity classifications are endless and can only be described by example: Fortune 500 firms that have not availed themselves of a firm's strategic planning offering; firms that have ordered a product or service from the firm or business partner and have not ordered a support service; newly chartered or funded institutions that fit the profile for a firm's consulting, education, or software service offering; the clients within an enterprise that have yet to avail themselves of a service offering that has shown good success in other parts of the enterprise; the follow-on clients from a strategic consulting effort within an enterprise.

The more complex the marketplace classification, the higher the risk of data becoming obsolete and, therefore, not believable. A high-level industry classification can be assigned once, will rarely change, and is essential for analyzing the firm's revenue performance against economic data and market research. Any detail below that must be accompanied by a commitment of administrative expenditure to keep the information current and, therefore, usable.

- **History.** Three sets of historical data need to be maintained for each client.
- *Engagement:* The historical status of each contract within each engagement with this client. Typically, the list shows the type of service performed, the type of contract used, the effort and revenue estimated and actually received, the dates and current status, and an indication of where to go for the detailed files. This is ideally a computerized list from the marketing and contract management systems.
- *Billing and collections:* A list of all invoices to the client and their status of payment. This is ideally a computerized list from the contract management and invoicing systems.
- *Resources:* A history of each person and vendor used or assigned on behalf of the client. Typically, the list shows the amount of effort and the dates, revenue received, expense incurred (particularly for vendors), location of work performed, and some indication of satisfaction level. This is ideally a computerized list from the contract management and resource systems.

The historical information that is kept concerning clients can be much more extensive than the list above. Accounting and legal practices may dictate very comprehensive archiving of the details of the client relationship. For instance, copies of invoices may be kept readily available for two to five years. The information just described is the minimum needed to support ongoing marketing and engagement relationships between an office and its current and potential clients.

Client Data Base Versus the Local Client File

The evolution of the major professional services firm as discussed in Chapter 1 is a clue to the current state of the art regarding computerized client data base systems. All but a very few of today's firms evolved from an established national or international business. Early in their own implementation of ordering and billing systems, they built client/customer data bases to support their various products and services. These client data base systems have undergone various levels of consolidation and improvement over the years. Consistent with the minimum investment strategy of forming the business, one (maybe even the most appropriate) was chosen for professional services.

As one would expect, the utility of client data base systems to a local office can vary widely from firm to firm. Many have a wide choice of information elements that can be stored regarding a client organization. The data may be under the control of a headquarters function outside the professional services offices, often even outside the professional services business organization. Its utility, particularly for complex people services, is very inflexible. At the other extreme are limited information data bases created solely to support accounting systems for basic people services that are old and provide no utility to professional services marketing.

A practical solution to increasing the utility of national client data and meeting the expanded needs of the local office is a two-level filing process that extracts relevant information from the national system on a periodic basis, say weekly. The primary base of information is a local file built onto the extracted national data. If the national file satisfies most of the need, the local file may be simply a printed profile kept in a manual file folder with the local information. If the national data requires considerable expansion, the local file may be computerized, with a supporting paper file of those components that are more easily maintained on hard copy.

As will be seen with all of the computer application systems that support professional services, the rapid growth and change in volumes and varieties of services has not been equally matched by new programming. Client data is merely the first of many examples.

Engagement and Contract Data Base

An extremely important computerized business system for the professional services office is the contract management system. This system contains an electronic inventory of all current, past, and potential engagements and contracts for the office. Architecturally, the contract management system forms a bridge between marketing support systems that manage general client information and the invoicing system that is triggered when a client payment is due.

The contract management system should contain a record of each finite agreement (contract) between the firm and the client. One contract might be for a class; others may be a period of consulting, the second phase of a systems integration project, or an individual support call. Additionally, the contract management system should be able to cluster a group of these individual contracts into an engagement that is a series of like or sequentially related contracts. Thus, engagements might be a set of the same class, an entire systems integration project, or all of the calls under a support agreement.

Later chapters will discuss the detailed control mechanisms needed to ensure that entries onto the contract management system are accurate and timely. The highest and best use of the system is to manage the entire life cycle of all engagements and contracts within engagements. This means entry of information to the contract management system at the beginning of pre-engagement, and the continued management and updating of the information through any post-engagement activities that change the status of the completed or terminated contract.

A contract management system that supports the complete engagement life cycle can provide an index of events to aid in client communications. A status report or a query to the contract management system lists those proposals and contracts for which corresponding communication control files should be in place. Additionally, the contract management system provides a base from which to manage the assignment and tracking of people assigned to the client and show the current point of contact.

Information about engagements and contracts, like information about clients, will be split between paper and electronic files. Figure 3-3 summarizes the information and where it is likely to be found.

Information carried by a contract management system might include the following.

Engagement Information
- **Client identifier.** The client identifier bridges to the client data base for this engagement. This may be a multilevel identifier that defines whether the local or national client enterprise has contract and/or fiduciary control over the engagement.
- **Engagement identifier.** As is the predilection of computer systems, a unique number will likely be assigned to identify this engagement.
- **Engagement period.** This is the actual from and to dates of an existing engagement or the probable dates of a proposed engagement.

Figure 3–3
Engagement and Contract Information

Engagement, Proposal, and Contract Data

Item	Paper?	Electronic?
Client identifier		✔
Engagement identifier		✔
Engagement period		✔
Territory		✔
Source of marketing lead		✔
Invoicing data		✔
Revenue/product identifier		✔
Type of engagement		✔
Engagement status		✔
Engagement correspondence	✔	✔
Request for proposal	✔	
Proposal information summary	✔	
Contract identifier		✔
Contract period		✔
Signature date		✔
Type of service (contract)		✔
Contract specific data		
Territory		✔
Lead source		✔
Invoicing		✔
Contract status		✔
Work title or project name		✔
Resource summary		✔
Pricing summary		✔
Billing schedule		✔
Minimum charges		✔
Review status		✔
Proposal/offering		
Checklist	✔	
Tasks, estimates, schedule	✔	✔
Pricing detail	✔	✔
Risk assessment	✔	✔
Vendor documents	✔	
Project plan	✔	✔
Offer letter	✔	✔
Agreement	✔	✔
Statement of work	✔	✔
Offer materials	✔	
Client documents	✔	
Change documentation	✔	

Figure 3–3
Engagement and Contract Information (concluded)

Engagement, Proposal, and Contract Data		
Item	Paper?	Electronic?
Client correspondence	✔	✔
Other correspondence	✔	✔
Deliverables	✔	
Status/progress reports	✔	
Labor/expense records	✔	✔
Review reports	✔	
Notes	✔	✔

- **Specific territory and source of marketing lead.** This information copies and qualifies the territory and lead source information carried in the client data base. Typically it specifies the individuals who are directly responsible for the success or failure of marketing and performance efforts in regard to this engagement. It may also contain textual information for status reporting.
- **Specific invoicing qualifiers.** This information qualifies the default invoice address, invoice terms, taxation controls, client purchasing identifiers, and invoice printing controls contained in the client data base.
- **Default revenue and product identification.** This information establishes the overall marketplace for this engagement to be further qualified at the contract level.
- **Type of engagement.** Very often the computerized contract management system has various paths available to enter contracts under an engagement. This information will assist the system to select the path that is most friendly to the user. This might indicate a series of classes, a schedule of software deliveries and billings, or a major set of systems integration contracts.
- **Engagement status.** This indicates whether this engagement is actively being pursued in the absence of any active proposals or contracts.

Proposal or Contract Information

- **Client/customer identifier.** This identifies whether the location of the actual work is different from the client that controls the decisions and payments for the engagement.
- **Contract identifier.** Again, the contract management system is obligated to assign a number. This number, however, will appear on all documents and correspondence to uniquely identify communication regarding this contract relationship.

- **Contract period.** This is the from and to date of the agreed upon contract period.
- **Client signature date.** This is the date of agreement to the terms of the contract and the date from which the client expects performance. Often the contract period begins with the latest date at which the firm will provide consulting resource, while the signature date is the earliest date at which the client will pay for consulting services.
- **Type of service/contract.** This indicates the specific type of agreement between the firm and the client. These are discussed in more detail in Chapter 4 and include the various terms and conditions for options of hourly rate, daily rate, fixed price, class, and incident relationships. This often triggers options in the contract management system to ask for corresponding pricing and billing information regarding this contract.
- **Override territory and lead source information.** This information will determine the specific marketing and performance territories that will receive credit for the revenue and sales for this contract.
- **Override revenue and product information.** This defines the marketplace characteristics for the contract, if different than the engagement. To complicate measurements, different units and people may get credit for the different contracts in an overall engagement. An easy example is the education center that receives all or part of the credit for a subset of classes taught at their site. There are a number of possibilities when the firm has competency centers. As will again be seen in Chapter 4, specific charges under this contract might further divide credit for revenue it generates.
- **Specific invoicing information.** This information includes specific purchase order numbers and billing reference information as requested by the client.
- **Contract status.** This usually indicates whether the contract is in effect and, if not, whether it is a proposal activity, whether it is completed/terminated, or whether it has been marked for some other reason of inactivity.
- **Point of contact.** This is the individual who currently manages communication for this contract. This information is likely to include names, telephone numbers, locations and electronic addresses, and some minimal definition regarding responsibility and tenure.
- **Title and type of work.** This information distinguishes this contract from other similar contracts and provides textual and coding data to assist in search and reporting.
- **Resources.** Depending on the sophistication of the contract management system, this information may be a summary of the total hours or days of effort or a breakdown of each for all sources and levels of consultants and contractors to be assigned.

- **Pricing.** Depending on the sophistication of the contract management system this information may be simply the rate and upper limit of the contract or a breakdown of each element of cost and its corresponding revenue component.
- **Billing schedule.** This information indicates the frequency of billing and the schedule of payments, if other than the actual work performed during the billing period.
- **Minimum charges.** This is the minimum to be charged in a billing period for retainer relationships.
- **Review status.** This information records the internal audit and/or external client satisfaction scoring for the contract.

Engagement File: Preperformance Materials

The key utility of an easy to use contract management system is the ability to list currently active engagements and their contracts simply and quickly at the local level. For every entry on the list is a corresponding physical file and assigned point of contact. As has been discussed earlier, the file may be a central paper file containing the original or at least copies of all communication, including hard copies of all electronically stored information. On the other hand, it may contain a set of indexes to a variety of paper and electronic storage media. Whatever form it takes, it is the inventory of everything communicated internally and externally concerning the individual contracts within a client engagement.

Typically, the engagement file is organized alphabetically by client and subdivided by a contract numbering scheme. The computer systems of most firms assign a client number to each client. These are useful to differentiate multiple client locations and the rare instance where two clients in the same territory have the same name. The client number is rarely needed, however, to index a local engagement file.

Very often, the engagement file is divided into three sections: proposal, open contracts, and closed or completed contracts. The auditors likely have fewer rules for the completeness of a proposal file versus that of an open contract file. Separation of these two eliminates unnecessary debates on the schedule for file reviews. Separation of closed contracts is simply a space management convenience.

The information contained in the engagement file for each contract is the following.

- **Engagement initiation correspondence, including client request for proposal.** This first section of the engagement file contains references to or actual copies of the correspondence that initiated the engagement. It should contain a copy of the key contact information that identifies the client organization to which this engagement will be marketed. The file may include a client request for proposal and associated correspondence, marketing lead source correspondence and marketing materials, and internal notes that are not specific to the individual contracts in the engagement.

- **Contract management information documents.** The first section of an individual contract section of the engagement file usually contains forms that were completed when this engagement and its initial contract were added to the contract management system. These may be the original entry documents, a computer list of the documents or a combination of both showing the progression of approval signatures that were required to complete the offer and agreement with the client.

These forms contain the information described as input to the contract management system. They are likely to contain more detail than is needed for the computerized tracking system. An example might be pricing assumptions. Whereas the computer system might require a summary of the subcontractor resources to be used and the average expected rate, the file might contain documents that list each vendor contract, the schedule of resources, and the rates to be paid. The file would need to contain special contractual language, special methods to be employed, risks and exposures, competitive analyses, and companion products and services from business alliances.

- **Offering package documents.** Each service offering from a firm has a prescribed set of documentation that is completed, reviewed, and approved prior to negotiating the agreement with a client. The amount of this paperwork is directly proportional to the risk and uncertainty of the offering. The simplest is a class or a published support service, that uses available facilities and no vendor resources. The other extreme is a systems integration offering that involves a wide variety of supplemental agreements and complex estimating and pricing assumptions. The following list contains potential offering package documents in the order of the most likely to be seen in a file.

- **Checklist.** The most common discipline (and training tool) for those that assemble an offering package is a checklist. They usually come in small, medium, large, and extra large to signal the size of the package to come, and act as a statement by the offering assembler of the relative risk of the proposed venture. The checklist has saved many consulting offices from serious embarrassment.

- **Task list, estimates, and staffing schedule.** The task list, its supporting estimates, and a staffing schedule are the input backup to pricing for labor services. These should be prepared for any offering of 10 hours or more. This material is included with the elaborate project plan for complex offerings involving deliverables and vendors.

- **Pricing sheets.** Any custom priced offerings, either fixed price, per day, or per hour, requires hours (days), material expenses, and travel expenses summarized for input to the appropriate pricing algorithm. These sheets develop individual price components for consultant employees, contract personnel, other firm employees, supplies and facilities, and travel. For systems integration, the sheets will also initiate price components for vendors.
- **Risk assessment.** Experienced firms have evolved rules and guidelines for calculating the risk uplift on custom priced offerings. A useful mechanism for managing pricing consistency across offices is a risk-scoring method for each type. This usually takes the form of a multiple choice questionnaire that establishes risk levels for the specific client and engagement. The risk level derived is used as a factor in the pricing algorithms. A medium risk may not change the rate on a per hour contract, but would greatly increase the calculation for a fixed price.
- **Vendor and partnership agreements, purchase orders, and correspondence.** A prudent business manager will have in place written and signed commitments from alliance partners and vendors before an offer is made to a client. File documents can include or refer to licensing, escrows, bonds, delivery, taxation, customs, confidentiality, and support service.
- **Comprehensive project plan and backup estimates.** For major efforts, particularly multicontract, multiphase projects, a comprehensive project plan will have been prepared as a framework for the specific tasks and estimates that make up this contract.
- **Offering documents.** The professional services offering (proposal) contains four elements: an offer letter, an agreement, a statement of work, and when needed, complementary offer materials. All of these combined are usually called the proposal and can be one page or a good size package.
- **Offer letter.** There should be only one offer letter, the last one. In reality there is likely to be a series of correspondence tracking negotiation to final agreement. At contract signature, all negotiation correspondence should be removed and filed separately in the correspondence section listed later.
- **Agreement(s).** The agreement defines the general terms and conditions of the services. In many cases a blanket agreement is executed once, and the individual contract agreement is merely a signature page associated with a specific statement of work. The more complex the offer, the larger the number of supplemental agreements. Most client relationships require at least some form of supplemental and specific confidentiality agreement. A systems integration contract is likely to have a dozen or more agreements under a composite signature page.
- **Statement of work.** Even the simplest of services has a statement of work. The text may be contained in a catalog for education or support services and

referenced by order number. If the work is unspecified consulting or a repetition of a previous service, the description is likely to be contained in the offer letter. For other than this, a document will be produced that describes the responsibilities of the firm, the responsibilities of the client, the work products or deliverables from the firm, and the completion criteria for the service.

• **Complementary offer materials ("sizzle").** If the firm is offering to a client that needs convincing of the firm's credentials, particularly if there is competition, the statement of work is packaged within a larger proposal that contains a strong argument for why the client would best be served by doing this business with this firm. Professional services proposals are often works of art, demonstrating the capabilities of the firm to document and communicate. It may be a colorful binder imprinted with the firm's logo, containing text and glossies that extol the methods and successes of the firm. It may include extensive text and figures on how the firm will meet the client's requirements. It often incorporates presentation media that summarize the major selling points of the firm's offer. It might be a point by point response to a client bid request. The experienced firm, however, makes a very clear distinction between those elements of the proposal that are marketing and that portion which is the statement of work for which the firm will be held legally accountable during performance.

Engagement File: Performance Materials

The contract sections of the engagement file grow weekly as performance events occur. These files are the first place anyone goes to see the status of ongoing communication.

• **Client documents.** Those materials collected from the client. Some documents may be of such sensitivity that they are stored only on client premises.

• **Changes and contract management modification information.** This section contains any formal correspondence and other signed documents that are subject to the change process established for the effort.

• **Client correspondence.** This section contains all other correspondence with the client.

• **Other correspondence.** This section contains correspondence that references this contract that was not exchanged with the client. This includes, but is not limited to, all correspondence with lead sources, vendors, and business alliances.

• **Deliverables.** An archive copy of each deliverable specified as such by the contract. Any professional services effort has work products. The majority of these are incidental to the intellectual effort and include written material, verbal presentations, software, and leadership. Some very specific work products are called out in client agreements as formal deliverables. Deliverables have a predefined form, a formal delivery process, and an agreed to completion criteria. A consulting team will produce many pieces of documentation that are incidental to the effort. These are interview results, drafts of deliverables, and presentations used to get understanding and agreement. Typically, the firm does not keep formal copies of incidental work products.

- **Status/progress reports.** This section contains the weekly and monthly status reports. There are usually weekly reports to the client, a monthly summary to the client and a monthly assessment that is internal to the office. In addition there may be weekly and monthly reports from vendors and alliance partners.
- **Labor records, reimbursable expense receipts, and billing summaries.** Auditing rules often require copies (or originals) of all billing substantiation to be filed with the contract.
- **Engagement/project review and audit reports.** This section contains formal reviews of the engagement by quality assurance and auditing staff.
- **Internal correspondence and notes.** This section contains written and electronic informal correspondence that should be retained for this contract or engagement.

There is a substantial difference between the amount of paper that collects for consulting versus that for custom development and systems integration. The former is likely to be no more than 10 to 50 pages, while the latter, which are major efforts, can occupy much of a file drawer. The engagement file is equally necessary for both, though, and will make the difference when other parts of the communication process break down.

SURVEYING CLIENT SATISFACTION

The satisfied client is most often the one who believes that the firm accomplished what it advertised it would. The firm that appears to have done what it said it would is the one that managed communication throughout. The more participants, the tougher this becomes and the more disciplined the process must become.

The top professional services firms do not rely solely on the mechanics of ongoing communication and the apparent acceptance of end products in their assessment of client satisfaction. A common practice is a client satisfaction survey.

These are usually one- to three-page questionnaires that ask the client to rank the firm as satisfactory or unsatisfactory in the areas where it would expect added value. Typically, these questions address the following topics.

- Did the firm produce quality end products?
- Did the consultants work well with the client staff?
- Did the lead consultant/project manager demonstrate the leadership needed?
- Was change managed and communicated well?
- Was schedule and cost managed effectively?
- Did the effort improve the client's environment?
- Would the client use the firm again?
- Would the client be a reference for the firm?

Only one of these questions relates to the quality of consulting. The remainder are directed at the firm's leadership and ability to meet expectation. A positive response is an affirmation that the client understood where the firm was leading it and that they got there. Taking the time to communicate well and keeping communication under control is the best way to put the client first.

THE CLIENT COMES FIRST

The subject of this chapter has been managing communication and, in particular, managing client expectation. Key points to remember are:

- No matter how diverse the reasons for engaging a firm, the client always expects leadership. The most important demonstration of this leadership is effective and controlled communication.
- Good communication is not simply writing and speaking well. It requires structure that includes points of contact, predefined media and methods, and disciplined information retention.
- Communication between a firm and client may involve extensive volumes of information during major engagements. The management of this information must start early and be well supported by information management tools.
- Client expectation is to be tested every day. Change management is the most effective method of determining and refining client expectation.
- Satisfied clients are those that see the end products they were led to believe they would receive. Satisfied clients acquire more services.

Many people communicate well. Not nearly as many communicate effectively. The difference is in the management of the communication process. Good communicators transfer their beliefs, while effective communicators also learn the beliefs of others.

Chapter 4

Revenue Management: Dividing Up the Green

R evenue is the easiest measurement to understand in any business. It is particularly easy to understand in professional services. In other businesses, revenue measurements are complicated by shipping and installation delays, back orders, returns, discounts, financing, and currency exchange. In professional services and particularly basic people services, you work, you bill, and you get paid. Because it is most easily understood, revenue is the most common measurement of choice.

Revenue is the gross income from billed people services and nonlabor expense recovery. Every person assigned to an engagement makes a contribution to the generation of revenue. It is easy to see how revenue billed might be one measurement of the success and value of a consultant. Carrying it further, the accumulated revenue derived by groups of people (consultants and contractors) can be a measurement of an individual manager's success.

Likewise, each engagement is intended to derive income in planned amounts over periods of quarters and years. The actual billing to a client measures the success of an engagement. Revenue billed to a group of clients becomes the measurement of success among account managers and industry managers. As we will see, segmentation of revenue into a measurement for groupings within the business is multidimensional and covers a number of variations.

Revenue occurs as a result of invoicing to clients. As we have discussed, invoicing is a highly sensitive part of the firm's relationship with its clients and is, therefore, very carefully controlled. A firm sends an invoice when it deserves payment for work performed. This makes revenue a very reliable short-term measurement of success. As we will see, this can be complicated by payment scheduling and the withholding of payments by clients on complex deals, but, in the main, revenue remains the simplest vehicle for comparing results against expectation.

The term *measurement* when used in business implies both risk and reward. Reward comes directly in the form of bonuses and commissions, and it comes indirectly through high performance ratings deriving salary and promotion. Risk is created by establishing an expectation of revenue or **quota** that is usually higher than one would choose for themselves, requiring the extraordinary to be successful. We will discuss later the various approaches for compensating consultants, managers, marketers, field executives, industry managers, and service offering managers for achieving success in meeting quotas.

First we will look at the definition of revenue as it applies to large professional services firms. This will lead to a review of revenue sources, looking at variety in contract vehicles, charging options, and crediting practices. We will compare the client's view of billing detail with what the firm needs for effective financial management. We will look at territories and compensation. Finally, we will review the revenue control process and focus on reporting needs to make revenue measurements visible.

DEFINITION OF REVENUE

The definition of when and how revenue is credited starts with the accounting practices of a firm. As in any business, professional services wants to credit income against cost and expense as early as possible. When and how this occurs is a combination of what is legal, what is practical for business computer systems and administration and what will best urge the field consulting offices to derive a maximum in current revenue for each person resource they have available.

The professional services business is not burdened by the need to recover past investment through its current revenue. For all practical purposes, all expenses of services business are current expenses and should be recovered through current revenue. This is not to say that a major firm may not build a facility to house its units or invest in software development. Generally, though, these are a small part of a professional services expense structure and have little influence on the rules for crediting revenue.

When a firm first starts out, it most likely accounts for its income on a cash basis (i.e., it doesn't count until the check from the client is in the bank). As it grows, it will move over to accrual base accounting. At that point it has to choose an easily understood set of conventions for determining when expected payment from a client can be counted as revenue.

The following discussion offers a workable approach that walks the fence between rewarding unwarranted optimism and punishing prudence and conservatism. More importantly it is fairly simple, and busy field executives don't have to waste a lot of time in debates with their business controls staff.

The first protocol should be that revenue is not revenue, unless it can be **invoiced.** Keeping the client satisfied is such a high priority, that the willingness to present a bill is the best test of whether income is deserved. This rule might cause an invoice to be sent in the middle of a client dispute, so that needed revenue gets on the books, but the occasion will be rare. More importantly it prevents counting revenue when the client would never have agreed that payment was deserved.

The next easiest protocol is professional services revenue will be credited when a service has been **accomplished.** Clients pay for intellectual value received. As soon as such value passes from a consultant to a client, service is being accomplished. In its simplest form, revenue under this definition is credited as soon as a consultant spends a minimum countable time on behalf of a client. As we will see, this is a very useful definition for basic services and can be an effective point of departure for the more complex services that include deliverables and progress payments.

Crediting Per Hour and Per Day Revenue

Let's first look at this protocol in the context of a basic consulting service. The client has contracted to receive intellectual assistance to its operations and planning. It has agreed to pay for this assistance on a per hour or per day basis plus compensate the consultant's firm for any travel or other out of pocket expenses. Although the agreement calls for work products and even specific deliverables to be developed, the charges for service are not linked to the timing of their delivery. For this basic service arrangement, revenue can be credited at the completion of each hour or day. Additionally, revenue can be credited at the time any out of pocket expense becomes payable.

This is revenue, because the firm believes that each increment of time worked brought value to the client and the firm deserves compensation for the cost of the consultant. It is prepared to send an invoice to that effect at any time and will, during its next billing cycle. It is prepared to defend its consultant in any arguments to the contrary from the client. It is also prepared to count this revenue on behalf of all those who share in its rewards, including payment of commissions and bonuses and measurements of successful performance.

Let's say the client refuses to pay the invoice, because it is dissatisfied with the service. The firm is facing an unpaid receivable and a wide variety of people have counted this revenue on behalf of themselves, their unit, the marketplace they track, and their service line of business. To reverse the revenue would mean a reversal of compensation and measurement to all parties. To write off the receivable means some lonely administrative and accounting function will suffer slings and arrows for not collecting on a client debt. What is needed is another protocol that qualifies as accomplished and provides guidance when the client is not as proud of the work as is the firm.

A concept that is consistent with professionalism and is reflected in the wide variety of rates charged by the firms is that of **best efforts.** Professional services gets paid for the skill and experience of its consultants and the strength of the firm's management and methods to back its people up. A standard of best efforts means that in the firm's opinion, its people accomplished the work (be it vague or specific) using the best leadership, best methods, best communication, best skills and experience, and best support from the firm that this client could expect.

To avoid disputes over payment, firms have become very adept in describing the concept of best efforts. Selling best efforts is another importance of the communication leadership described in Chapter 3. Clients often need encouragement in recognizing these elements of professionalism in the people they are buying.

Ultimately, the opinion regarding whether a best effort was performed is an internal one, and often independent of the decision to press the client for fulfillment of its debt. It is a judgment of quality, and consultants should be very conscious of the standard set for their daily efforts. It helps them to see the value in getting positive confirmation that the client sees their professionalism as clearly as they do.

In this invoice payment situation, the firms who consistently perform well and bring that reputation with them will probably not credit the revenue (deduct the amount on the next client invoice); they will insist that the moneys are owed. If the client still refuses to pay, it becomes a collections problem and might ultimately require write-off (where it becomes an expense and will reduce net profit at the time the write-off occurs). The firm might choose to resolve the issue with a hint of mea culpa and perform some pro bono service to pacify the client into making payment.

Few businesses actually credit revenue to their general ledger more frequently than once per month. Revenue accumulated per day, per hour, or against a payable expense is trial revenue to be finalized at the next revenue closing. We will discuss the revenue administration process later in the chapter.

Crediting Fixed-Price Revenue

You will learn that the recurring theme in this book is that fixed price complicates things (all too often beyond its expected return in profits). A first example can be seen in crediting revenue.

During a fixed-price contract, payment will not coincide with work, except by coincidence. The purpose of a fixed-price agreement is for the client to make predetermined payments at scheduled dates or at the time of milestones, regardless of how many hours of work have actually been delivered. Only when a fixed-price contract and all of its corresponding work begins and ends in one billing period does revenue and cost coincide.

Crediting is tricky. Accounting wants to match revenue to cost. Prudent management and the definition of revenue wants to match revenue with invoicing and payment. The cleanest and easiest is to be consistent and credit with the invoice. The practice has some built-in discipline that outweighs the problems it creates.

By crediting only when an invoice is issued, revenue and cost are not synchronized and profit fluctuates greatly. An example is an engagement that runs for six months and is billed in equal amounts at the end of the second, fourth, and sixth months. The cost builds steadily through the fourth month, peaks and holds constant in the fifth month, and falls to zero at the end of the sixth month. The profit is negative after the first month, very positive after the second month, very negative after the third month, and so on. Over the life of the engagement it will look like a very erratic heart trace.

The temptation to complicate the process by smoothing the revenue credit through the zero months is intense. This requires an accounting practice that will anticipate future invoices and average their effect in those months prior to their issuance. This seems to fix the accounting problem by bringing revenue into coincidence with cost.

When people get measured and compensated for revenue credited this way, smoothing can have some rather unpleasant side effects.

- Managers can more easily agree to defer invoicing when performance disputes arise, since they have been paid ahead for future invoicing.

- Fixed-price efforts are notorious for overrunning the estimated hours that were the basis for cost in the price. This overrun will most likely occur in the last 20 percent of whatever time frame had been committed to the effort. Profit will be front end loaded, providing no incentive for early cost containment. Most revenue incentives will be paid long before profitability tumbles, thus rewarding bad project management.

- In the very complex services, a significant cost is that of products and vendors. When revenue is smoothed, there is no incentive for managers to schedule progress payments around these charges and, in fact, profit can now fluctuate because cost is not smoothed.

These side effects can be minimized by separating compensation for revenue from accounting for revenue (i.e., pay commissions when invoiced, while smoothing revenue for profit computation). This is even more complicated. It requires two sets of revenue books and keeping one is tough enough for most offices.

It simply makes for less effort and debate to credit revenue from any source when it is invoiced. Prudent business managers, particularly ones being measured on both revenue and profit, will not readily agree to large gaps between cost and corresponding income. A useful deterrent is a requirement that senior executive approval is required for spacing of more than three or four months in progress payments or the gap between the start of work and a one-time payment. Entrepreneurs are easily guided when going upstairs can be avoided.

Most offices have a mix of hourly (daily) and fixed-price engagements. In any one period (month), a scheduled payment from a fixed-price deal (or the cost without payment) will vary the profit line, but the accumulation of all income and expense over three months will be much smoother, and reasonably smooth from quarter to quarter. This certainly is acceptable in light of the problems and added complexity of overt revenue smoothing.

We will see in Chapter 8 how this subject arises again when relating revenue per hour and cost per hour. There we will discuss spreadsheet techniques that can assist in spreading revenue on fixed price-contracts, but only when this additional work is necessary and justified. As we will see, the measurement of specific engagement profitability is part of this justification.

Crediting Prepayments

Another common debate is whether up front payments (payments before work begins) or end of fiscal year prepayments by a client are revenue and deserve credit and compensation. Both of these are very sensitive, because they imply that a client has agreed to pay for work yet to be performed. The risk of collusion between a firm employee and a client can be very great and, of course, it goes against the protocol that credits revenue only upon accomplishment.

A prepayment for work yet to be performed should not be credited as revenue (nor should it be accrued for smoothing purposes, if such is a common practice). It should flow as a negative accounts receivable and cash. Most billing systems will support some sort of cash receipt with no corresponding accounts receivable.

When the real invoice for work accomplished is issued by the system, the client is instructed not to pay it, or it is captured prior to delivery (some systems have an invoice suppression feature for this purpose). Someone must then manually apply the invoice against the negative receivable and, internally, the revenue is now credited.

In a case where real cost was incurred prior to a contract agreement and the client received value and best efforts through the proposal process, the firm deserves compensation and should credit a prepayment as revenue. This should trigger corresponding people compensation and be income against cost and expense. This extends to the situation in complex labor and nonlabor services where a firm has been invoiced for up front payments for products and vendor commitments and deserves recovery for this cost on behalf of the client.

Prepayment situations should be made very visible. This visibility provides much of the protection from fraud. A management review and approval step might be appropriate, but only if the billing computer systems are not sophisticated enough to raise the needed visibility.

Crediting Retainer Revenue

Professional services firms charge retainer fees in situations where resources are to be provided on call. These may be to follow up on problems that arise after implementation of new business and system procedures. These may be to provide short response maintenance to systems and procedures because of unforeseen changes in usage or environment. These may be to keep people and machine resources in place in the event of disaster.

A retainer payment is not a prepayment. The firm is asking the client to pay compensation for the cost of keeping people *more* readily available. The firm is no longer free to assign the retained resource as it sees fit and where it can always generate the most compensating revenue.

REVENUE TRIGGERS AND TYPES OF SERVICES

Professional services are offered to clients under a number of contracting vehicles. We will use the term **type of service** to denote a professional services offering with a set of terms and conditions. Terms and conditions define the firm's commitment to deliver service, the client's commitment to pay for the service, an agreement of how the engagement will end, and protections for both parties from unethical practices of the other. A distinguishing feature of contract terms is how and when clients will be billed. Therefore, types of services represent the various ways in which invoicing is triggered and revenue credited.

Each type of service we will discuss is a balance between:

- Doing enough work that provides value to the client, to where it is a reasonable expectation that the client will pay the bill.

FIGURE 4-1
Relationship Between Invoicing and Types of Services

Revenue Trigger Versus Type of Service						
	Type of Service (Contractual Agreement)					
	Hourly/Daily Services		**Fixed Price Services**		**Labor & Nonlabor Services**	
Invoice (Billing) Triggers	Time & materials	Managed	Client attended	Event	Product support	Systems integration
Per hour/per day						
Catalog rate	✔					
Custom rate		✔				✔
Scheduled payment		✔	✔		✔	✔
Charge (at time of expense)	✔	✔	✔	✔	✔	✔
Per client person			✔			
Retainer	✔	✔		✔		

- Generating enough revenue to cover actual cost and expense to stay in business.

Basic people services firms will offer as few of the alternatives as they can, subject to pressures from their best clients and competition in general. Only full-service firms offer all of these. The variety of terms and conditions, and corresponding billing options, has a profound effect on the workload required to administer the business.

Figure 4-1 is a table of six types of services that may be offered by a firm, related to up to six ways to trigger an invoice in that billing period. The types of services are grouped into three categories of progressively increasing contractual complexity: hourly/daily services, fixed-price services, and combined labor and nonlabor services. As can be seen, each type of service has more than one way in which an invoice can be triggered and revenue obtained.

Invoice Triggers

Before discussing the types of services, let's summarize the actions that can trigger billing. A line item on an invoice can result from any of the following.

1. **The completion of an hour or a day (or acceptable portion) of work.** The amount on this invoice reflects the accumulated hours or days at a rate over a period since the last billing cycle. Invoices can contain a single, one-line summary of all work in the period, a line for every week, or a line for every day. Charges can name the person. Charges can be a line per person with a single rate for all people, a line per person with a separate rate for each person, or lines for each type of work performed by each person with corresponding rates. Rates charged may be standard catalog rates, catalog rates with volume discounts, or rates customized to the specific engagement.

2. **At the beginning of a period in which a scheduled charge will be billed to a client as progress payment against work being performed.** Scheduled payments can be negotiated uniquely for each contract and be fixed once in place, be estimated for the contract and adjusted as performance occurs, or be standard in the contract such as all at completion, equal monthly payments, or a one-third preliminary payment with the remainder at completion.

3. **Upon incurring an expense on behalf of a client that is subject to recovery through specific charge.** These can be for either labor or nonlabor expense. It may result from the completion of a packaged service such as a product installation. It may be as a result of a service call to fix something. It may be for travel. It could be for completion by a vendor or delivery of a product under systems integration.

4. **Attendance of a client individual at a service offering.** This is usually the attendance of client people at a class. It may be billed ahead or at completion. Each participant might be charged a different amount.

5. **At the beginning of a period in which a client has incurred a surcharge to retain the availability of firm resources.** The retainer charge is in lieu of actual charges for services under some minimum amount. For example, the retainer might be $500 per month and will be charged each month that actual hourly, daily, or service event (call) charges accumulate to less than $500. Otherwise the charge for the month will be the actual charges over $500.

Flexible payment terms do not in and of themselves create complexity and associated administrative workload. Sole proprietors use these same invoice triggers. An engagement for basic people services from a small office with a client might be as follows.

1. One of the consultants is paid $130 per hour to assist in the design of a new employee compensation method.

2. The same consultant and occasionally two others with like skill are paid $1,500 per day to conduct user group sessions to gather requirements and review results from the employee compensation methods project.

3. The client's people pay $500 each to attend a class on employee compensation administration offered on firm premises.
4. The firm charges $30,000 for the installation of its standard methodology, charged one time at completion.
5. The consultant in examples 1 and 2 has been traveling on occasion to remote client locations. The consultant uses a client corporate travel function for air and hotel arrangements, but uses a personal credit card for meals and incidentals. The firm charges these plus an administrative fee to the client following reimbursement to the consultant.
6. The client is charged $500 per month or actual hours times $100, whichever is higher, for coding changes to a firm developed employee compensation computer program.

Growth in any size firm that does not have business computer systems that accommodate these options will be restricted. The entrepreneurs of professional services must have this flexibility to make deals that fit the needs of the client situation. When the number of consultants reaches 25 or more, billing has to be automated and all of these options have to be supported.

Types of Service (Contractual Agreements)

The real complexity of the professional services business is in the variety of contractual vehicles offered and the corresponding intricacies in the manner in which work is performed. Contractual agreements for services fall into three overlapping groups as seen in Figure 4-1: **hourly/daily services, fixed price services, and combined labor and nonlabor services.**

Hourly/daily services are people (labor) services with incidental, nonlabor expense recovery where the firm gets paid for every best effort hour worked. Agreements types are:

• **Hourly time and materials.** Consultants assist the client on an hourly basis at a single rate per hour or rates for level of consultant value. The client owes payment for all hours of best effort service regardless of schedules or estimates. The client is responsible for recovery of any expenses it directs the firm to incur in excess of normal firm cost of a consultant. Often the client pays discounted rates for large blocks of estimated services. The firm produces incidental work products under client direction and is not committed to specific deliverables. The minimum service is usually at least one hour, though time above one hour can be charged as portions of an hour.

Assistance is the key concept in the contractual terms for time and materials, which is the preferred contract for basic people services and covers items 1, 2, and 5 in the earlier multiservice example. The client is in charge of the work effort and directs the consultants. The firm has no responsibility for the outcome of the effort or its effect on the client's business. The firm is, however, responsible for the professional performance of their people, both consultants and subcontractors, and must demonstrate skill, experience, and personal leadership. The client is only committed to pay when best efforts are performed.

• **Daily time and materials.** Same as above at rates per day. The minimum service is usually at least one day, though charges above one day can be charged as portions of a day.

• **Hourly services with a retainer fee.** The firm has agreed to keep consultants readily available to perform hourly time and material services. Specific agreement is made concerning which consultants or equivalent capability will be available, hourly rates when service is performed, and how responsive the service will be. In payment for the availability of support, the client will pay a minimum fee on a regular basis. Item 6 in the basic services example would be under this agreement.

• **Daily services with a retainer fee.** Same as daily services at rates per day.

• **Hourly managed services with committed deliverables.** The firm has assumed responsibility to perform services per hour with specific schedules, estimates, and deliverable end products. Charges per hour may be a single rate for all consultants and subcontractors, separate rates based on the experience and expected value of each type of individual, separate rates for the type of work performed at its relative value and difficulty, and combinations of all of these. The rate(s) charged to the client are usually customized to the engagement. They are derived from adding up the estimated labor cost and expenses for the effort and determining the total income needed by the firm. Total income is a trade-off between what the firm believes will be the client's value received (and what that is worth) versus what the firm must realize in profit, taking into consideration its risk of not meeting its estimated effort. This total income needed is then divided by the estimated hours of work to determine rates.

Hourly managed services are the most popular vehicle for complex people services, most notably custom software. Management of the effort brings a number of additional responsibilities for the firm, which are not in time and materials. The firm is now committed to the quality of all work performed, including that of client personnel, and is held responsible for the quality of those end products it names as deliverables.

Most firms define management quality in terms of the basic elements of their project management methods. The proof of a firm's ability to win debates regarding project management quality is how well it performs change control. The right job will get extensions when work exceeds estimates or schedule, and will get deliverables accepted upon delivery. Failures in change management result in pro bono work and reversed charges.

Firms may include travel in the total cost which gets recovered through the rate. The firm may recover client directed travel expenses as a separate charge or a combination of both. The decision usually hinges on how predictable the travel will be and whether the higher rate will cause sticker shock.

- **Daily managed services with committed deliverables.** Same as hourly managed services at rates per day.
- **Managed services with a retainer fee.** The same charging concept as time and materials retainer fee, but with more responsibility regarding management, deliverables, and warranties. Maintenance of previously delivered software with specific acceptance criteria is an example.

Fixed price services are people (labor) services with incidental nonlabor expense recovery, where the firm gets paid at intervals that may not coincide with how much work has been performed and may not vary when the work level is different than estimated.

- **Managed services with a one-time charge.** The firm has committed to a specific service with specific end results and schedule. Typically, the service is scheduled to begin at the availability of the resources and will complete in a relatively short period (less than three months). Often the start of the service is dependent upon the delivery of products and materials that are outside of the firm's control. Examples include software installation or upgrading of procedures made necessary by pending issuance of revised government regulations. Clients are reluctant to pay for extra charges such as travel and materials under a one-time charge agreement. Prior agreement as to what constitutes an unplanned expense must be in place in order for additional expenses to be recovered.

Most one-time charge offerings are standard services with published prices. The firm is very specific in the responsibilities placed on the commitments of the firm. This allows them the flexibility to find and assign resources against the uncertainty of other delivery schedules and to manage the delivery of the service with little risk of surprises and misunderstandings. This is the only complex service in the basic services example (item 4).

- **Managed services with progress payments.** The firm has contracted for a managed service with deliverables, schedules, and acceptance terms and conditions. The service project plan has defined checkpoints that demonstrate progress toward completion of the effort. The agreement defines a payment schedule that charges the client for value received, while giving the firm at least minimum compensation for cost incurred.

The favorite schedule for the firm is even increments of the total price invoiced at each billing period over the planned life of the effort. At the other end of the scale are complex payment structures that are scheduled against expected approvals for deliverables, acquisition and disengagement of subcontractors, estimated monthly progress, and specific major expenditure.

This is a very risky venture for the firm and it is likely to assign the best project manager it can to the project. Management of the effort includes regular review jointly by the firm and the client to determine whether the scheduled payment structure is on track with the actual events of the engagement. Unplanned expenses such as extraordinary travel may be added to the next scheduled payment or more likely billed as a separate charge as it occurs. The profitability of the office will hinge on the ability of this project manager to get overruns declared changes and added to progress payments.

- **Client participation services.** The firm will provide a specific service with designated end results at a specific place on a specific date or dates. The client is charged for each participant while the service is being offered. Typically, the participant charge recovers all firm costs for facility, materials, and of course, its people. Truly extraordinary expenses might be billed to a client that requested special treatment for its participants. The most common use is education charges, as in item 3 in the basic services example. Often, the firm stipulates a minimum participation as a prerequisite for initiating the service.

- **Event service.** The firm will initiate a charge each time a predefined event occurs that uses people. The initiation of the service may or may not require prior client approval depending upon specifics in the agreement. The most common event is a maintenance service call. An event might be one of a series of product installations at different locations. The firm will usually have a level of service to meet under terms of the agreement and have measures of quality. Event agreements are very limited in scope and usually have provisions that will activate one of the managed services contracts when the client wishes more. Needed parts and other vendor contracted services (electrician support, etc.) are usually separate charges.

- **Event service with a retainer fee.** The firm has committed resources to be available for an event service. The client pays a regular charge for the availability of these resources. The agreement specifies a maximum incident level beyond which the firm will charge for events not covered within the regular retainer fee structure.

Combined labor and nonlabor services are complex offerings where the firm incurs cost and expense to obtain products (such as equipment and software) and other vendors (such as construction contractors) to be combined with its people into a service for which it takes prime responsibility.

- **Product support services.** The firm purchases a product that requires installation and support services and delivers this product to the client through the efforts of its people. This is a packaged deal for a fixed price, usually with a single charge at completion or two charges, one following commitment to the purchase of the product and another at completion. Another approach is to treat the installation services as a fixed-price managed service, bill accordingly, and charge for the product separately when the client pays the vendor (or internally, if purchased through its parent). Travel expenses are usually charged separately. These packaged services are most often at advertised prices that cannot anticipate the expense of transporting people to the installation location.

• **Systems integration.** The firm performs the combination of labor and product services described in Chapter 1. The engagement is usually a combination of per hour and fixed-price offerings, plus specific charges.

Since systems integration and the software portion of the product support services have evolved so recently, agreements for these services are still in their infancy. As is typical of new things, service firms are using combinations of old and new contracting approaches to satisfy the expediency of making these deals and getting on with these projects. The key difference between these services and those of basic and complex people services is the high percentage of nonlabor generated income and corresponding cost. These will be treated very differently from basic people services in later chapters on profit and productivity.

INCOME DIFFERENTIATION

Lest we forget, the most important purpose of revenue is to offset cost and expense, leaving profit. Revenue reported as income takes a different form than revenue reported for measurement purposes. Measurements are related to territories and markets, and sum revenue on behalf of the people that manage these business segments. Income, on the other hand, is summed into categories that align with elements of cost. For professional services, costs and offsetting income fall into the broad categories of labor and nonlabor.

Figure 4-2 is an income statement of planned versus actual revenue for a firm offering complex people services. The statement is through the first four months of the year. The firm performs consulting, custom development, and education. It incurs cost for labor and nonlabor travel in all three services, and for a nonlabor cost of materials in its education business. As you can see, it is slightly ahead of plan through the first quarter, but has fallen behind in the first month of the second quarter.

Labor generated revenue segments that best fit with cost segments in professional services are:

• **Consultants:** The income generated by consultants of the office of the firm that delivers the service to the client. This may be further broken down by consultant levels when revenue data of that detail is readily available (e.g., where every consultant charges a different rate).

FIGURE 4-2
Income Statement for Complex People Services

Professional Services Income Statement

		Quarter 1 ($000)		Quarter 2 ($000)		Quarter 3 ($000)		Quarter 4 ($000)		Total Year ($000)	
		Plan	Actual	Plan	1-May	Plan	Actual	Plan	Actual	Plan	YTD
Income											
Consulting	Consultants	340.0	335.1	285.0	132.5	365.0		475.0		1465	468
	Management	0.0	5.2	62.0	9.9	52.0		54.0		168	15
	Contractors	0.0	0.0	0.0	0.0	0.0		0.0		0	0
	Borrowed	74.0	71.8	74.0	24.2	74.0		74.0		296	96
	Travel (nonlabor)	10.0	8.3	10.0	4.1	10.0		10.0		40	12
	Product (nonlabor)	0.0	0.0	0.0	0.0	0.0		0.0		0	0
	TOTAL	424.0	420.4	431.0	170.6	501.0		613.0		1969	591
Custom Development	Consultants	503.0	497.7	657.0	190.4	544.0		824.0		2528	688
	Management	142.0	133.8	157.0	53.5	161.0		181.0		641	187
	Contractors	636.0	643.8	636.0	197.7	636.0		636.0		2544	841
	Borrowed	148.0	156.9	148.0	46.8	74.0		74.0		444	204
	Travel (nonlabor)	42.9	43.0	47.9	14.7	42.5		51.5		185	58
	Product (nonlabor)	0.0	0.0	0.0	0.0	0.0		0.0		0	0
	TOTAL	1471.9	1475.2	1645.9	503.0	1457.5		1766.5		6342	1978
Education	Consultants	185.0	182.9	205.0	78.5	200.0		285.0		875	261
	Management	0.0	0.0	0.0	0.0	0.0		0.0		0	0
	Contractors	0.0	0.0	0.0	0.0	0.0		0.0		0	0
	Borrowed	74.0	77.3	74.0	25.6	74.0		74.0		296	103
	Travel (nonlabor)	2.5	2.8	2.5	1.7	2.5		2.5		10	5
	Product (nonlabor)	10.0	9.4	10.0	4.8	10.0		10.0		40	14
	TOTAL	271.5	272.4	291.5	110.6	286.5		371.5		1221	383
Total Income	Labor	2102.0	2104.5	2298.0	759.0	2180.0		2677.0		9257	2863
	Nonlabor	65.4	63.5	70.4	25.3	65.0		74.0		275	89
	TOTAL	2167.4	2168.0	2368.4	784.2	2245.0		2751.0		9532	2952

- **Managers:** The income generated by managers or principals. They are usually differentiated from consultants, because they are expected to bill less at higher rates and are usually paid differently.
- **Contracted labor:** Income generated by people under contract from outside the firm or its parent.
- **Borrowed labor:** Income from people on assignment from other units in the firm or its parent.

Nonlabor income segments that best fit with cost segments are:

- **Travel and other incidental expense recovery.** Most labor services have incidental costs, particularly travel, that are directly attributable to engagements. When these costs are very inconsistent across engagements or build to above 3 percent of total direct cost, they begin to distort analysis of cost per person and profitability between engagements. To match incidental direct cost to its corresponding income, expense recovery revenue needs to be separated from labor generated revenue.

Separation is easy when travel is billed as its own charge. More often than not, though, it is incorporated into a custom rate or a fixed price. In these cases, pricing assumptions that show the relative amounts of labor and nonlabor cost that went into the charge to the client can be used as a ratio of labor to nonlabor in revenue. Although not precise, it is sufficient for purposes of resource productivity and engagement profitability purposes (which are not very precise either).

- **Product.** Product support and systems integration services have significant direct cost specific to each engagement when products are purchased and resold with the offering. On a smaller scale, education services usually have class materials that are ancillary products through the classes. The portion of income for a product must be separated from labor and matched with the corresponding cost of each to ensure that both are making expected profit. Again, pricing assumptions may be needed to separate the product portion of a packaged price.

- **Vendor** (other than subcontractor). Direct vendor costs may be as high as 80 percent of the total cost of a complex labor and nonlabor service. Matching the two cost components to their corresponding income components is an essential part of managing profit for these services. Additionally, clients often want to see a breakdown of their payments into components. Later we will talk about taxes and why taxation may force separation of labor and nonlabor income.

There are two important footnotes to segmenting revenue by cost component. Going to the trouble of breaking out revenue by people groups and not recording all hours for consultants is absurd. Hours worked are often not collected for fixed-price engagements, because they serve no billing purpose (see labor claiming in this chapter). The purpose of income and cost segmentation is to determine revenue and cost per hour. Without hours, there is no computation.

The second footnote is to again point out the utility of using pricing assumptions as a simple mechanism for separating revenue by cost component. The fortunate ones are those firms where this data is retained in the contract management system and the income separation occurs automatically.

BILLING: WHAT THE CLIENT SEES AND WHAT THE OFFICE NEEDS

We have discussed a variety of ways in which revenue is credited and then segmented for profit analysis. We will be discussing further revenue segmentation for territory evaluation and for compensation later. It is useful to look at what detail a client may want to see on their billings and what further information the firm has that the client need not see.

Figure 4-3 is a portion of a billing register (a report that is common to the business control of most firms and which will be discussed again in that context later). Each line on the report is an element of revenue. The report is highlighted in bold for examples of what a client may see versus what the firm will always need to see. You will notice that varying options are illustrated to show the variety of demands placed on firms by their clients for disclosure.

Notice that for Wadi Power, the client sees each week's hours, while at Vermin Foods, another hourly contract, the client sees a summary of all consultant and subcontractor time and a separate line for travel. For the two fixed-price contracts, the client sees no hours worked, but sees travel on one, but not the other. In the case of Vulgar Sales, the client received a bill for a progress payment, even though no work was performed during the month.

Obviously, firms do not provide clients with a recipe of invoice options. The variety in Figure 4-3 was to illustrate that firms vary widely between themselves in the detail offered to their clients. They all, however, need the detail shown for internal tracking of the components of revenue.

CREDITING REVENUE TO TERRITORIES

So far we have discussed revenue crediting for purposes of measuring profit, and its extended use in revenue and cost productivity analysis. A more visible (and emotionally charged) purpose of revenue measurement is to directly or in-

FIGURE 4-3
Billing Register: What the Client Sees on an Invoice

Detailed Billing Register

TEAM	CLIENT NO	CLIENT	ENGAGE NO	CONTR NO	TYP SVC	BUS TYP	IND	ACT-IVITY	DATE ENTER	CHARGE WEEK	PER NO	DESCRIPTION	PER OFF	PER TYP	UNITS	HR DY	HR RATE	REV TYP	SUB TOTAL	BILLED
ZOO	9412313	VERMIN FOOD	A9908	C0006	MS	CUS	PROC	10	920212	920207	991101	TP BARNUM	ZEN	S	39.5	HR	117.00	L	$4,621.50	
								20	920212	920207	127238	WK AHOLIC	ZEN	C	41.0	HR	117.00	L	$4,797.00	
								30	920213	920207	321654	OL SUDDEN	ZEN	C	31.0	HR	117.00	L	$3,627.00	
								10	920218	920214	991101	TP BARNUM	ZEN	S	40.0	HR	117.00	L	$4,680.00	
								20	920219	920214	127238	WK AHOLIC	ZEN	C	32.0	HR	117.00	L	$3,744.00	
								30	920219	920214	321654	OL SUDDEN	ZEN	C	32.0	HR	117.00	L	$3,744.00	
								10	920226	920221	991101	TP BARNUM	ZEN	S	37.5	HR	117.00	L	$4,387.50	
								20	920227	920221	127238	WK AHOLIC	ZEN	C	43.0	HR	117.00	L	$5,031.00	
								30	920227	920221	321654	OL SUDDEN	ZEN	C	36.0	HR	117.00	L	$4,212.00	
								10	920302	920228	991101	TP BARNUM	ZEN	S	39.5	HR	117.00	L	$4,621.50	
								20	920302	920228	127238	WK AHOLIC	ZEN	C	41.0	HR	117.00	L	$4,797.00	
								30	920302	920228	321654	OL SUDDEN	ZEN	C	31.0	HR	117.00	L	$3,627.00	
												CONSULTANT CHARGE							$51,889.50	
									920217	920214		WK AHOLIC TRAVEL	ZEN		44.5	HR	117.00	L	$1,743.78	$53,633.28
	9413002	VULGAR SALES	B0113	C9486	FPP	CON	DIST													
												PROGRESS PAYMENT						L	$15,000.00	
												PROGRESS PAYMENT						NL	$2,600.00	$17,600.00
	9544710	WADI POWER	A8888	C7176	TM	CON	UTIL													
								10	920211	920131	567123	UP DOWN	ZEN	B	33.5	HR	130.00	L	$4,355.00	
								10	920212	920207	567123	UP DOWN	ZEN	B	28.0	HR	130.00	L	$3,640.00	
								10	920218	920214	22344	RE NGU	ZEN	C	12.5	HR	140.00	L	$1,750.00	
								10	920221	920221	567123	UP DOWN	ZEN	B	38.0	HR	130.00	L	$4,940.00	
								10	920302	920228	567123	UP DOWN	ZEN	B	22.5	HR	130.00	L	$2,925.00	
												CONSULTANT CHARGE			134.5	HR			$17,610.00	$17,610.00
	9580202	WAFFLE IRON	B0006	C3420	CP	EDU	MFG													
								40	920213	920207	546554	BF RANKLYNN	BMV	C	8.5	HR				
								50	920227	920221	546554	BF RANKLYNN	BMV	C	33.0	HR				
									920207			PROGRESS PAYMENT						L	$45,000.00	
									920228			BF RANKLYNN TRAVEL						NL	$1,227.78	
												BF RANKLYNN TRAVEL						NL	$1,465.33	
												ED MATERIALS						NL	$590.00	$48,193.11

Legend:
Type of Service (TYP SVC): MS = Hourly managed, FPP = Fixed price, progress, TM = Time & materials CP = Client participation
Business Type (BUS TYP): CUS = Custom development, CON = Consulting, EDU = Education
Activity: 10 = General consulting, 20 = Architect, 30 = Project management, 40 = Class preparation 50 = Teaching

directly compensate people for their performance. In direct compensation people will receive commissions and bonuses for achievement of revenue against quota. Indirect compensation can occur when meeting revenue objectives affects a person's performance evaluation and subsequent salary potential.

Territory measurements are grouped into three categories.

1. *Client ownership and market.* These are territories whose measurement is based on the market that contains the client. It includes the performance of client owners (account managers) and industry segments.

2. *Business type.* These are territories that are measured by revenue achievements in professional services markets.

3. *Resource and component.* These are territories that measure individual offering revenue, such as a specific class, or a specific consulting service unique from other services, such as project management or session leadership.

In order to identify revenue generated on behalf of one of these territories, the administrative process has to be able to relate line items on the bill to each territory to which it applies. Figure 4-4 shows how this might be done. It shows the natural hierarchy of information about a client, engagements, contracts, and charges. The corresponding level at which each territory might be identified is also shown. This identification needs to be part of the data bases for clients and engagements as discussed in Chapter 3.

Only those measurements that compensate local office executives will get attention from their administrative and business controls staffs. Those that are for people who manage cross sections of the business, such as business type and resource and component territory managers will get short shrift from local administration and rightly so. It is the responsibility of the business to invest in business computer support that automates the collection of other than local territory identification information, untouched by human hands.

Client Ownership Territories

We discussed client ownership in Chapter 3. An office receives a revenue quota for the clients it owns and passes this quota to managers and marketers within the office by dividing the body of clients among them. These assignments spread the workload and create competition. The individuals receive revenue credit for each of the client accounts they are assigned. These assignments usually start with some underlying logic like geography or common business characteristics, but over time territories take on a life of their own.

FIGURE 4-4
Identifying Territories with Revenue

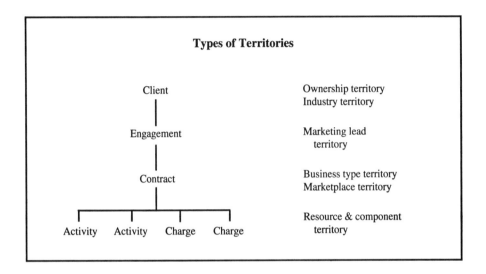

Revenue compensation comes in many forms. The simplest is a commission paid as a percentage of revenue billed. This should be capped by a specific maximum amount that can be earned in one year or at a percentage of the person's annual base salary.

A more complex approach is to assign a monthly revenue objective to be generated by the set of client accounts. A bonus is paid periodically based on whether accumulated revenue for the year to that point is below, at, or above expectation (quota). The amount of the bonus usually accelerates as attainment moves well above quota. Each periodic payment may be a prepayment against a final computed bonus at year end. If the payments to date are lower than the total year's attainment would pay, more is paid up to maximums as described for commissions. If the periodic payments were too much, then money is taken back (as a credit against future bonuses or from salary).

Compensation should motivate people to get good business and to perform engagements to the benefit of both the client and the firm. In Chapter 7 we will talk about a revenue compensation option that encourages people to see that successful execution is equally important to bringing in the green.

The management structure above these individuals is likewise measured and compensated for the revenue billed to the collection of clients below them. This roll up of client revenue can continue upward to a number of levels, depending upon the height of the firm's middle executive structure.

The firm may pay compensation to businesses for marketing leads to their professional services offices. This may be other units in the parent of the firm such as accounting offices or software marketing offices. Compensation for marketing leads usually takes the form of a payment for the potential revenue to be billed, computed as a percentage of the engagement value to which the client commits (again subject to maximums). There are probably cases where the firm and marketing lead relationship is close enough that compensation occurs on a continuous basis through the life of the engagement, similar to that paid to members of the firm.

Groupings of clients within industry classification are important to professional services. Strong credentials in an industry mean sustained revenue from that group of clients. For this reason, industry classification is a common characteristic for local assignment of clients as just described. It is also a common cross-sectional measurement for the entire firm.

An industry manager is one measured on the accumulated revenue of all clients in a segment. Very often, these executives offer emphasis bonuses to office executives as an incentive to grow. (Emphasis bonuses are an incentive to generate revenue in a very specific business area or for a specific service offering.) If the firm has industry competency centers, their performance will be measured against the year by year revenue across the business in their segments.

Business Type Territories

In Chapter 1 the broad lines of business that have evolved in professional services were identified. Firms continue to measure their share of these markets and react to the conclusions they draw. Senior executives will have individual incentives to grow in a particular line of business. Pricing guidelines will change to reap an advantage in share or to correct a loss of share. As in industry segment management, local office executives may get emphasis bonuses for growing a particular line of business.

The best way to focus attention on how the business is prospering in its separate markets is to state income by these markets. The income statement in Figure 4-3 and all others in the book lists income by business type. This is done for the same reason any business compares its product line to the sum of their competitors and against their own performance in previous years. It is simply good business management.

Resource and Component Territories

A common practice is to pay bonuses for new offerings. An offering in the services business has a very specific methodology and end result. These can be a class, a strategic plan for a new client, the installation of a specific product, use of a high-leverage skill such as project manager, or the first time introduction of new methodology to a client.

Keeping track of these can be a problem. They are reflected in the lowest level of revenue information, as illustrated in Figure 4-4. If data collection is not automatic, verification becomes a problem. The benefit of tracking these segments definitely outweighs the cost. The bonuses are effective for introducing innovations, particularly when offices must incur loss of revenue to get people trained. The ongoing tracking of how well they are accepted and grow allows quick reaction to take advantage of very successful offerings and scrap losers.

REVENUE PROCESSING

We will now turn to the administration and control of revenue. We will be expanding on the weekly and monthly cycles described in Chapter 2. Our focus will be on the primary purpose of revenue control—invoice quality. When invoices are accurate and timely, all other control needs fall in place. Invoice quality reflects on the professionalism of the firm and is a window through which clients can view its internal management.

In this section, we will cover labor claiming as it applies to the completeness and accuracy of billing. We will look at the mechanics of billing audit in advance to improve short-term forecasting. The latter part of the section covers such subjects as revenue reporting and taxation.

Revenue Recording

As might be expected, the revenue entry process is divided into recording labor for consultants and contractors and triggering the billing to compensate for nonlabor expenses as they are incurred. Typically, 90 percent of the effort is workload in support of labor claiming.

In this chapter, we will focus only on the revenue aspects of labor claiming. In Chapter 5, we will look at the total subject of utilization and its relationship to profit management. Figure 4-5 is an example of a labor claiming sheet in professional services. These are (should be) completed by consultants and managers (principals) for all portions of the work week and by contractors and borrowed people for the time they are assigned to engagements.

FIGURE 4–5
Services Labor Claiming Sheet

Services Labor Activity Sheet

02 / 07 / 92   3 7 4 8 5 9   C A L H O M   E T   Z E N   D
Week Ending   Person No.   Last Name   Init   Office Mgr

Hours	Contract	Activity	Day	Rate	Comments
— — . — —	— — — — —	— — — —	— —	— — — . — —	_____
27 . 0	C 1 7 3 1	3 0			*Project management at Vaccine Du Pox*
11 . 0	D 2 2 1 4	5 0			*Teaching at Der Wunderwiener*
2 . 0	C 0 0 0 2	9 0			*Find problem at Vermin Foods*
8 . 0		1 1 1 1			*Attended class*
— — . — —	— — — — —	— — — —	— —	— — — . — —	_____
— — . — —	— — — — —	— — — —	— —	— — — . — —	_____
— — . — —	— — — — —	— — — —	— —	— — — . — —	_____
48 . 0	— — — — —	— — — —	— —	— — — . — —	_____

Legend:
Activity: 30 = Project management
           50 = Teaching
           90 = Service call
           1111 = Classroom education (for the consultant)

Assuming that contract numbers are unique, the labor claiming capability in the contract management and resource management systems should be able to link the information on each line to the appropriate engagement. Similarly, the systems should link to more information about the person through a number assigned for each.

The individual records how many hours were spent during the period (in this example, the entire week) performing particular activities. The activity may be billable work related to a contract as seen on the first three lines of the example. The entry could be for assignment to a contract where no billing occurred. As with the fourth line in the example, the sheet may contain off-contract related activities (i.e., spent on vacations, illness, internal office work that brings no direct revenue, education, or marketing).

In the example, this consultant put in a 48-hour week, of which 40 hours were billable. The other 8 hours were spent in a one-day class. The consultant's billable time was divided between project management, teaching, and a service call.

If the terms of the contract are per hour or per day, the labor claimed will result in immediate revenue credit for the period and will appear on the next client invoice. The 27 hours of project management might fall in that category. If fixed price, the labor claimed does not directly affect billing but implies cost and affects engagement profitability as discussed in Chapter 9.

Consultants may need to enter the rate to be charged. These can vary by person or by activity within a contract, and certainly between contracts. A smart contract management system can link labor entries to appropriate contract information and avoid entry of rates. This is preferable, since busy consultants are notorious for forgetting such things.

In a weekly labor claiming process, the consultants and subcontractors are usually urged to complete their previous week's labor sheets on Monday. The administrative staff wants to get these through management review and approval by Tuesday and entered and edited by Wednesday, so that on Thursday they can audit the source documents against a trial version of the billing.

Following this weekly discipline serves two purposes. It avoids the last minute rush of labor billing at month end with its guaranteed errors, and it allows the staff to verify invoice quality with plenty of time to make corrections.

Figure 4-3 was an example of this report.

Nonlabor Revenue Control

Nonlabor revenue entry reacts to actions in the expense control process, described later in the book. Consultants will complete travel expense accounts on each Monday with their labor claiming sheets. Invoices will arrive from vendors. Products and materials may be delivered. Completion notices for support work and rosters from classes are received.

Each of these activities is reviewed to determine whether charges are due a client. Given the weekly process, Monday is a good day for entry of charges. These will then appear on the Thursday trial audit for correction.

Revenue Review

Four kinds of problems will show up when reviewing the trial billing.

- Differences when compared to the source document (labor claiming sheet or nonlabor expense item), usually indicating incorrect entry.
- Wrong consultant or wrong nonlabor item charged to a contract. Some systems have elaborate protections to avoid charging an incorrect contract. These rarely screen out more than would be picked up in the visual check and always slow down the entry process.
- Strange financial results such as extremely high or low amounts. These indicate incorrect rates stored in the system or entered by the individual.
- Ill-timed progress payments or one-time charges. One case can be an incorrect payment schedule due to an entry error. The other case is the more subtle one, where management must consciously decide whether the bill should be sent, based on the status of the engagement

A popular innovation in labor claiming systems is to have the consultant or, even subcontractor, enter their own labor directly. This does not eliminate the control steps above, and in fact makes them more critical. The errors will multiply, but the savings in entry workload have presumably been justified.

By keeping to the weekly schedule, billing derived from labor claiming can be entered, corrected (either the labor record or the underlying contract or person data), and audited by close of business on Thursday. This leaves Friday as a buffer against short weeks and as a day to pursue any problems.

A final benefit of processing revenue on a weekly basis is the ability to make accurate short-term forecasts. Services can be a quick reaction business. Knowing how much revenue is flowing by mid-month allows cost decisions that benefit in more consistent profit. Managing profit is a lot easier when revenue is not a mystery game.

Revenue Closing

At some point all revenue recorded is assembled by a billing system and invoices are created with appropriate credits to the books. This is usually once per month, but some firms invoice semimonthly, biweekly, and even weekly. Because revenue is a universal measurement and directly affects personal income, there is always a strong incentive to get as much into a billing cycle as time, workload, and events will allow. This last minute activity is terminated by rules and procedures that surround the **cutoff** and the **closing** of a revenue cycle.

The revenue cutoff is the date and time after which the accounting process will no longer credit a revenue activity for the period being invoiced. Consulting, and now professional services, has traditionally been a weekly work delivery process. As we just discussed, labor recording usually occurs at the end of a week. For this reason, most billing cutoff occurs on a weekly (Friday) basis, usually one or two hours after the firm's most western office closes.

The revenue closing is the last moment that revenue claims can be entered for activity that occurred before the cutoff. It is essentially a period of grace to allow labor from the last week before the cutoff to be processed (collected, entered, audited, and corrected).

For those that invoice on a semimonthly or monthly basis, the gap between cutoff and closing is not so regular. Typically, the closing will occur one or two days before or after the 1st and/or the 15th of the calendar month. This means that some months, the offices have only one day to enter, review, and correct revenue entries, if they are to get full credit for all revenue deserved in that period.

With modern systems, the machine collection of revenue and the printing of invoices occurs within hours of closing. Very often, the office can see a graphic image of the actual client invoice on the next day. A good practice is to scan these images one last time to ensure that the client will see no surprises.

The final step in this process is to transfer the revenue invoiced (and the corresponding accounts receivable) to the general ledger of the office and, through roll ups, to the partnership/corporation. In Chapter 6 we will look at the resulting income and expense statement.

Revenue Reporting

Four groups of reports support revenue measurements. Typically, these reports contain information through the previous closing, which for most firms is monthly. As we saw earlier, period to date reports or "trials" are also often available, but these are usually considered estimates of revenue generation with the prospect that the information may change before closing and actual client invoicing. The revenue report groups are as follows.

1. *Invoice registers and detailed billing.* These reports recap the invoices sent to clients. Typically they show both data that appears on the invoice and addi-

tional accounting data that indicate how the revenue will be applied to the general ledger and various territories.

Most firms require an audit of the detailed billing to ensure invoice quality and protect against fraudulent credits. The weekly review of trial revenue reports is often the first level of this audit, with a comparison of final totals by the client as the finishing review.

The detailed billing reports are also formatted to support revenue sharing that occurs under resource sharing (cross-territory) agreements. This will be discussed in more detail in Chapter 9.

Figure 4-6 is another example of a billing register, similar to that in Figure 4-3. In this example, six clients receive invoices this month. As can be seen, the office has a variety of services being performed for each client, with Sawyer Rafts receiving services on four contracts under an engagement.

This report shows an example of a systems integration bill. The client, Surf Sand, does not see the detailed hours for the project manager, I. M. Atecky. The client does get a progress bill for the labor and is individually charged for the vendor and product expenses that are being recovered at this checkpoint.

2. *Attainment reports.* Revenue attainment reports list revenue credited for commissions and/or quota for each territory. These may be for organizational territories (marketing personnel, consultants, their management, offices, regions, or areas). These also may be to inform offices of payments to sources of marketing leads, showing what revenue qualified for compensation.

As shown in Figure 4-7, attainment is typically expressed in revenue credit for the period just ended, year to date, and the ratio of year-to-date accumulated revenue credit to the quota accumulation expected by this point in the year. The report is at a higher level than the detailed billing, but adds information that indicates which business segments will also be receiving potential credit for this revenue.

Notice that the revenue for Sawyer Rafts (C9622) in Figure 4-7 is lower than the amount invoiced in Figure 4-6 by the amount listed as "K Kong Act Travel." This indicates that the firm does not compensate its people for revenue that is not profitable (actual travel being a travel expense recovered with no markup).

3. *Marketplace reports.* These are reports sorted and formatted for each territory that the firm tracks. To save trees, these are usually produced on a quarterly basis and lend themselves well to graphic representation.

4. *Revenue by resource reports:* These are reports that analyze the revenue received against various sources of cost. The most common is revenue from firm employees versus revenue from subcontractors.

Obviously, the variety and utility of revenue reports depends heavily on the quality and utility of the contract management and billing systems used by the firm and its offices. The detailed reports in Figures 4-6 and 4-7 are fairly common. If there is a data base that contains the information listed on the detailed reports, query tools provide a mechanism to select and graph revenue history in a variety of cross sections. As a last resort, the resourceful local office can extract line items from the detailed reports and enter them into spreadsheets to achieve much of what has been described.

Taxation of professional services

Professional services is fortunate to be able to avoid much of the complexity involved in sales and excise taxes. A few states and municipalities tax services, and in these jurisdictions, professional services firms are obliged to add tax to invoices and, correspondingly, pay the appropriate government for monies collected.

More complex taxation hinges on whether the firm acts as a broker or reseller during the execution of complex engagements involving delivery of components that are taxable.

The following discussion is to highlight the issues involved in taxation. Tax accountants and attorneys must be consulted when the probability of taxation is high. The following can provide a checklist for deciding whether to involve tax experts.

1. If the only charges are for labor related expenses and the tax jurisdiction of the client (location where the work is performed and the invoice is paid) clearly does not tax the sale of general services, little time should be spent on this subject. Most jurisdictions do not tax professional labor services, because it would mean the taxation of attorney's fees.

2. If the charges are to be invoiced to a location in a taxing jurisdiction different from where the work is performed and one of the two locales taxes the service or any other part of the charge, get an opinion.

3. If the agreement with the client is for services, but includes the reselling of equipment and software purchased with appropriate taxes paid, no further taxation applies subject to items 1 and 2. This assumes that the firm takes asset ownership with the associated accounting that may be required. Again, the major issue here can be taxing jurisdiction, considering that the source of the product being delivered under the service is probably different from the point of delivery, which can be different from the invoicing location. Reconciling these differences needs an expert opinion.

FIGURE 4-6
Detailed Billing Report (Invoice Register)

Detailed Billing Register

TEAM	CLIENT NO	CLIENT	ENGAGE NO	CONTR NO	TYP SVC	BUS TYP	IND	ACT-IVITY	DATE ENTER	CHARGE WEEK	PER NO	DESCRIPTION	PER OFF	PER TYP	UNITS	HR DY	RATE	REV TYP	SUB TOTAL	BILLED
ZOT	7979008	SAWYER RAFTS	A4599	C2930	TM	CON	TRAN	20	920212	920207	357044	LO ANBEHOLD	ZEN	C	27.5	HR	143.00	L	$3,932.50	
								20	920219	920214	357044	LO ANBEHOLD	ZEN	C	39.5	HR	143.00	L	$5,648.50	
								20	920226	920221	357044	LO ANBEHOLD	ZEN	C	46.0	HR	143.00	L	$6,578.00	
								20	920302	920228	357044	LO ANBEHOLD	ZEN	C	27.0	HR	143.00	L	$3,861.00	
									920217	920207		LO ANBEHOLD TRAVEL						NL	$1,002.67	
									920244	920214		LO ANBEHOLD TRAVEL						NL	$844.56	$21,867.23
	7979008	SAWYER RAFTS	A4599	C2957	TM	CON	TRAN						ZEN	C	140.0	HR				
								60	920219	920214	773399	EL CID	ZEN	C	1.5	DY	1500.00	L	$2,250.00	
								60	920302	920228	357044	LO ANBEHOLD	ZEN	C	1.0	DY	1500.00	L	$1,500.00	$3,750.00
	7979008	SAWYER RAFTS	A4599	C4879	FP	PI	TRAN					EMP COMP PACKAGE			2.5	DY		NL	$30,000.00	$30,000.00
	7979008	SAWYER RAFTS	A4599	C9622	E	CON	TRAN	90	920211	920124	621843	K KONG	ZEN	S	7.5	HR			$0.00	
								90	920228	920221	621843	K KONG	ZEN	S	5.5	HR			$0.00	
												SERVICE CALL						L	$850.00	
												SERVICE CALL						L	$850.00	
												K KONG ACT TRAVEL			13.0	HR		NL	$777.77	$2,477.77
	8102885	SURF SAND	A2183	B9899	SI	SI	DIST	30	920212	920207	110220	IM ATECKY	ZEN	M	49.0	HR			$0.00	
								30	920219	920214	110220	IM ATECKY	ZEN	M	54.0	HR			$0.00	
								30	920226	920221	110220	IM ATECKY	ZEN	M	43.0	HR			$0.00	
								30	920302	920228	110220	IM ATECKY	ZEN	M	39.0	HR			$0.00	
												PROGRESS PAYMENT						L	$133,334.00	
												WAREHOUSE CONST						NL	$47,000.00	
												NETWORK EQUIP						NL	$124,250.00	
												SAND SOFTWARE						NL	$33,800.00	$338,384.00

FIGURE 4-6
Detailed Billing Report (Invoice Register) (concluded)

Detailed Billing Register

TEAM NO	CLIENT NO	CLIENT	ENGAGE NO	CONTR NO	TYP SVC	BUS TYP	IND	ACT-IVITY	DATE ENTER	CHARGE WEEK	PER NO	DESCRIPTION	PER OFF	PER TYP	UNITS	HR DY	RATE	REV TYP	SUB TOTAL	BILLED
															185.0	HR				
ZOO	9412313	VERMIN FOODS A9908		C0006	MS	CUS	PROC	10	920212	920207	991101	TP BARNUM	ZEN	S	39.5	HR	117.00	L	$4,621.50	
								20	920212	920207	127238	WK AHOLIC	ZEN	C	41.0	HR	117.00	L	$4,797.00	
								30	920213	920207	321654	OL SUDDEN	ZEN	C	31.0	HR	117.00	L	$3,627.00	
								10	920218	920214	991101	TP BARNUM	ZEN	S	40.0	HR	117.00	L	$4,680.00	
								20	920219	920214	127238	WK AHOLIC	ZEN	C	32.0	HR	117.00	L	$3,744.00	
								30	920219	920214	321654	OL SUDDEN	ZEN	C	32.0	HR	117.00	L	$3,744.00	
								10	920226	920221	991101	TP BARNUM	ZEN	S	37.5	HR	117.00	L	$4,387.50	
								20	920227	920221	127238	WK AHOLIC	ZEN	C	43.0	HR	117.00	L	$5,031.00	
								30	920227	920221	321654	OL SUDDEN	ZEN	C	36.0	HR	117.00	L	$4,212.00	
								10	920302	920228	991101	TP BARNUM	ZEN	S	39.5	HR	117.00	L	$4,621.50	
								20	920302	920228	127238	WK AHOLIC	ZEN	C	41.0	HR	117.00	L	$4,797.00	
								30	920302	920228	321654	OL SUDDEN	ZEN	C	31.0	HR	117.00	L	$3,627.00	
										920228		CONSULTANT CHARGE			443.5	HR			$51,889.50	
									920017	920214		WK AHOLIC TRAVEL							$1,743.78	$53,633.28
	9413002	VULGAR SALES B0113		C9486	FPP	CON	DIST					PROGRESS PAYMENT						L	$15,000.00	
												PROGRESS PAYMENT						NL	$2,600.00	$17,600.00
	9544710	WADI POWER A8888		C7176	TM	CON	UTIL	10	920211	920131	567123	UP DOWN	ZEN	B	33.5	HR	130.00	L	$4,355.00	
								10	920212	920207	567123	UP DOWN	ZEN	B	28.0	HR	130.00	L	$3,640.00	
								10	920218	920214	223344	RE NGU	ZEN	C	12.5	HR	140.00	L	$1,750.00	
								10	920227	920221	56712	UP DOWN	ZEN	B	38.0	HR	130.00	L	$4,940.00	
								10	920302	920228	56712	UP DOWN	ZEN	B	22.5	HR	130.00	L	$2,925.00	
										920228		CONSULTANT CHARGE			134.5				$17,610.00	$17,610.00
	9580202	WAFFLE I RON B0006		C8420	CP	EDU	MFG	40	920213	920207	546554	BF RANKLYNN	BMW	C	8.5	HR				
								50	920227	920221	546554	BF RANKLYNN	BMW	C	33.0	HR				
										920207		PROGRESS PAYMENT						L	$45,000.00	
												BF RANKLYNN TRAVEL						NL	$1,227.78	
										920228		BF RANKLYNN TRAVEL						NL	$1,465.33	
												ED MATERIALS						NL	$500.00	$48,193.11

Legend:
Type of Service (TYP SVC): MS = Hourly managed, FPP = Fixed price, progress, TM = Time & materials, CP = Client participation, FP = Fixed price, one payment, E = Event

Business Type (BUS TYP): CUS = Custom development, CON = Consulting, EDU = Education, PI = Product installation, SI = Systems integration

Activity: 10 = General consulting, 20 = Architect, 30 = Project management, 40 = Class preparation 50 = Teaching, 60 = Session leader, 90 = Problem call

FIGURE 4-7
Revenue Attainment Report (for Compensation)

Services Attainment Report

OFFICE	TEAM	CLIENT NO	CLIENT	ENGAGE NO	CONTR NO	MEASUREMENT REVENUE	YTD MEASUREMENT REVENUE	YTD QUOTA	ATTAIN
ZEN	ZOT	7979008	SAWYER RAFTS	A4599	C2930	$21,867.23			
					C2957	$3,750.00			
					C4879	$3,000.00			
					C9622	$1,700.00			
						$338,384.00			
		8102885	SURF SAND	A2183	B9899	$368,701.23	$409,556.23	$450,000.00	91%
	ZOO	9412313	VERMIN FOODS	A9908	C0006	$53,633.28			
		9413002	VULGAR SALES	B0113	C9486	$17,600.00			
		9544710	WADI POWER	A8888	C7176	$17,610.00			
		9580202	WAFFLE IRON	B0006	C8420	$48,193.11			
						$137,036.39	$226,309.54	$200,000.00	113%
						$505,737.62	$635,865.77	$650,000.00	98%

4. If any assets pass to the client via the service contract and the firm
   does not take asset control, or pay taxes at the source, the firm is
   responsible for seeing that appropriate taxes are invoiced and paid to
   the appropriate jurisdiction. This will require an opinion.

DIVIDING UP THE GREEN

In this chapter we have examined everyone's favorite measurement. We have
looked at how to define it, credit it, account for it, and compensate for it. Revenue is easy to understand, so everyone tries to get a piece of it. Some key
things to remember are:

- Dividing revenue into measurements must first serve the need to understand profit and, in the professional services business, the profitability
  of resources. Once this is taken care of, revenue can be reorganized to
  measure territories, markets, and service offerings. Relative revenue
  (this year to last year, actual to quota) will always be a safe basis for
  compensating people for managing growth.

- Revenue measurements should not be used to the exclusion of all others. Profit is equally important and, in the professional services business, not that much more difficult to understand and administer. The
  other three measurements of utilization, backlog, and productivity
  supplement revenue and profit by providing means to forecast and
  make corrections.

- Variety in billing clients is what makes professional services an entrepreneur's business. The revenue management process shouldn't restrict
  this. If the need to measure everything using revenue as a base causes
  the business to reduce billing options, then some measurements must
  go. It is foolish to allow the complexity of measurements to become a
  limitation in the freedom to meet client needs.

- Fixed-price contracts with scheduled payment schedules are the beginning of most complexity in professional services. This complexity is
  most easily avoided by timing payments to correspond closely to expenditure of resources. Growth in fixed-price business should be accompanied by corresponding layers of business controls.

- Having a very smart contract management system allows a firm to
  have variety in client options and variety in who gets measured by
  revenue. There will be good pay back from managing market share and

tracking the introduction of new offerings. This is ample justification for investment in good business computer systems.

The underlying message in this chapter is, don't spend all your administrative resources on revenue management. It is important, but it can be made too important. The emphasis should be on invoice quality. All other revenue administration and distribution activities are incremental to an effective billing process. When clients refuse to pay, a complex revenue distribution process will contribute little to the business.

Chapter 5
Utilization Management

U tilization tracking is the inventory analysis of the professional services business. All firms manage utilization, from the smallest basic people services business to the largest systems integration provider. Weekly review of utilization is the first and easiest step toward managing the cost of people. A convenient utilization management information system, coupled with resource skills inventory and availability calendar systems, provides the essential set of tools for the effective people management so necessary in a people business.

In this chapter we will be examining utilization measurements and resource skills inventory in detail. We will begin with definitions of terms associated with people inventory management, along with computations that define utilization as a measurement. We will then look at the variety of labor resources that a people services office may have at its disposal, particularly when the professional services business of a firm is in association with other enterprises of a parent corporation. We will then carry this discussion of resource categories into types of labor and how to build a people services business plan. We will finish by discussing the information needed to manage labor resource use and availability, the systems and business processes needed, and the issues that surround the measurement and incentive of the consultant.

CALCULATING UTILIZATION

The term *utilization* when applied to people is the dividing of their available time into discreet segments, expressed as a percentage. There are a number of ways to calculate a person's availability. Certainly, the maximum time any person is available is 24 hours per day, 168 hours per week and 8,736 hours per year. Few, if any, use a 168-hour week, since viewing the human as a 100 percent utilizable resource is not as popular as it once was. To get appropriate granularity, though, 100 percent utilization should be near the maximum reasonable use of the time a person could devote to work.

The common baseline for work time is the 40-hour work week, known as **available time.** This computes to a 2,080-hour work year. For those who track in days, available time is 5 days per week and 260 days per year.

In Chapter 8 we will be discussing a variation of available time used to analyze the productivity of the firm's consultants versus subcontractors. This is called **effective available time** and normalizes the work week for comparisons of productivity between these two choices of resource. Effective available time reduces the 40-hour work week by obligated personal time such as holidays, average vacation, minimum education, and minimum employee meetings.

Most firms measure utilization on a weekly basis and do not try to match weeks to months. The average work month is 176 hours, but within a year, there are five 200-hour months and seven 160-hour months. Monthly utilization is, however, important to project managers when determining the staffing needed on engagements (projects) of long duration. The value in person months of one person is computed by multiplying the expected billable utilization for that person times 176 hours. Billable utilization varies widely among different types of consultants.

Utilization varies widely from week to week through the work year. Summer vacations raise the level of personal time utilization and lower the amount of billed utilization. High concentrations of time devoted to professional education often occur in May and November. Plotting weekly and year-to-date utilization provides a valuable profile of historical levels of time distribution. This is important input for the planning activity described later in this chapter and for the engagement staffing previously mentioned.

The total hours worked in a week by most professionals is greater than 40 hours. Overtime is an expectation of all professionals, but people sensitive firms are concerned when overtime exceeds 7 percent to 10 percent on a consistent basis. A utilization of 107 percent of available time is a common planning target from which to break out billable, personal, and business investment time objectives. Figure 5-1 illustrates four examples of expected time distribution for consultants. The variety of these examples emphasizes how different utilization expectations can be from office to office. As one can see, the typical consultant might be billed 55 percent to 85 percent of a work year and record work and personal hours that total 105 percent to 125 percent of available time.

As discussed in Chapter 4, all people who contribute to revenue record their work time each week. If the only requirements were to measure and invoice revenue, only that time directly applied to efforts which produce revenue would need to be recorded. The measurement of utilization requires that all time be recorded, regardless of whether the time was devoted to work that derives revenue.

FIGURE 5-1
Examples of Available Time Utilization for Consultants

Category of Utilization	Consultant Utilization Distribution Example:			
Consultant Utilization (2,080-Hour Work Year)	A	B	C	D
Billed	82%	55%	58%	85%
Assigned, not billed	3%	3%	9%	5%
Personal				
Holiday/vacation	5%	5%	8%	5%
Education	5%	10%	10%	5%
Other	5%	5%	5%	5%
Investment	5%	27%	20%	20%
TOTAL	105%	105%	110%	125%

Example A: Moderate rate, medium skill staff

Example B: High rate specialty staff

Example C: Large multiservice staff

Example D: Large project

Later in this chapter we will discuss who within a firm are the minimum set of people considered inventory and included in utilization measurements. Many firms have everyone in the firm record their time each week. The administrative workload to enter labor to a contract management and billing system is easiest to manage when the workload is constant. When only those who bill that week turn in sheets, the workload is variable and considerable time is wasted determining whether all time sheets are in. An efficient time recording system will usually support growth in the number of people being tracked with very small increments of additional entry time.

The weekly cycle should be as regular as clockwork. Each management unit ought to see weekly, quarterly, and year-to-date utilization reports each Monday morning. As will be discussed, a key operation in a professional services office is the regular review by the management and marketing staff of assignment tactics for engagements and investments in the weeks ahead. As Figure 5-1 illustrated, no office plans to waste available consultant time by having people on the bench. The sad alternative to good utilization management is more and more consultant overtime late in the year and stretching available time to make up for waste in previous months.

CATEGORIES OF UTILIZATION

The use of people in a professional services firm is divided between **engagement time** and **nonengagement time**. Engagement time is any time devoted to the satisfaction of client expectations. It can be before contract signature, during execution, and after completion. It can be directly billable, indirectly billable as in fixed-price activities, or it can be nonbillable work by trainees, those performing rework, those managing nonbillable activities, or any number of areas where nonbillable time contributes to the expected work products of an engagement.

Nonengagement time is all other available time that is separate from the performance of engagements. This includes time off, marketing, administration, nonengagement travel, education, and a myriad of other activities to which consultants might be assigned outside of engagements. The number of nonengagement labor codes to choose from is often an absorbing intellectual subject in a firm. Too few codes, and insufficient data is available to analyze historical trends in education, administration, marketing, and other essential support and investment activities in the office. Too many codes, and the consultants play pick a number when deciding among similar choices.

The amount of time expected from an individual toward engagement time is **billable utilization.** The corresponding expenditure of this time is **billed utilization** or **assigned, not billed, utilization.** The difference between expected billable and actual billed utilization is the difference between actual and planned use of people resources. This translates directly to a difference in cost of labor necessary to deliver each hour. The higher the billed utilization of an office, the lower is the cost of each hour that brings in revenue.

Most labor claiming and utilization systems allow for the designation of an **activity** that is associated with each line item of time. If an engagement or contract is recorded with the activity, the time is engagement time within the expected billable utilization of the individual. Activities can be skill related, such as project leading, teaching, programming, consulting on a particular business process, analyzing the problems of a particular product, or people managing. Activities can be process related such as analyzing requirements, planning, developing external process design documentation, analyzing information flow, developing software, and testing. Activities can be event related, such as meetings and engagement related travel.

A special set of activities are defined for those consultants who are assigned to an engagement, but are not billable. There are an uncomfortably wide number of instances where consultants receive no revenue for their efforts. Some are positive; most are negative. Some examples are listed below.

Positive Reasons	*Negative Reasons*
On-site people management	Nonrecoverable travel time
Project audits	Rework
Postengagement reviews	Managing a failed subcontractor
Follow-on marketing	Consultant replacement training
	Nonbilled trainee time

As we will see later, assigned, not billed, time is considered billable utilization for resource planning purposes, but is in its own category for utilization tracking and price and productivity analysis. Assigned, not billed, activities are particularly important on hourly and daily contracts, since the client often wants an accounting of nonbilled time on the invoice. They can be just as important on fixed-price engagements to support revenue proration among assigned consultants for productivity and profitability computations.

Nonengagement utilization can be grouped into three broad categories: **personal, business investment,** and **administration.** Personal investment includes all time needed by the individual and management to satisfy personal needs and to grow as a professional. Examples of personal activities are:

Holiday	Classroom education
Vacation	Self-study education
Illness	Employee/manager meeting
Personal business	Compensatory time off

Business investment is either **marketing** or **service office improvement** activities. The tendency is not to be too granular in describing these activities. Marketing support is usually the highest priority allocation of available business investment time. Consultants are asked to estimate, interview client personnel, write proposal detail, and be seen at client marketing sessions. (This may be recorded as assigned, not billed, when consultants perform these activities to get more work from current clients.)

When marketing needs are filled, investment is made in improving the efficiency of the office, its consulting methods and its range of offerings. Just as marketing efforts require a business case, so also do service office improvement projects. In most cases these have been proposed, approved, and placed on the shelf awaiting an available consultant. It is not unusual for these projects to take months to complete and to be implemented in pieces by a number of different people.

Administration is a catchall for both planned and unplanned nonbilled activities. The planned activities include minimum time to keep people informed of the state of the business, to keep people motivated and to perform essential business management tasks. The unplanned activities are a result of both fate and foible.

Planned	*Unplanned*
General business meeting	Emergency closing
Relocation	Unpaid absence
New employee orientation	Not assigned (on the bench)
Nonengagement travel	
Administrative tasks	
People management	

Time recording should be kept as simple as possible. A consultant should not be required to spend more than 15 minutes per week on the administrative task of labor recording. The temptation is to continually expand the number of categories into which time is to be divided. Its purpose is to get more detailed history for a finer analysis of time usage. All too often, it merely causes more time to be spent by consultants to create data no one believes.

CLASSIFICATION OF PEOPLE INVENTORY

Rarely does a firm expect the same utilization from all segments of its staff. As a result, the professional services business uses inventory classification with much the same purpose as a product business. Inventory classification provides a means to plan and track people usage in groups that have common attributes such as expected rates per hour and how much of their available time can be billed.

People inventory has approximately six broad classes and a number of sub-classifications. The classes represent variations in the cost of the person, the source of the person, and the degree to which the person is fully or partially revenue generating. Throughout this chapter, we will be reviewing examples of utilization plans, utilization tracking reports, and availability calendars. Figure 5-2 introduces the categories of people inventory that appear in these examples.

These classifications of people are described as follows.

1. **Consultants.** These are the primary revenue producing staff of an office. Usually this classification includes no managers of people, but may include project leaders who bill full time. Typical subclassifications define the consultant's experience level and revenue potential. It may also define specific assignment responsibilities such as project manager.

2. **Direct managers/partners.** These are partially revenue producing personnel, who also have people management, business management, and senior staff responsibilities. Their subclassifications are specific to their title such as

FIGURE 5-2
Examples of People Inventory Classifications

People Classifications		
Resource Class	*Description*	*Planned*
Consultants		
New trainee	College hire—1st six months	Yes
Trainee	Trainee consultant	Yes
Associate	Associate consultant	Yes
Consultant	Consultant	Yes
Intern	Retrained professional—1st six months	Yes
Senior	Senior consultant	Yes
Management		
Project	Project manager/quality assurance	Yes
Consulting	Consulting services manager	Yes
Senior	Senior manager/partner	Yes
Contractors		
Sub	Subcontractor	Yes
Temp	Supplemental professional	Yes
Borrowed		
Consultant	Consultant level	Yes
Senior	Senior consultant level	Yes
Indirect (Local and Nonlocal)		
Marketing	Marketing personnel	No
Staff	Nonmanagement personnel	No

partner, consulting services manager, branch manager, and quality assurance staff.

3. **Contractors.** These are people who are not paid regular salary and benefits by the firm. The subclassifications include hourly contractors from vendors and supplemental payroll employees on temporary staff. Contractors record time for each week they are assigned. They are paid for only those hours they work. Their utilization of available time in a week will be slightly less than 100 percent, because of the personal hours they may require. (Of course, they are not paid for the time off.)

4. **Borrowed/internally rented.** These are people who are assigned from other divisions of the firm. Their expense is usually recovered through expense transfer. The subclassifications are often similar to consultants. These are not consultants shared by offices within the services line organization, but are people from parts of the company that are not part of the firm's base inventory of direct people (i.e., from a development unit of the firm's parent or from a cost center unit, such as a competency center).

5. **Local indirect personnel.** These are the employees of the firm who are not assigned to billable jobs and whose expense is distributed across the office. They may claim labor only when they are called upon to bill or they may claim for the purpose of analyzing support workload distribution. Their subclassifications are usually specific to their job such as marketing representative, administrative staff, and business manager.

6. **Nonlocal indirect personnel.** These are staff above the local office or partnership in organizational hierarchy. Their expense is distributed across a number of offices. When they bill, it is at very high and selective rates and they probably only claim labor when they bill. Their subclassifications are usually by job title.

UTILIZATION PLANNING AND FORECASTING

Utilization management begins with a plan. Utilization planning is the basis for all other planning in professional services. Annual revenue targets are established nationally by projecting head count (the number of people in the firm), applying average utilization percentages to get hours or days that can be delivered to clients, and multiplying the result by average rates. Annual expense plans key off of the same head count assumptions in the computation of people cost.

National revenue planning always seems to take a number of twists and turns before final targets are established. The plan is adjusted for economic forecasts of inflation and overall economic outlook. Forecasts for new offerings that are to be announced and nonlabor revenue components are added. Adjustments are made for widely differing regional economic outlooks. By the time local management sees the targets, any basis in current head count and utilization sometimes seems totally lost.

The first step a manager needs to take upon receiving new revenue targets is to build a new utilization plan. The purpose is to quantify any difference between the new expectation and a plan based on current staff, its expected utilization in hours, and revenue generated from those hours at current rates. This is known as the business as usual plan. Assuming for this exercise that this business has only labor generated revenue, any shortfall between the business as usual plan and the assigned targets must come from some combination of higher utilization, more people, or higher average rates.

The professional services office executive will try a number of iterations before finally settling on a combination that meets the nationally assigned quota. This iterative process is illustrated on the following pages. It follows three repetitions of the plan process to find an acceptable business mix and growth to achieve targets.

There is one note concerning utilization and revenue planning for product support services, systems integration, and any other business with sizable non-labor generated revenue. The following process is no different for these businesses. It is, however, only part of the process that includes additional iterations for the nonlabor portion of the business. Chapter 6 expands on this exercise for a systems integration example and covers the all-important topic of shifting mix to optimize margin.

The first iteration of the local utilization plan is to see if an unusual growth in people resources will be necessary to meet revenue targets. We start with our business as usual plan using current resources and last year's attrition and hiring. As a starting point, we are assuming constant labor costs with correspondingly constant prices through the plan period. This also assumes that our current prices per hour yield an acceptable profit per hour.

Initial Utilization Plan (Business As Usual)

Utilization planning lends itself very well to spreadsheets. The spreadsheet in Figure 5-3 is a summary of the initial utilization plan for the year. (Later illustrations will show more detail.) The plan provides the expected head count by person classification for each 13-week period and a summary for the year. The business of this office has been approximately two-thirds custom development, 20 percent consulting, and 12 percent education. Slightly over one-half of the revenue is generated by consultants and managers, with the remainder from contractors, borrowed people, and a small amount of travel and education material expense recovery. Planned billable utilization for each classification of resource is based upon actual performance of the previous year. These are:

- Consultants: 63 percent

- Management: 40 percent

- Contractors: 95 percent

- Borrowed: 90 percent

The planning process produces an estimate of the number of hours that can be generated by each classification of resource and how these hours translate to revenue during each of the 13-week periods. With current average revenue rates and current business mix as an assumption, our business as usual plan would provide an estimate of over $8.3 million generated through labor.

Some key assumptions that help understand the plan are as follows.

FIGURE 5-3
Summary Utilization Plan (Business As Usual)

Business As Usual Staffing and Utilization Plan

		Previous Year	Weeks 1–13 Plan	Weeks 14–26 Plan	Weeks 27–39 Plan	Weeks 40–52 Plan	Total Year Plan
Consultants	Ave util	0.63	0.62	0.67	0.53	0.75	0.64
	Ave rate	128	126	127	130	129	128
	Ave hcount	23.7	22.5	21.5	24.5	23.5	23.0
	End hcount	23	22	21	24	23	23
	Hours	30,900	7,290	7,537	6,721	9,217	30,766
	Revenue ($000)	3,955	918	955	871	1,189	3,933
Management	Ave util	0.40	0.36	0.41	0.40	0.44	0.40
	Ave rate	188	188	188	188	188	188
	Ave hcount	3.5	4	4	4	4	4
	End hcount	4	4	4	4	4	4
	Hours	2,912	749	853	832	915	3,349
	Revenue ($000)	547	141	160	156	172	630
Contractors	Ave util	0.95	0.95	0.95	0.95	0.95	0.95
	Ave rate	117	117	117	117	117	117
	Ave hcount	11	11	11	11	11	11
	End hcount	11	11	11	11	11	11
	Hours	21,736	5,434	5,434	5,434	5,434	21,736
	Revenue ($000)	2,543	636	636	636	636	2,543
Borrowed	Ave util	0.90	0.90	0.90	0.90	0.90	0.90
	Ave rate	158	158	158	158	158	158
	Ave hcount	4	4	4	4	4	4
	End hcount	4	4	4	4	4	4
	Hours	7,488	1,872	1,872	1,872	1,872	7,488
	Revenue ($000)	1,183	296	296	296	296	1,183
Total	End hcount	42	41	40	43	42	42
	Hours	63,036	15,345	15,696	14,859	17,438	63,339
	Revenue ($000)	8,228	1,990	2,047	1,959	2,293	8,288

1. Consultant attrition is four per year which is replaced by hiring college graduates into a training and internship program during June.
2. Utilization in the first three months is down due to kick-off meetings and engagements that ended in December and early January.
3. Utilization is very low in the third period due to summer vacations and the effect of four newly hired, nonbillable people.
4. Utilization is high in the fall when marketing and other investment activity levels are low and when trainees begin to bill part of their time.
5. Contractors and borrowed personnel are on short-term assignments and do not take vacations or attend education until they are free.

Adjusting the Utilization Plan

The revenue target our office has been given is $9.5 million. We have been generating slightly over $250,000 from the recovery of extraordinary travel expenses and from the sale of materials during education offerings. Keeping inflation out of it, we need to generate another $920,000 from labor. In order to increase revenue production, an executive has three options.

- Increase utilization. Assuming there has been negligible assigned, not billed, and on the bench time, this will require a reduction in investment activities or an increase in overtime.
- Raise all or selected rates.
- Add people.

All three of these alternatives require cooperation from the marketplace. Clients must be willing to buy more services or pay higher rates for the same services, or more clients need to be found.

In the next iteration of the plan, we will selectively increase utilization and rates. Our lower rate consultants are in great demand and we have a backlog of engagements where these people can be placed. Our senior consultants have a solid reputation with the clients who use them on a regular basis. To reflect these market conditions, we will increase the expected utilization for our staff in a range of 1 percent to 6 percent. We will raise our average rates for seniors and management by $19 and $14 per hour, respectively (for an overall rate increase for consultants and managers of 3 percent).

Figure 5-4 illustrates our revised utilization plan. To highlight the effect of our changes, the plan is now carried to the consultant subclassification level. The increase in associate utilization takes effect immediately, because we have backlog. Raising high-end rates is more gradual as current engagements are completed and new rates are put into effect.

FIGURE 5-4
Detailed Plan (Adjusted for Utilization and Rates)

Adjusted Staffing and Utilization Plan (Without Growth)

		Previous Year	Weeks 1–13 Plan	Weeks 14–26 Plan	Weeks 27–39 Plan	Weeks 40–52 Plan	Total Year Plan
New Trainee	Ave util	0.00	0.00	0.00	0.00	0.00	0.00
	Ave rate	85	85	85	85	85	85
	Ave hcount	2	0	0	4	2	1.5
	End hcount	4	0	0	4	2	2
	Hours	0	0	0	0	0	0
	Revenue ($000)	0	0	0	0	0	0
Trainee	Ave util	0.56	0.53	0.58	0.58	0.61	0.57
	Ave rate	85	85	85	85	85	85
	Ave hcount	2.5	4	3	1	2	2.5
	End hcount	0	4	3	1	2	2
	Hours	2,912	1,102	905	302	634	2,943
	Revenue ($000)	248	94	77	26	54	250
Associate	Ave util	0.78	0.76	0.80	0.80	0.96	0.84
	Ave rate	117	117	117	117	117	117
	Ave hcount	7.5	6	7	8	9	7.5
	End hcount	6	6	7	8	9	9
	Hours	12,168	2,371	2,912	3,328	4,493	13,104
	Revenue ($000)	1,424	277	341	389	526	1,533
Consultant	Ave util	0.68	0.65	0.70	0.60	0.82	0.69
	Ave rate	135	135	135	135	135	135
	Ave hcount	8.2	9.5	8.5	7.5	6.5	8.0
	End hcount	10	9	8	7	6	6
	Hours	11,598	3,211	3,094	2,340	2,772	11,417
	Revenue ($000)	1,566	433	418	316	374	1,541
Intern	Ave util	0.42	0.42	0.42	0.42	0.42	0.42
	Ave rate	135	135	135	135	135	135
	Ave hcount	0	0	0	0	0	0
	End hcount	0	0	0	0	0	0
	Hours	0	0	0	0	0	0
	Revenue ($000)	0	0	0	0	0	0

FIGURE 5-4
Detailed Plan (Adjusted for Utilization and Rates) (concluded)

Adjusted Staffing and Utilization Plan (Without Growth)		Previous Year	Weeks 1–13 Plan	Weeks 14–26 Plan	Weeks 27–39 Plan	Weeks 40–52 Plan	Total Year Plan
Senior	Ave util	0.58	0.54	0.59	0.51	0.80	0.62
	Ave rate	170	185	190	190	190	189
	Ave hcount	3.5	3	3	4	4	3.5
	End hcount	3	3	3	4	4	4
	Hours	4,222	842	920	1,061	1,664	4,488
	Revenue ($000)	718	156	175	202	316	848
Consultants	Ave util	0.63	0.64	0.70	0.55	0.78	0.67
	Ave rate	128	128	129	133	133	131
	Ave hcount	23.7	22.5	21.5	24.5	23.5	23.0
	End hcount	23	22	21	24	23	23
	Hours	30,900	7,527	7,831	7,030	9,563	31,951
	Revenue ($000)	3,955	960	1,010	932	1,270	4,173
Management	Ave util	0.40	0.38	0.42	0.41	0.46	0.42
	Ave rate	188	190	205	205	205	202
	Ave hcount	3.5	4	4	4	4	4
	End hcount	4	4	4	4	4	4
	Hours	2,912	790	874	853	957	3,474
	Revenue ($000)	547	150	179	175	196	700
Contractors	End hcount	11	11	11	11	11	11
	Hours	21,736	5,434	5,434	5,434	5,434	21,736
	Revenue ($000)	2,543	636	636	636	636	2,543
Borrowed	End hcount	4	4	4	4	4	4
	Hours	7,488	1,872	1,872	1,872	1,872	7,488
	Revenue ($000)	1,183	296	296	296	296	1,183
Total	End hcount	42	41	40	43	42	42
	Hours	63,036	15,623	16,011	15,189	17,826	64,649
	Revenue ($000)	8,228	2,042	2,121	2,039	2,398	8,599

3% increases in consultant and management utilization and rates yields a 4% increase in revenue.

We increase associate consultant utilization by 6 percent with minor increases in all others. We gradually increase senior consultant and management billing rates. Overall utilization went from 60 percent to 63 percent for consultants and managers, while their combined rates went from $134 to $137 per hour. Potential revenue production increased by approximately $311,000. In Chapter 6 we will see that this is a very profitable plan, but doesn't yet meet the revenue goal of $9.5 million.

Key assumptions that help understand this plan iteration are as follows.

1. Four trainees are on staff from the previous June. All have finished training and are partially billable.

2. Of the four college graduates hired in this plan, two require four months to become partially billable, while the other two will be in training until the end of the year.

3. During the year, four trainees will be promoted to associate, one associate to consultant, and one consultant to senior.

In the next and final iteration of the plan, we will need to add staff. Before proceeding, it would be well to summarize some key points about utilization planning that have been illustrated so far.

1. Utilization is seasonal. January is lower, because meetings are necessary to communicate the business objectives, compensation changes, organizational changes, and recognition that logically flow from one year to the next. June through August are lower to reflect vacations. December is lower for the holidays. March through May and September through November are high billing months, because of early year marketing emphasis and the spring and fall demands from clients to complete work by midyear and year end.

2. Younger people work longer hours and are more prepared to go long distances to do the job. Therefore, younger professionals can be asked to work more overtime. Increasing utilization over historical averages always increases overtime on the short term. Experienced people are needed for marketing and working with trainees. The annual revenue per person among each level of consultant may not vary by more than $20,000 due to high utilization at lower rates versus lower utilization at higher rates.

3. Subcontractors are a performance risk, but can command high enough rates and utilization to be clear choices for filling the gap in a revenue shortfall. The example could have been revised to meet objectives by simply increasing the subcontractor resource content by 35 percent at the same average rates. The ratio of contractors to permanent staff should be kept below 1 to 3 and the business as usual plan is already high at 1 to 2.5. To raise the contractor mix above this level, the office must be prepared to reduce the utilization of con-

sultants and managers to provide adequate supervision and perform rework that results from too high subcontractor concentration.

4. Senior managers and partners are not reliable revenue sources. They are too important to the momentum of the business to be sacrificed to high utilization. They are more important in demonstrating special expertise for which clients are very willing to pay extremely high rates for a few hours of amazing insight.

5. Borrowed resources can be the best short-term compromise between permanent employees and subcontractors, assuming there is a readily available source. Their knowledge of specialized business offerings and their high expertise command higher than average rates. One must be careful to avoid agreeing to restrictions on their availability when assigned away from their home base. These strings can lower their utilization and, thus, profitability.

6. The effect of increasing utilization and rates for the permanent staff is diluted in the complex services business with contractors and borrowed people generating large amounts of revenue, and little ability to change their production of hours. In the basic services business, small changes in rates and utilization are much more dramatic. In Figure 5-5, a $5.5 million annual revenue is generated by an office that performs 80 percent consulting and 20 percent education and uses only permanent staff. It has a higher average rate ($149 per hour), because its clients will accept substantially fewer associates and no trainees. It replaces attrition by hiring experienced professionals. Notice that the same increases in utilization and rate generate twice the increase in revenue as was experienced for the complex services office.

Utilization Planning in a Growing Office

The final plan iteration involves adding people to the office beyond those needed to cover attrition. When the numbers of people needed to meet revenue objectives must grow, the difficulty factor for head count and utilization planning goes up quickly. Marketing and management time must be increased to meet the demands of hiring, orienting, training, and marketing these people. Every person new to the office has a period of low utilization before they can meet the standards of their peers. In a perfect world, the office would hire fully qualified professionals at salaries commensurate with their billing rate potential and begin billing them within days of their arrival. Unfortunately, the supply of qualified people to hire is far below the demand for such people. (That's in good times. In bad times there are always lots of good people, but you can't afford to hire them.)

Each firm has traditional sources of new consultants and their business mix sets their priorities among the sources. Three major sources are described here

FIGURE 5-5
Impact of Improved Utilization on Basic Services

Impact of Small Changes in Utilization and Rate (Basic Services)—Business as Usual Plan

		Previous Year	Weeks 1–13 Plan	Weeks 14–26 Plan	Weeks 27–39 Plan	Weeks 40–52 Plan	Total Year Plan
Consultants	Ave util	0.65	0.60	0.64	0.56	0.79	0.65
	Ave rate	146	146	147	146	147	146
	Ave hcount	25.7	26	25.5	26	26.5	26.0
	End hcount	26	26	25	27	26	26
	Hours	34,686	8,050	8,479	7,582	10,954	35,064
	Revenue ($000)	5,066	1,174	1,248	1,104	1,606	5,132
Management	Ave util	0.40	0.36	0.41	0.40	0.44	0.40
	Ave rate	188	188	188	188	188	188
	Ave hcount	3	3	3	3	3	3
	End hcount	3	3	3	3	3	3
	Hours	2,496	562	640	624	686	2,512
	Revenue ($000)	469	106	120	117	129	472
Total	End hcount	29	29	28	30	29	29
	Hours	37,182	8,611	9,118	8,206	11,640	37,575
	Revenue ($000)	5,535	1,279	1,369	1,221	1,735	5,604

Impact of Small Changes in Utilization and Rate (Basic Services)—Improved Utilization and Rates

		Previous Year	Weeks 1–13 Plan	Weeks 14–26 Plan	Weeks 27–39 Plan	Weeks 40–52 Plan	Total Year Plan
Consultants	Ave util	0.65	0.62	0.67	0.59	0.84	0.68
	Ave rate	146	152	155	154	156	154
	Ave hcount	25.7	26	25.5	26	26.5	26.0
	End hcount	26	26	25	27	26	26
	Hours	34,686	8,434	8,861	8,024	11,575	36,894
	Revenue ($000)	5,066	1,279	1,376	1,232	1,801	5,688
Management	Ave util	0.40	0.38	0.42	0.41	0.46	0.42
	Ave rate	188	190	205	205	205	202
	Ave hcount	3	3	3	3	3	3
	End hcount	3	3	3	3	3	3
	Hours	2,496	593	655	640	718	2,605
	Revenue ($000)	469	113	134	131	147	525
Total	End hcount	29	29	28	30	29	29
	Hours	37,182	9,027	9,516	8,663	12,293	39,499
	Revenue ($000)	5,535	1,391	1,511	1,363	1,948	6,2130

3% increase in utilization and 5% increase in rates yields an 11% increase in revenue.

with corresponding assumptions regarding utilization and billable rates to be considered when using them in a plan:

- **Professional hiring.** Newly hired, experienced professionals can be billable within days of employment. Usually the only delays are for training in office methods and practices and any personal time to become settled. A conservative planning assumption can assume 50 percent normal utilization in the first month, followed by normal utilization. Their billable rates will reflect their level, although as we will see in Chapter 6 they may create short-term profitability issues, because of relocation expenses and high beginning salaries.
- **Transferring/retraining.** Transferred employees from other parts of a business have a wide variety of qualifications, but rarely are billable immediately. If they are being transferred for assignment to an ongoing project, they are likely to be fully billable within two months. If they are being transferred for retraining, they will be likely to require up to three months before any billing occurs and another three months of 50 percent billing. In the examples, these are termed "Interns."
- **College hiring.** Newly hired employees from college campuses are usually targeted for very specific work and training programs. The majority are MBA graduates who have sufficient understanding of general business to be marginally effective on consulting and development engagements. The individual typically attends a crash orientation and training program of one to four months before assignment. Most firms have a trainee rate that is charged when the individual is making a contribution that meets client satisfaction. Their utilization can vary between 30 percent and 60 percent of normal utilization.

The practice of using trainees in professional services business varies widely. Most firms hire from colleges only to refresh the staff and replace attrition. Many firms use no trainees at all, relying for growth on various means to obtain experienced personnel. Many firms grow by acquiring smaller firms with proven professional talent. Only a few very large firms can afford to hire college people to fuel growth.

When building a plan that contains acquisition of new people, it is helpful to split each subclassification into those who are fully billable and those who are learning. The resulting average utilization will reflect learning curve periods and will be more accurate.

In the next plan, Figure 5-6, the addition of people has increased revenue production to $9.3 million, which reaches the target for labor generated income. This is a growth of 12 percent over the previous year. We have added eight consultants for a 30 percent increase in our permanent staff (we also let one borrowed person go to make room for the growth). We chose not to increase contractors and brought their ratio to permanent staff back to a more comfortable level. We also carried forward some of the increases in utilization and rates from the adjusted plan (Figure 5-4).

FIGURE 5-6
Detailed Growth Plan

Staffing and Utilization Plan with Growth in Number of Consultants

		Previous Year	Weeks 1–13 Plan	Weeks 14–26 Plan	Weeks 27–39 Plan	Weeks 40–52 Plan	Total Year Plan
New Trainee	Ave util	0.00	0.00	0.00	0.00	0.00	0.00
	Ave rate	85	85	85	85	85	85
	Ave hcount	2	0	0	4	2	1.5
	End hcount	4	0	0	4	2	2
	Hours	0	0	0	0	0	0
	Revenue ($000)	0	0	0	0	0	0
Trainee	Ave util	0.56	0.53	0.58	0.58	0.61	0.57
	Ave rate	85	85	85	85	85	85
	Ave hcount	2.5	4	3	1	2	2.5
	End hcount	0	4	3	1	2	2
	Hours	2,912	1,102	905	302	634	2,943
	Revenue ($000)	248	94	77	26	54	250
Associate	Ave util	0.78	0.75	0.76	0.77	0.94	0.82
	Ave rate	117	117	117	117	117	117
	Ave hcount	7.5	6.5	8	9.5	11	8.8
	End hcount	6	7	8	10	11	11
	Hours	12,168	2,535	3,162	3,804	5,377	14,877
	Revenue ($000)	1,424	297	370	445	629	1,741
Consultant	Ave util	0.68	0.64	0.69	0.59	0.81	0.69
	Ave rate	135	135	135	135	135	135
	Ave hcount	8.2	10	10	10.5	11.5	10.5
	End hcount	10	10	10	10	11	11
	Hours	11,598	3,328	3,588	3,221	4,844	14,981
	Revenue ($000)	1,566	449	484	435	654	2,022
Intern	Ave util	0.42	0.42	0.42	0.42	0.42	0.42
	Ave rate	135	135	135	135	135	135
	Ave hcount	0	1	3	2	0	1.5
	End hcount	0	2	4	2	0	0
	Hours	0	218	655	437	0	1,310
	Revenue ($000)	0	29	88	59	0	177

FIGURE 5-6
Detailed Growth Plan (concluded)

Staffing and Utilization Plan with Growth in Number of Consultants

		Previous Year	Weeks 1–13 Plan	Weeks 14–26 Plan	Weeks 27–39 Plan	Weeks 40–52 Plan	Total Year Plan
Senior	Ave util	0.58	0.52	0.57	0.48	0.74	0.58
	Ave rate	170	185	190	190	190	189
	Ave hcount	3.5	3	2	4	4	3.3
	End hcount	3	3	2	4	4	4
	Hours	4,222	811	593	998	1,539	3,942
	Revenue ($000)	718	150	113	190	292	745
Consultants	Ave util	0.63	0.63	0.66	0.54	0.78	0.65
	Ave rate	128	127	127	132	131	130
	Ave hcount	23.7	24.5	26	⌐1	30.5	28.0
	End hcount	23	26	27		30	30
	Hours	30,900	7,995	8,902	8,7⌐2	12,394	38,054
	Revenue ($000)	3,955	1,019	1,132	1,154	1,629	4,935
Management	Ave util	0.40	0.36	0.41	0.40	0.44	0.40
	Ave rate	188	190	205	205	205	202
	Ave hcount	3.5	4	5	5	5	4.75
	End hcount	4	4	5	5	5	5
	Hours	2,912	749	1,066	1,040	1,144	3,999
	Revenue ($000)	547	142	219	213	235	809
Contractors	Ave util	0.95	0.95	0.95	0.95	0.95	0.95
	Ave rate	117	117	117	117	117	117
	Ave hcount	11	11	11	11	11	11
	End hcount	11	11	11	11	11	11
	Hours	21,736	5,434	5,434	5,434	5,434	21,736
	Revenue ($000)	2,543	636	636	636	636	2,543
Borrowed	Ave util	0.90	0.90	0.90	0.90	0.90	0.90
	Ave rate	158	158	158	158	158	158
	Ave hcount	4	4	4	3	3	3.5
	End hcount	4	4	4	3	3	3
	Hours	7,488	1,872	1,872	1,404	1,404	6,552
	Revenue ($000)	1,183	296	296	222	222	1,035
Total	End hcount	42	45	47	50	49	49
	Hours	63,036	16,050	17,274	16,640	20,376	70,340
	Revenue ($000)	8,228	2,093	2,282	2,225	2,722	9,322

Utilization grew, but by only 1 percent over last year. The increased utilization among associates is almost completely offset by the learning curves for new people, particularly the interns. Overall rates for consultants and managers were still raised by 3 percent, with the expectation that the marketplace will support them. Staff growth accounts for an 8 percent increase in revenue. Key additional assumptions in the growth plan are as follows.

1. The majority of the new consultant staff is acquired in the first four months. Of the new staff acquired in the year, half are transfers and half are professional hires. No transfers are acquired after May. (The four college graduates were still hired in June.)

2. Managers have significant staffing, planning, and marketing work early in the year, but are free to bill later in the year.

3. Associate consultant utilization is raised as planned to compensate for the lower utilization from hiring and internships. Senior consultant rates are raised, but their utilization was kept at previous year levels to allow them to train new people.

In the next chapter, we will expand this exercise to determine whether this plan is profitable. Growth creates a period of lower profitability proportional to the correspondingly lower utilization in bringing people up to marketable competence. We will look at what happens to profit when we plan for 30 percent growth. When costs are computed, we can then determine whether other actions, such as further price increases or changes in contractor levels will be needed to finance growth.

Labor generated revenue is half the work when planning for product support and systems integration businesses. Forecasting revenue generated by nonlabor sources, such as products installed and other vendors, can be equally time consuming. Revenue planning for these components is a function of forecasting how many engagements will incur the cost of nonlabor components and then determining how much to charge to bring in a corresponding profit. We will take this up in the next chapter, but it should be immediately obvious that reliable history on ratios of people revenue to nonlabor revenue would be very helpful in determining how much the combined business could generate.

There is a final point. Some will argue that detailed labor resource utilization planning and tracking is overkill when labor represents less than 25 percent to 30 percent of professional services revenue (systems integration, facilities management). It goes without saying that careful and time consuming analysis of the cost versus the corresponding revenue for vendor and product components is very necessary to ensure profitability. The corresponding analysis of labor profitability is no less important, and utilization tracking remains the simplest indicator of labor profitability. It provides the necessary history about levels of education and investment needed for planning labor. Utilization data is needed in the computation of labor cost rates that makes up half the profitability analysis for systems integration. This data is a natural and painless by-product when labor claiming and utilization tracking are practiced.

UTILIZATION TRACKING

Utilization tracking is simply the ongoing measurement of actual hours expended against expected hours to be available and utilized for each type of labor. Tracking is at the resource subclassification level. Specific actions to address problems of low utilization usually require tracking and reporting by an individual and manager.

Typically, utilization reports are produced weekly or at least biweekly. Later we will review management actions that are taken when weekly utilization is compared with availability, skills, and marketing forecasts. Other utilization analysis is performed less frequently to compare overall progress against plan and to make tactical decisions regarding pace of recruiting, marketing investment, and supply and demand issues.

Utilization reports can be agonizingly detailed and voluminous. Ideally, the report shows the distribution of available time by every activity, for every week, and for every person. The ideal report would then be summarized by quarter, year to date, class of resource, subclass of resource, unit manager, engagement and nonengagement time, and work activity. Unfortunately, such a report would be ten feet wide and fifty feet long.

The practical approach is to build and maintain a base spreadsheet for each management unit containing its people by resource classification by week. Each unit's utilization is tracked separately. The information in these unit spreadsheets can be incorporated into higher level spreadsheets that compute utilization summaries when needed for each of the groupings.

Actual hours are entered into the lowest level spreadsheet and summed to the higher levels. Often this involves entry of labor data to both a billing system and a utilization system. With better system support, the single entry of labor claiming data to a billing system can be bridged to utilization spreadsheets. The better systems also provide a common data base for all labor data for query and analysis of national trends in where and how hours are being spent.

The following illustrations are high-level summaries of actual hours spent by a unit of consultants, contractors, and borrowed people. Activities have been accumulated into five groups.

- **Client billed:** Time worked for direct revenue. These correspond to the expected hours in the utilization plan.

- **Client assigned, not billed:** Time worked for no direct revenue while assigned on engagements.

- **Personal:** Time spent on basic personal activities of holidays, vacations, education, personal business, employee/manager meetings, and so on.

- **Business investment:** Time spent in marketing, development, quality control, and so on.

- **Administration:** Time spent in all other nonbilling activities such as unrecovered travel, general meetings, administration, outings, and so on.

The following examples are a quarterly and year-to-date summary of actual hours against our quarterly plan. Utilization is summarized also for each of these five activity groups by consultant subclassification and by management, contractors, and borrowed labor resources. Left to the imagination is each manager's corresponding detailed spreadsheet that provides this data for each person assigned in a unit.

Both examples are a view of the business as of seven weeks into the second quarter (week ending May 15). The plan numbers are from our growth plan in Figure 5-6. Included in the summary report are the utilization data for the week just ending to show current hours in comparison with accumulated hours for the first two quarters. In the first illustration (Figure 5-7), a business downturn has occurred in the first quarter of the year, but business may be improving in the second quarter.

The track of actual utilization against planned utilization highlights a problem of over-supply. Lower than expected demand has caused utilization to be down for all types of people. The office increased staffing as planned during the first quarter, but has ceased hiring in the second quarter and let go three contractors and one of its borrowed people. Utilization has risen slightly in the second quarter, indicating that demand might come back from its earlier low. The office has responded by increasing associate, contractor, and borrowed people overtime, while assigning the experienced staff to assist in finding more business.

The office is 3,800 hours below plan which represents nearly $500,000 in lost revenue. Assigned, not billed, time is high, indicating heavy pro bono work to demonstrate value to existing clients (in anticipation of more billable work). Managers are working considerable overtime, particularly on behalf of marketing.

The options available to the field executive depend on whether the office decides to make profit margin against lower revenue (and growth) for the year or accept lower profit and margin in order to make the revenue and growth target. The choices are as follows.

- **Achieve profit margin (and maybe profit target).** Freeze staff levels and overachieve utilization through overtime and deferred education, but not meet the revenue target. Stop intended college hiring, but continue any further professional hiring that is supported by demand. Bring back contractors and borrowed people, as needed, but not at levels that would strain the ability of managers to focus on getting more business.

- **Achieve revenue at lower profit margin.** Continue to increase staff, but add more than those planned as demand rises in order to make up for lower production early in the year. Bring back contractors and borrowed people as needed, but not at levels that would strain managers focused on getting people and performing extensive marketing.

- **Achieve profit margin and increased revenue.** Increase only subcontractor and borrowed people while overachieving utilization through overtime and deferred education. This alternative assumes that current projects are sufficiently large to accommodate subcontractors and that clients will be willing to accept the substitution. Stop college hiring. Use managers to direct contractors and temporary people and to bill only occasionally at very high rates.

The first is the most likely choice to make. Most firms will defer growth for short-term profit, unless a parent business is willing to subsidize the growth. By not hiring the college people, this office will ransom the future to make current profit (hopefully, the office hasn't already made hiring commitments in April). The second approach avoids ransoming the future, but may ransom the office executive's job by not making profit.

The third choice risks all, including client satisfaction to make profit and increase revenue results (an entrepreneur's dream come true). It is a good choice, if demand continues to grow and it does not bring lower quality performance and its associated client dissatisfaction. It is a bad choice for the future, though, because it may raise the revenue record of the office without a permanent increase in the staff needed to sustain that revenue.

The second illustration (Figure 5-8) shows slower than planned recruiting. In this example, an opposite set of decisions faces the field executive. Recruiting has gone very slowly and the current staff is working major overtime to meet client demand. Presumably, the office has exercised all approaches to acquiring permanent staff and must now decide whether to be satisfied with a lower revenue attainment. The office clearly should be very profitable so far this year and can likely continue an overachievement in profits. Unfortunately, it is losing an opportunity to grow in a demand market.

FIGURE 5-7
Planned Versus Actual Utilization—Business Downturn

Actual Utilization: Business Downturn

1st Quarter: Weeks 1-13

	Ave Hcount	Billed Hours	Util YTD	Assigned, Not Billed Hours	Util YTD	Personal Hours	Util YTD	Investment Hours	Util YTD	Administration Hours	Util YTD	Total Hours	Util YTD
Trainee	4.0	853.00	0.41	36.00	0.02	927.00	0.45	142.00	0.07	153.00	0.07	2,111.00	1.01
Plan	4.0	1,102.00	0.53	0.00	0.00	850.00	0.41	100.00	0.05	120.00	0.06	2,172.00	1.04
Associate	6.5	2,273.50	0.67	27.00	0.01	473.00	0.14	329.00	0.10	299.50	0.09	3,402.00	1.01
Plan	6.5	2,535.00	0.75	0.00	0.00	450.00	0.13	400.00	0.12	270.00	0.08	3,655.00	1.08
Consultant	10.0	2,685.00	0.52	94.50	0.02	512.50	0.10	1,823.50	0.35	409.00	0.08	5,524.50	1.06
Plan	10.0	3,328.00	0.64	0.00	0.00	250.00	0.05	1,500.00	0.29	360.00	0.07	5,438.00	1.05
Intern	1.0	93.00	0.18	114.00	0.22	411.00	0.79	0.00	0.00	83.00	0.16	701.00	1.35
Plan	1.0	218.00	0.42	0.00	0.00	400.00	0.77	0.00	0.00	44.00	0.08	662.00	1.27
Senior	3.0	793.00	0.51	17.00	0.01	161.00	0.10	533.00	0.34	253.50	0.16	1,757.50	1.13
Plan	3.0	811.00	0.52	0.00	0.00	160.00	0.10	400.00	0.26	200.00	0.13	1,571.00	1.01
Consultants	24.5	6,697.50	0.53	288.50	0.02	2,484.50	0.20	2,827.50	0.22	1,198.00	0.09	13,496.00	1.06
Plan	24.5	7,994.00	0.63	0.00	0.00	2,110.00	0.17	2,400.00	0.19	994.00	0.08	13,498.00	1.06
Management	4.0	419.00	0.20	112.50	0.05	96.00	0.05	789.00	0.38	1,004.50	0.48	2,421.00	1.16
Plan	4.0	749.00	0.36	0.00	0.00	80.00	0.04	500.00	0.24	840.00	0.40	2,169.00	1.04
Contractors	9.5	4,817.50	0.98	0.00	0.00							4,817.50	0.98
Plan	11.0	5,434.00	0.95	0.00	0.00							5,434.00	0.95
Borrowed	3.5	1,371.00	0.75	211.00	0.12	43.00	0.02	0.00	0.00	101.00	0.06	1,726.00	0.95
Plan	4.0	1,872.00	0.90	0.00	0.00	0.00	0.00	0.00	0.00	84.00	0.04	1,956.00	0.94
TOTAL	41.5	13,305.00		612.00		2,623.50		3,616.50		2,303.50		22,460.50	
Plan	43.5	16,049.00		0.00		2,190.00		2,900.00		1,918.00		23,057.00	

7 Weeks of 2nd Quarter: Weeks 14-20

	Ave Hcount	Billed Hours	Util YTD	Assigned, Not Billed Hours	Util YTD	Personal Hours	Util YTD	Investment Hours	Util YTD	Administration Hours	Util YTD	Total Hours	Util YTD
Trainee	3.0	562.00	0.67	44.00	0.05	328.00	0.39	19.00	0.02	47.00	0.06	1,000.00	1.19
Plan	3.0	540.00	0.64	0.00	0.00	334.00	0.40	56.00	0.07	42.00	0.05	972.00	1.16
Associate	8.0	1,997.50	0.89	137.00	0.06	227.00	0.10	162.00	0.07	123.50	0.06	2,647.00	1.18
Plan	8.0	2,020.00	0.90	0.00	0.00	220.00	0.10	224.00	0.10	112.00	0.05	2,576.00	1.15
Consultant	10.0	2,003.00	0.72	328.50	0.12	82.00	0.03	562.00	0.20	152.00	0.05	3,127.50	1.12
Plan	10.0	2,100.00	0.75	0.00	0.00	140.00	0.05	700.00	0.25	140.00	0.05	3,080.00	1.10
Intern	4.0	387.00	0.35	243.00	0.22	583.50	0.52	0.00	0.00	83.00	0.07	1,296.50	1.16
Plan	4.0	525.00	0.47	0.00	0.00	672.00	0.60	0.00	0.00	56.00	0.05	1,253.00	1.12

FIGURE 5-7
Planned Versus Actual Utilization—Business Downturn (concluded)

Actual Utilization: Business Downturn

	Plan		7 Weeks of 2nd Quarter: Weeks 14–20 (continued)				Total
Senior	2.0	329.50 0.59	68.00 0.12	32.00 0.06	111.50 0.20	79.00 0.14	620.00 1.11
Plan	2.0	365.00 0.65	0.00 0.00	28.00 0.05	140.00 0.25	56.00 0.10	589.00 1.05
Consultants	27.0	5,279.00 0.70 0.59	820.50 0.11 0.05	1,252.50 0.17 0.18	854.50 0.11 0.18	484.50 0.06 0.08	8,691.00 1.15 1.09
Plan	27.0	5,550.00 0.73 0.67	0.00 0.00	1,394.00 0.18 0.17	1,120.00 0.15 0.17	406.00 0.05 0.07	8,470.00 1.12 1.08
Management	5.0	641.00 0.46 0.30	262.00 0.19 0.11	24.00 0.02 0.03	257.00 0.18 0.30	483.00 0.35 0.43	1,667.00 1.19 1.17
Plan	5.0	690.00 0.49 0.41	0.00 0.00	40.00 0.03 0.03	462.00 0.33 0.28	420.00 0.30 0.36	1,612.00 1.15 1.09
Contractors	8.0	2,296.00 1.03 0.99	0.00 0.00	0.00 0.00	0.00 0.00	0.00 0.00	2,296.00 1.03 0.99
Plan	11.0	2,925.00 0.95 0.95	0.00 0.00	0.00 0.00	0.00 0.00	0.00 0.00	2,925.00 0.95 0.95
Borrowed	3.0	892.50 1.06 0.85	9.50 0.01	21.00 0.03 0.02	23.50 0.03 0.01	17.50 0.02 0.04	964.00 1.15 1.01
Plan	4.0	1,020.00 0.91 0.90	0.00 0.00	0.00 0.00	0.00 0.00	42.00 0.04 0.04	1,062.00 0.95 0.94
TOTAL	43.0	9,108.50	1,092.00	1,297.50	1,135.00	985.00	13,618.00
Plan	47.0	10,185.00	0.00	1,434.00	1,582.00	868.00	14,069.00

Previous Week

							Total
Trainee	3.0	78.50 0.65	7.50 0.06	52.00 0.43	0.00 0.00	4.00 0.03	142.00 1.18
Associate	8.0	307.00 0.96	18.50 0.06	41.00 0.13	6.00 0.02	12.50 0.04	385.00 1.20
Consultant	10.0	273.00 0.68	27.50 0.07	82.00 0.21	67.50 0.17	17.50 0.04	467.50 1.17
Intern	4.0	73.00 0.46	12.00 0.08	87.00 0.54	3.00 0.02	14.00 0.09	189.00 1.18
Senior	2.0	78.00 0.98	0.00 0.00	0.00 0.00	12.00 0.15	4.00 0.05	94.00 1.18
Consultants	27.0	809.50 0.75	65.50 0.06	262.00 0.24	88.50 0.08	52.00 0.05	1,277.50 1.18
Management	5.0	76.00 0.38	12.50 0.06	1.50 0.01	104.00 0.52	49.00 0.25	243.00 1.22
Contractors	8.0	360.00 1.13	0.00 0.00	0.00 0.00	0.00 0.00	0.00 0.00	360.00 1.13
Borrowed	3.0	132.00 1.10	0.00 0.00	2.00 0.02	3.00 0.03	4.50 0.04	141.50 1.18
TOTAL	43.0	1,377.50	78.00	265.50	195.50	105.50	2,022.00

FIGURE 5-8
Planned Versus Actual Utilization—Recruiting Problems

Actual Utilization: Staffing Below Plan

1st Quarter: Weeks 1-13

	Ave Hcount	Billed Hours	Util YTD	Assigned, Not Billed Hours	Util YTD	Personal Hours	Util YTD	Investment Hours	Util YTD	Administration Hours	Util YTD	Total Hours	Util YTD
Trainee	4.0	1,111.00	0.53	29.00	0.01	848.00	0.41	78.50	0.04	133.00	0.06	2,199.50	1.06
Plan	4.0	1,102.00	0.53	0.00	0.00	850.00	0.41	100.00	0.05	120.00	0.06	2,172.00	1.04
Associate	6.0	2,363.00	0.76	27.00	0.01	449.00	0.14	329.00	0.11	262.50	0.08	3,430.50	1.10
Plan	6.5	2,535.00	0.75	0.00	0.00	450.00	0.13	400.00	0.12	270.00	0.08	3,655.00	1.08
Consultant	9.5	3,237.50	0.66	87.50	0.02	227.50	0.05	1,477.00	0.30	359.00	0.07	5,388.50	1.09
Plan	10.0	3,328.00	0.64	0.00	0.00	250.00	0.05	1,500.00	0.29	360.00	0.07	5,438.00	1.05
Intern	1.0	127.00	0.24	103.50	0.20	352.00	0.68	0.00	0.00	83.00	0.16	665.50	1.28
Plan	1.0	218.00	0.42	0.00	0.00	400.00	0.77	0.00	0.00	44.00	0.08	662.00	1.27
Senior	3.0	793.00	0.51	17.00	0.01	161.00	0.10	417.00	0.27	253.50	0.16	1,641.50	1.05
Plan	3.0	811.00	0.52	0.00	0.00	160.00	0.10	400.00	0.27	200.00	0.13	1,571.00	1.01
Consultants	23.5	7,631.50	0.62	264.00	0.02	2,037.50	0.17	2,301.50	0.19	1,091.00	0.09	13,325.50	1.09
Plan	24.5	7,994.00	0.63	0.00	0.00	2,110.00	0.17	2,400.00	0.19	994.00	0.08	13,498.00	1.06
Management	4.0	688.00	0.33	12.50	0.01	82.00	0.04	479.00	0.23	1,004.50	0.50	2,306.00	1.11
Plan	4.0	749.00	0.36	0.00	0.00	80.00	0.04	500.00	0.24	840.00	0.40	2,169.00	1.04
Contractors	11.0	5.44	6.00	0.95	0.00	0.00		0.00	0.00		5.43	5,446.00	0.95
Plan	11.0	5,434.00	0.95	0.00	0.00	0.00		0.00	0.00	4.00	0.04	4.00	0.95
Borrowed	4.0	1,907.50	0.92	43.00	0.02	27.00	0.01	0.00	0.00	87.00	0.04	2,064.50	0.99
Plan	4.0	1,872.00	0.90	0.00	0.00	0.00	0.00	0.00	0.00	84.00	0.04	1,956.00	0.94
TOTAL	42.5	15,673.00		319.50		2,146.50		2,780.50		2,222.50		23,142.00	
Plan	43.5	16,049.00		0.00		2,190.00		2,900.00		1,918.00		23,057.00	

7 Weeks of 2nd Quarter: Weeks 14-20

	Ave Hcount	Billed Hours	Util YTD	Assigned, Not Billed Hours	Util YTD	Personal Hours	Util YTD	Investment Hours	Util YTD	Administration Hours	Util YTD	Total Hours	Util YTD
Trainee	3.0	628.50	0.75	0.00	0.00	324.00	0.39	0.00	0.00	47.00	0.06	999.50	1.19
Plan	3.0	540.00	0.64	0.00	0.01	334.00	0.40	56.00	0.07	42.00	0.05	972.00	1.16
Associate	7.0	1,793.00	0.91	24.50	0.01	218.00	0.11	162.00	0.08	109.00	0.06	2,306.50	1.18
Plan	8.0	2,020.00	0.90	0.00	0.00	220.00	0.10	224.00	0.10	112.00	0.05	2,576.00	1.15
Consultant	9.0	1,919.00	0.76	127.50	0.05	127.00	0.05	562.00	0.22	152.00	0.06	2,887.50	1.15
Plan	10.0	2,100.00	0.75	0.00	0.00	140.00	0.05	700.00	0.25	140.00	0.05	3,080.00	1.10
Intern	2.0	195.00	0.35	91.50	0.16	353.50	0.63	0.00	0.00	29.00	0.05	669.00	1.19
Plan	4.0	525.00	0.47	0.00	0.00	672.00	0.60	0.00	0.00	56.00	0.05	1,253.00	1.12

FIGURE 5-8
Planned Versus Actual Utilization—Recruiting Problems (concluded)

Actual Utilization: Staffing Below Plan

7 Weeks of 2nd Quarter: Weeks 14-20 (concluded)

	Ave Hcount	Billed Hours	Billed Util	Billed YTD	Assigned, Not Billed Hours	ANB Util	ANB YTD	Personal Hours	Personal Util	Personal YTD	Investment Hours	Investment Util	Investment YTD	Administration Hours	Admin Util	Admin YTD	Total Hours	Total Util	Total YTD
Senior	**3.0**	**601.00**	**0.72**		**17.00**	**0.02**		**49.00**	**0.06**		**122.50**	**0.15**		**99.00**	**0.12**		**888.50**	**1.06**	
Plan	2.0	365.00	0.65		0.00	0.00		28.00	0.05		140.00	0.25		56.00	0.10		589.00	1.05	
Consultants	**24.0**	**5,136.50**	**0.76**	**0.67**	**260.50**	**0.04**	**0.03**	**1,071.50**	**0.16**	**0.16**	**846.50**	**0.13**	**0.17**	**436.00**	**0.06**	**0.08**	**7,751.00**	**1.15**	**1.11**
Plan	27.0	5,550.00	0.73	0.67	0.00	0.00	0.00	1,394.00	0.18	0.17	1,120.00	0.15	0.17	406.00	0.05	0.07	8,470.00	1.12	1.08
Management	**4.0**	**534.00**	**0.48**	**0.38**	**11.50**	**0.01**	**0.01**	**24.00**	**0.02**	**0.03**	**257.00**	**0.23**	**0.23**	**483.00**	**0.43**	**0.48**	**1,309.50**	**1.17**	**1.13**
Plan	5.0	690.00	0.49	0.41	0.00	0.00	0.00	24.00	0.03	0.03	462.00	0.33	0.28	420.00	0.30	0.36	1,612.00	1.15	1.09
Contractors	**11.0**	**2,951.00**	**0.96**	**0.95**	**0.00**	**0.00**	**0.00**				**0.00**	**0.00**	**0.00**				**2,951.00**	**0.96**	**0.95**
Plan	11.0	2,925.00	0.95	0.95	0.00	0.00	0.00				0.00	0.00	0.00				2,925.00	0.95	0.95
Borrowed	**4.0**	**1,064.00**	**0.95**	**0.93**	**3.50**	**0.00**	**0.01**	**20.50**	**0.02**	**0.01**	**0.00**	**0.00**	**0.00**	**58.50**	**0.05**	**0.05**	**1,146.50**	**1.02**	**1.00**
Plan	4.0	1,020.00	0.91	0.90	0.00	0.00	0.00	0.00	0.00	0.00	0.00	0.00	0.00	42.00	0.04	0.04	1,062.00	0.95	0.94
TOTAL	**43.0**	**9,685.50**			**275.50**			**1,116.00**			**1,103.50**			**997.50**			**13,158.00**		
Plan	47.0	10,185.00			0.00			1,434.00			1,582.00			868.00			14,069.00		

Previous Week

	Ave Hcount	Billed Hours	Billed Util	Assigned, Not Billed Hours	ANB Util	Personal Hours	Personal Util	Investment Hours	Investment Util	Administration Hours	Admin Util	Total Hours	Total Util
Trainee	3.0	117.50	0.98	1.00	0.01	36.00	0.30	0.00	0.00	6.50	0.05	161.00	1.34
Associate	7.0	282.00	1.01	0.0	0.00	28.00	0.10	24.00	0.09	12.50	0.04	346.50	1.24
Consultant	9.0	288.00	0.80	22.50	0.06	16.00	0.04	67.50	0.19	17.50	0.05	411.50	1.14
Intern	2.0	30.00	0.38	18.00	0.23	48.00	0.60	2.00	0.03	3.00	0.04	101.00	1.26
Senior	3.0	114.50	0.95	0.00	0.00	0.00	0.00	12.00	0.10	4.00	0.03	130.50	1.09
Consultants	24.0	832.00	0.87	41.50	0.04	128.00	0.13	105.50	0.11	43.50	0.05	1,150.50	1.20
Management	4.0	76.00	0.48	1.00	0.01	1.50	0.01	42.00	0.26	72.00	0.45	192.50	1.20
Contractors	11.0	459.00	1.04	0.00	0.00			0.00	0.00			459.00	1.04
Borrowed	4.0	147.00	0.92	0.00	0.00	2.00	0.01			4.50	0.03	153.50	0.96
TOTAL	43.0	1,514.00		42.50		131.50		147.50		120.00		1,955.50	

Many of the staff (including all of the managers) are working 10 or more hours of overtime each week. Education time is below plan and contractors are also working long hours. Management is spending considerable time in recruiting, and marketing is far below planned levels. Interns are not performing well (substantial rework), because managers and seniors are too busy to give them adequate training.

The office in this example is also faced with a common issue in the people business: How long can it sustain the overtime performance of its staff, before quality deteriorates? The capacity of the human machine is totally unpredictable. Consultants are usually at top performance when under sustained pressure and working long hours. There is a limit, however, and it is different for each person and their family situation at the time. It requires highly sensitive managers to know when to give them a break, even for no other purpose than to go to a thought-provoking class.

The objective of the office in the second illustration should be to use the short-term earnings overachievement to finance investment in growth. This is done by raising rates to modify demand, use even more short-term resources to continue a strong revenue stream, increase college hiring, and put resources on prospecting for projects of longer duration that allow flexibility in how to add staff in the future. In order of priority, the office should:

- Convince clients to accept more contractors.
- Increase college campus recruiting and the corresponding mix of young, high-potential consultants.
- Increase marketing in large project opportunities that support the use of more subcontractors.
- Market for systems integration or other revenue sources that do not rely entirely on labor as a revenue source

These actions should be taken carefully to avoid overspending the accumulated earnings or overtaxing management. Clients might be willing to accept less experienced people, if the offer includes a senior consultant to provide nonbillable leadership. In Chapter 6, we will look at the current cost structure of this office to see how much investment can be funded. Additionally, this office is a prime candidate for the cross-territory resource sharing topic in Chapter 9.

PLANNING AND TRACKING AVAILABILITY

A common companion tracking mechanism to utilization is that of availability.

Availability tracking is the maintenance of a daily calendar for each billable resource in an office, showing committed client engagement assignments, committed personal time to be taken, committed investment assignments (marketing, project reviews, office improvement, new offering development), potential client assignments, and short-term assignments in lieu of any of the above.

Availability tracking predicts utilization in the foreseeable future (usually six to eight weeks) and forecasts differences between planned and potential utilization. It supports testing the effect of alternative assignments on overall utilization. As will be seen later, it also serves as a working document for regular resource management decisions.

The following example is a typical availability planning and tracking chart. Each person (consultant, manager, subcontractor, and borrowed) is represented by two lines: current engagement and nonengagement assignments through the previous week and those committed for the next three weeks; and backup assignments in case committed assignments do not materialize (clients do not sign, a seat doesn't open up in a fully enrolled class). People currently on board or known to be incoming members of the staff are represented by their initials. People that need to be obtained are represented by NEW1, NEW2, and so on. These are replaced with initials when they have been recruited.

Each day in Figure 5-9 is coded with the primary assignment for that day. The coding in this example is as follows.

- **Initials:** The client or internal project.
- **E:** Education, including travel to class.
- **H/V:** Holiday or vacation.
- **P:** Any other personal time of more than five hours.
- **M/Initials:** Marketing, specific to the client indicated (no initials represents general marketing support). Marketing activities include estimating and proposal review.
- **A:** Nonbillable activities such as internal meetings, administration, office improvement projects with no specific revenue objective, management, and so on.
- **OTB:** Unassigned, that is, on the bench.

The committed assignment line has two additional columns following each Friday. These columns contain the expected number of hours to be billed and the expected number of hours to be assigned for utilization purposes. This second number contains billable hours plus assigned, not billed, hours. The signif-

FIGURE 5-9
Availability Tracking Calendar

Availability Calendar	Level	Level	Last Week	Week 1	Week 2	Week 3
P. Graph	M	A	A FV FV P A A A IV XP	6.00 8.00 XP XP A IV A A A OTB A	12.00 16.00 A A A SR A A OTB A	0.00 0.00
L.O. Anbehold	C	SR SR	SR SR E SR SR SR SR SR	25.00 40.00 E E E E E	0.00 8.00 / 4.00 8.00 OTB IV IV IV IV OTB IV	8.00 8.00 / 20.00 40.00
D.R. Bill	AC	E E	E E E OTB OTB OTB	0.00 0.00 OTB OTB v v v v	0.00 0.00 OTB ZF v v E E	0.00 0.00 / 16.00 24.00 OTB ZF
B.O. Derrick	SC	DW DW	DW DW DW v DW v	0.00 0.00 DW DW A DW DW DW DW DW	40.00 40.00 DW DW DW DW DW DW	40.00 40.00
A.L. Ectricity	C	DW DW	DW A A A DW DW	24.00 24.00 A A E A DW DW DW DW	16.00 16.00 DW DW DW DW DW DW	0.00 40.00
M. Ezze-Forta	C	DW DW	WI DW DW DW WI DW	38.00 40.00 DW E E DW DW DW WI DW	8.00 8.00 P DW XP DW DW DW WI DW	38.00 40.00
L.F. Tern	AC	VS VS	VS VS VS VS VS YS	20.00 40.00 VS VS XP XP M M XP XP XP	24.00 40.00 XP XP M M XP XP PTB	16.00 16.00
R.A. Zamatazz	C	M M	WI M M M WI M	6.00 8.00 M M M M M M M M	0.00 0.00 / 40.00 40.00 M ZF M ZF M ZF M ZF	6.00 8.00 / 40.00 40.00 M ZF M ZF
K. Kong	SUB	SR SR	SR SR 16.00 16.00	SR SR	16.00 16.00 SR	24.00 16.00 16.00
R. Rednose	SUB	DW DW	DW DW DW DW DW DW	40.00		
E.T. Calhom	B	XN XN	XN XN XN XN XN XN	40.00 40.00 XN XN XN XN XN XN	40.00 40.00 / 6.00 XN IV XN IV XN IV	40.00 40.00 XN XN IV IV
NEW1	C			IV	40.00 40.00 IV IV	IV IV
NEW2	AC				ZF	40.00 40.00 ZF ZF
				215 216	246 264	360 416

icance of this second column will be discussed later in this chapter (Measuring Revenue Utilization).

The availability example in Figure 5-8 corresponds to the first example of utilization tracking, that of the business downturn. As can be seen, there are some people who have both committed and backup assignments, while others have neither. Notice that Ezze-Forta and Calhom have multiple clients, while Bill and Zamatazz are not assigned. In addition, internal projects that started up during the period of business downturn are now conflicting with revenue opportunities (i.e., Ectricity's time away from client DW).

The challenge facing the office in this example is typical of an environment of mixed demand for professional services. When business is up, an office never seems to have enough people regardless of skill and experience. When business is mixed, particularly after a slow period, there is wide disparity among consultants who can be placed almost anywhere and those who are simply not in demand. Assuming the people on the bench have skills that will be marketable, the office that weathers this situation is the one that can quickly reassign internal and marketing work away from those in demand to those who are not. Offices that do not take the trouble to track both utilization and availability will often get rid of valuable people, simply because they did not appear to be working.

SKILLS INVENTORY

A third necessary piece of managing utilization is a personal skills and experience inventory. It contains a simple means to define the marketable characteristics of a billable person. It uses a coding structure that relates an individual's competency to the skills and experiences needed by potential assignments. A useable skills inventory is a shorthand description of an office's marketable people.

Each element of competency has a short description and a grade level. The description is abbreviated to save space, but not so short as to be confused with other similar areas of competency. An example of a skill and experience needed by a marketable consultant is:

> PLANLDR: Leads planning sessions and is experienced in at least three session formats.

A common method of defining a level of a skill is to assign a grade for the skill based upon the individual's ability to demonstrate the skill or experience. The following is an example of grade leveling for a skill.

Level 4: An expert in the skill among peers. Able to act as a personal mentor to others and assess performance regarding the skill.

Level 3: Fully proficient and can teach the skill. Can bill for the performance of the skill without supervision.

Level 2: Proficient and can bill for the skill under the supervision of a more skilled individual.

Level 1: Formally trained in the skill or has equivalent on the job exposure.

Staying with the PLANLDR example, trained session leaders after their first client planning session would be Level 2. One who has directed a variety of sessions would be a Level 3. Presumably, the training focuses on multiple session formats and by achievement of Level 3, the individual has conducted the three or more different types of sessions.

Skills and experiences can be graded in similar manners. Skills usually require formal or informal training to increase grade level. Grading of experiences relates to the number of times the experience has occurred. The highest level of an experience is that point where further repetitions add no more to the competency of top performers. An example would be project auditing, where qualification for a first assignment would be a Level 1, one successful project audit might be a Level 2, and auditing of four projects of varying phases and risks would be a Level 4.

Offices that maintain skill inventories usually have an assessment sheet that lists all relevant skills and experiences that pertain to its client market. The staff reassesses themselves at least once per year and assessments are kept in a data base for quick reference when an individual is being considered for assignment. Very often, the person's formal education and career development plan are also updated at the same time to forecast the skill and experience levels that will be attainable in the next year.

Figure 5-10 is an example of a partial skill inventory for a project manager. The purpose of the example is to show the wide variety of skill areas that most consultants need to have.

Skills coding and assessment has a number of other uses in a professional services office.

- It provides a standardized structure for defining the competence of resources needed to staff new engagements or for increasing the staff on existing engagements.

- It provides a convenient means to assess the capabilities of candidates for employment or newly assigned subcontractors.

FIGURE 5-10
Partial Skill and Experience Inventory

Project Manager Skills/Experience Inventory			
Skill/Experience	*Level*	*Skill/Experience*	*Level*
(Methods)		(Technical)	
STRATPLAN	2	PRISM	3
REQMTPLAN	3	IBMAS400	3
DESIGNPLAN	4	DECVAX	4
PLANINTEG	3	EMAIL	3
2WAYTRACK	4	YOURDUN	4
4WAYTRACK	3		
DOCDELIV	4		
SWDELIV	2	(Personal)	
HRCHNGCTL	4	WRITING	3
FPCHNGCTL	3	VERBAL	4
BUCHANON	2	PEOPLEMGT	2
		SUBMGT	3
(Industry)		PROBMGT	4
FINBANK	4	SITLDRSHP	2
MFGSHOP	3		

- It can be a national standard of competency for offering and receiving people shared between offices to alleviate resource imbalances.

The next section discusses approaches to computerizing skill and experience inventory data.

COMPUTER SYSTEM SUPPORT FOR UTILIZATION MANAGEMENT

When a staff is small, utilization tracking, availability tracking, and skills inventory can easily be administered through manual entry to spreadsheet, word processor, and data base, respectively. When a firm grows to many large offices, further computer system support becomes essential. The following is a discussion of one of many approaches to simplify the compilation of the variety of reports managers need and to reduce the reentry of employee, client, and hours data among different data bases.

At issue for any computer system that supports utilization and skills inventory is whether the data is solely for local management use or for use nationally. Utilization measurements can be a short-term indicator of national business health for executive actions prior to the availability of financial statements. Similarly, skills data can indicate what competency is most in demand by region, where key people are located when new ventures are under consideration and what education might be in demand.

Neither of these reasons for a national view of this data inspires much enthusiasm among local field executives. Having national management looking over one's shoulder and second-guessing why one chooses low utilization to stimulate sales or develop a key new offering is irritating at best. To also give the national organization the ability to identify one's best people for the purpose of recruitment elsewhere breeds paranoia.

On the other hand, a good national contract management and billing system can provide a high degree of assistance to utilization analysis. It can eliminate dual entry of labor data. It can provide extensive analysis of labor history by activity, type of service, business type, and client industry designation. A local office can save hours of research and independent planning, when it is able to inquire on such prospect estimating challenges as:

- Where and how often business process consulting is being provided on a per hour basis for manufacturers of auto parts.

- How many hours are historically needed to provide user interface design for an application software system for auto parts warehousing when offered on a fixed-price, multiphased engagement.

For national data to be trustworthy, it must be accurate and timely. This means that the local data from which it is derived has the local executive's attention. Raw data used by the local office will be accurate and timely. Giving up ownership to the local office also gives up the right to authorize its distribution. Given this principle, the following rules ought to apply.

- Billing data and the corresponding hours recorded during weekly labor claiming is national data. Its accurate recording is crucial to local client satisfaction and to local profitability analysis of both hourly and fixed-price engagements. National utilization trends can be computed from billing data.

- Availability data is local data. Its timeliness and accuracy is a local need. The people it describes are committed locally and their availability outside of the territory is at the discretion of local management.

- Skills and supporting resume data, education plans and career development plans are local data, but statistics of local skill levels should be available nationally. Most firms have personnel systems that can be accessed only by authorized local managers and a few selected national staff who prepare personnel statistics and government reporting. The same rules apply to skills data.

- Individual skills/experience and corresponding levels are entered into a national system, but can be played back only on local reports.

FIGURE 5-11
Computerized Labor Resource Management

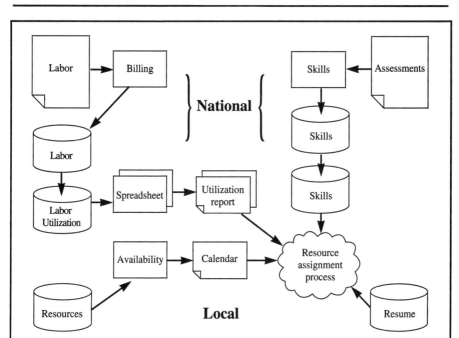

- Skill and experience categories are defined and administered nationally to create consistency for statistical purposes.

- Reports of skill demographics by office are available nationally, but the identity of the individuals are screened. National trends can be analyzed; requests for special resources can be directed to specific local executives for consideration within the context of local commitments; and local management that hoards highly skilled people, while achieving consistently low utilization, can be called to the carpet.

Figure 5-11 is a compromise among many alternatives for a computer system that meets the rules and requirements listed above. It is a combination of two national data bases and a series of local data bases, text files, and spreadsheets.

The components of the system are as follows.

- **Hours and activities data base.** As weekly labor sheets are recorded, the detailed hours by activity and engagement are stored for each individual who submits a report that week. Assuming this is a national contract management system, this data is used as input to national utilization reports and is down loaded to local systems for importation to spreadsheets.

It is important to note that this data provides the hours used, but not the hours available needed for utilization computation. National hours available can be estimated from data supplied by a personnel or payroll system.

- **Local labor resource data base.** This contains a record for each person committed to the local business, including consultants, managers, subcontractors, and people borrowed. It defines organization relationships and levels, and contains a 52-week projection of expected utilization and average billing rates.

- **Resume data base.** This contains resumes of each individual in the local labor data base for use in engagement proposals. Often resume systems are sophisticated enough to produce both internal resumes with dates, client names, and other confidential data, as well as, external resumes that characterize the experience, rather than listing specifics.

- **Availability calendar.** This is an expansion of the resource data base that contains the daily history and near term projections of actual, projected, and alternative assignments.

- **National skills/experience data base.** This contains the current skill level for each person for each standard skill or experience of Level 1 or greater. These are down loaded on request to a corresponding local data base from which reports can be produced. The more sophisticated skills systems provide for a current and planned skill level as input to reports showing future skill trends and implied demands on education centers. National demographics are reported from this data base.

- **Labor summary data base.** This is the combined data from resource, availability, and labor claiming in a single weekly history record for each person. Activity data is summarized into the key utilization analysis categories for that office. Typical categories might be: billed hourly; worked against a fixed price; assigned to client, but did not bill; vacation; holiday; education; and support to marketing. Ideally, all activities can be summarized into less than 20 categories that will be tracked and forecasted.

- **Utilization spreadsheets.** These are series of spreadsheets built from importation of data from labor utilization. They contain both planned and actual hours. Each represents a different reporting format such as: year to date for all subcategories; week by week, actual, and forecasted by billed, assigned, not billed, and not billable; any of the above, summarized for all classes of people resources; any of the above for subclasses or by individual; any of the above by manager or engagement.

The variety of computer support for people resource management in professional services firms at least equals the number of firms themselves. These systems have been slow in their evolution, because they are not necessary to the fundamental accounting process. They lend themselves to local implementation, which encourages pieces being built in a variety of places with little ability to integrate them. Therefore, it is unlikely that all of these systems exist in that form in one firm. It is probable, though, that most of the function is there in a combination of systematized and manual processes.

SUMMARY OF THE UTILIZATION MANAGEMENT PROCESS

Now that we have seen what utilization management reports look like and what tools are available to make the computations and produce the reports, let's review the entire process.

Annual Planning. At least once per year, field executives and their management staff prepare a forecast of the hours people resources will spend in broad categories of activities that correspond to work that directly derives revenue and time spent that is nonbillable. Although the activities performed may be in the tens to hundreds, the planning and tracking categories should be less than 20 and be only those that need year-to-year trend analysis.

The annual plan is carried to the individual level. This includes all known staff and contains slotting for staff that will be recruited as the year proceeds. This data is translated into what will eventually be a 52-week projection of known assignments, assumed assignments, and planned time on personal and educational activities. The annual plan is summarized into a week-by-week expectation of hours and utilization for each of the labor subclasses.

Weekly Labor Recording and Utilization Reporting. Each week, all people (or at least all who were assigned to a client) complete a labor recording sheet. The hours and activities from these sheets are summarized into the 20 or less planning and tracking categories for each individual within each manager unit, broken out by classification of people among levels of consultants, contractors, and so on.

The utilization of available time for each of these categories is computed and a series of reports are produced that show current and year-to-date utilization as compared to the plan.

Weekly or Biweekly Resource Review. On a weekly or biweekly basis, the management and marketing staff meet to plan the assignment of resources for the office. Input to the meeting is the utilization reports, the previous availability calendar, skills inventory reports, and a projection of marketing actions and potential sales (to be discussed in detail in Chapter 7).

During this meeting a revised availability calendar is developed covering the next two or more weeks. A number of issues and opportunities are addressed.

- Individuals with sustained low utilization are noted and actions are initiated. Actions might include emphasis marketing of the skills not in demand, short-term retraining, special projects, or a performance review.

- Individuals with sustained high utilization are noted and actions are initiated. Actions might include putting additional resources on the engagement, an official thank you to those with the highest utilization, or an engagement review.

- Requirements to increase or decrease resources on existing engagements and specific assignments are noted on the calendar.

- Requirements to staff new or potential engagements are scheduled on the calendar.

- Every person who remains without a scheduled assignment or activity on any day is tentatively assigned to time off, education, marketing support, or office improvement projects.

- Any people or engagement assignments that are left unresolved are assigned as an action to be taken by a specific manager.

Periodic Skills and Experience Update. At least once per year, each individual in the office updates their skills assessment and their resume. At this time, the individual should also remake their education plan and request enrollment in formal classes that have long lead times for acceptance. (As these are approved and acknowledged, they can be entered onto the calendar.) The individual may also be required to reassess his or her career development plan and jointly with management make any agreed changes. All of these are entered into the skills inventory, resume, education, and personnel systems as appropriate, with new reports generated.

Periodic Office Assessment. An important part of any measurement process is perspective. The analogy about being in the trees and not seeing the forest is very appropriate to utilization. Before the end of the second and third quarters, the field executive should rerun the high-level planning exercise that is illustrated in Figures 5-3 through 5-6. This causes one to probe whether current staffing makes sense against corresponding marketing assessments and current financial results. Up to this point, attention is alerted when results deviate from plan. The purpose of this exercise is to make sure its the right plan.

UTILIZATION MEASUREMENTS AND INCENTIVES

Most people in the professional services business carry some form of utilization measurement. This measurement may appear in their performance plan. It may also result in commissions or bonuses. Performance plan measurements are very often viewed negatively by the one being measured, since underachievement most often carries a penalty. For this reason, utilization is often an onerous topic among those who believe that quality work on behalf of the client should be the only measure of a professional.

Managers should always be measured on utilization, particularly where they can influence the level of effort on engagements and take an active role in obtaining extensions. A good balance between performance objectives and financial incentives is to measure a manager's performance quality on utilization and pay bonus or commission on profit results. Measurement bars (stated levels of expected utilization for the unit being managed) are set to inspire the manager to nurture the people, enrich their jobs with both billable and nonbillable assignments, and still drive for maximum revenue generation. The profit incentive balances one's instincts between good people management and the needs of the business.

Consultants should not be measured directly on utilization percentage, because they rarely control enough of the environment to be fairly judged on this area of their performance. The best consultant is someone who has made time for successful work experiences, lots of education (classroom, self-study, and on the job), a stable and fulfilling personal life, and associations with other professionals that have knowledge, style, and perspective that broaden one's own approach to the profession. The result is a billable person who can command the highest rates through proven quality and accumulated competence. Utilization measurements tend to keep people in one place, where they bill the most (today).

A more appropriate performance objective for consultants is balanced time. This conveys an expected distribution of hours that meets a standard for revenue generation, personal growth, and personal nourishment. An example might be the following.

Achieve a distribution of work hours in a 12-month period, that has a minimum of:

- 160 hours devoted to classroom and self-study education.
- 120 hours devoted to vacations, holidays, and personal time.

- 100 hours devoted to office communications and administration.

And expend the remaining hours in the best manner to generate billable revenue, with a minimum of:

- 1,270 hours derived from assignments that benefit the business.

The degree to which the individual can overachieve all components of this distribution is the difference between the average performer and the above average performer. This approach also works well with the other elements of a performance plan that likely measure client performance and satisfaction, quality of work products, business contributions through marketing, and new methods and personal leadership. For those who feel they must have some objective utilization measurement for consultants, the following might be added to the previous example.

Achieve at least 85 percent billable utilization while assigned full time to engagements.

The only warning to be given here is that every measurement needs a tracking system. The variety of utilization reports is varied enough for the necessities of managing assignments and profitability. Adding more reports to quantify individual performance may have diminishing returns.

MEASURING REVENUE UTILIZATION (REALIZATION)

Throughout this chapter we have been discussing billable utilization. We defined three categories: billed; assigned, not billed; and nonbillable. Billable utilization is the addition of the first two categories. We need to close this chapter with an expanded discussion of an individual who is assigned and not billing, and how this becomes much more complex when an office takes on systems integration.

A consultant or manager may be assigned, but not billing by design or by fate. When by design, the pricing for the engagement has accommodated the cost of the nonbilling people into the rates of others, or the total price. When by fate, events have caused additional hours to be spent and the original rate or price cannot recover the extra cost and still make profit.

In traditional consulting and custom development, there are some occasions when assigned people do not bill by design. Managers do not bill when performing firm related duties, such as business and people management (outside of the specific client), marketing support, and reviews of other engagements. Often, trainees do not bill when assigned in internships that lead to billing after qualification. Each of these examples is in a separate resource subclass, so the assigned, not billed time can be planned for and easily explained when it occurs.

The predominant reason behind unplanned assigned, not billed, time is re-work. Its risk may be anticipated in the price, but a quality firm does not ac-knowledge rework with estimated hours.

With systems integration, professional services firms have seen another di-mension in tracking assigned, not billed, time. The firm is a prime contractor for one or more other vendors. Recovering the cost of a vendor is a separate revenue stream from the labor cost consultants who manage vendor perform-ance. Often this is not billed or billed at a significant discount, with a corre-spondingly higher profit made against the nonlabor cost. Likewise, if the vendor fails to meet commitments, the time of consultants to take corrective action is often not billed (or billed at discount).

Some firms change the definition of billable utilization to revenue generat-ing and nonrevenue generating. Revenue generating time may have subclasses—revenue generation at full value versus discounted value. Nonreve-nue generating time may be broken down to track the cause.

Realization management, as this is called, is intended to give a more accu-rate view of whether people resources are being assigned to revenue bearing work in systems integration, than can be determined from simple utilization percentages. This becomes particularly true when people are repeatedly moved from traditional work to systems integration (or product support) and back again. Their time assigned, not billed, distorts the overall office utilization and reduces the ability to use utilization to track whether resources are assigned in a profitable manner.

WHERE'S CHARLIE?

The purpose of this chapter was to emphasize that managing professional serv-ices in a large office requires very close observation of where people resources are assigned. Too often, a resource plan is generated in January, and managers wake up in April to a large number of wasted hours in February and March that could have been avoided. Key topics to consider on the subject of manag-ing people resources are:

- In professional services, the people are the inventory of the business. Utilization analysis is the inventory management process that deter-mines where people time (and energy) is being spent. It is then the basis for revenue and profit planning.

- Utilization is not just the determination of how much time is devoted to clients. It is important to know the resource commitments to education, marketing, internal projects and administration. Even more important is being conscious of the time to be given to the people for their personal needs.

- The utilization plan is the starting point for business planning in professional services. The planning process is iterative, starting with business as usual that reflects current staffing, utilization, and rates.

- Utilization is a professional responsibility of consultants, but is not necessarily a good performance measurement. Managers should be measured on the billed utilization of those they manage.

We have discussed relatively simple tools for tracking a very large amount of data about where people are spending their time. As with any simple approach, there are an infinite number of ways to make it too complex and, thus, convince oneself that it is not worth the trouble.

We will see that knowing where hours are spent is critical to later discussions of profit and productivity analysis. Consultants quickly lose confidence and credibility in a management staff that can't figure out what the optimum levels of billing ought to be. Finally, clients tend to ask very direct and embarrassing questions (Where's Charlie?) when poor attention to assignments causes consultants to disappear and reappear like ghosts.

Managing utilization is a basic. It will change as the business moves in and out of fixed-price contracts and systems integration, but as long as the value of a consultant is the hours that can be delivered, utilization tracking will live on.

Chapter 6

Making Money

T he underlying purpose of all professional services measurements is to maximize profit. Profit is itself a measurement and its purpose is to keep score, since actions taken as a result of revenue and utilization measurements will affect profit immediately.

These immediate profits are also very simple to understand and compute. They are current income less current expense with little, if any, complications from apportionments of R & D, recovery of development, depreciation, warranty expenses, and other items that are often repaid out of profits. This month's income is compensation for this month's expenses and not an annuity to compensate for previous expense in products, facilities and equipment, or in anticipation of future expense.

This simple relationship between income and expense allows the delegation of net profit management and its specific measurement to the office level in the large firms (where it always is in the small firm). This is desirable in any business, since the marketplace is usually the final arbiter of business success. Being close to the client provides an up to the minute report card on the competitiveness of a firm's services and what it must provide in resources and accept as risk to ensure satisfaction.

An office executive with net profit authority can balance immediate profitability against immediate client satisfaction. Professional services managers will alter their income stream by agreeing to changes on existing engagements. They will decide how much to expend in resources to meet commitments for service quality, regardless of price and minimum legal commitment. The professional services manager with net profit measurements consciously understands the personal risk in accepting a low margin to price competitively and often chooses to pass up bad business.

The right and ability to price to the local market is the key competitive weapon of a local executive in a large professional services firm. It allows these firms to compete with the dozens of small firms in a metropolitan area. Local executives can find ways to offset the higher overhead of a large firm with valuable support services and the ability to acquire key people. Most importantly, these professional services office executives can both estimate the expected work and needed resources for new business and determine the most profitable price for the offering within the context of their own local financial structure.

Using net profit as a measurement prevents the local professional services executive from ignoring the higher overhead of the firm and charging only that needed to recover local cost, or to simply meet a revenue target. The manager measured by net profit lives and dies by the sword when a low-margin deal is mismanaged.

A complex services business requires a much closer track of month-to-month profit than basic services. Both types of businesses need to track revenue and utilization at least every other week. When, in basic services, these are performing better than expectation, profit is almost always on track and may require detailed analysis no more often than quarterly. With complex services (and certainly with complex labor and nonlabor services), the cost trade-offs between resource choices that also affect profit are too plentiful to ignore. For these businesses, profit analysis is a monthly obligation. Of course, when either revenue or utilization is not tracking, profit analysis is a must.

In this chapter we will discuss the following key topics.

- Planning, measurement, and control of direct cost and indirect expense for basic people services, complex people services, and labor and non-labor services.
- Allocation of indirect support expenses.
- Relationships between pricing and profit.
- Compensation for making profit.

We will begin with an analysis of typical income and expense statements (I & E) for professional services offices. We will define each element of the cost and expense structure and how these should be administered and controlled. We will return to the planning process of Chapter 5 and each of our business as usual, adjusted, and growth plans will be assessed for profitability. These examples of profit planning will range from basic people services to systems integration, and will include the effect of 30 percent growth on profits. We will also return to our situations of business downturn and slow hiring to see how these have affected profit and add some more data to the executive decision-making process.

The chapter proceeds to a discussion of the estimating and pricing process for professional services. It will focus on how to use the income and expense data to develop pricing components. The discussion also looks at various approaches to compensating field managers for net profit performance.

PROFESSIONAL SERVICES PROFIT COMPUTATION

There are a variety of ways to divide expenses against revenue to compute gross and net profit for a professional services office. The method described in this book is designed to complement the further computation of revenue and cost productivity rates that are introduced in this chapter and discussed in detail in Chapter 8. What is described here is a useful format for an office. The top of the business may use an entirely different format for its accounting purposes and this format should not inhibit a roll up of this office I & E to a national statement. Figure 6-1 illustrates the major elements of an income and expense statement for a professional services office.

Each of these line items will be discussed, followed later in the chapter by examples that illustrate actual values for various mixes of consultant, subcontractor, and nonlabor generated income. As is common with accounting statements, illustrations of income and expense can be at various levels of summary and detail. Three levels will be used in this chapter and will be identified as follows.

- **Summary.** Summary level equates to the line item detail in Figure 6-1.

- **Detail.** Detail level contains a further breakdown of the lowest level into major income and expense items. These might be considered account categories in a typical chart of accounts.

- **Subsidiary.** A subsidiary statement is at the detail level, but for a subset of the income and corresponding expense. An example will be the income and expense for the education portion of a combined consulting and education office.

Most of the examples in the chapter will be at the detail level, showing planned and actual for each quarter of the year. To further illustrate how income and expense vary depending on the business mix, the chapter will contain data from the following four simulated professional services businesses.

1. Office A (Basic Services): $6 million annual revenue business from consulting and education with only permanent staff. The office is not adding to its base of 29 consultants and managers. Eighty percent of its revenues are generated through consulting and 5 percent comes from nonlabor sources (this includes education materials that are sold separately).

2. Office B (Complex Services): $9 million annual revenue business from consulting, education, and custom development using both subcontractors and borrowed people to supplement its permanent consultant

FIGURE 6-1
Services Office Income and Expense Statement

Professional Services Income & Expense

Income
Labor generated revenue
Nonlabor generated revenue
Total income

Expense
Direct cost
 Direct labor
  Direct compensation
  Other direct costs
  Borrowed labor
  Vendor labor
 Direct nonlabor
  Direct travel/materials
  Transfer cost
  Vendor product cost
  Nonlabor apportionment
 Total direct cost

(Gross profit)

Indirect expense
 Selling
  Marketing compensation
  Marketing expenses
 Administration
  Administration compensation
  Office services
  Facilities
  Business computer services
 Other indirect expenses
 Total indirect expense

(Net earnings before allocation)

Allocated indirect expense

(Net earnings before tax)

staff. It is intending to grow 12 percent per year in revenues, while maintaining consistent profit levels.

3. Office C (Complex Labor and Nonlabor Services): $10 million annual revenue business from consulting, education, custom development, and product support. This office has additional income over Office B for software that it purchases internally from a development unit and resells in association with its product support services. It is using the margins from people services to bolster profits from selling its software at discount.

4. Office D (Complex Labor and Nonlabor Services): $13 million annual revenue business from all services, including systems integration with major expenses and corresponding revenue from purchases and delivery of equipment, software, and associated vendor services.

Income

Professional services income is derived primarily from billings for direct people services, secondarily from equipment, software, and materials delivered in conjunction with people services, and lastly from incidental sources such as interest and rental derived from managing cash and facilities. As we saw in Chapter 4, revenue can be segmented by market and territory. For purposes of profit computation and analysis, revenue must be divided further into labor generated and nonlabor generated.

Figure 6-2 is an example of revenue detail for Office A and Office C. This illustration contains plan data in preparation for tracking actual revenue as it is recorded. Income from consulting and custom development is labor generated, with a small amount of recovery from client-directed travel expenses. Approximately 4 percent of the income from education in Office A is generated through sale of materials, while over half of the revenue from product support services and 15 percent of all revenue in Office C is generated through the resale of software products.

In all examples shown, we will segment revenue by labor and nonlabor and by business mix. It emphasizes the differences in complexity between basic and complex services, but is, in fact, a common way in which firms divide their income. These examples could have chosen territory or industry as a basis of segmentation, which are also common.

The income illustrated above varies by the seasonality discussed for utilization in Chapter 5. The revenue from product sales causes the peaks and valleys for the complex services to be less pronounced. The fourth quarter is very strong for both businesses, showing a financial phenomenon that is consistent across the professional services business.

FIGURE 6–2
Income Plan Detail Comparing Basic and Complex Services

Comparing Income Plans: Basic Versus Complex Services

		Quarter 1 Plan ($000)	Quarter 2 Plan ($000)	Quarter 3 Plan ($000)	Quarter 4 Plan ($000)	Total Year Plan ($000)
Income Plan for a Basic People Services Business						
Consulting	Consultants	908.0	956.0	857.0	1,232.0	3,953
	Management	106.0	120.0	117.0	129.0	472
	Travel (nonlabor)	40.6	43.0	39.0	54.4	177
	Product (nonlabor)	0.0	0.0	0.0	0.0	0
	TOTAL	1,054.6	1,119.0	1,013.0	1,415.4	4,602
Education	Consultants	266.0	293.0	247.0	374.0	1,180
	Management	0.0	0.0	0.0	0.0	0
	Travel (nonlabor)	2.7	2.9	2.5	3.7	12
	Product (nonlabor)	12.0	12.0	12.0	12.0	48
	TOTAL	280.7	307.9	261.5	389.7	1,240
Total Income	Labor	1,280.0	1,369.0	1,221.0	1,735.0	5,605
	Nonlabor	55.2	58.0	53.4	70.2	237
	TOTAL	1,335.2	1,427.0	1,274.4	1,805.2	5,842
Income Plan for a Complex Product Support Services Business						
Consulting	Consultants	215.0	225.0	216.0	300.0	956
	Management	28.0	64.0	63.0	69.0	224
	Contractors	0.0	0.0	0.0	0.0	0
	Borrowed	148.0	148.0	148.0	148.0	592
	Travel (nonlabor)	15.6	17.5	17.1	20.7	71
	Product (nonlabor)	0.0	0.0	0.0	0.0	0
	TOTAL	406.6	454.5	444.1	537.7	1,843
Education	Consultants	127.0	128.0	113.0	152.0	520
	Management	0.0	0.0	0.0	0.0	0
	Contractors	0.0	0.0	0.0	0.0	0
	Borrowed	118.0	118.0	118.0	118.0	472
	Travel (nonlabor)	2.5	2.5	2.3	2.7	10
	Product (nonlabor)	12.0	12.0	12.0	12.0	48
	TOTAL	259.5	260.5	245.3	284.7	1,050
Custom Development	Consultants	378.0	400.0	371.0	498.0	1,647
	Management	113.0	96.0	94.0	103.0	406
	Contractors	509.0	509.0	509.0	509.0	2,036
	Borrowed	30.0	30.0	30.0	30.0	120
	Travel (nonlabor)	30.9	31.1	30.1	34.2	126
	Product (nonlabor)	0.0	0.0	0.0	0.0	0
	TOTAL	1,060.9	1,066.1	1,034.1	1,174.2	4,335
Product Support	Consultants	198.0	202.0	171.0	239.0	810
	Management	0.0	0.0	0.0	0.0	0
	Contractors	127.0	127.0	127.0	127.0	508
	Borrowed	0.0	0.0	0.0	0.0	0
	Travel (nonlabor)	9.8	9.9	8.9	11.0	40
	Product (nonlabor)	400.0	400.0	400.0	400.0	1,600
	TOTAL	734.8	738.9	706.9	777.0	2,958
Total Income	Labor	1,991	2,047	1,960	2,293	8,291
	Nonlabor	471	473	470	481	1,895
	TOTAL	2,462	2,520	2,430	2,774	10,186

Direct Cost

Direct costs include all those incurred to deliver revenue generating service. Typically these are the costs for all people other than marketing and administration, and for products and materials resold to clients under contract.

People costs can be specific to the payment of wages and benefits, reimbursement of employee incurred travel and living expenses, fees for education and other professional development expenses, or payments for contracted and borrowed resources. People costs can also include apportioned costs for facilities to house direct personal and recruiting expenses that are allocated among engagements.

Managers (other than those specific to marketing and business control) should be considered direct cost. All line managers, including the office executive, are potentially billable. Their hours and cost should be included in the utilization and direct cost pool. It is also simpler, as it eliminates additional pro rata of cost and expense among managers who bill and those who don't.

Nonlabor direct costs are for the purchase (or internal transfer) of equipment, software, and materials that are delivered to clients under service agreements. These costs include freight and off-site storage costs and may also include maintenance services, if incurred during the life of the engagement. Nonlabor costs may also include apportioned costs for a common library, storage facilities, distribution services, and administrative labor used to support product and vendor generated revenue.

Direct labor cost is composed of the following detail line items.

- **Direct compensation** is the salary, benefits, commissions, and bonuses paid to consultants, their direct management up to and including the field office manager, and any staff personnel who are expected to bill a portion of their available time. Often, these expenses are incurred in organization units where costs are budgeted and tracked by manager.

- **Other direct costs** include reimbursements of nonengagement travel, education, professional associations, and other expenses associated with the delivery of people services and the maintenance of professional credentials. It includes those costs incurred to recruit and hire new employees.

  Other direct costs also include apportioned facilities and administrative services costs to house and support direct personnel. A definition of apportioned cost is that expense which stops when all consultants, borrowed people, and subcontractors disappear. These costs, which include office rental, telephones, technical materials, facility services, and consultant computing support, are usually incurred in general accounts for the entire office and are manually apportioned. The apportionment should be simple, such as the ratio of consultant office square footage to all other rented square footage.

- **Borrowed and supplemental labor** costs are incurred through direct salary payments or salary transfers. Included in these expenses are any direct reimbursements for travel specific to borrowed people.
- **Vendor labor** payments are for subcontractors, including labor fees and travel expense reimbursements.

Apportioned facilities and services costs for contractors, supplemental, and borrowed people might be broken out separately for each, but its further detail is usually not worth the effort. As a general rule they are housed at a client location and draw on a negligible amount of the resources of the office.

Direct nonlabor cost is the cost of products, materials, and other vendor services that are delivered to clients and generate revenue separately from people services under professional services contracts. These costs are divided into the following detail line items.

- **Engagement travel** is the reimbursement of client directed travel and other extraordinary expenses incurred by people while working on an engagement. The income to offset these costs may be built into the price charged for the labor or may be charged separately.
- **Transfer costs** are company internal charges for equipment, software, and materials, including specific freight and storage charges. In a detailed cost ledger, these would be tracked as separate line items for each group of products.
- **Vendor product** is payment for purchases of equipment, software, and materials, including specific freight and storage charges and taxes. These payments also may include maintenance and installation fees.
- **Apportioned nonlabor** is prorated on-site storage and administrative support costs associated with the distribution of revenue generating equipment, software, and materials. These costs might be the labor and facilities costs for a library of documents and software. These would be accumulated for a specific organization unit in the expense ledger and apportioned by the simplest technique available (ratio of storage space used, ratio of administrative people time or head count, or percentage of revenue generated).

Direct cost is likely to be between 75 percent and 85 percent of the total expense of an office, without allocations (as discussed later). A small office has a proportionately smaller overhead in marketing and administration. A large office needs proportionately more such services to keep it going, particularly marketing. A very large systems integration office requires substantial overhead services, particularly administration. Direct cost tends to grow linearly, while overhead grows in increments, causing the ratio of the two to vary over time.

Figure 6-3 contains the direct cost and gross profit plan for a basic services office (Office A). Direct cost is 62 percent of revenue, giving a 38 percent gross profit. Labor to nonlabor cost is 14.7 to 1, while the corresponding revenue ratio is 23.6 to 1. Notice that the cost of a library and its distribution is apportioned as a direct nonlabor cost.

Besides the obvious cost of nonlabor versus its corresponding revenue (which we will take up later under profit planning), there does not seem to be any glaring cost issues in this plan. Recruiting costs add to lower utilization to make the summer a very poor profit period. Facilities costs include a separate cubicle for each consultant. These could be replaced by common areas where consultants only get desk space when they are not assigned to client premises. This reduces the space assigned to each consultant from 50 to 30 square feet for a corresponding improvement in gross profit of 1 percent, including any minor construction costs.

Gross Profit

Gross profit (total income minus direct cost) is used to indicate the relative financial value of income generating resources, both labor and nonlabor. It is not particularly accurate as a measurement of an office or its management, since it does not include all of the expenses that the office executive can control. Gross margin (gross profit divided by income) is used to compare one source of income with another or one business plan to another. The accuracy of these comparisons require that all other expenses, not in those listed so far, will be constant between the resources or plans being compared.

Gross margin is heavily affected by utilization levels and by rates and is a good test of how changes in these will affect overall financial performance. You will notice that the gross margin for our business plan is 38 percent. By making the plan improvements described in Figure 5-5 (which illustrated the impact of changes in utilization and rate on a basic services business), the gross margin improves to 42 percent against an increase in income of 11 percent. This additional 4 percent in profit carries through to increased net profit, making gross profit analysis a simple tool to judge the effect of revenue plan iterations.

Differences in relative gross profit will be used later to judge the productivity of resources and guide choices between levels and sources of people. Gross

FIGURE 6–3
Cost and Gross Profit Plan for Basic Services

Cost and Gross Profit Plan for a Basic Services Office		Quarter 1 Plan ($000)	Quarter 2 Plan ($000)	Quarter 3 Plan ($000)	Quarter 4 Plan ($000)	Total Year Plan ($000)
Direct Comp	Salaries	513.0	512.9	524.4	534.9	
	Benefits	101.5	99.8	101.5	103.3	
	Commissions	113.6	114.5	116.2	117.9	
	Other comp	7.3	7.1	7.3	7.4	
	TOTAL	735.3	734.2	749.3	763.4	2,982
Other Direct Costs	Travel/commute	8.7	8.6	8.7	8.9	
	Education/fees	68.8	67.5	68.8	70.0	
	Recruiting	10.0	10.0	30.0	0.0	
	Facilities	19.8	16.9	19.8	17.6	
	TOTAL	107.2	103.0	127.2	96.5	434
Direct Labor	TOTAL	842.5	837.2	876.6	859.8	3,416
Direct Travel	TOTAL	36.7	39.1	35.2	49.5	160
Transfer Cost	TOTAL	8.4	8.4	8.4	8.4	34
Vendor Product	TOTAL	0.0	0.0	0.0	0.0	0
Nonlabor Apportion	Salary	2.1	2.1	2.1	2.1	
	Benefits	1.1	1.1	1.1	1.1	
	Commissions	0.0	0.0	0.0	0.0	
	Other comp	0.0	0.0	0.0	0.2	
	Facilities	5.9	5.2	5.9	5.2	
	Services/shipping	0.9	0.9	0.9	0.9	
	TOTAL	10.0	9.2	10.0	9.5	39
Direct Nonlabor	TOTAL	55.1	56.7	53.6	67.3	233
Total Direct Cost		897.6	893.9	930.2	927.2	3,649
Gross Profit		437.6	533.1	344.2	878.0	2,193
	Margin	33%	37%	27%	49%	38%

profit is used to compute engagement profitability and is a key consideration in
pricing. Even though it is not a good measurement of an office, it can be used
as a relative measure between first-line consulting services unit managers in an
office. Finally, gross profit is used to compare business segments in a large of-

fice, to ensure that consulting, education, and systems integration are each contributing their share to the success of the office.

Indirect Expense

Indirect expenses are those costs (incurred directly by the office) that contribute equally to the earning of every dollar of revenue, regardless of its source. These are the selling and administrative expenses of the office, plus any support costs that apply equally to labor generated and nonlabor generated revenue, such as business computer charges and support staff salaries and expenses.

Selling expense is the cost of the marketing function in the office. It is composed of two parts.

- **Marketing compensation** is the salaries, benefits, commissions, and bonuses for directly compensated marketing personnel. These costs also include recruiting, training, and housing of marketing personnel.

- **Marketing expenses** are all other expenses incurred in the marketing function for travel, materials, promotions, advertising, computer support, and telephones. These expenses include payments to sources of marketing leads.

Administration is the cost of the office staff, their supplies and equipment, and the computer systems that supply business processing support, including the following.

- **Administration compensation** is the salaries, benefits, and other compensation for administrative staff and management. These costs include those for recruiting and training these personnel.

- **Office services** are the costs of contract administrative staff and reproduction, mail, and other office support services (many of these are supplied under contract by the facility landlord).

- **Facilities** are the costs of office space, equipment, supplies, telecommunications, and computerized office services.

- **Business computer services** are the charges for the business computer applications to administer and control the business, or the costs of a local computer operation, if processing is done locally.

Other indirect expense includes miscellaneous expenses, such as general meetings and outings for the entire office. Depending on the practices of the firm, other indirect expense might also contain an allocation of the office's share of geographic support expenses, such as quality assurance, middle executive compensation, and business controls staff.

Net Earnings (Profit) Before Allocation (NEBA)

NEBA is a measure of profit generation within a major firm, where part of the indirect expense can be controlled by the local executive and some is simply an allocation. It is total income for the office minus direct costs and indirect expenses. It should include direct charge of costs incurred by the firm to directly support the office. It doesn't include general corporate or partnership expenses which have no direct bearing on the performance of any offices and which can be allocated across all offices.

NEBA is an excellent measurement of local executives when it contains that income and those expenses that can be controlled. Some expenses seem fixed when they are not. Any expense, such as facilities, business computer charges, telecommunications, and office services that is incurred by head count or usage is controllable. The rate of charge is likely to be a matter of some debate, but the relative amount of these charges between offices and their effect on profit is well within the influence of local management by virtue of their control of staff size and pricing. Direct engagement support by headquarters or a competency center should be in an office's expense (in fact, in direct cost). New offering development that has no immediate revenue benefit to offices should not be charged to office expense.

Because NEBA is a result of the business direction provided by local management, it is commonly used to measure and pay profit commissions and bonuses for professional services office executives. Local management get to live and die by their own swords when empowered to hire and price and then are measured by NEBA. Using NEBA, though, rather than true net profit, shields local executives from being skewered by untimely increases in the overhead of the national business.

Allocated Expense

Allocations recover the overhead expenses of the firm over which the local executives have no cost control. Accounting practices usually allocate overhead as a uniform percentage of revenue. Therefore, if revenue generated this year was $100 million and overhead expense was $10 million, each office would receive an allocation expense of $0.10 for every $1 of revenue they have earned.

Before systems integration and other services where revenue is generated both through labor and nonlabor services, allocation was often by head count. The premise behind head count allocations was that labor revenue should be directly proportional to current head count and that low utilization should not be rewarded with a lower allocation. Avoiding endless debates on allocation methodology is another reason why NEBA has become the preferred office executive measurement and bonus trigger.

Large parts of an allocated overhead are general purpose computer and telecommunications services, such as payroll, personnel, accounts receivable, general ledger, leased voice and data networks, and electronic mail forwarding. The cost to charge these services by specific usage is often prohibitive (companies have more than wiped out the savings in consolidating services by developing complicated and expensive charge out systems).

The allocation covers the compensation of personnel and general expenses of finance and planning, new methods research and development, and employee development. Finally, it pays the salaries of the top executives and their support staff.

Net Earnings Before Tax (NEBT)

Net earnings before tax (NEBT) is total income minus direct, indirect, and allocated expense. Net profit margin is NEBT divided by total income. A prosperous professional services office should realize a net profit margin of 10 percent to 15 percent. An office growing at 30 percent per year is likely to see profits in the 8-percent to 10-percent range.

As stated above, NEBT is most important in analyzing pricing. Because of fluctuations in allocated expense beyond the control of the field executive, NEBT is not the best measurement of local management. We will see later how NEBT influences the decisions of local managers.

Figure 6-4 contains the expense plan for our basic services office culminating in projected net profit. The base business as usual plan generates a 27 percent NEBA and a 12 percent NEBT (allocated expense is planned at 15 percent of revenue). This is probably somewhat below target. No further opportunities for expense reduction stand out beyond the reduction in consultant office space mentioned earlier. This plan has a marketing staff of one and an administrative staff of two, which leaves little room for further cuts.

PROFIT PLANNING

The detailed income and expense statement is the tool used by a professional services field executive to forecast and manage profitability. As in utilization management, income and expense lends itself well to spreadsheets. Utilization and I & E spreadsheets are often linked to reduce entry. This becomes increasingly helpful when analyzing productivity rates as discussed in Chapter 8.

FIGURE 6–4
Expense and Net Profit Plan for Basic Services

		Quarter 1 Plan ($000)	Quarter 2 Plan ($000)	Quarter 3 Plan ($000)	Quarter 4 Plan ($000)	Total Year Plan ($000)
Expense and Net Profit Plan for a Basic Services Office						
Marketing Comp	Salary	17.0	17.1	17.2	17.3	
	Benefits	3.5	3.5	3.5	3.5	
	Commissions	4.3	4.3	4.3	4.3	
	Other comp	0.0	0.0	0.0	0.0	
	Recruiting	0.0	0.0	0.0	0.0	
	Education	1.3	1.3	1.3	1.3	
	Facilities	2.1	1.9	2.1	1.9	
	TOTAL	28.1	28.0	28.4	28.2	113
Marketing Expenses	Travel	7.7	7.7	7.7	7.7	
	Materials	3.0	3.0	3.0	3.0	
	Promo/advertising	0.0	10.0	0.0	0.0	
	TOTAL	10.7	20.7	10.7	10.7	53
Selling	TOTAL	38.9	48.7	39.1	39.0	166
Admin Comp	Salary	15.3	15.5	15.6	15.8	
	Benefits	6.0	6.0	6.0	6.0	
	Commissions	0.0	0.0	0.0	0.0	
	Other comp	1.5	1.5	1.6	1.6	
	Supplemental	0.0	0.0	0.0	0.0	
	Recruiting	0.0	0.0	0.0	0.0	
	Education	1.3	1.3	1.3	1.3	
	Travel	0.0	0.0	0.0	0.0	
	TOTAL	24.0	24.2	24.4	24.6	97
Office Services	Vendor personnel	4.7	4.7	4.7	8.3	
	Vendor services	0.0	0.0	0.0	0.0	
	Supplies	3.0	3.0	3.0	3.0	
	TOTAL	7.7	7.7	7.7	11.3	34
Facilities	Rental/occupancy	39.7	39.4	39.7	40.0	
	Services	7.9	7.9	7.9	8.0	
	Telecomm	2.6	2.6	2.6	2.7	
	Equipment/furn	7.3	0.0	7.3	0.0	
	Direct apportion	−19.8	−16.9	−19.8	−17.6	
	Nonlabor apportion	−5.9	−5.2	−5.9	−5.2	
	Marketing apportion	−2.1	−1.9	−2.1	−1.9	
	TOTAL	29.7	25.9	29.7	25.9	111
Business Comp Serv	TOTAL	26.7	28.5	25.5	36.1	117
Administration	TOTAL	88.1	86.4	87.3	97.9	360
Other Indirect	Meetings	3.5	3.5	3.5	3.5	
	Regional apportion	22.8	22.8	22.8	22.8	
	Miscellaneous	1.0	1.0	1.0	1.0	
	TOTAL	27.3	27.3	27.3	27.3	109
Indirect Expense	TOTAL	154.3	162.4	153.7	164.2	635
Net Earnings (NEBA)		283.3	370.6	190.5	713.8	1,558
	Margin	21%	26%	15%	40%	27%
Allocated Expense	TOTAL	200.3	214.0	191.2	270.8	876
Net Earnings (NEBT)		83.0	156.6	−0.6	443.1	682
	Margin	6%	11%	0%	25%	12%

In this section we will review a series of income and expense examples. Each will represent a progressively more complex business mix. The first will be the basic people services business (Office A) where we have made improvement in utilization and rates to bring net profit in line with objectives. This will include an example of how to use a subsidiary statement in planning. Next we will return to the complex people services planning exercises of Chapter 5 and show the corresponding income and expense plans. Finally, we will look at a complex systems integration plan.

Basic Services

Figure 6-5 is a summary plan for the same office as described in Figures 6-2 through 6-4 (basic people services). In this case we have increased utilization and raised selected rates as discussed in Chapter 5. To recap, Office A is a 26-consultant and 3-manager office with 1 marketer and 2 administrative personnel. It reports to a regional executive along with 3 other offices, who has a staff of 3. Most of the billing is per hour, with most education charged per participant or at a fixed price. Average utilization for consultants is 68 percent, for both consultants and managers is 65 percent, and the average rate charged in the office is $157 per hour. After these adjustments, the office now has a business plan to derive a NEBA of 38 percent and NEBT of 17 percent.

This is likely a very acceptable plan. It assumes that the higher rates can be sold and that backlog will grow to absorb the increased utilization. This means more marketing and you will notice that selling expense between this plan and the business as usual plan in Figure 6-4 has increased from $166,000 to $183,000 (10 percent). This was in more promotion and not additional marketers. One more marketing person would drop net profit back to 13 percent.

A clear drag on profit is from education materials. These are $48,000 of the $62,000 that we receive in nonlabor income under education. Simple arithmetic shows that transfer cost plus nonlabor apportioned expense (the library) is more than the revenue by $25,000. The education people tell us that they can't sell the materials for any more, but that they are considered a strong competitive edge in selling our education services. Figure 6-6 looks at a subsidiary income and expense plan for the education business by itself. The purpose is to see if profits from labor carry the loss from the materials.

As you can see, the total education business makes a healthy profit, particularly since we are using the higher rates for senior people from our adjusted plan. The materials, taken by themselves, lose 35 percent in gross profit, but are more than made up for by a 42 percent gross profit for labor generated revenue.

FIGURE 6–5
Summary Income and Expense Plan: Basic Services Office

	Adjusted Income & Expense Plan for a Basic Services Office				
		Quarter 1 Plan ($000)	Quarter 2 Plan ($000)	Quarter 3 Plan ($000)	Quarter 4 Plan ($000)	Total Year Plan ($000)
Income						
	Consulting	1,138.8	1,224.1	1,118.0	1,567.3	5,048
	Education	311.0	348.3	302.9	457.4	1,420
	Labor	1,391.0	1,510.0	1,363.0	1,948.0	6,212
	Nonlabor	58.8	62.4	57.9	76.7	256
	TOTAL INCOME	1,449.8	1,572.4	1,420.9	2,024.7	6.468
Direct Cost						
	Direct comp	758.0	757.1	772.6	787.0	3,075
	Other direct costs	107.2	103.0	127.2	96.5	434
	DIRECT LABOR	865.2	860.1	899.8	883.4	3,509
	Direct travel	39.7	42.8	39.0	55.0	177
	Transfer cost	8.4	8.4	8.4	8.4	34
	Nonlabor apportion	10.0	9.2	10.0	9.5	39
	DIRECT NONLABOR	58.1	60.5	57.4	72.9	249
	TOTAL DIRECT COST	923.4	920.6	957.2	956.3	3,757
	Gross Profit	526.4	651.9	463.7	1,068.4	2,710
	Margin	36%	41%	33%	53%	42%
Indirect Expense						
	Marketing comp	29.0	28.8	29.2	29.1	116
	Marketing expenses	16.7	21.7	16.7	11.7	67
	SELLING	45.7	50.6	46.0	40.8	183
	Admin comp	24.0	24.2	24.4	24.6	97
	Office services	7.7	7.7	7.7	11.3	34
	Facilities	29.7	25.9	29.7	25.9	111
	Business comp serv	29.0	31.4	28.4	40.5	129
	ADMINISTRATION	90.4	89.3	90.2	102.3	372
	OTHER INDIRECT	29.2	29.2	29.2	29.2	117
	INDIRECT EXP TOTAL	165.3	169.1	165.4	172.3	672
	Net Earnings (NEBA)	361.1	482.8	298.3	896.1	2,038
	Margin	25%	31%	21%	44%	32%
Allocated Expense	TOTAL	217.5	235.9	213.1	303.7	970
	Net Earnings (NEBT)	143.6	246.9	85.1	592.4	1,068
	Margin	10%	16%	6%	29%	17%

FIGURE 6-6
Subsidiary Income and Expense for an Education Business

Income & Expense Plan for Education					
		Quarter 1 Plan ($000)	Quarter 2 Plan ($000)	Quarter 3 Plan ($000)	Quarter 4 Plan ($000)	Total Year Plan ($000)
Income						
	Education	311.0	348.3	302.9	457.4	1,420
	Labor	296.0	333.0	288.0	441.0	1,358
	Nonlabor	15.0	15.3	14.9	16.4	62
	TOTAL INCOME	311.0	348.3	302.9	457.4	1,420
Direct Cost						
	Direct comp	159.0	161.4	162.8	164.1	647
	Other direct costs	33.6	32.9	53.8	23.0	143
	DIRECT LABOR	192.6	194.3	216.6	187.1	791
	Direct travel	2.5	2.8	2.4	3.7	12
	Transfer cost	8.4	8.4	8.4	8.4	34
	Nonlabor apportion	9.9	9.2	9.9	9.5	38
	DIRECT NONLABOR	20.8	20.4	20.8	21.6	84
	TOTAL DIRECT COST	213.4	214.7	237.3	208.7	874
	Gross Profit	97.6	133.6	65.5	248.7	545
	Margin	31%	38%	22%	54%	38%
Indirect Expense						
	INDIRECT EXP TOTAL	31.2	33.5	31.1	33.4	129
	Net Earnings (NEBA)	66.4	100.2	34.5	215.3	416
	Margin	21%	29%	11%	47%	29%
Allocated Expense	TOTAL	46.6	52.2	45.4	68.6	213
	Net Earnings (NEBT)	19.8 0	47.9	-11.0	146.7	203
	Margin	6%	14%	-4%	32%	14%

Complex Services without Growth

This first example of income and expense was relatively simple. It provided for a healthy profit margin and all revenue and cost was from permanent staff. In our next example we will look at a complex services office that is not growing, and which uses contractors and borrowed people to supplement its labor resources. Later we will expand our planning to include growth in people and, finally, the addition of the vendor products and services of systems integration.

We will be using the office portrayed in Figures 5-3, 5-4, and 5-6 and described as Office B earlier in this chapter. Our purpose is to test whether our staffing and utilization plan iterations from the previous chapter were each profitable.

As you recall, our first plan exercise was business as usual. In this plan, we maintained staffing levels from year to year, only replacing attrition with high-potential college hires, and we kept our rates constant against market conditions and competition. As Figure 6-7 shows, the business as usual plan is profitable at a 38 percent gross profit and a 12 percent net profit. Notice that income includes that for custom development and borrowed and vendor labor costs appear under direct cost.

This is probably a perfect plan when economic conditions are uncertain. Any business would be delighted with 12 percent net during tough times. It allows business to go on without the risk of higher rates and more people and does not depend on as yet unproven utilization levels. The problem, as presented in Chapter 5, is that $8.3 million, now $8.6 million, is not up to the revenue objective of $9.5 million. Presumably, economic conditions favor higher revenue generation.

A plan objective of 12 percent net is acceptable, but not great, if economic conditions strongly favor the services of this office. In Chapter 5, our lower level people were in demand and we determined that our higher level people could command higher rates. This led us to an adjusted plan with increased utilization and rates. Our expectation was that the adjusted plan would also satisfy any profit problems in our business as usual plan.

As can be seen from Figure 6-8, it is indeed a very healthy profit generator. Gross profit is now up 2 percent to 40 percent and net profit is up a corresponding 2 percent to 14 percent. As in the corresponding adjustment exercise for the basic services office, we have increased marketing promotion expenses to ensure that utilization of our people and our new rates will be met with corresponding demand by our clients.

Again, increases in utilization and rates for a complex services business has less overall effect than comparable increases in a basic services business. This results from having 30 percent to 40 percent of the people resources supplied through contractors. We chose not to increase their average rates. If we had, we would have seen more than a 2 percent increase in profit. Usually the market is less receptive to increases in subcontractor rates, and they are raised only when actual placement of contractors on engagements is demonstrating a sustained increase in rates across the professional services marketplace.

The adjusted plan is a solid plan for a no-growth business. No-growth professional services is almost an oxymoron, but, even so, parent companies have been known to freeze growth in their people services units. Since our objective is to grow (and the $8.9 million generated by this plan is still short of that goal), this plan serves as an excellent base for another iteration that brings more people onto the staff. It can also serve as a fallback plan in the event that people become difficult to acquire.

FIGURE 6-7
Income and Expense Plan Summary for Complex Services

		Quarter 1 Plan ($000)	Quarter 2 Plan ($000)	Quarter 3 Plan ($000)	Quarter 4 Plan ($000)	Total Year Plan ($000)
Income & Expense Plan for a Complex Services Office						
Income						
	Consulting	406.6	454.5	444.1	537.7	1,843
	Education	259.5	260.5	245.3	284.7	1,050
	Custom development	1,395.7	1,404.9	1,341.1	1,551.2	5,693
	Labor	1,991.0	2,047.0	1,960.0	2,293.0	8,291
	Nonlabor	70.7	72.9	70.5	80.6	295
	TOTAL INCOME	2,061.7	2,119.9	2,030.5	2,373.6	8,586
Direct Cost						
	Direct comp	596.5	581.5	637.4	624.5	2,440
	Other direct costs	89.2	83.6	116.5	90.7	380
	Borrowed labor	198.5	198.5	198.5	198.5	794
	Vendor labor	353.2	353.2	353.2	353.2	1,413
	DIRECT LABOR	1,237.3	1,216.8	1,305.5	1,266.8	5,026
	Direct travel	49.9	51.7	49.7	58.3	210
	Transfer cost	8.4	8.4	8.4	8.4	34
	Nonlabor apportion	10.6	9.9	10.6	10.1	41
	DIRECT NONLABOR	68.9	70.0	68.7	76.8	284
	TOTAL DIRECT COST	1,306.2	1,286.8	1,374.2	1,343.6	5,311
	Gross Profit	755.6	833.1	656.2	1,030.0	3,275
	Margin	37%	39%	32%	43%	38%
Indirect Expense						
	Marketing comp	56.7	56.4	57.2	56.9	227
	Marketing expenses	28.8	39.1	28.6	30.3	127
	SELLING	85.5	95.5	85.8	87.3	354
	Admin comp	38.1	43.4	43.6	38.9	164
	Office services	7.7	7.7	7.7	7.7	31
	Facilities	40.5	36.1	40.7	36.1	153
	Business comp serv	41.2	42.4	40.6	47.5	172
	ADMINISTRATION	127.6	129.6	132.7	130.3	520
	OTHER INDIRECT	27.3	27.3	27.3	27.3	109
	INDIRECT EXP TOTAL	240.3	252.4	245.8	244.8	983
	Net Earnings (NEBA)	515.2	580.6	410.4	785.2	2,291
	Margin	25%	27%	20%	33%	27%
Allocated Expense	TOTAL	309.3	318.0	304.6	356.0	1,288
	Net Earnings (NEBT)	206.0	262.7	105.8	429.1	1,004
	Margin	10%	12%	5%	18%	12%

FIGURE 6-8
Income and Expense Plan with Adjusted Utilization and Rates

		Quarter 1 Plan ($000)	Quarter 2 Plan ($000)	Quarter 3 Plan ($000)	Quarter 4 Plan ($000)	Total Year Plan ($000)
Adjusted Income & Expense for a Complex Services Office						
Income						
	Consulting	424.3	481.5	475.3	584.5	1,966
	Education	265.5	268.5	256.4	302.9	1,093
	Custom development	1,424.5	1,446.1	1,381.2	1,594.4	5,846
	Labor	2,042.0	2,121.0	2,040.0	2,398.0	8,601
	Nonlabor	72.3	75.2	72.9	83.8	304
	TOTAL INCOME	2,114.3	2,196.2	2,112.9	2,481.8	8,905
Direct Cost						
	Direct comp	596.5	581.5	637.4	624.5	2,440
	Other direct costs	89.2	83.6	116.5	90.7	380
	Borrowed labor	198.5	198.5	198.5	198.5	794
	Vendor labor	353.2	353.2	353.2	353.2	1,413
	DIRECT LABOR	1,237.3	1,216.8	1,305.5	1,266.8	5,026
	Direct travel	51.3	53.7	51.8	61.0	218
	Transfer cost	8.4	8.4	8.4	8.4	34
	Nonlabor apportion	10.6	9.9	10.6	10.1	41
	DIRECT NONLABOR	70.2	72.0	70.8	79.5	292
	TOTAL DIRECT COST	1,307.5	1,288.8	1,376.3	1,346.3	5,319
	Gross Profit	806.8	907.4	736.6	1,135.5	3,586
	Margin	38%	41%	35%	46%	40%
Indirect Expense						
	Marketing comp	56.7	56.4	57.2	56.9	227
	Marketing expenses	35.1	40.5	35.0	31.9	142
	SELLING	91.7	96.9	92.2	88.8	370
	Admin comp	38.1	43.4	43.6	38.9	164
	Offices services	7.7	7.7	7.7	7.7	31
	Facilities	40.5	36.1	40.7	36.1	153
	Business comp serv	42.3	43.9	42.3	49.6	178
	ADMINISTRATION	128.6	131.2	134.3	132.4	527
	OTHER INDIRECT	27.3	27.3	27.3	27.3	109
	INDIRECT EXP TOTAL	247.6	255.3	253.9	248.6	1,005
	Net Earnings (NEBA)	559.2	652.1	482.7	886.9	2,581
	Margin	26%	30%	23%	36%	29%
Allocated Expense	TOTAL	317.1	329.4	316.9	372.3	1,336
	Net Earnings (NEBT)	242.0	322.6	165.8	514.7	1,245
	Margin	11%	15%	8%	21%	14%

Complex Services with Growth

In our third planning iteration we determined how many people we needed to add on top of the adjusted plan in order to make the $9.3 million revenue objective. This is a plan for at least 12 percent revenue growth. Our concern was whether this plan remained profitable as we absorbed the lower utilization of interns and the costs of recruiting and moving the new people to locations, where their services can be used.

Figures 6-9, 6-10, and 6-11 are the detailed income and expenses for a growth plan. The plan satisfies our revenue objective of $9.5 million, in fact it overachieves by $147,000 or 1.5 percent. Custom development generates two-thirds of the income, while consulting and education, with their correspondingly higher rates, generate 22 percent and 12 percent, respectively. With a net increase in staff of seven, we expect to achieve a gross profit of 37 percent and a net profit of 12 percent (back to the levels of a business as usual plan).

Adding people has brought with it a significant recruiting cost. This is particularly true, since we chose to recruit half of our new staff from our parent company and incurred the corresponding moving and living costs of internal relocations. We have retained the higher marketing expenses of the adjusted plan, in order to stimulate the demand we will need and we are paying some outside parties for leads to new clients. We have chosen not to add an additional marketer at this time (an additional marketing person would cost us another 2 percent from our net profit). We have chosen to employ a temporary administrative person at $8,900 per quarter, rather than hire another permanent administrative person at $13,700 per quarter.

Under this plan, earnings will also grow 12 percent over business as usual, and last year's $1,004,000. This is likely to be a very acceptable plan. It is aggressive, but it starts out with a profit projection that leaves a lot of room for trouble. It actually reduces the ratio of contractors to permanent staff, which lowers performance risk and provides room to increase contractors, if business is even stronger than expected. Since all but two of the new people will be fully productive by the end of the year, this plan provides a solid base for additional revenue growth in the next year simply from higher overall utilization.

Notice that the division of average head count (from Figure 5-6) into total direct employee cost (direct compensation plus other direct costs) computes an average permanent staff cost of approximately $9,121 per month, including managers. The transfer cost of borrowed specialists is $90 per hour in this office example, plus the cost of their temporary assignment (cost transfer). This makes borrowed people more than $1\frac{1}{2}$ times as costly as their direct employee counterparts. Borrowed people command a higher average rate for their expertise, but, as will be seen in Chapter 8, a fully utilized direct employee is a better

FIGURE 6-9
Detailed Income Plan for a Growing Business

		Quarter 1 Plan ($000)	Quarter 2 Plan ($000)	Quarter 3 Plan ($000)	Quarter 4 Plan ($000)	Total Year Plan ($000)
Growth Income Plan						
Consulting	Consultants	254.0	274.0	311.0	402.0	1,241
	Management	28.0	87.0	85.0	94.0	294
	Contractors	0.0	0.0	0.0	0.0	0
	Borrowed	148.0	148.0	111.0	111.0	518
	Travel (nonlabor)	17.2	20.4	20.3	24.3	82
	Product (nonlabor)	0.0	0.0	0.0	0.0	0
	TOTAL	447.2	529.4	527.3	631.3	2,135
Education	Consultants	157.0	179.0	187.0	219.0	742
	Management	0.0	0.0	0.0	0.0	0
	Contractors	0.0	0.0	0.0	0.0	0
	Borrowed	118.0	118.0	89.0	89.0	414
	Travel (nonlabor)	2.8	3.0	2.8	3.1	12
	Product (nonlabor)	12.0	12.0	12.0	12.0	48
	TOTAL	289.8	312.0	290.8	323.1	1,216
Custom Development	Consultants	607.0	679.0	656.0	1,009.0	2,951
	Management	114.0	131.0	128.0	141.0	514
	Contractors	636.0	636.0	636.0	636.0	2,544
	Borrowed	30.0	30.0	22.0	22.0	104
	Travel (nonlabor)	41.6	44.3	43.3	54.2	183
	Product (nonlabor)	0.0	0.0	0.0	0.0	0
	TOTAL	1,428.6	1,520.3	1,485.3	1,862.2	6,296
Total Income	Labor	2,092.0	2,282.0	2,225.0	2,723.0	9,322
	Nonlabor	73.6	79.6	78.3	93.6	325
	TOTAL	2,165.6	2,361.6	2,303.3	2,816.6	9,647

financial deal to the office than a correspondingly fully utilized borrowed person.

This give and take between risk, profitability and total revenue goal is at the heart of business planning for the large professional services office. In the examples, we have made it easy for ourselves by going for only 12 percent growth. In reality, quota increases are often 30 percent and more. To grow 30 percent in our example complex services office, we would have added 15 people to our permanent staff, with a heavy emphasis on professional hiring in the immediate locations where people are needed, and 4 additional contractors. Our resulting revenue would reach $11.1 million, but our gross profit would drop to 34 percent, while net would be at 8 percent. Actual earnings would decrease by 13 percent to $875,000.

FIGURE 6-10
Detailed Cost Plan for a Growing Business

Growth Cost and Gross Profit Plan		Quarter 1 Plan ($000)	Quarter 2 Plan ($000)	Quarter 3 Plan ($000)	Quarter 4 Plan ($000)	Total Year Plan ($000)
Direct Comp	Salaries	447.0	492.5	567.2	566.0	
	Benefits	99.8	108.5	126.0	124.3	
	Commissions	80.3	86.5	100.5	105.5	
	Other comp	7.1	7.8	9.0	8.9	
	TOTAL	634.2	695.3	802.7	804.6	2,937
Other Direct Costs	Travel/commute	9.8	10.5	11.7	11.6	
	Education/fees	66.3	71.3	83.8	82.5	
	Recruiting	110.0	105.0	25.0	0.0	
	Facilities	20.5	19.2	26.0	22.5	
	TOTAL	206.5	206.0	146.4	116.5	675
Borrowed Labor	Salary transfer	168.5	168.5	126.4	126.4	
	Supplemental	0.0	0.0	0.0	0.0	
	Cost transfer	30.0	30.0	22.5	22.5	
	TOTAL	198.5	198.5	148.9	148.9	695
Vendor Labor	Vendor labor	353.2	353.2	353.2	353.2	
	Travel reimburse	0.0	0.0	0.0	0.0	
	TOTAL	353.2	353.2	353.2	353.2	1,413
Direct Labor	TOTAL	1,392.4	1,452.9	1,451.2	1,423.2	5,720
Direct Travel	TOTAL	52.3	57.5	56.4	69.4	236
Transfer Cost	TOTAL	8.4	8.4	8.4	8.4	34
Nonlabor Apportn	Salary	2.1	2.1	2.1	2.1	
	Benefits	1.1	1.1	1.1	1.1	
	Commissions	0.0	0.0	0.0	0.0	
	Other comp	0.0	0.0	0.0	0.2	
	Facilities	6.5	5.8	6.5	5.8	
	Services/shipping	0.9	0.9	0.9	0.9	
	TOTAL	10.6	9.8	10.6	10.0	41
Direct Nonlabor	TOTAL	71.3	75.7	75.4	87.8	310
Total Direct Cost		1,463.7	1,528.6	1,526.6	1,511.0	6,030
Gross Profit		701.9	833.0	776.7	1,305.6	3,617
	Margin	32%	35%	34%	46%	37%

Significant growth and high profitability can be accomplished, though, when market demand is high and professional people with ready skills and experience can be hired without relocation costs. This is why large firms choose to acquire small local firms as a means to expand into new geography, and why Andersen, Ernst & Young, and IBM are able to profitably grow using the base

FIGURE 6–11
Detailed Expense Plan for a Growing Business

Growth Expense and Net Profit Plan

		Quarter 1 Plan ($000)	Quarter 2 Plan ($000)	Quarter 3 Plan ($000)	Quarter 4 Plan ($000)	Total Year Plan ($000)
Marketing Comp	Salary	34.0	34.2	34.4	34.6	
	Benefits	7.0	7.0	7.0	7.0	
	Commissions	8.5	8.6	8.6	8.7	
	Other comp	0.0	0.0	0.0	0.0	
	Recruiting	0.0	0.0	0.0	0.0	
	Education	2.5	2.5	2.5	2.5	
	Facilities	4.7	4.1	4.7	4.1	
	TOTAL	56.7	56.4	57.2	56.9	227
Marketing Expenses	Travel	15.5	15.5	15.5	15.5	
	Materials	4.0	4.0	4.0	4.0	
	Lead sources	10.8	11.8	11.5	14.1	
	Promo/advertising	5.0	10.0	5.0	0.0	
	TOTAL	35.3	41.3	36.0	33.6	146
Selling	TOTAL	92.0	97.7	93.2	90.4	373
Admin Comp	Salary	24.3	24.6	24.8	25.1	
	Benefits	9.5	9.5	9.5	9.5	
	Commissions	0.0	0.0	0.0	0.0	
	Other comp	2.4	2.5	2.5	2.5	
	Supplemental	0.0	5.0	5.0	0.0	
	Recruiting	0.0	0.0	0.0	0.0	
	Education	1.9	1.9	1.9	1.9	
	Travel	0.0	0.0	0.0	0.0	
	TOTAL	38.1	43.4	43.6	38.9	164
Office Services	Vendor personnel	8.9	8.9	8.9	8.9	
	Vendor services	0.0	0.0	0.0	0.0	
	Supplies	3.0	3.0	3.0	3.0	
	TOTAL	11.9	11.9	11.9	11.9	48
Facilities	Rental/occupancy	45.4	48.1	50.7	50.5	
	Services	9.1	9.6	10.1	10.1	
	Telecomm	9.8	10.0	10.4	10.3	
	Equipment/furn	8.1	0.0	9.8	0.0	
	Direct apportion	−20.5	−19.2	−26.0	−22.5	
	Nonlabor apportion	−6.5	−5.8	−6.5	−5.8	
	Marketing apportion	−4.7	−4.1	−4.7	−4.1	
	TOTAL	40.7	38.6	43.7	38.5	161
Business Comp Serv	TOTAL	43.3	47.2	46.1	56.3	193
Administration	TOTAL	133.9	141.0	145.3	145.6	566
	Meetings	3.5	3.5	3.5	3.5	
	Regional apportion	22.8	22.8	22.8	22.8	
	Miscellaneous	1.0	1.0	1.0	1.0	
Other Indirect	TOTAL	27.3	27.3	27.3	27.3	109
Indirect Expense	TOTAL	253.2	266.0	265.8	263.4	1,048
Net Earnings (NEBA)		448.7	567.0	510.9	1,042.2	2,569
	Margin	21%	24%	22%	37%	27%
Allocated Expense	TOTAL	324.8	354.2	345.5	422.5	1,447
Net Earnings (NEBT)		123.8	212.7	165.4	619.7	1,122
	Margin	6%	9%	7%	22%	12%

of accounting and systems people that are already resident in a geographically dispersed parent business.

Product Support and Systems Integration Planning

Another way to grow at 30 percent or more is to take on systems integration deals. These are usually engagements of many hundreds of thousands of dollars over one- to two-year periods. They may be one large project in one location or a series of moderate-sized engagements that build and propagate a system across many locations. Unfortunately, this adds another dimension to planning—significant amounts of nonlabor income and expense.

Three broad categories of services that involve translating nonlabor cost into revenue are the following.

• The office buys software from its parent and/or business partners and installs the software under a client engagement. The offer is usually a fixed price for a standard service that includes both labor and the product, and an accompanying uniquely priced offering to customize the product and its use for this client.

Very often the professional services business is only one of multiple channels used by the company to distribute its products. The professional services business "buys" the product internally, saving the product unit some distribution cost and selling expense. The professional services unit then marks up the product, adds value added services and creates an engagement price to deliver, install, and customize the product. The professional services channel is in competition with other outlets for the product and gets an internal price that is slightly below the best discounted price the company offers to its largest distributors and volume customers.

At the office level, more profit comes from the value added services than the product. The people services business can be priced to bring 15 percent to 18 percent net while the combined business may bring 8 percent. If the product has strong competition, the company with the best value added services will be the most profitable when product price discounting begins in earnest.

• The office supplies a lead professional who manages the efforts of another vendor to perform a combined physical and intellectual installation of equipment. An example would be the planning, construction, installation, testing, and training for new workstations in an existing office area. The client is charged a fixed price by the professional services firm, which pays a fixed price to the construction vendor.

• The office project team acts as prime contractor for a variety of equipment and software vendors to design and build a complex information systems application. The engagement with the client provides for a single periodic invoice from the firm for all participating suppliers, with the firm taking a markup for its role as project manager and prime contractor.

Although it sounds more complex, the simplest way to manage combined labor and nonlabor generated revenue in sizable relative components is to view them as two separate businesses. This is done by isolating the nonlabor generated component within the profit tracking process and continually being aware of the relative drag on profit by either component. By making this isolation, it allows the office to continue to react to weekly changes in the labor business, without its performance being clouded by the nonlabor business.

Figure 6-12 is a summary plan for an office with two large systems integration (SI) deals and a small product support business. The SI engagements are each $5 million over two years and they will generate $2 million in nonlabor revenue this year for equipment, software, and construction services which the office acquires and delivers as prime contractor. The office is in the process of marketing a third deal that will start late in the third quarter, but will require only labor services for requirements and design in its first six months. These three engagements are also markets for the firm's software business (which generates an additional $450,000 per quarter for this office).

The plan forecasts $13.8 million in revenue, including nearly $3.9 million from nonlabor sources. In addition to $2.1 million from systems integration nonlabor, the office expects $1.1 million in resales from its own products. The $13.8 million in revenue is expected to net 6 percent or $882,000.

Notice that the revenue pattern from quarter to quarter for systems integration can be very different from traditional services. Scheduled milestones and corresponding client billing is heavily concentrated in the middle of the year. Labor milestone billing is scheduled at approximately three-month intervals, so the revenue stream is actually smoother than it might be (the month-by-month revenue stream will look extremely ragged). Correspondingly, though, the cost stream shows peaks where the vendors have billed the firm at the same milestones (vendor product is now a cost line). Since cost and compensating revenue for the large milestone payments to the vendor are kept in synch, gross profit is fairly constant until it blooms during the last quarter as a result of higher utilization.

The office has anticipated the growth in the systems integration business by the end of the year. A team of eight is hired for the new project in the fourth quarter. By the end of the year the office has four marketers and four administrative people. If the sale of the new contract does not materialize, the office can back off on much of this growth.

Systems integration distorts the natural rhythms of the business. This can be seen by comparing the labor and nonlabor revenue lines. Compare the revenue

FIGURE 6–12
Income and Expense Plan for Systems Integration

Income & Expense Plan for a Systems Integration Office					
		Quarter 1 Plan ($000)	Quarter 2 Plan ($000)	Quarter 3 Plan ($000)	Quarter 4 Plan ($000)	Total Year Plan ($000)

		Quarter 1 Plan ($000)	Quarter 2 Plan ($000)	Quarter 3 Plan ($000)	Quarter 4 Plan ($000)	Total Year Plan ($000)
Income						
	Consulting	339.0	333.8	368.2	526.2	1,567
	Education	263.5	259.5	270.6	414.0	1,207
	Custom development	724.1	776.6	745.7	862.1	3,109
	Product support	377.4	414.5	473.8	533.8	1,800
	Systems integration	921.4	2,104.9	1.380.5	1,689.9	6,097
	Labor	2,062.0	2,243.0	2,310.0	3,294.0	9,909
	Nonlabor	563.5	1,646.3	928.7	732.0	3,870
	TOTAL INCOME	2,625.5	3,889.3	3,238.7	4,026.0	13,779
Direct Cost						
	Direct comp	634.2	695.3	840.2	1,009.2	3,179
	Other direct costs	205.8	205.5	252.8	165.9	830
	Borrowed labor	198.5	198.5	198.5	198.5	794
	Vendor labor	357.6	357.6	357.6	422.6	1,495
	DIRECT LABOR	1,396.0	1,456.9	1,649.1	1,796.1	6,298
	Direct travel	116.0	131.1	137.4	216.8	601
	Transfer cost	179.4	179.4	217.4	236.4	813
	Vendor product	142.5	941.3	360.0	123.8	1,568
	Nonlabor apportion	25.9	24.4	26.0	24.6	101
	DIRECT NONLABOR	463.8	1,276.2	740.8	601.5	3,082
	TOTAL DIRECT COST	1,859.8	2,733.1	2,389.9	2,397.7	9,380
	Gross Profit	765.7	1,156.2	848.8	1,628.4	4,399
	Margin	29%	30%	26%	40%	32%
Indirect Expense						
	Marketing comp	84.8	103.5	114.0	113.5	416
	Marketing expenses	45.3	60.5	56.2	55.1	217
	SELLING	130.1	164.1	170.1	168.6	633
	Admin comp	42.7	48.0	63.1	58.0	212
	Office services	11.9	11.9	11.9	11.9	48
	Facilities	40.7	39.0	48.2	45.6	173
	Business comp serv	52.5	77.8	64.8	80.5	276
	ADMINISTRATION	147.7	176.7	187.9	196.0	708
	OTHER INDIRECT	27.3	27.3	27.3	27.3	109
	INDIRECT EXP TOTAL	305.2	368.1	385.4 .	391.9	1,451
	Net Earnings (NEBA)	460.5	788.1	463.5	1,236.4	2,949
	Margin	18%	20%	14%	31%	21%
Allocated Expense	TOTAL	393.8	583.4	485.8	603.9	2,067
	Net Earnings (NEBT)	66.7	204.8	−22.4	632.5	882
	Margin	3%	5%	−1%	16%	6%

segmentation by business type. For our systems integration office, labor revenue (and corresponding resources) are distributed as follows.

- Consulting: 15 percent
- Education: 12 percent
- Custom development: 30 percent
- Product support: 8 percent
- Systems integration: 35 percent

This distribution when both labor and nonlabor generated revenue are combined is as follows.

- Consulting: 11 percent
- Education: 9 percent
- Custom development: 23 percent
- Product support: 13 percent
- Systems integration: 44 percent

The best way to keep this distortion from diluting the effectiveness of revenue, utilization, backlog, and productivity measurements is to treat labor and nonlabor as two separate businesses. We already know that they represent $9.9 million and $3.9 million revenue streams. Their relative costs are easy to pick out; they are $6.3 million and $3.1 million, respectively. This means we are getting a 36 percent gross profit on labor and 21 percent on nonlabor (this compares favorably to the 37 percent we are getting for labor in our complex services office and 38 percent in a basic services office).

For net profit computation, we will simply distribute expense by revenue. As a result, our NEBA and NEBT for labor and nonlabor are 25 percent, 10 percent, 21 percent, and –4 percent. By keeping these separate, the office executive can make decisions for the higher margin labor business based on continued use of utilization, backlog, and productivity tools. The nonlabor business is one of forecasting and managing milestones that bring large revenue payments. Nonlabor profitability also requires careful coordination and timing of expense.

The spreadsheets in the figures make business separation for systems integration much easier. We discussed the only real difficulty in Chapter 4—separating the two when they are part of fixed-price payments. Hopefully this discussion shows that a good estimate of the relative parts of fixed-price payment is all that is needed. We will look later at how pricing data helps this estimate.

MANAGING PROFIT

The planning exercise just completed is the prelude to managing profit. The real work begins by the end of the first quarter and continues through the eleventh month. Recording of actual revenue and expense is a monthly control activity. The frequency of analyzing profit depends upon the business mix and effectiveness of revenue and utilization controls. Profitability analysis will need to be performed:

- After February for all offices of any mix to determine whether cost and expense assumptions are holding true. Key areas of concern are changes to annualized employee benefit costs, increases in rental or occupancy rates, and changes in business computer service charges. Very often these changes do not show up until the end of February as headquarters functions debate final budgets through January and beyond.

- After March, June, and September for those basic and complex services offices that have disciplined revenue and utilization management and have very little fixed-price engagement billing.

- Every two months for those with over 25 percent fixed price billing, but less than 5 percent from nonlabor.

- Every month after February for all others.

Tracking Actual Profit

The income and expense spreadsheet serves as a monthly profit tracking mechanism. Actual billed revenue is bridged or transcribed from the final detailed billing report and is broken down by labor and nonlabor. Later we will discuss the further distribution of revenue by resource type for pricing and productivity purposes. Expense is bridged or transcribed from detailed expense ledger reports.

Two examples of actual income and expense performance are given here. These correspond to the two actual utilization examples in Chapter 5: a first quarter business slowdown with a partial recovery in the second quarter (Figure 5-7) and an inability to hire or transfer enough professionals in a strong demand market (Figure 5-8), respectively.

We reported on utilization data in the seventh week of the year (mid-May). Our profit data in this chapter will be as of the last monthly cycle, or the end of April. Each of the two spreadsheets shows actual income and expenses for the full first quarter, the year to date (through April), and for April itself. The plan base for both of these actual performance examples is the growth plan described in Figures 6-9 to 6-11.

Executive decisions resulting from revenue and profit problems are greatly influenced by how one is paid. We will assume that the management staff is compensated for both revenue and profit, while the marketing staff is compensated for revenue and backlog. The profit measurement will be on net earnings before allocation (NEBA) and the plan numbers are the performance expectations.

Effect of a business downturn on profit.   As you recall from our first utilization scenario, the first quarter ends with consultant utilization down an average of 10 percent against plan, but has come back to be only 3 percent under plan by the seventh week of the second quarter. In fact, utilization has reached a comfortable 75 percent in the third week of May, but vacation season is about to take its toll.

We have reduced our staff by three contractors and one of our borrowed people. We were unable to disengage from hiring and transfer commitments through April 1. We gave requirements to college recruiting and four offers have been made on our behalf.

Our staff, particularly contractors and borrowed people, is working at or above capacity as of last week. We can expect that both revenue and profit are well below plan and it will be very unlikely that we can make our annual revenue objective. We need to know whether we can make our profit margin against the reduced revenue and use this information to further evaluate our choices from Chapter 5.

As can be seen in Figure 6-13, year-to-date income is down by 16 percent through the first quarter. April saw $684,000 in revenue which is up 13 percent from the average for each of the previous months, but is still only 87 percent of the average revenue needed from each month in the second quarter. Year-to-date (YTD) gross and net profit (NEBA) are 24 percent and 10 percent, respectively, against corresponding expectations of approximately 33 percent and 23 percent.

NEBA margin for April is up 1 percent over the first quarter. In a professional services business, it is very difficult to see trends from one month of financial data, but the second quarter does appear much improved. April had relocation costs for the last two interns. By spreading that over the entire quarter, April's net would grow to 22 percent, two points below plan. Revenue is at 77 percent of a flat plan (dividing annual objective by 12 equal monthly amounts). This is more like 80 percent of the real plan, since 53 percent of the revenue was planned for the second half of the year.

FIGURE 6–13
Actual Income and Expense in a Business Downturn

Actual Income & Expense During a Business Downturn

		Quarter 1 Plan ($000)	Quarter 1 Actual ($000)	Quarter 2 Plan ($000)	Quarter 2 Actual ($000)	Quarter 3 Plan ($000)	Quarter 3 Actual ($000)	Quarter 4 Plan ($000)	Quarter 4 Actual ($000)	Total Year Plan ($000)	Total Year YTD ($000)	April ($000)
Income												
	Consulting	447.2	369.5	529.4	527.3	631.3		2,135		503		133.6
	Education	289.8	210.3	312.0	290.8	323.1		1,216		291		81.2
	Custom development	1,428.6	1,230.6	1,520.3	1,485.3	1,862.2		6,296		1,700		469.0
	Labor	2,092.0	1,704.0	2,282.0	2,225.0	2,723.0		9,322		2,357		653.0
	Nonlabor	73.6	106.4	79.6	78.3	93.6		325		137		30.8
	TOTAL INCOME	2,165.6	1,810.4	2,361.6	2,303.3	2,816.6		9,647		2,494		683.8
Direct Cost												
	Direct comp	634.2	581.4	695.3	802.7	804.6		2,937		799		217.4
	Other direct costs	206.5	195.8	206.0	146.4	116.5		675		341		144.9
	Borrowed labor	198.5	186.1	198.5	148.9	148.9		695		241		54.7
	Vendor labor	353.2	310.3	353.2	353.2	353.2		1,413		396		86.1
	DIRECT LABOR	1,392.4	1,273.6	1,452.9	1,451.2	1,423.2		5,720		1,777		503.1
	Direct travel	52.3	79.0	57.5	56.4	69.4		236		101		22.4
	Transfer cost	8.4	9.4	8.4	8.4	8.4		34		13		3.1
	Nonlabor apportion	10.6	11.3	9.8	10.6	10.0		41		16		5.1
	DIRECT NONLABOR	71.3	99.7	75.7	75.4	87.8		310		130		30.6
	TOTAL DIRECT COST	1,463.7	1,373.3	1,528.6	1,526.6	1,511.0		6,030		1,907		533.7
	Gross Profit	701.9	437.1	833.0	776.7	1,305.6		3,617		587		150.1
	Margin	32%	24%	35%	34%	46%		37%		24%		22%
Indirect Expense												
	Marketing comp	56.7	48.1	56.4	57.2	56.9		227		63		15.3
	Marketing expenses	35.3	41.9	41.3	36.0	33.6		146		57		14.9
	SELLING	92.0	90.0	97.7	93.2	90.4		373		120		30.2
	Admin comp	38.1	37.3	43.4	43.6	38.9		164		48		11.2
	Office services	11.9	6.3	11.9	11.9	11.9		48		7		0.6
	Facilities	40.7	44.2	38.6	43.7	38.5		161		58		14.0
	Business comp serv	43.3	43.4	47.2	46.1	56.3		193		49		5.4
	ADMINISTRATION	133.9	131.3	141.0	145.3	145.6		566		162		31.1
	OTHER INDIRECT	27.3	26.0	27.3	27.3	27.3		109		34		8.2
	INDIRECT EXP TOTAL	253.2	247.2	266.0	265.8	263.4		1,048		317		69.6
	Net Earnings (NEBA)	448.7	189.8	567.0	510.9	1,042.2		2,569		270		80.5
	Margin	21%	10%	24%	22%	37%		27%		11%		12%
Allocated Expense	TOTAL	324.8	298.7	354.2	345.5	422.5		1,447		299		112.8
	Net Earnings (NEBT)	123.8	-108.9	212.7	165.4	619.7		1,122		-28		-32.3
	Margin	6%	-6%	9%	7%	22%		12%		-1%		-5%

Consulting and education have suffered most in the downturn due to increases and a view by clients that they are now discretionary activities. Travel is higher as the office goes farther afield to find business. The rate increases have been deferred and average rates have actually decreased slightly.

The beginning of the year has also brought its customary good news and bad news. Facility costs in our local area have gone up an additional $5 per square foot. Benefits are slightly lower than plan assumptions, and contractor rates have gone down in our area, due to the slump. Allocated expense is running at a higher percentage of revenue than planned, but this does not concern our executive who is measured on NEBA (it will have some effect on pricing later this year, as we will discuss later).

Our first question: Can this office make a profit margin of 27 percent NEBA (its objective) against a reduced revenue objective? A spreadsheet analysis shows that if the office stays with the people it currently has and the utilization it is currently getting, it will end the year at 25 percent NEBA against 86 percent of its revenue plan. This assumes that utilization will get back to plan for the second half of the year and bonuses (commissions) are reduced commensurate with lower revenue and profit.

Further action and a little luck is required. If all four college graduates accept our offers (or cannot be diverted to another office), there is little we can do to make profit. If none of the four are hired, we will make our 27 percent NEBA against 86 percent of revenue.

If two accept our offers, we should then take two other actions that will improve profit. We can drop all temporary administrative personnel and ask managers to spend their weekends and evenings performing business control tasks. Secondly, we can reduce all remaining education by 50 percent. Both of these are unpleasant, increase risk, and can reduce business flexibility. The actions also may mean survival for this year.

On the positive side, demand may continue to increase. The office can carefully add contractors and borrowed people at least back to the levels before the downturn. If done before the end of the third quarter, the office can probably make over 90 percent of its revenue and bring back administrative support.

Meeting its revenue target is still a big jump. Increasing utilization to the levels needed risks attrition at a time the office can least afford it. The costs of hiring in the latter part of the year are rarely compensated by enough increased revenue by year end. Adding large numbers of contractors is even more risky and invites high levels of rework and client dissatisfaction. This office should not be driven to grow this year, much as its executives might be tempted to do so.

Clearly, the choice here was profit. The office sacrificed some of the future by delaying the hiring of fresh, young talent. It lost some compensation by choosing not to drive for an out of reach revenue goal. Clearly the choice here is to live to fight another day.

Effect of slow hiring on profit. The other scenario we discussed in Chapter 5 deals with the decisions in an office where demand is high, but new staff is not available fast enough. The office has been unable to find qualified professionals to hire (the plan called for three by May 1), and has only been able to transfer in two of four people from the parent company (and these two will require considerable retraining). In the meantime, average utilization of the staff has zoomed to 87 percent in the middle of May.

The year-to-date income and expense for this office is illustrated by Figure 6-14. As we expected, revenue is under plan (88 percent of a flat plan and approximately 90 percent of a seasonal plan). We would expect profit to be well ahead of plan, and gross profit is running 2 percent above expectation, but NEBA is not. We are not generating enough revenue to carry indirect expense. April NEBA was very healthy, but again one month of information is not reliable.

Custom development has suffered the most from the lack of additional people. High demand has allowed us to implement our rate increases and we are increasing our average rates at all levels. Unfortunately, the demand is encouraging our contractors to increase their rates also. Again, the increased allocation has caused our NEBT to be lower.

At current head count levels, 3 percent higher overall utilization, slightly higher rates, and no additional contractors, the office will finish the year at $9.1 million (94 percent of plan). Assuming it continues on its plan to hire four college graduates, this will translate to a 27.3 percent NEBA versus a 26.6 percent NEBA (the decimal places start to become important). This allows for the higher profit bonuses. As can be seen, the higher utilization and rates barely carry the overhead of the office at these lower revenue levels.

If the office can get a combination of five contractors and borrowed people under contract by the end of the third quarter, the office can make its revenue objective and bring in nearly 30 percent in NEBA. The profit would actually be $355,000 more than the profit currently in the plan. The executive of this office can use these as investment funds and still be able to deliver needed earnings to the firm.

Approximately 20 percent should be used to go back to the campuses and hire more college people. Another 5 percent to 10 percent should be used to increase education among the staff by reducing their use in marketing activities. Twenty percent can be used to add a marketer to make up for the loss of consultant resource, with the express purpose of finding large projects for next year.

FIGURE 6–14
Actual Income and Expense During Slow Staffing

Actual Income & Expense During Staffing Difficulties

	Quarter 1 Plan ($000)	Quarter 1 Actual ($000)	Quarter 2 Plan ($000)	Quarter 2 Actual ($000)	Quarter 3 Plan ($000)	Quarter 3 Actual ($000)	Quarter 4 Plan ($000)	Quarter 4 Actual ($000)	Total Year Plan ($000)	YTD ($000)	April ($000)
Income											
Consulting	447.2	437.8	529.4		527.3		631.3		2,135	609	171.0
Education	289.8	291.2	312.0		290.8		323.1		1,216	395	103.5
Custom development	1,428.6	1,380.7	1,520.3		1,485.3		1,862.2		6,296	1,829	447.9
Labor	2,092.0	2,047.0	2,282.0		2,225.0		2,723.0		9,322	2,748	701.0
Nonlabor	73.6	62.6	79.6		78.3		93.6		325	84	21.4
TOTAL INCOME	2,165.6	2,109.6	2,361.6		2,303.3		2,816.6		9,647	2,832	722.4
Direct Cost											
Direct comp	634.2	623.0	695.3		802.7		804.6		2,937	830	206.8
Other direct costs	206.5	188.1	206.0		146.4		116.5		675	206	18.3
Borrowed labor	198.5	205.1	198.5		148.9		148.9		695	273	67.5
Vendor labor	353.2	357.6	353.2		353.2		353.2		1,413	476	117.9
DIRECT LABOR	1,392.4	1,373.8	1,452.9		1,451.2		1,423.2		5,720	1,784	410.4
Direct travel	52.3	41.8	57.5		56.4		69.4		236	56	14.4
Transfer cost	8.4	9.4	8.4		8.4		8.4		34	13	3.2
Nonlabor apportion	10.6	11.4	9.8		10.6		10.0		41	16	5.1
DIRECT NONLABOR	71.3	62.5	75.7		75.4		87.8		310	85	22.6
TOTAL DIRECT COST	1,463.7	1,436.4	1,528.6		1,526.6		1,511.0		6,030	1,869	433.0
Gross Profit	701.9	673.2	833.0		776.7		1,305.6		3,617	963	289.4
Margin	32%	32%	35%		34%		46%		37%	34%	40%
Indirect Expense											
Marketing comp	56.7	59.6	56.4		57.2		56.9		227	76	16.2
Marketing expenses	35.3	34.5	41.3		36.0		33.6		146	46	11.2
SELLING	92.0	94.2	97.7		93.2		90.4		373	122	27.4
Admin comp	38.1	38.9	43.4		43.6		38.9		164	51	11.9
Offices services	11.9	11.6	11.9		11.9		11.9		48	15	3.3
Facilities	40.7	44.4	38.6		43.7		38.5		161	58	13.2
Business comp serv	43.3	44.3	47.2		46.1		56.3		193	49	5.0
ADMINISTRATION	133.9	139.1	141.0		145.3		145.6		566	173	33.4
OTHER INDIRECT	27.3	29.0	27.3		27.3		27.3		109	38	9.1
INDIRECT EXP TOTAL	253.2	262.3	266.0		265.8		263.4		1,048	332	69.9
Net Earnings (NEBA)	448.7	410.9	567.0		510.9		1,042.2		2,569	630	219.5
Margin	21%	19%	24%		22%		37%		27%	22%	30%
Allocated Expense TOTAL	324.8	348.1	354.2		345.5		422.5		1,447	348	119.2
Net Earnings (NEBT)	123.8	62.8	212.7		165.4		619.7		1,122	282	100.3
Margin	6%	3%	9%		7%		22%	12%	10%	14%	

There is one note of caution. The increase in allocated expense is a potential conflict for the office that is able to exceed its NEBA objective. The top of the business may want to get part of their lost NEBT back. It is well to plan to spend enough of the windfall to position the office for growth, but be prepared to make a contribution to overall firm profits as well.

Given the opportunities of this office, a decision to simply make the profit plan would be very conservative. An entrepreneur in this situation does not give up on growth. Eventually, people will become available. Continuing to expand the client base and the breadth of one's staff will pay off when that happens.

Expense Controls

We discussed earlier that profit is bimonthly or quarterly in many businesses. This can be the case when they have good revenue and utilization controls. They also need good expense controls. An office can't wait one to two months to find out what errors have been made in expense transactions. Most business systems report expenses on a monthly expense ledger that is audited locally to discover errors. If the expense process is prone to error, the correction process may also be the same. It can be very frustrating to try to analyze profitability knowing that expense data is still in question.

The best defense against expense errors becoming a confusing blur is to have a disciplined weekly expense control process that focuses on those transactions that are most likely to distort profit. As will be seen, such an expense control process not only reduces uncertainty about expenses already incurred, it increases consciousness about expenses yet to occur.

Three categories of expense require constant inspection and scrutiny.

• **Employee reimbursed expenses.** These are incidental expenses for travel, supplies, meeting arrangements, and entertainment that are incurred by the employee (either directly or through credit cards) and must be both reimbursed and distributed. Distribution will be to direct travel if for a specific engagement travel expense or to employee travel: direct cost, if consultant and management; indirect expense, if marketing and administration.

Comprehensive identification of the purpose of an expense is not the first priority of a busy consultant. In fact, simply getting a consultant to complete an expense reimbursement request for monies owed to them can be a frustrating exercise for management and administration. The advent of company credit cards (where the bill is paid by the firm, not the employee) has made the expense control problem even worse. The only workable process is to make the weekly completion of labor and time recording, weekly status reports and expense reimbursement accounting a ritualistic activity that all do every week, and for which one gets points on a performance evaluation when done regularly.

The real problem occurs when this high-volume accounting activity is entered into the expense reimbursement system and makes its way into the expense ledger. A typical office may have 20 to 30 of these per week and some will inevitably be charged to the wrong accounts. More than half contain expenses direct to an engagement, which may trigger compensating billable charges to a client in the next billing period. The consultant who completes the expense reimbursement may not know the appropriate coding that ensures correct distribution of the expense.

Ultimately, the general ledger expense detail (and billing detail for the recoverable expenses) will need to be reconciled against the original expense account. This can be very time consuming, particularly when it only represents about 4 percent of the total expense of an office. As we will discuss, there are some techniques that will spread the workload and make the accuracy commensurate with the time spent.

• **Intrafirm expense transfers.** An office in a medium to large firm sees tens to hundreds of individual internal charges to its expense ledger each month from other units in the firm. These are for rent, services, supplies, telecommunications, education, and a number of other support functions to an office that is part of a greater corporate entity. The charges are initiated by units outside of the office, and only become known when the expense system reports them on the ledger. In many cases, erroneous charges can only be corrected or reversed if identified immediately. Those that are regular in nature can be compared against the plan after February and usually require little further attention.

Two types of charges are not regular and require close attention—debits for the salary recovery of personnel borrowed by an office from another unit and transfer charges for products and materials that generate nonlabor income from engagements. Typically, these charges are irregular, significant, and often occur asynchronously.

For example, four people borrowed from a center work 1,200 hours over two months in the second quarter. The office receives $190,000 in revenue for their efforts. Their center waits until late in the third quarter to transfer (debit) $108,000 in salary recovery to our office. Profit will appear to be 4 percent better at midyear than it really is. An aggressive entrepreneur will invest profits to expand. This one is due a third quarter surprise.

The same scenario can be played the other way. A $100,000 product transfer charge prior to its corresponding revenue might bring unnecessary and time consuming focus on a profitability situation that doesn't exist.

Some expense ledger systems provide a daily or weekly view of debits (and credits) that are accumulating against the current month's books. Many do not, and most issuers of the debits seem to wait until the end of the month to enter them, anyway. On the other hand, the office knows when the expense is committed: when the borrowed person completes a labor claiming or expense recovery document and when the product or materials are received. As we will see, these are opportune times to get control of the expense long before the actual charge is felt.

• **Vendor payments.** Similar to internal charges, some vendor charges for office services and supplies are regular and require little scrutiny. There are, however, significant vendor payments that are not regular and require close control. These are for contracted labor and vendor supplied products and services that require compensating billing to clients. These have the same expense to revenue timing problems. They also may have been incorrectly billed or incorrectly paid. This means that both their invoices and subsequent payments need scrutiny.

Many firms have subcontractors administer their labor distribution just as though they are employee consultants. It falls to the sophistication of the contract management and billing business system to determine whether the time is billed directly to the client or becomes part of the accumulated hours of a fixed price or other indirectly billed activity. This usually requires contracted people to fill out two labor distributions each week—one for the firm to bill the engagement and one for their home firm. The invoice from the vendor is then reviewed for discrepancies.

An invoice from a vendor for service or product usually requires a direct distribution to one or more engagements and the triggering of a compensating revenue billing activity. Professional services offices try to avoid building asset inventory of vendor products and usually have arrangements where the product remains in vendor stock until shipped to the firm or client for immediate use or installation. In any event, the action of paying the invoice and billing the client are two separate actions, one based upon fair dealing with the vendor and its cash needs and the other based upon contractual terms with the client. The two may not come together.

The more difficult control problem for these large individual expenses is the built-in delays in a firm's accounts payable process. Typically, a vendor will invoice within 30 days of the delivery of the people, service, or product. The firm's accounts payable process (including approval of the invoice by the local office) may take another 30 to 60 days. This means that the actual expense will not occur until some time after the corresponding service performance event and its compensating revenue action. For a business that incurs most of its expense in direct relation to revenue, this administrative delay can be very misleading.

Each of these expense anomalies can be managed with a simple expense log. Maintaining a local log is likely a duplication of the services provided by the firm's expense ledger system and is probably a duplicate entry. It is well worth it, though, to avoid the timing issues just listed. Using simple data base software, data entry will be quick and the local lists that can be produced will actually make expense auditing less time consuming. Most importantly, it provides an accurate and current list of all committed expenses, regardless of whether they are to be in the ledger for this month.

Figure 6-15 is an example of such a log. Each employee expense claim, time record for borrowed or contracted people, receipt of internal material/product, and invoice for vendor people, services, or product is listed in the log. The log contains coding information that will allow sorting and selecting of the items as they will ultimately appear on the detailed expense ledger for easy audit. Additionally, the record contains the engagement to which a direct expense applies and the month in which the compensating revenue should appear. Where hours are involved, the record contains enough information to reconcile labor claiming records against internal transfers or vendor invoices.

The log contains some items that appear on the billing detail illustrated in Figure 4-6. The expected expenses for contractors, such as Kong and borrowed people, such as Ranklynn contain hours as well as amounts. Transfers also show from where the transfer is expected for sorting and selection purposes. Notice that an invoice to Vaporware for an expense incurred and correspondingly billed to a client three months ago was overpaid by $20,000. The log becomes the means to track the delay between an expense being incurred and the actual expense appearing in the ledger. In the event that the actual expense in the ledger is incorrect and a corresponding remedy action is taken, another entry is made in the log that awaits confirmation of the correction.

Each month, the log is compared to the ledger and marked when found. Those remaining or in error become information to the profit analysis process. This reduces the surprises and gives a clearer picture of actual profit performance.

Other uses of the log are as follows.

- **Expense accrual.** Those expenses for which revenue has been generated, but which are not in the expense ledger can be accrued. These are fully reversed each month and do not appear in the last statement of the year. The expense list in November provides a clue to any expenses that might carry over into next year's plan.

FIGURE 6-15
Local Expense Control Log

Expense Control Log

In Dept	In Account	Engage No	Contr No	Out Dept	Out Account	Amount	Date Incur	Date Logged	Invoice Month	Ledger Month	Name	Description	Invoice Amount	Acc?	Trouble?
		A3577	B4799	ZEN	92-0043	$37,886.22	911227	911231	9112	9202	Vaporware	Product-Vaccine	$49,850.00		Pd-#39,886.22
LLJ	13-1289	A4599	C4879	ZEN	92-0542	$22,800.00	920201	920114	9202		Internal	Product-Sawyer	$30,000.00		
		A2183	B9899	ZEN	92-0521	$36,950.00	920122	920122	9202		Rock Constr	Vendor-Surf Sand	$47,000.00		
		A4599	C9622	ZEN	92-0524	$1,564.00	920124	920124		9202	Person Tech	Kong 17.0 hours			
BMV	75-0612	B0006	C8420	ZEN	92-0612	$1,465.33	920207	920207	9202		Ranklynn	Travel-Waffle	$1,465.33		
		A2183	B9899	ZEN	92-0521	$96,915.00	920212	920212	9202		NetNet	Vendor-Surf Sand	$124,250.00		
		A9908	C0006	ZEN	92-0612	$1,429.90	920217	920214	9202		Aholic	Travel-Vermin	$1,743.78		
		A4599	C2930	ZEN	92-0612	$852.27	920207	920217	9202		Anbehold	Travel-Sawyer Rafts	$1,002.67		
		A2183	B9899	ZEN	94-0543	$25,688.00	920315	920217	9202		Sand Software	Product-Surf Sand	$33,800.00	Y	
		A4599	C2930	ZEN	92-0612	$751.66	920214	920224	9202		Anbehold	Travel-Sawyer Rafts	$844.56		
BMV	75-0677	B0006	C8420	ZEN	92-0677	$3,735.00	920221	920227	9202		Ranklynn	41.5 hours			
		A4599	C9622	ZEN	92-0612	$668.88	920221	920228	9202		Kong	Travel-Sawyer	$777.77		
BMV	75-0612	B0006	C8420	ZEN	92-0612	$1,227.78	920228	920228	9202		Ranklynn	Travel-Waffle	$1,227.78		
		A9908	C0006	ZEN	92-0524	$10,172.50	920228	920228			Person Tech	Barnum 156.5 hours			Y
		A4599	C0006	ZEN	92-0524	$1,196.00	920228	920228			Person Tech	Kong 13 hours			Y

- **Supplier relations.** It is always helpful in negotiations with suppliers (internal and vendor) to know up to the minute charges they have issued. A list of past and current expenses is a helpful tool when there are delays and inaccuracies in the systems and processes of both firms.

Three significant areas of expense have been ignored in this discussion—salary, commissions, and benefits. Clearly these major expenses need scrutiny, but in a different way. These expenses are usually a result of activity in payroll and billing systems. We discussed commissions audit in Chapter 4 and it is not to be taken lightly. Payroll data control is a key people management responsibility of all first line managers. Payroll changes (pay rate, reporting unit, tax location, etc.) require promptness and accuracy. When they are inaccurate, salary and benefit expense accrual may become a necessity.

Expense control does not need to be a second decimal place accuracy process (as long as significant expenses are audited eventually to ensure fair dealings with vendors and employees). The purpose is to avoid distortions in net profit computation and corresponding incorrect actions. Plus or minus a few thousand is not going to make much difference when it takes tens of thousands to influence profit.

PRICING

The quality of the price of a professional services engagement has a great influence on its success. A price that adequately compensates the firm is one that allows for flexible management and will cover many mistakes. When the price doesn't cover all the real work, doesn't anticipate all of the actual kinds of resources needed, and doesn't anticipate the real risk, it will be at the root of many bad decisions and mismanagement.

A price should allow the person or the team to focus on getting the work done to the client's satisfaction. A good price results from a thorough effort to bring together all facts and suppositions about an engagement. It reflects an assessment of the width in the range of least cost and most cost to complete the work. It reflects a conscious decision to be or to not be profitable to get the business, while being realistic in what will actually be needed to perform successfully.

Pricing of professional services has two independent components—estimating and valuation. Estimating is the determination of resources needed to perform the engagement, and valuation is the determination of the amount and method of charge to the client.

A number of fine works have been written on the subject of project management and most deal extensively with the subject of estimating. All to often, though, we ignore our guru's on this subject and focus only on valuation, using what we think the market will bear as our basis. There is nothing wrong with making a market-based decision on price. The business management error is in not doing the estimating work needed to assess the real effort. Everyone needs to be prepared to support the work and be aware of how the engagement will really affect profitability.

In the following discussion, we will spend a moment on estimating to carry forward important points from other sources and then focus in more depth on valuation. The relative treatment of the two subjects is in no way intended to represent their relative importance. A bad price almost always starts with a bad estimate, while a good estimate is the first step toward the successful management of an engagement.

Estimating

In its final form, an estimate is a scheduled list of people, travel events, and nonlabor product and service expenses that will be needed to successfully meet the client's expectation for an engagement. As is discussed extensively in the texts on this subject, an estimate is rarely a single finite quantity for any of these components. In fact, the most useful estimates are a range of the optimal and worst case quantities of each of these over the scheduled life of the effort.

The amount of work needed to develop an estimate is directly proportional to how much is known about the effort. A strategic design effort, where very little is known concerning the outcome beyond who to talk to is less work to estimate than that for building a very specific information system based on a design document. In the first case, the client has little tangible expectation of the final product and is prepared to accept a wide range in estimated work and schedule, as long as a creditable process is executed to get to the work done. In the second case, the client has a very finite expectation of the end product and is probably comparing firms on the detail of their understanding of the work involved and their relative productivity in getting the job done.

Engagements are usually multiple phases. The first phase takes what was learned prior to the engagement and produces detail that supports refined estimating of the next phase. The first phase can likely be estimated within a range of plus or minus 10 percent of the work and risks. A second phase is usually an extrapolation of the first and may range plus or minus 100 percent. An extrapolated third phase will often range from 500 percent to 1,000 percent.

The tasks to be performed on a small engagement and those on a large engagement are usually very similar and their estimates may look very alike. Only the size and duration is different. Both will have detailed tasks listed for the first phase and will use extrapolation for other phases. The effect of wide ranges in the small estimate tend not to have the sticker shock of those same ranges (percentages) on large engagements.

The first phase estimates must be backed by a detailed description of documentation to be produced, the detailed steps (tasks) needed to get to those end products and have them accepted by the client, the number of hours (optimum and worst case) needed to execute the steps, the type of person needed to execute each step, and a network diagram that determines the calendar needed to efficiently and safely complete the phase. Each task estimate is backed by a count of the "things" that compose the work in that task. These may be interviews to be performed, meetings to be attended, functions to be documented, orientation and training sessions to be conducted, or screens and reports to be designed. Finally, the estimate is summarized into a schedule of milestones for view by the client and into the form just described for valuation.

The estimate for the second phase will be backed by any of a variety of data that are input to estimating models used by the firm. Most extrapolate from the first phase. Many are based on counts of elements that might make up the final process installed and used by the client. The accuracy and usability of later phase estimating models is one of the key success factors for a large professional services firm. These models are most effective when they are based upon empirical data collected from a variety of engagements and compute both the optimum and worst case levels of resource needed to execute the phase.

These extrapolation techniques are also used to qualify a client's ability to pay during early marketing of an engagement. Simply knowing that a client will continue to talk when faced with a price at the upper end of an extrapolation range (or won't talk at the lowest end) is a significant step forward toward building an agreement.

Marketing qualification using extrapolation techniques is not estimating. All of the detailed work toward the estimating items just discussed is still left to do. The secret is to use a qualification range that makes the real estimate seem low.

Price Valuation

Price valuation is performed in two steps. The first is the bottom up computation that builds cost and return around the resource estimate to determine the best financial price. The second is the reconciliation of the best market price to the financial price when they differ.

Most firms have national pricing. The local field executive has varying degrees of authority to develop unique price valuations or to modify national pricing. Those with the least authority change estimates to get to a market price. Those with full authority to price to local cost and expense will change price valuation and profit expectation to get a market price. The key is how well each understood the process and how conscious they will be on how the real cost of the engagement will affect their profits.

The initial costing process is relatively straightforward and uses the income, expense, and utilization spreadsheets from this chapter and Chapter 5. We will be using the spreadsheet for Office D, our systems integration office, because it provides significant labor and nonlabor data. The exercise would be the same for any office we chose, only varying by the percentage of indirect expense that is allocated to labor and nonlabor.

The process is illustrated in Figure 6-16. Each component is listed. For labor we have our consultants and managers (direct staff), people we plan to borrow, and contractors. For nonlabor we have a vendor and travel. Using the planned costs for Office D divided by the planned hours in each labor resource category, we calculate a cost per hour. This is multiplied by estimated hours. We take the percentage of indirect expense that applies to labor (divided by the ratio of labor revenue to total revenue), divide that by the total planned hours for all labor resources, and get an indirect expense rate that we also multiply by the estimated hours.

The cost per hour for our own staff is weighted by the estimated distribution of trainee to manager people on the engagement. In this case we use consultant compensation as a base and weight associates and trainees lower and seniors and managers higher, based on the ratio of their compensation to that of consultants. Our total cost plus expense (burdened) amount for labor resources is $758,214 for 8,000 hours. At the bottom of the figure, the fully loaded cost per hour for each type of resource has been summarized. This is cost per *delivered* hour, not cost per available hour. In Chapter 8, we will examine the distinction between these and see how various decisions are affected by the use of both. Pricing is best served by the use of cost per delivered hour to obtain needed revenue per delivered hour.

The process to compute a nonlabor burdened cost is much the same, except the cost will be what we actually expect to pay for the travel and vendor. The indirect expense added to the resulting cost is applied based on how much our planned indirect expense for nonlabor (total indirect expense times nonlabor revenue divided by total revenue) must be carried by this engagement. This is simply the ratio of this cost to planned direct nonlabor cost times nonlabor indirect expense. We compute $975,001 burdened cost for nonlabor.

FIGURE 6-16
Computation of a Best Financial Price

			Price Components					
	Annual Cost ($000)	Annual Hours	Cost Per Hour	Weight	Hours	Labor Cost	Labor Burden	Total
Direct staff	$4,009	45,251	$88.59	1.012	4,500	$403,439	$61,875	$465,314
Borrowed	710	7,488	94.81	1.000	500	47,405	6,875	54,280
Contractor	1,495	22,724	65.79	1.000	3,000	197,370	41,250	238,620
			Total hours		8,000	Burdened labor cost		$758,214

Risk factor: Low (5%) for hourly, best effort   Profit (30%): $324,949
Medium (25%) for fixed price   Profit (50%): $758,214

Labor hourly price: $1,085,000; $135.50 per hour
Labor fixed price: $1,515,000

Nonlabor cost $843,000 (Vendor: $795,000)
(Travel: 48,000)
Nonlabor burden   132,001
Burdened nonlabor cost $975,001

Risk factor: Low for fixed price (10%)   Profit (30%): $417,858

Nonlabor price: $1,393,000

Labor weighting:

	Cost Factor	% of Hours	Weight
Trainee	.73	10%	.073
Associate	.80	30%	.240
Consultant	1.00	40%	.400
Senior	1.33	10%	.133
Manager	1.66	10%	.166
			1.012

Indirect expense factor = $13.75 per hour for labor

The estimates have been summarized for this engagement. They were likely laid out month by month and expressed in a range of optimum to maximum. This valuation exercise will be performed more than once to see what happens to the financial price when using different amounts of the range and inflation factors, if the schedule goes beyond this year. As would be expected, the later in the current year, the more deviation between planned and actual cost and expense. Most offices adjust their pricing with new factors about three times per year, with a fourth set predicting next year.

It is very important to make sure management time associated with delivery of nonlabor components is estimated as part of the overall management needed for the effort. Any materials and supplies should be in the nonlabor price component. That ensures that their risk and profit are considered correctly in our next step, regardless of whether they are in the final price.

Adding profit and risk is the subjective part of financial price valuation. As we discussed earlier, risk is the probability that these costs are low compared to what the effort will really cost. The profit uplift that we will use is the addition of the profit we normally expect after all cost and local indirect expense is covered, plus an amount to further hedge our risk.

Most firms have a formal risk assessment process. The purpose is to score the relative risk, based upon degrees of innovation, stability of technology, stability of the client's business, the number of decision makers, the length of the schedule, the slope of the resource manning curve, and the terms and conditions of payment and warranty. In most cases the risk is summarized as high, medium, or low, or a specific percentage. Its effect on the price is very subjective, and it usually depends on the judgment of very experienced professional services professionals.

Our planned NEBA for labor and nonlabor in Office D are 27 percent and 23 percent, respectively. The risk of not meeting our cost estimate for labor is 5 percent, if performed on a per hour, best effort basis, where we only risk rework. The risk rises to 25 percent, if we use a fixed price, where we might substantially overrun, if not managed and staffed very well. The risk of our vendor performing badly, requiring us to incur cost above vendor charges is 10 percent.

Quantification of the risk added to the profit is your choice. In this example, two-thirds of the risk is added to the price, reflecting a belief that the risk is in cost, not in expense. As a result, the profit for labor is 30 percent for hourly and 50 percent for fixed price, while the profit for nonlabor is 30 percent. The uplift is incorporated by simply dividing the burdened cost by one minus the decimal profit, and rounding to a nice presentable number. As a result our per hour rate would be $135.50 per hour or a fixed price of $1,515,000. We would like to charge $1,393,000 for nonlabor.

The next step in the valuation is to make the marketplace decision. We should have a reasonable understanding of the client's expectation (hopefully, we were the source of that expectation), what our competition might be offering, and the market price structure in general. If we don't like this price, there are a number of steps we can take.

- We can reduce the estimate by asking the client to do more. This is the most potent of choices in a noncompetitive situation and not out of the running when all competitive offers are higher than the client wanted. Most clients do not actually face the price performance question of using their own people versus that of a firm until they see the price. Asking them to add one person for a corresponding reduction in total price of around $150,000 to $200,000 might sound like a good face-saving choice.

- We can reduce the estimate by reducing the work. We can eliminate functions or we can eliminate end products. Every project has too many things to do for the price being charged. Most of those will be eliminated through change management during the effort. Some can be eliminated at the outset, if the price is too high.

- We can reduce the estimate by using a lower end of the estimate range. We will increase the risk accordingly, but often not in the same proportions. The risk of not making estimates is usually the risk of not managing changes to perfection. A high- or low-end estimate is usually equally makeable with good management (Parkinson's Law).

- We can change the financial computation by adding more contractors or more lower level direct staff. We will increase the risk, and that should be added back to the computation.

- We can reduce our profit. We can even make it negative. The decision is whether we want the business badly enough. If we take this approach, we should reset all of the other compromises we took, except delegating to the client. We must staff this effort as it requires and manage it as though we had received our higher price. If we reduce the resources to make back part of our lower profit, we will magnify the risk and its resulting cost overruns by amounts approaching infinity.

In our example, we still have to choose a payment schedule for the fixed-price option. It may be equal amounts each month, or it may be quarterly progress payments. Either way we should be paid for the vendor services on the same schedule that the vendor charges us. The hourly option may be broken out by each of our resource levels or in groupings. Many of these may be negotiated across the table from the client once our total price is agreed to.

As we mentioned earlier, an office needs to change its pricing factors at least three times per year. In October, the firm builds a set based on the actual plan and next year's preliminary plan. In February, these are updated based on first quarter actual expenses. In July, the factors are assessed again to see if the assumptions for the year are holding true.

Pricing is not an exact science, because estimating is not an exact science. The true value of this exercise is that we are being forced to continually revisit the cost structure of the office and the relative profitability of different resource and charge method options. The options offered barely scratch the surface of ways to meet the client's price demands and do not sacrifice the ability to be financially successful. Keeping records of hours, revenues, and expenses as illustrated in the last three chapters makes these choices meaningful and quantifiable.

COMPENSATING FOR PROFIT

Dividing up year-end profits among the top managers is a time honored tradition in the people services business. Most consulting firms are partnerships, where profit distribution is a right of ownership. The newer firms formed from parent corporations have had to design profit compensation for this new business, often different from corresponding incentives in their core businesses.

Distributing part of financial gain to managers makes sense as a way to increase their earnings proportional to benefits they bring to the success of the business. Profit is more than a financial measurement in services, though. It is a quality measurement.

Executives will not be consistently profitable, if they do not satisfy their clients by delivering qualified people, who communicate and manage well. Anyone can make short-term profit by charging under the market, staffing with less than the needed resources, providing less than the needed management, and delivering barely acceptable work. Over time, though, clients will either turn away (and they talk to each other) or will demand more than the office can afford to give. Making profit over the long term is a reflection of good performance and people management, rather than simply financial management.

For this reason, all managers in professional services should be compensated for profit contribution, not just owners. Profit compensation needs to be more than simply dividing year-end earnings. It should reward (or penalize) decisions made progressively throughout the year. It also needs to be in balance with revenue incentives.

A simple approach is to divide the management share of variable compensation into three parts for all managers and a fourth part for owners.

1. Approximately 40 percent of quarterly bonuses should go to all managers as an incentive for meeting revenue objectives as described in Chapter 4.

2. Approximately 40 percent of quarterly bonuses should go to all managers as an incentive for meeting current year-to-date NEBA objectives.

3. Approximately 20 percent of quarterly bonuses should go to all managers as a discretionary award for something special (major marketing win, completing a tough engagement, or solving a difficult employee issue).

4. For owners, a year-end distribution of overachievement of NEBA should occur. In our second example of profit tracking (office with staffing difficulties), bonuses were paid each quarter, the executive invested much of the projected 30 percent NEBA in more marketing and education, reserved some for the firm, and still had 1 percent of NEBA left over.

The quarterly payments for all but the award are advanced payments against the total year as also described in Chapter 4. The firm can choose to put the managers at risk by paying less than full salary and compensate for revenue and profit on a sliding scale that starts a little below 100 percent of quota achievement and moves upward at a rising curve (this blunts the effect of moderate underachievement and accelerates the effect of overachievement).

Compensating all managers for both profit and revenue growth causes a balance in driving for more business and settling for good business. It causes managers to satisfy clients without giving away the store at the end. It makes managers rely on the quality of their people, while making sure that their people are well utilized and well cared for.

MAKING MONEY

The purpose of this chapter was to provide a practical approach to recording income and expense for professional services; then to show how useful the information can be. The plan is important, because it forces the executive to make conscious choices among resources, pricing intent, and overall financial direction. Tracking is important, because it shows entrepreneurs how much latitude they have when their instinct says to charge or lay back. The chapter also intended to illustrate the maxim: If you don't have a plan, how will you know when you arrive?

Key points to consider from this chapter are:

- Profit measurements for professional services are simpler than those for products. Most of the cost and expense is incurred at service delivery, making it very practical to delegate profit authority.

- Net earnings before allocation (NEBA) is a useful measurement in a national firm with investment activities carried on by its headquarters.

NEBA insulates the local offices from financial actions that do not directly relate to profit delivery, and financial actions over which the office executive has no control.

- The frequency of profit analysis increases with diversity.
- Profit analysis and pricing are linked by the computation of cost per resource. Pricing is more dependent on good estimating than on accurate price valuation.

The few hours per month needed to keep a local office spreadsheet is a small price to pay for the confidence of knowing the probable effect of key decisions. Certainly, the office with the broader variety of services and personnel will have more to keep track of. On the other hand, this same data can take away much of the thrashing caused by guesswork and indecision on day-to-day pricing and resource actions. All offices ought to keep track of both hours and financial data. Successful entrepreneurs have confidence in their actions. Having the information when you need it gives that confidence.

Chapter 7

Backlog Management: Knowing When to Sell

B acklog provides near term revenue forecasting in professional services. Each active engagement in an office carries a commitment of funding from a client. The sum of these commitments forms a basis for predicting revenue.

Forecasting serves two purposes in a people services business. It confirms or denies the income plan and causes management to make corresponding decisions regarding expenditures. Secondly, it triggers an evaluation of marketing requirements. A rich forecast of revenue relieves pressure on short-term marketing. A lean forecast, particularly a lean near term forecast, suggests a serious look at marketing strength and effectiveness. It is on this second use of forecasting that we will be focusing our attention.

We need to separate the subjects of revenue planning and revenue forecasting. Planning, as covered in earlier chapters, uses people resource utilization to determine how much revenue can be generated by the office in the future. Planning assumes that the demand for these resources will be there when needed and that income is only constrained by supply. Forecasting considers demand from existing clients as its basis. If people are fully utilized, the forecast may be later reduced accordingly. Using the supply of available hours to develop a near term forecast is wishful thinking.

Revenue history is also not a particularly good basis for forecasting professional services. Previous buying patterns tell little in a business that is made up of unique engagements with clients. A previous engagement might be a guide to clients with similar needs, but it and all other engagements at the time tell us little about revenue potential in the future.

Backlog is the difference between how much funding clients have committed to our active engagements and how much we have invoiced. Backlog has four levels—contractually committed, funded, probable, and potential. Backlog can be expressed as a sum of all potential revenue or an adjusted amount for only the current year. Backlog can be expressed in both revenue and hours.

Marketing in professional services is performed by the managers (principals) of the office, dedicated marketers (very often a group of one), and that minimum amount of consultant time that an office may assign. Marketing levels are discretionary and the office executive needs tools that trigger changes to these levels. Backlog analysis is one of these tools.

Firms often provide compensation for building backlog. The purpose is to reward marketers for influencing clients into making larger funding commitments. This is particularly important when a firm is expanding into new territories, where committed backlog can justify aggressive hiring and relocations to build a staff.

We begin this chapter with a general discussion of marketing resources. We look at a way to assess marketing productivity. We then move to the computation of backlog and making adjustments to ensure that the computation is for near term client demand. The result will be a revenue forecast for the remainder of the current year. We will then use the result to assess whether marketing is generating enough new client funding as we invoice our engagements.

The chapter goes on to cover other subjects related to prospect tracking, making next month's forecast, using marketing information in weekly assignment reviews, and using backlog information for engagement reviews. At the end of the chapter we will take up the subject of backlog compensation.

MARKETING INVESTMENT DECISION

In the people services business, marketing is an investment activity. There needs to be a clear business case to increase the level of marketing in an office, and marketing expenditure should be quickly reduced when sustainable demand is strong. Office executives need two decision triggers built into their thought process.

- **What symptoms indicate a need to change levels of marketing?** The office needs an ongoing review and measurement process that determines whether marketing is creating tangible demand for the current and future resources of the office. This process needs to be simple, since good marketing people are not mentally conditioned to participate in administratively complicated practices.

- **What indicates that enough ergs of marketing energy are being applied?** The office executive must have a sense of how much marketing resource is needed to make a positive and lasting change to demand and to quickly stabilize or rein in the marketing investment when it has satisfied its purpose.

Ongoing Marketing

Every business has a base level of marketing activity and corresponding marketing expense. This subsistence level of marketing is not discretionary in normal conditions of demand. It is in place to keep the market for a firm's product and services refreshed with new buyers, as current ones run out. The people services business is no different.

Every professional services office has an ongoing level of marketing performed by the top manager (office executive, managing partner, practice leader) and one or more dedicated marketing people. Office executives typically spend 25 percent of their time in selling, over and above the influence time they spend with their clients while performing and managing engagements. Since most engagements are the result of follow-on work with existing clients, this selling and influence time of executives is the key to sustaining a steady practice.

Some offices perform all marketing with managers that split their time with people and engagement management. Others dedicate people to marketing, either experienced consultants or managers. Within this base marketing resource is the prospecting function of an office. It is the necessary time needed to meet and qualify new clients and to develop proposals. The time needed varies, but the function always has some work to do, be it following up on a lead or preparing an offer.

The highest level of dedicated marketing is in those offices that respond to bid requests. Many firms avoid formal bid situations just for this reason. Any firm whose clientele includes governments or government funded enterprises will need a large proposal generation resource. These clients require formal bids for all new and most follow-on engagements.

The level of marketing needed to sustain an office is determined through very inexact science. Chapter 10 refers to some excellent texts on the subject of professional services marketing. Each gives guidance on how much of the resource of an office should be devoted to marketing. In the discussion here, we will focus on testing whether results from marketing activity should trigger changes in the level of marketing regardless of whether it is above or below subsistence.

Sales Planning

A sale in professional services is the formal commitment of funding by a client. Sales planning establishes objectives for creating new funding commitments from clients as invoicing uses up previous commitments. For a steady-state business, sales need to equal the amount of invoicing for a year, and most offices build a sales plan that slightly exceeds the revenue plan for each quarter to be a little ahead in committed business.

In a growing business, increases in sales volumes need to anticipate increases in revenue volumes. Throughout this chapter we will be using our systems integration office as the example for marketing and backlog management. It provides a growth plan that demands higher than subsistence level marketing and it has a wide business mix to illustrate some of the unique characteristics of professional services forecasting.

The planned revenue by quarter for our systems integration office was $2.6 million, $3.9 million, $3.2 million, and $4 million. Since the plan was developed during the final quarter of the previous year, we can assume that sales in that period support our first quarter revenue need. We should build a sales plan that meets revenue needs one quarter ahead and that anticipates continuing growth into the next year. Sales for the first, second, and third quarters should be $3.9 million, $3.2 million, and $4 million, respectively. Since this is a 30 percent growth plan, the sales for the fourth quarter should be 30 percent higher than the revenue of this year's first quarter, or $3.4 million.

Notice that the sum of the four sales objectives equals $14.5 million, whereas our revenue objective for the year is $13.8 million. We are growing sales in anticipation of revenue growth by approximately three months. If we sell faster, we run the risk of needing people sooner than we can acquire or free them. This is still very conservative planning, since it builds a backlog of client commitments well in advance of revenue needs.

Tracking Marketing Activity

Sales tracking is the recording of sales performance against plan. In its simplest form, the track of sales is used to calculate whether new contract commitments add up to planned quarterly volumes. When sales fall behind for a full quarter, action is clearly warranted.

Tracking marketing activity serves other purposes, though. It provides a measure of marketing resource productivity. It makes visible the mix of opportunities and assignments that will face the people in an office and triggers actions to prepare the staff accordingly. As we will see later, it provides further information for the forecasting process.

The simplest and most universal technique for making marketing visible is an activity log that is updated weekly and lists every known marketing opportunity for the office. Figure 7-1 shows an example of such a log. It shows all client marketing situations that are active, with the newest identified situations grouped together (March). As you can see, the office has 13 deals working, has sold 1 this month, and has lost 1 this month. Notice also that the log contains all client marketing situations that were brought to conclusion over the previous three months, with the total sales for each of those months.

Marketing in this office is assigned to two dedicated people and to the management staff (the managers who own the responsibility to close a deal are indicated by an asterisk). In general the dedicated marketers have new clients, and managers have their existing clients. An exception might be a major proposal required for the next phase of an engagement, where the manager cannot commit the attention needed to lead the effort (Vermin Foods illustrates this situation).

Each active line item shows whether the deal is in the pre-offering (PP), proposal and offering development (P), or offered and presignature (O) phase of the marketing process. Inactive deals are identified as abandoned prior to offering (A), signed successfully (S), or lost (L). Inactive deals stay on the log for statistical purposes during the rolling four-month analysis period.

Each line item contains two dates on which the engagement might start. The start date of an offering often receives as much attention during client negotiation as price. The first date is when the client wants to start, the second is when the office can start. During periods of excess supply and lower demand, the latter is usually earlier than the former. In periods of high demand and tight supply of resources, these are usually reversed. By the time of the signature, they are theoretically the same.

The probability of signature (Odds) is usually a very subjective piece of information. Marketing is an inherently hopeful activity, so medium means, "I don't know, but it is worth continuing to pursue." Low usually means it is lost, but not completely dead.

The notes on next action are the best clue as to where this deal is moving. If a client-supported event is planned, then the deal is probably alive and may need resources. If it is waiting for something, it is suspect. The exception would be a major bid that is grinding its way through an approval and purchase confirmation process.

Eleven active deals in this list will be carried into April. Four of these look fairly good. They are:

- Zamindar Financial. We have chosen to do the work of a proposal in anticipation of a product decision. Presumably this means we believe the product decision will be favorable and justifies our offer being in place. Our price is very specific, indicating that pricing has occurred and is within client acceptance parameters.

- 1st Vitiate. The offer has been made and we are still meeting with the client.

- Zenana Furnishings. The client wants the work even sooner than we can get an offer out.

FIGURE 7-1
Marketing Activity Log

Resp	Stat	Engag No	Contr No	Client	Log Date	Amount	Client Start Date	Bus Typ	Typ Svc	Odds	Office Start Date	Notes
Active												
*1A	O	A3458	C6935	Yataghan Weapons	911016	$1,096,000.00	920309	CUS	FPP	9203	920309	*Signed*
NT	PP	B1010	C9436	Zareba Construction	911218	$2,000,000.00	920501	SI	FPP	M	920701	*Needs final est. ROE sub 2/14. 5 competitors.*
SS	O	A9908	C9571	Vermin Foods	920113	$256,200.00	920401	CUS	MS	M	920420	*Prop sub 3/10. Awaiting Dec. 3 competitors.*
SS	O	B3219	D0133	Zeppelin Airways	920131	$19,440.00	920801	CON	FP	M	920801	*Prop sub 2/26. Depends on bus. paid. selection due 4/1.*
*1A	P	B3224	D0152	Zamindar Finance	920131	$97,220.00	920501	CUS	MS	H	920504	*Prop due 4/2. Needs software dec. due 4/7.*
SS	O	B3256	D0244	1st Vitiate	920131	$1,385,215.00	920701	SI	FPP	H	920701	*Prop sub 4/13. Client call 4/3. One competitor.*
*PG	O	B3489	D0286	Zebrass Pets	920211	$15,552.00	920213	EDU	FP	9203	920213	*Prop sub 2/12 for classes in March. Lost. Not funded.*
					MARCH							
*KK	PP	A4610	D0533	High Flying S & L	920305	$67,152.00	920901	CUS	FP	L	920601	*Kowalski to follow up. May be premature.*
SS	P	B3219	D0464	Zeppelin Airways	920306	$45,500.00	920901	CON	TM	H	920901	*Awaiting technology dec by 5/16.*
*PG	P	B3591	D0313	Zenana Furnishings	920316	$15,535.00	920401	EDU	TM	H	920408	*Client call 4/1. Want classes next week.*
*PP	PP	B3726	D0443	Zuchetto Hats	920320	$3,240.00	920501	CUS	TM	M	920518	*Awaiting funding dec due 4/10.*
NT	PP			Yemen Air Services	920330	$12,000,000.00	920901	SI	MS	M	920901	*Client call on 4/7. Needs wavy team.*
*PP	O	A3891	C7428	Yawls 'R' Boats	920331	$135,200.00	920323	CON	TM	H	920323	*Need coverage for last week's hours, plus 4 months.*
					Signed	*$1,096,000.00*						
Inactive												
SS	S	A0007	Y4789	Slim Pickers	910219	$4,980,000.00	911202	SI	FPP	9112	911202	*Signed*
NT	S	A1104	C8294	Yam Tubas	910805	$106,600.00	920102	PI	FP	9112	920102	*Signed*
NT	S	A1104	C8606	Yam Tubas	910917	$131,400.00	920102	CUS	MS	9112	920102	*Signed*
*PG	S	A0099	C7420	Der Wunderweiner	911202	$152,012.00	911209	CUS	MS	9112	911209	*Signed*
*1A	S	B1412	C8700	Xenon Natural Gas	911203	$55,160.00	911216	CUS	TM	9112	911216	*Signed*
SS	S	B0113	C9486	Vulgar Sales	911016	$52,800.00	920205	CON	FPP	9112	920205	*Signed*
					SIGNED	$5,477,972.00						
NT	L	A2183	B9894	Surf Sand	911101	$73,200.00	920101	PI	FP	9201		*Lost. Client chose another product.*
*1A	S	A2209	C0151	Vaccine Du Pox	911112	$73,450.00	920102	CON	TM	9201	920102	*Signed*
*1A	S	A4578	C4845	Wivern Footwear	911126	$64,740.00	920127	CON	TM	9201	920127	*Signed*
					SIGNED	$138,190.00						
SS	L		C8814	Jam Boxes	910923	$247,120.00	920128	CON	FPP	9202		*Lost on price to competition.*
SS	A		C8702	Slease Pubs	911002	$1,250,000.00	911201	CUS	MS	9202		*Chose not to bid.*
*PG	S	B0006	C8983	Waffle Iron & Steel	911120	$49,500.00	920401	EDU	FP	9202	920401	*Signed*
					SIGNED	$49,500.00						

FIGURE 7-2
Marketing Productivity Analysis

	Active Deals	Added Deals New Engage	Exist Engage	Won	Amount	Loss	Abandon
		Marketing Productivity Analysis					
December	12	0	2	6	$5,477,972	0	0
January	10	3	1	2	138,190	1	0
February	10	1	2	1	49,500	1	1
March	13	2	4	1	1,096,000	1	0

New/Follow = 7/9; $6,366,800/$394,862
Win/Loss = 10/4
1Q Sales = $1,283,690

- Yawls 'R' Boats. The work has already extended beyond the previous contract level and the client clearly wants us to stay there and go on.

Of the remaining, most are waiting for action (it would appear that a high probability is premature for Zeppelin Airways) or are very early in the marketing process (particularly Zareba Construction and Yemen Air Services). The current sales forecast for April from the four listed above is $1,535,950.

Sales for the first quarter were $1,283,690 or 33 percent of our $3.9 million plan objective. On the other hand, December sales were $5.5 million, and our second quarter looks to be starting off nicely. The five-month period will see $8.3 million in sales, which is well ahead of even a six-month requirement to replace client funding commitments and to grow the funding base. Clearly, further analysis is needed to see if it is sufficient.

The marketing activity log is input to another tool for assessing levels of marketing—the productivity trend analysis. Common selling productivity indicators are the number of concurrent deals that are actively being pursued and the ratio of wins to losses. Figure 7-2 contains summary statistics of marketing productivity for the last four months. Active deals fell off in January after a successful December, but they have built back to a comparable level going into April. The ratio of wins to losses is 2.25, showing that we sign nearly 70 percent of the opportunities we pursue.

Neither of these statistics are cause for alarm and are, in fact, indicators of very healthy marketing. Typically, win/loss ratios in professional services are very high (70 percent to 80 percent). This is because well over half of an office's sales come from more work at current engagements. In the analysis, 9 of 16 wins were follow-on, but the value of follow-on commitments was only 6 percent of the new funding. An office should see a much higher level of follow-on sales.

The productivity analysis tells us that we are staying up with the work and the quality of our prospects is sufficient. The next thing we want to know is how long the office can be sustained by the funding commitments our marketing is bringing us.

Backlog Analysis

Backlog analysis is our test of whether marketing has been sufficient to meet our near revenue needs. As defined earlier, professional services backlog is counted in two ways.

- **Revenue:** The accumulated amounts that remain to be billed on each contract within active engagements in the office. The client has made a commitment to accept invoicing up to a certain limit (which may or may not be the actual amount funded). The revenue backlog amount for an engagement is the difference between the client commitment and the amount invoiced to date.

- **Hours/days:** The accumulated work remaining to be performed on the active engagements in the office expressed in hours or days. The consultant (team leader) has periodically established the number of hours or days that this engagement requires to meet client expectation. Usually this is two figures: the official version as communicated to the client and the unofficial version as believed by the consultants. The hours backlog amount for an engagement is the difference between total estimated hours/days and those expended through the previous week's labor claiming.

Figure 7-3 is an example of a backlog report for professional services. As mentioned earlier, the example contains a very broad mix of services in order to later illustrate forecasting variety. Each entry is an active contract within an engagement and shows when it started, when it should end, its client committed revenue value (both labor and other charges), its estimated hours (official), and the amount invoiced since inception. In addition, the report shows the labor and nonlabor amounts left to be invoiced, the official hours not used, and an unofficial estimate of the hours needed to complete the work. Days (daily rate contracts) have been converted to hours to make the information consistent.

To save room on the report, the funded amount and the billed amount contain both labor and nonlabor, whereas the backlog amounts for each are broken out. Billed travel expense comprises most of the nonlabor backlog on all but product installation (PI) and systems integration (SI). Notice that an excess

FIGURE 7-3
Unadjusted Backlog of Committed Client Funding

Professional Services Backlog—Unadjusted

CLIENT	CLIENT NO	ENGAG NO	CONTR NO	LAST INV DATE	START DATE	END DATE	BUS TYP	TYP SVC	HOURS	AMOUNT	BILLED AMOUNT	LABOR BACKLOG AMOUNT	N/L BACKLOG AMOUNT	HOURS REM	HOURS EST
SAWYER RAFTS	7979008	A4599	C2930	9203	910826	920430	CON	TM	104.0	139,200	118,300	16,900	324	130.0	210.0
SAWYER RAFTS	7979008	A4599	C2957	9203	910826	920430	CON	TM	552.0	103,500	100,500	3,000	0	16.0	0.0
SAWYER RAFTS	7979008	A4599	C4879	9202	911001	920229	PI	FP	30.0	30,000	30,000	0	0	-217.0	0.0
SAWYER RAFTS	7979008	A4599	C9622	9202	911201	930531	CON	E	144.0	36,000	9,762	12,900	13,338	96.0	24.0
SLIM PICKERS	7982011	A0007	Y4789	9203	911202	940131	SI	FPP	26,400.0	4,980,000	1,000,000	3,150,000	830,000	22,424.0	23,950.0
SURF SAND	8102885	A2183	B8899	9203	910617	930701	SI	FPP	15,600.0	2,856,200	1,271,722	914,528	669,950	7,201.0	7,980.0
VACCINE DU POX	9411600	A2209	C0092	9110	900912	911230	CON	TM	565.0	73,450	70,785	2,665	0	20.5	0.0
VACCINE DU POX	9411600	A2209	C0151	9201	920101	920630	CON	TM	90.0	11,700	9,295	2,405	0	18.5	0.0
VERMIN FOODS	9412313	A9908	C0006	9202	900701	920201	CUS	MS	23,122.0	2,723,124	2,720,396	15,035	1,733	128.5	0.0
VULGAR SALES	9413002	B0113	C9486	9203	920205	920630	CON	FPP	320.0	52,800	35,200	17,600	0	60.0	72.0
WADI POWER & LIGHT	9544710	A8888	C7176	9203	910821	920630	CON	TM	360.0	46,800	29,900	16,900	0	130.0	380.0
WAFER SNACKS	9566027	B1476	C9831	9203	911108	920228	CUS	MS	1,410.0	229,140	215,678	6,160	7,302	40.0	0.0
WAFFLE IRON & STEEL	9580202	B0006	C8420	9202	910901	920330	EDU	FP	150.0	45,000	51,214	0	0	92.0	76.0
WAFFLE IRON & STEEL	9580202	B0006	C8983		920101	920330	EDU	FP	150.0	49,500	0	45,000	4,500	150.0	130.0
WIVERN FOOTWEAR	9586541	A4578	C3908	9202	901230	911231	CON	FP	120.0	16,200	16,200	0	0	13.0	0.0
WIVERN FOOTWEAR	9586541	A4578	C4845	9203	920125	920501	CON	TM	520.0	64,740	64,285	455	0	3.5	800.0
DER WUNDERWIENER	9594051	A0099	C7420	9203	910801	920730	CUS	MS	5,646.0	688,812	586,393	102,419	0	839.5	652.0
XANTIPPE PHARMACOLOGICAL	9602235	A2099	C6237	9203	910703	921228	CUS	TM	5,200.0	691,000	469,372	216,450	5,172	1,665.0	1,665.0
XANTIPPE PHARMACOLOGICAL	9602235	A2099	C9285	9203	911204	921130	PI	FPP	450.0	81,100	19,500	39,000	22,600	-227.0	12.0
HIGH FLYING S & L	9611111	A4610	C8057	9203	910901	930830	CUS	MS	40,000.0	4,480,000	731,556	3,814,160	34,055	34,055.0	34,291.0
XENOGAMY BIOTECHNOLOGY	9622459	B0101	C7649	9203	911115	920531	CUS	MS	2,912.5	406,013	145,950	259,958	105	1,897.5	2,336.0
XENON NATURAL GAS	9622539	B1412	C8700	9203	911212	920615	CUS	TM	932.0	121,160	60,060	61,100	0	470.0	470.0
YAM TUBAS	9809624	A1104	C8294		920102	920518	PI	FP	820.0	106,600	0	106,600	0	211.0	253.0
YAM TUBAS	9809624	A1104	C8606	9203	920102	920430	CUS	MS	900.0	131,400	76,358	55,042	0	377.0	752.0
YANKEE NOODLES	9810029	A0005	C6233	9202	910724	911231	CON	TM	330.0	42,900	31,330	11,570	0	89.0	0.0
YATAGHAN WEAPONS	9818400	A3458	C6935	9203	910828	920316	CON	TM	400.0	52,600	30,990	21,610	0	162.0	0.0
YATAGHAN WEAPONS	9818400	A3458	C9894	9203	920307	930630	CUS	FPP	8,000.0	1,096,000	0	1,096,000	0	7,633.5	7,620.0
YAWLS 'R' BOATS	9827100	A3891	C7428	9203	911001	920930	CON	TM	3,154.0	410,020	698,750	0	0	-22.0	1,300.0
YAWLS 'R' BOATS	9827100	A3891	C7456	9111	910101	920930	EDU	FP	255.0	42,080	42,080	0	0	216.0	215.0
COURSE		E2132			920414	920417	EDU	S	64.0	17,600	17,600	0	0	64.0	64.0
COURSE		E2732			920420	920423	EDU	S	100.0	21,750	21,750	0	0	100.0	100.0
									138,800.5	19,846,389	8,674,926	9,987,457	1,055,024	77,836.5	83,352
									HOURS	AMOUNT	BILLED	BACKLOG	TOTAL $13,042,481	HOURS	HOURS

of billed travel has caused the billed amount to be higher than the funding amount on Waffle Iron & Steel. The follow-on contract has been increased accordingly.

The unadjusted backlog amount is $13 million. If all of this could be invoiced in the next 12 months, we would have almost a year's worth of revenue committed by our clients. Notice, though, that five of the contracts go beyond this year. Notice also that there is not consistent agreement between the backlog of hours and the estimated hours needed to complete.

Another measure of marketing health is whether an office has at least one offer outstanding to a client for every two active engagements. This office appears to have 18 active engagements (Sawyer Rafts, Vaccine Du Pox, Waffle Iron & Steel, Wivern Footwear, Xantippe Pharmacological, Yam Tubas, Yataghan Weapons, and Yawls 'R' Boats are each single engagements with more than one contract). Advanced payments have been received from students (type of service [TYP SVC], S) for two classes being held in April that are not in the engagement count. If all of these are truly active engagements, our ratio would appear to be 7 to 18, based on those offered and very soon to be offered from our marketing activity log.

Annualizing Backlog

Annualizing engagement backlog is a process of estimating how much of the remaining revenue and hours will be expended in the current measurement year. If the end date on the engagement is before the end of the measurement period, we can assume in this exercise that all of it will count for revenue this year. When the end date is beyond the period, the backlog needs to be divided into current and future year segments. Three methods are common.

1. Assign an equal share to each of the remaining months of the engagement and multiply by the number of those months that fall in this year. This is a simple and effective approach when the level of staffing will remain constant throughout the remaining life of the engagement.

2. Compute the revenue and hours per person for the preceding month. Develop a quick schedule of staffing through the remaining months of the engagement and total the person months for this year. Then multiply the person months for this year by the revenue per person and hours per person computed for last month. This is less simple, but is an effective forecasting tool when staffing levels vary. It does assume that the relative mix of resource types (associate, senior, contractor) will remain reasonably constant.

3. Use the detailed engagement plan to compute revenue to be billed and hours to be expended over the remaining months of the year. Obviously, this third approach to annualizing backlog is necessary only when the engagement has such a variety in revenue and hours from month to month that neither of the first two averaging choices can be used. Very large systems integration engagements are certain to fall into this category.

Fixed-price engagements usually require two different approaches—one for revenue and another for hours. The revenue is usually on a fixed schedule. The schedule is unique to the engagement and only requires judgment as to whether the work is still on that schedule, particularly if a payment is due in December. Hours will be annualized based on any of these techniques that best spread the estimate to complete.

In Figure 7-3, engagements for Sawyer Rafts, Slim Pickers, Surf Sand, High Flying Savings & Loan, and Yataghan Weapons will extend beyond this year. The event contract under Sawyer Rafts is very small and justifies little intellectual energy. We will assume it contributes no revenue this year and deal with it again later, when we look at potential backlog.

High Flying is hourly and would bill $225,000 and use 2,020 hours per month, if staffing were even over its remaining 17 months. It has billed an average of $122,000 and 1,000 hours per month in its first six months. $200,000 and 2,000 hours per month is a conservative forecast for the nine months of the current year using an equal period distribution. This gives a labor backlog of $1,800,000 and hours of 18,000. Although nonlabor billing has occurred on this engagement, the backlog shows none remaining.

Yataghan is fixed price with five equal quarterly payments of $219,200. Two payments are expected this year for $438,400 in labor backlog. The project plan estimates that 2,250 hours will be expended in the remaining months of the year.

Slim Pickers and Surf Sand are systems integration engagements. They are both invoiced through regular progress payments for labor and milestone initiated payments to recover vendor and product costs. The project teams for both are a stable mix of people with constant staffing over the life of the engagements. Slim Pickers should invoice three of seven $400,000 labor payments this year and two nonlabor checkpoint payments of $415,000. Surf Sand invoices $44,000 per month for labor and will have one nonlabor payment of $333,000 due. The two teams will expend 12,600 and 5,850 hours, respectively.

Annualizing backlog can seem tedious, particularly near the end of the year when most engagements carry into the next year. If the analysis is done regularly (once per quarter), the same criteria will usually apply each time to long running engagements, making them easier to repeat.

Good, Bad, and Additional Backlog

Once the backlog is annualized, an assessment of its integrity needs to be made. A number of factors can change the revenue potential for an engagement. We have already seen that the estimated number of hours to complete the work can be very different than those funded under the contract. Bad backlog is where less revenue will be achieved. Typical bad conditions that must be assessed and for which backlog is adjusted include:

- Early completion and/or underrun of the estimated work needed to complete the engagement on an hourly or daily contract. This is a good problem. The client will be delighted, but the business will come up short on expected revenue.

- An overrun of the work without a corresponding increase or extension of the revenue flow. This does not affect the revenue backlog, but it detracts from the ability to shift resources to other engagements and may affect overall revenue backlog. Obviously, it has implications regarding profitability.

- Inability to expend all hours in the time frame remaining, because no additional resources can be hired, borrowed, or transferred, and all other resources are at maximum utilization. A serious supply problem may require a general extension of all engagements with corresponding reduced revenue flow and hours expended.

- A rapidly deteriorating local economy. Slow changes in economic conditions can usually be traded off between engagements that will accelerate and ones that will slow. A local economy that is dropping off the edge of the table will inevitably mean the canceling of work. Often the backlog needs to be discounted by some percent that applies the probable effect of the slow down.

Good backlog is where the revenue and hours remaining can be counted on for the year. A common result of backlog analysis is finding contracts that not only have good backlog, but they have a high potential for follow-on.

Figure 7-4 shows the result of analyzing our backlog, reducing to zero all that were bad, confirming and annualizing those that were good, and noting those where follow-on opportunity might exist and should be added to our marketing activity log for assignment.

Fifteen contracts required no adjustment. With the 5 we discussed that were annualized, we have 19 contracts among 15 engagements with solid backlog. Seven hourly and daily contracts with no further work have had their backlog

FIGURE 7-4
Adjusted Backlog

Professional Services Backlog—Adjusted

CLIENT	CONTR NO	END DATE	BUS TYP	TYP SVC	HOURS	AMOUNT	BILLED AMOUNT	LABOR BACKLOG AMOUNT	N/L BACKLOG AMOUNT	HOURS REM	HOURS EST	ADJUSTED BACKLOG AMOUNT	ADDITION AMOUNT	ADJSTD HOURS
SAWYER RAFTS	C2930	920430	CON	TM	104.0	139,200	118,300	16,900	324	130.0	210.0	16,900	12,400	210.0
SAWYER RAFTS	C2957	920430	CON	TM	552.0	103,500	100,500	3,000	0	16.0	0.0	0		0.0
SAWYER RAFTS	C4879	920229	PI	FP	30.0	30,000	30,000	0	0	-217.0	0.0	0		0.0
SAWYER RAFTS	C9622	930531	CON	E	144.0	36,000	9,762	12,900	13,338	96.0	24.0	0	6,600	24.0
SLIM PICKERS	Y4789	940131	SI	FPP	26,400.0	4,980,000	1,000,000	3,150,000	830,000	22,424.0	23,950.0	865,000		12,600.0
SURF SAND	B9999	930701	SI	FPP	15,600.0	2,856,200	1,271,722	914,528	669,950	7,201.0	7,980.0	729,000		5,850.0
VACCINE DU POX	C0092	911230	CON	TM	565.0	73,450	70,785	2,665	0	20.5	0.0	0		0.0
VACCINE DU POX	C0151	920630	CON	TM	90.0	11,700	9,295	2,405	0	18.5	0.0	0		0.0
VERMIN FOODS	C0006	920201	CUS	MS	23,122.0	2,723,124	2,720,396	15,035	1,733	128.5	0.0	0		0.0
VULGAR SALES	C9486	920430	CON	FPP	320.0	52,800	35,200	17,600	0	60.0	72.0	17,600		72.0
WADI POWER & LIGHT	C7176	920630	CON	TM	360.0	46,800	29,900	16,900	0	130.0	380.0	16,900	34,000	380.0
WAFER SNACKS	C9831	920228	CUS	MS	1,410.0	229,140	215,678	6,160	7,302	40.0	0.0	0		0.0
WAFFLE IRON & STEEL	C8420	920330	EDU	FP	150.0	45,000	51,214	0	0	92.0	76.0	0		76.0
WAFFLE IRON & STEEL	C8983	920330	EDU	FP	150.0	49,500	0	45,000	4,500	150.0	130.0	49,500		130.0
WIVERN FOOTWEAR	C3908	911231	CON	FP	120.0	16,200	16,200	0	0	13.0	0.0	0		0.0
WIVERN FOOTWEAR	C4845	920501	CON	FP	520.0	64,740	64,285	455	0	3.5	800.0	455	100,000	800.0
DER WUNDERWIENER	C7420	920730	CUS	MS	5,646.0	688,812	586,393	102,419	0	839.5	652.0	79,544		652.0
XANTIPPE PHARMACOLOGICAL	C6237	921228	CUS	TM	5,200.0	691,000	469,372	216,450	5,172	1,665.0	1,665.0	221,622		1,665.0
XANTIPPE PHARMACOLOGICAL	C9285	921130	PI	FPP	450.0	81,100	19,500	39,000	22,600	-227.0	12.0	61,600		12.0
HIGH FLYING S & L	C8057	930830	CUS	MS	40,000.0	4,480,000	731,556	3,814,160	0	34,055.0	34,291.0	1,800,000		18,000.0
XENOGAMY BIOTECHNOLOGY	C7649	920531	CUS	MS	2,912.5	406,013	145,950	259,958	105	1,897.5	2,336.0	260,063	10,300	2,336.0
XENON NATURAL GAS	C8700	920615	CUS	TM	932.0	121,160	60,060	61,100	0	470.0	470.0	61,100		470.0
YAM TUBAS	C8294	920518	PI	FP	820.0	106,600	0	106,600	0	211.0	253.0	106,600		253.0
YAM TUBAS	C8606	920430	CUS	MS	900.0	131,400	76,358	55,042	0	377.0	752.0	55,042	54,750	752.0
YANKEE NOODLES	C6233	911231	CON	TM	330.0	42,900	31,330	11,570	0	89.0	0.0	0		0.0
YATAGHAN WEAPONS	C6935	920316	CON	TM	400.0	52,600	30,990	21,610	0	162.0	0.0	0		0.0
YATAGHAN WEAPONS	C9894	930630	CUS	FPP	8,000.0	1,096,000	698,750	1,096,000	0	7,633.5	7,620.0	438,400		2,250.0
YAWLS 'R' BOATS	C7428	920930	CON	TM	3,154.0	410,020	42,080	0	0	-22.0	1,300.0	2,860	166,140	1,300.0
YAWLS 'R' BOATS	C7456	920930	EDU	FP	255.0	42,080	42,080	0	0	216.0	215.0	0		215.0
COURSE	E2132	920417	EDU	S	64.0	17,600	17,600	0	0	64.0	64.0	0	0	64.0
COURSE	E2732	920423	EDU	S	100.0	21,750	21,750	0	0	100.0	100.0	0	0	100.0
					138,800.5	19,846,389	8,674,926	9,987,457	1,555,024	77,836.5	83,352.0	4,782,186	384,190	48,211.0 HOURS

ADJUSTED BACKLOG $4,782,186
ADDITION $384,190

reduced to zero—Sawyer Rafts (C2957), both Vaccine's, Vermin, Wafer, Yankee, and Yataghan (C6935).

The following engagements have unique backlog problems.

- Sawyer Rafts and Xantippe Pharmacological (C9285) have required substantially more work under their fixed prices, but billing will not be delayed beyond this year. Xantippe is a close call, since completion and final payment is expected in November.
- Der Wunderwiener is going to underrun its funding. The client will likely be delighted and might agree to more work, but the backlog must be adjusted down to $79,544.
- Yawls 'R' Boats is 22 hours beyond current funding. Since this is time and materials, we are owed for those hours and this represents real backlog of $2,860.

The backlog adjustment process has identified seven opportunities for more revenue this year. Only one of these, Yawls, is on the marketing forecast. These follow-on opportunities are as follows.

- The consultant on Sawyer Rafts (C2930) estimates an additional 80 hours. The effort has seen more travel than originally estimated. The remaining effort should bring a total of $12,400 in combined labor and nonlabor.
- The Sawyer Rafts event contract (C9622) was conservatively annualized at zero. A more optimistic view is three more calls which bring $6,600 in combined labor and nonlabor revenue.
- Wadi Power and Wivern Footwear each have time and materials estimates that are higher than currently funded. The consultants see these as opportunities for more labor revenue.
- Xenogamy will also require more travel to complete the effort; actual nonlabor billing has run over the original estimate.
- Yam Tubas (C8606) is a managed hourly contract. It is expected to overrun its current funding. Good change control will bring that as revenue and may even lay the groundwork for more follow-on.

Computing Coverage

Our adjusted revenue backlog is $4,879,476 on 15 engagements with backlogged hours of 48,211. We have the comfort of knowing that 35 percent of our annual revenue objective is in solid backlog. That is better than the one quarter advance that was the basis of our sales plan. We can also see that our actual ratio of offerings to engagements is 7 to 15 and will improve further when we formalize the additional opportunities we just identified. We complete our analysis by determining how much of our annual revenue objective is covered by client funding and how much more we need to market.

Computing coverage sums four backlog and forecast components. The computation begins with the actual revenue invoiced so far this year. To this is added the adjusted backlog, giving us an assured level of coverage. To this is further added the additional backlog we would see from high potential follow-on and sales (adjusted to reflect this year's revenue only).

Figure 7-5 illustrates how this computation was made for our office. Revenue so far this year is $3,201,487. The sum of it and our solid backlog is 60 percent of our annual revenue plan. Adding our high-potential additional backlog gives us a total estimated funding of $10 million or 76 percent of our annual plan.

We will see next how this will be used in a marketing investment decision. There is debate of some intellectual intensity as to what constitutes comfortable backlog. Some argue that an office should have three months of future billing in its backlog. Others argue that the amount of backlog is irrelevant and that its diversity to cover all resources in the office is more important. The key is whether the office has enough of its resources covered for the next 60 to 90 days and that there is enough potential in marketing activities to react, if this coverage begins to deteriorate. A 76 percent coverage in the second quarter would be considered by most to be very comfortable.

Making the Investment Decision

We have computed how much of the needed revenue can be achieved with no further investment in marketing. We have analyzed the productivity of our marketing. The only other concern we can have is whether backlog is growing and at the right rate. Figure 7-6 is a graph of backlog over the last six months. The curve is the three-month average. The upper dotted line is the slope of backlog growth over that period. We know that March had a single large engagement sale, so we have drawn another more conservative dotted line that averages February and March sales into a lower three-month average.

Both dotted lines show that backlog is growing. In Figure 7-7 the two dotted lines are plotted with a corresponding graph showing actual growth in revenue for the six months. Even the more conservative plot of backlog growth is nicely keeping pace with revenue growth.

The executive for this office now has three important pieces toward a decision to increase or decrease marketing investment.

FIGURE 7-5
Services Revenue Funding Coverage Computation

Services Revenue Coverage ($000)	
Year to date	$3,201
Adjusted backlog	4,782
	$7,983
Coverage	60%
Follow-on (additional)	384
New (marketing)	1,679
	$10,046
Coverage	76%

1. The marketing resource has been sufficient to grow the number of active deals, and the ratio of offers to engagements seems healthy.

2. Backlog is growing and appears to be growing with revenue.

3. Annual revenue is 76 percent covered with nine months to go.

This situation leaves little doubt that marketing is functioning well in this office. An entrepreneur's first instinct will be to leave it alone and let the business build under the momentum that is in place. An executive is always reluctant to fix something that is not broken.

There is a profitability opportunity, though, that should not be ignored and which was the justification for performing this analysis in the first place. This executive is getting signals that a short-term reduction in marketing may not impact revenue. It could be an opportunity to bank some additional profit during the second quarter as a hedge against the unknown later in the year.

The executive has any of the following options and would probably take them in the following order.

- Reduce discretionary time being spent by consultants on marketing. The time they devote to estimates cannot be eliminated, but that which is devoted to survey teams can be reduced by simply stretching out the survey periods and reducing the number of consultants used. Clearly, this won't occur until each consultant completes work on offerings that are in process.

- Temporarily curtail specialized marketing activities that were put in place to stimulate a wider business mix. Obviously, any of these that

FIGURE 7-6
Backlog Growth

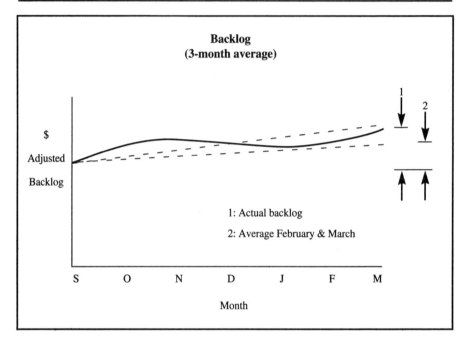

1: Actual backlog

2: Average February & March

are just beginning to identify solid prospects, or have substantially
increased backlog, should be left in place. Those that are taking people
off billing and are showing only marginal success should be looked at
very closely. (An example might be a consultant who is making calls in
a specific industry to stimulate interest in a unique skill, but has no
proposals in the works.)

- Reduce time managers may be spending in marketing, and carefully
  increase their levels of billing. Specifically reduce the number of cold
  calls assigned to lower level managers, causing the office to become
  temporarily less responsive to requests to meet with new clients. Reducing management attention to marketing should not reduce their attention to the engagements they manage, where their marketing time with
  existing clients is mixed with making sure that on-site consultants receive support.

- Temporarily reduce base marketing levels. This is not a recommendation to dismantle marketing, particularly on this evidence alone. Ongoing contacts are essential to the long-term existence of the office. Even

FIGURE 7-7
Backlog Growth Versus Revenue Growth

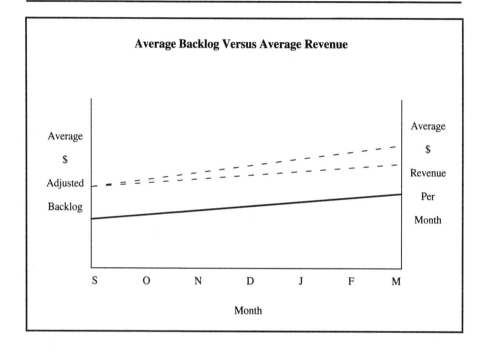

momentary disconnections of the marketing contacts can mean months of work to reconnect before effective leads begin to flow again. Someone has to assure new clients and alliance partners that the office will be responsive to them (eventually).

It is not out of line, though, for marketing people to bill on occasion. Teaching is an excellent short-term revenue assignment for marketers. Temporary, crisis project management is not an unheard of assignment for a marketer. People who are good marketers in professional services are also good project managers, and a project in crisis refreshes their feel for what it is like to be on the firing line. Also, if the project goes under, it doesn't besmirch the resume of someone else in the office.

Finally, this is the time for the office executive to get some billing. The top person is also the top consultant on the staff and inducing a temporary lull in marketing frenzy is the time to be visible to key, long-term clients.

All good marketing programs are run on instinct. Entrepreneurs worth their salt can sense when marketing is not getting the job done. It is much harder to sense when marketing can be abated, and the tools just described give counsel to the decision. The entrepreneur must not become dependent on the tools and lose contact with the voice inside them. The tools cannot speak to quality: Can the business being sold be successfully performed? Is marketing bringing opportunities that are suited to the resources of the office? Assessing marketing quality and taking improvement actions should be a very high priority in making the investment decisions just described.

This leads us to the other side of this coin. Does the process change when instinct and analysis points to marketing performing at less than needed strength. The process doesn't change, but the choices of actions are reversed. Most importantly the office executive needs to quickly get disentangled from billing commitments, do the same for any others in the base marketing resource of the office, and make marketing momentum a very high priority.

The executive has another issue to deal with when marketing falls behind— the capabilities of those who have been marketing. Extra investment will not help an inherently bad marketing program. The books on professional services marketing referenced in Chapter 10 will be very helpful. They give valuable advice on the marketing process and marketing people. This will help determine whether the office is investing in the wrong things. That chapter also offers some observations on qualities of good marketing people, in the event that the executive chooses to change personnel assignments.

Assuming the marketing program is correct and the base personnel assigned are effective, the tough decision is deciding how much to increase resources. The executive will likely choose the reverse order of the list, progressively increasing the dedicated base level, the amount of manager time, levels of specialized prospecting, and the general level of consultant marketing. The executive needs to be convinced that an increase in people hours (and corresponding expense) will generate offsetting revenue. The office may be better off accepting lower revenue, if the expense of increased marketing itself eliminates year-end profits.

Knowing when and how much marketing to add to generate not only compensating, but accelerated near term revenue is one of the toughest decisions an executive has to make. Experience helps, because one can try what has worked in the past. One caution, though, before throwing a lot of people at the problem, size the total effort.

Labor tracking tells us how many hours we spend in marketing. Backlog analysis tells us how effective the effort has been in net sales contribution month by month. The division of hours into net sales provides a rough productivity factor for sizing marketing.

If each hour of marketing brings $2,500 in net sales, an increase in average sales by $.5 million will need more than one person and less than two. If, in periods of high net sales, the productivity factor goes substantially lower, adding more people isn't the answer. On the other hand, if the productivity factor stays within range of the average factor in high net sales periods (or even gets higher), then adding resources will generate more new business.

Testing the effect of increasing marketing investment on profitability is fairly easy when an office uses the spreadsheets described in Chapters 5 and 6. The analysis requires two iterations.

- Make a projection of the decreasing backlog to the end of the year. Plot the corresponding effect on revenue. First, it should go flat; then decrease. Insert the new revenue projection in the spreadsheet and determine its effect on profit. This represents the cost of taking no action and allowing lower marketing investment to eventually reduce revenue.

- Run iterations of the spreadsheets with varying combinations of marketing staff. Short-term staffing with billable people may reduce short-term revenue (reduced utilization). Any staffing of new marketing people increases expense. Judgment, instinct, and productivity data provide estimates of revenue that can result from each combination of increased marketing staff. Each iteration is compared with the base case (doing nothing), to see what makes good business sense.

The analysis is inexact, but it does give some help in deciding whether to be conservative or aggressive. Usually the case is fairly clear. If additional hours will build backlog and result in only a short-term profit problem, then a discretionary increase makes sense. If an increase in marketing brings down profit, regardless of whether it is effective in increasing revenue, the investment is probably too late, and reduced revenue is likely to be the best choice.

There is a strong resistance to viewing marketing analytically. Certainly, the instinctual judgments of where and when to apply resources in marketing should not be hampered by administrative detail. The tracking just described is painless, though. It is a logical by-product of normal business tracking and gives a comforting 20 percent factual component to go with 80 percent judgment, when running a fast-paced professional services marketing program.

MONTHLY FORECAST

No manager at any level gets to go for long without making a revenue forecast. Each level of management tests the next lower level by demanding forecasts and then judging their accuracy. The motivation is threefold: a genuine need to see how the business will be performing against plan; gathering data for their own upward forecast; and making those managers that report to them go through the same hammering they are getting from their managers.

The forecast in professional services is made from backlog information. It combines three pieces of information about each engagement.

1. How much was billed in the previous month?
2. How much of the backlog can be billed in the next month?
3. Are there any constraints on resources that would prevent billing in the next month?

Figure 7-8 is a forecast for the office we have been working with in this chapter. Combined labor and nonlabor billing was $1.075 million in the previous month. This is right on the average billing we need in the early part of the year to make our revenue objective. Each engagement is listed with its corresponding contribution to last month's revenue (for all contracts under the engagement). One month of backlog has then been spread by week for each to make the forecast.

Notice that the forecast for the coming month is down by over $300,000. Most of the reason is a milestone payment in the previous month on Surf Sand. The coming month contains no major scheduled payments (scheduled payments are listed in the first week). The rest of the forecast reflects the normal increases and decreases one would see in professional services businesses of any complexity.

The engagements with hourly contracts are those with labor billing every week. Vermin has finished, but weekly billing on High Flying will increase as resources are shifted to that effort (the first week wasn't quite as successful as planned). Clearing all but the hourly and daily contracts from the forecast, the previous month and current month revenue would be $582,528 and $537,940, respectively. Most of the difference is a nonlabor charge on High Flying in the previous month.

Forecasting for hourly engagements is just as we see in this example—laying out a weekly estimate of how much resource can be applied and comparing it with the previous month. It is unusual that there would be significant differences from one month to the next that cannot be explained by the abrupt beginning or ending of contracts.

The education business requires an enrollment process for effective forecasting. In our example, the revenue for the previous month is from advanced payments for classes in the current month, while the revenue in the current month is billing for enrollments by students in future months. The enrollment process

FIGURE 7-8
One Month Revenue Forecast

		Previous Month		Week 1		Week 2		Week 3		Week 4		Total Month		Total
		Labor	Nonlabor	Labor	Nonlabor	Labor	Nonlabor	Labor	Nonlabor	Labor	Nonlabor	Labor	Nonlabor	
Sawyer Rafts	A4599	25,470	32,625	4,000	900	4,000	900	4,000	900	4,000	0	16,000	2,700	18,700
Actual				3,984	1,102							3,984	1,102	5,086
Slim Pickers	A0007	0	0	0	0	0	0	0	0	0	0	0	0	0
Actual			.											0
Surf Sand	A2183	133,330	205,050	133,330	0	0	0	0	0	0	0	133,330	0	133,330
Actual				133,330	0							133,330	0	133,330
Vermin Foods	A9908	51,890	1,745	0	2,150	0	0	0	0	0	0	0	2,150	2,150
Actual				0	2,152							0	2,152	2,152
Vulgar Sales	B0113	15,000	2,600	15,000	0	0	0	0	0	0	2,600	15,000	2,600	17,600
Actual				15,000	0							15,000	0	15,000
Wadi Power & Light	A8888	17,610	0	4,200	0	4,200	0	4,200	0	4,200	0	16,800	0	16,800
Actual				4,214	0							4,214	0	4,214
Waffle Iron & Steel	B0006	45,000	3,195	0	0	0	0	0	0	0	1,500	0	1,500	1,500
Actual				0	0							0	0	0
Wivern Footwear	A4578	18,720		4,700	0	4,700	0	4,700	0	4,700	0	14,100	0	14,100
Actual				4,682	0							4,682	0	4,682
Der Wunderwiener	A0099	54,170		13,900	0	13,900	0	13,900	0	13,900	0	55,600	0	55,600
Actual				13,900	0							13,900	0	13,900
Xantippe Pharmacological	A2099	39,780	960	24,700	240	5,200	240	5,200	240	7,800	480	42,900	1,200	44,100
Actual				24,646	288							24,646	288	24,934
High Flying S & L	A4610	114,688	32,060	34,000	0	38,300	0	38,300	0	38,300	0	148,900	0	148,900
Actual				31,544	0							31,544	0	31,544
Xenogamy Biotechnology	B0101	133,165	2,895	34,500	1,500	34,500	0	34,500	1,500	34,500	0	138,000	3,000	141,000
Actual				35,687	2,146							35,687	2,146	37,833
Xenon Natural Gas	B1412	19,560		4,700	0	4,700	0	4,700	0	4,700	0	14,100	0	14,100
Actual				4,722	0							4,722	0	4,722
Yam Tubas	A1104	48,180		11,970	0	8,980	0	11,970	0	11,970	0	44,890	0	44,890
Actual				11,982	0							11,982	0	11,982
Yataghan Weapons	A3458	0	0	0	0	0	0	0	0	0	0	0	0	0
Actual				0	0							0	0	0
Yawls 'R' Boats	A3891	37,655		9,400	0	9,400	0	9,400	0	9,400	0	37,600	0	37,600
Actual				9,523	0							9,523	0	9,523
Education		39,350		0	0	0	0	0	0	44,000	0	44,000	0	44,000
Actual				9,300								9,300	0	9,300
NEW				0	0	0	0	0	0	15,535	0	15,535	0	15,535
Actual				0								0	0	0
TOTAL		793,568	281,130	294,400	4,790	127,880	1,140	126,170	2,640	188,305	4,580	736,755	13,150	749,905
Actual				302,514	5,688	0	0	0	0	0	0	302,514	5,688	308,202

creates its own forecast—only qualified by whether minimum class levels will force cancellation of existing enrollments. As with hourly business, there should be easy explanations for why the forecast will change greatly from month to month.

The fixed price, product, and systems integration will always have major differences in revenue from month to month. The backlog of each must be examined individually to determine what billing is scheduled in the next month. These large variations can screen real problems in the revenue stream.

In the example in Figure 7-8, the hourly revenue lost when Vermin ended is not being transferred to other engagements. We will likely see utilization fall below plan in the first two weeks. The management staff may wish to move even more hours over to High Flying, if the effort can be accelerated. Otherwise, something needs to be sold.

USING AN HOURS FORECAST

Professional services backlog is both revenue and hours. The hours forecast serves two purposes.

- It is compared with the staffing plan to determine whether overall people resources will be available to meet demand.
- It is used to highlight potential problems on engagements.

In our adjusted backlog we determined that 48,200 hours are estimated as needed resource underlying the revenue that is assured for the remaining nine months. The staffing plan for this office provides 59,547 hours during the same period to billable work. At this point, the staffing plan is sufficient to meet demand and the additional marketing to get 24 percent more revenue backlog would seem to adequately support the remaining resource supply. As the year progresses, this comparison becomes much more critical. That same plan calls for 24,900 hours to be delivered to billable activities in the fourth quarter, showing the characteristic late-year increase in utilization for a professional services office. A backlog of less than that number of hours is cause for great concern.

For an hourly or daily business, the probability that revenue backlog and hours backlog be out of synchronization in the last months of the year is very low. For a heavily fixed-price business, it can be very likely. It is very easy for payments to be skewed to the end of the year, while work occurs earlier in the year. If profit is not an issue (late year payments may generate enough income against expense to be very profitable), then the office should be marketing these resources elsewhere. This is a wonderful opportunity, not to be missed. If profitability is in danger, then additional revenue generated through extra utilization takes on even more meaning.

A once per month backlog review is a simple discipline for raising questions about current engagements. It shouldn't be used to look over the shoulders of consultants and managers. Asking engagement leaders for their estimates to complete can appear threatening. Penalizing them will naturally cause data (particularly hours) to be reported to avoid pain, rather than highlight anomalies.

The following are observations that can be made from backlog and the questions that might be raised accordingly.

- **Hours and revenue are over 90 percent of contracted levels and scheduled completion is less than one month.** What is the marketing plan for this client? Should senior management take any actions to further ensure client satisfaction of the engagement?

- **Revenue is over 90 percent of contracted levels, scheduled completion is one month away, but hours are visibly less than 90 percent of expected levels.** If it is a fixed price, are more resources needed to finish for a high client satisfaction level? If combined labor and nonlabor, are resources sufficient to finish on time? Again, what is the marketing plan for this client, and are there actions to be taken by senior management?

- **Calendar is within 20 percent of the end of the contract period, while revenue and hours are noticeably less than 80 percent expended.** If the effort is on schedule and the client is satisfied, what is the marketing plan to capitalize on this success story? If the effort is behind schedule, what resources are needed?

- **Scheduled start has occurred, but no hours are being expended.** If the effort is behind schedule, what resources are necessary?

- **Schedule is more than 50 percent expended and the average resources per month to use up remaining hours substantially exceeds current staffing.** If current staffing is sufficient and estimates will be underrun, how do we capitalize on this success story? If current staffing is insufficient, what demands will be placed on the utilization of consultants in the office? Will the client accept a higher number of subcontractors?

- **Schedule is more than 50 percent expended and the average resources per month to use up remaining hours is substantially fewer than current staffing.** Would a project review be helpful?

With any analysis like this there is an obvious temptation to use it as a club. A regular show and tell by engagement leaders to the office executive is the most sensible way to avoid this. Real problems will surface in these formal engagement reviews. Backlog analysis and any other form of administrative review will then take care of the small stuff.

WEEKLY MARKETING REVIEW

A prudent executive keeps a close finger on marketing activity. Marketers are most effective when they are allowed to run freely after potential deals. This freedom needs to be punctuated by regular and friendly checkpoints that comfort management that the process is bringing good business, and reward the marketer with needed resources to get the job done.

The most reliable mechanism is a weekly review of the marketing activity log that includes all participants in the marketing process. Typically, these are all managers (other than those assigned full time to projects) and each member assigned to marketing staff. The review can be a conference call, since few of these people will be in the same place at the same time.

Before the call, the marketing staff distributes the activity log (Figure 7-1), and the management staff distributes the assignment calendar (Figure 5-9). The purpose of the review is to fill in the blanks on the log and calendar. Carrying on with our exercise of this chapter, four clients will be added to the marketing log, where follow-on opportunities deserve attention. Additionally, the Yemen Air Services deal needs a survey team.

In less than one hour, each of these items should have a new action item and every person in the office should have an assignment. Each person leaves the call with his or her own marked up copy of the log and calendar. If at any time during the week, one of the parties finds the action plan going awry, others dependent on the action are well known and can be brought together (electronic communication is invaluable for this type of coordination).

The office executive can participate, listen in, or choose to have a summary delivered with an updated version of the two control documents. Most executives are also a marketing resource and need to take assignments like anyone else. On the other hand, the rest of the management staff ought to be allowed to make judgments on assignments and their own commitments as they see best. The office executive will always have to be a tie breaker in disputes.

SALES INCENTIVES

Many firms pay commissions or bonuses as an incentive to add signed business to the backlog. Obviously, this additional expense only makes sense when the revenue stream needs to grow on a sustained basis and the investment in marketing is major and ongoing.

Sales incentives take many forms.

- **Closing bonus.** The individual(s) who has primary responsibility for the client receives a prescribed bonus, paid upon client signature of an engagement. It may be only for new engagements. It may be only for engagement commitments above a certain dollar amount or number of hours/days. The payment is usually a percentage of the amount of new commitment by the client up to some maximum amount.

- **Line of service bonus.** The individual(s) who has primary responsibility for the account receives a bonus for the first or each sale of a specific service offering to a client. These are used to encourage marketers to take time to sell offerings that need extraordinary effort in qualifying, proposing, and closing. New offerings fall in this category, because their selling process has to be learned and few, if any, references are available to expedite client acceptance. Offerings with higher profitability, such as education, often have special bonuses.

- **New account bonuses.** An individual who gets a specified number of signatures from completely new clients receives a prescribed bonus. The bonus may be based on the number of new accounts or on accumulated new backlog.

- **Revenue commission advance.** Selected individuals who receive commissions for billed revenue are paid a portion of those commissions at the time the engagement is signed. If the full amount of the engagement is not billed, the individuals receive a debit at engagement completion against their commissions to reflect the difference between the advance and the amount actually billed. On long engagements, personnel will change and the liability for the advance is transferred to the new person on the account.

The revenue commission advance is a very effective incentive for marketers of professional services. Having a liability against the advance encourages the marketer to structure engagements that will be executed successfully and to remain interested in the engagement.

More than half of the success of an engagement lies in the hands of those who structure and sell the deal. As we have discussed, new clients and large new engagements with existing clients are most often the responsibility of dedicated marketers. The good ones want to be paid well for successful selling and should be. An office must avoid rewarding bad business. Keeping the marketer's income at risk while engagements are being performed is a way to pay well and also see that the marketer builds performable deals.

KNOWING WHEN TO SELL

An effective marketing program is a very high priority for a professional services executive. Balancing expense to results is a constant challenge. In this chapter we have looked at relatively simple tools for analyzing marketing resource levels and productivity.

Some important things to remember from this chapter are:

- Determining whether sufficient energy is being expended in marketing will always be a very subjective call. The more monthly revenue fluctuations an office sees, the tougher it gets to trust instincts and experience.

- The decision to increase or decrease marketing effort and expense is aided by input from an assessment of backlog, a judgment of how backlog is changing, and an understanding of marketing productivity.

- Backlog is both a forecasting tool and an engagement analysis method.

- Marketing efforts should be recognized by their effect on the amount and quality of backlog.

We have focused on the most complex of business mixes in this discussion, because our example office is the one that most needs the tools we described. How much an executive with a simpler business mix chooses to back off from the level of control described is largely a matter of style. Certainly, basic people services executives who are themselves the dedicated marketers in their businesses are already very close to the marketing action. Only if they find themselves too deep in the trees, should they want to implement these controls.

The main premise behind these controls is valid for all. Marketing is an investment. Increasing or decreasing the level of marketing investment is an important decision; instinct with the right information leads to the right decision.

Chapter 8

Measuring Productivity

P roductivity in the professional services business is measured by changes in the revenue per hour (effective revenue) and the cost per hour (effective cost) of its people. The objective of a professional services executive is to increase the effective revenue of each person at a faster rate than the increase in effective cost. Maintaining revenue and cost productivity is part of a three-ball juggling act that includes pricing competitively and attracting top people. A manager must keep focus on all three.

Growth is a fourth ball that can easily blur one's vision. It particularly screens concentration on productivity. This chapter is devoted to tools that will increase the luminescence of productivity.

Productivity computations can be integrated into the professional services income and expense statement (I & E). The I & E spreadsheet provides separate tracking of revenue, cost, and expense productivity of consultants, managers, and contractors every month. These factors are then used to analyze profitability among resource groups and compute the accumulated profitability of engagements.

Revenue productivity is additionally the companion measurement with utilization for evaluating fixed-price business. Whereas utilization tells managers whether resources are busy, revenue per hour indicates whether revenue production is consistent with the effort expended, particularly near the final stages of the engagement.

In this chapter we will present productivity measurements and their use in layers of simple to complex. These layers correspond to progressively more complex mixes of business and types of service as follows.

- Per hour consulting.

- Fixed–price consulting.

- Mixed price terms consulting.

- Mixed price terms systems integration.

For each layer, we will look at computation of effective revenue and cost via the I & E and where to use the results to modify pricing and to analyze engagement profitability. We will look at examples of engagement profitability computations and discuss the typical profit profile of an engagement.

COMPUTING REVENUE AND COST PER PERSON

Most firms begin their annual financial planning with a revenue per year, direct cost per year, and total expense per year assumption for their people inventory. This allows the planners to use simple multiplication against various levels of head count to develop a high-level plan. There is, however, wide variety in how these three factors are computed and expressed.

Some planners develop individual factors for each type of resource (levels of consultants, levels of management, categories of contracted and borrowed personnel). Some planners go to the other extreme and develop factors only for consultants, leveraged by revenue and cost for managers, contractors, and borrowed people.

Once the plan is in place, routine productivity analysis becomes a cornerstone to the regular measurement of business success. Four purposes are served in the computation and analysis of productivity factors.

1. Track actual revenue, cost, and expense factors against plan assumptions. Assuming pricing is based from these plan assumptions, this is a quick test as to whether pricing is having a positive or negative effect on current financial results.

2. Compute relative profitability by type of resource. Junior consultants cost less than experienced consultants, but also bill less per hour, while experienced consultants charge more and attain lower utilization. The analysis allows each type to be isolated from the overall office profit computation and to be analyzed for its separate and unique profitability.

3. Compute average cost and expense per hour for use in measuring engagement profitability. The one-month gross and net profit on an engagement is the revenue billed for that month minus the number of people hours times the average cost and average expense, respectively, for each type of person used on the engagement. The overall profitability is the accumulated gross and net profits for each month of the engagement from its inception.

4. Compare the relative profitability of each type of resource that might be applied against a given revenue opportunity. Standard cost and expense per person factors for consultants versus contractors or borrowed people can assist in the decision of whom to use on an existing engagement, where the rate or fixed price is a given. A contractor that needs half again more hours with corresponding management to do a job may not be cheaper than borrowing an expensive internal resource, even though the direct rate is less.

We have already seen that the revenue stream for a people services business varies widely from month to month, based on the seasonality of utilization. We have also seen that cost and expense can vary month by month for an office that is growing through people acquisition. (We will take up the considerable effect of nonlabor revenue and cost as a separate subject.) Because revenue, cost, and expense productivity factors vary month by month, it is important to analyze and compare them month by month.

Productivity computation starts with revenue distribution. Labor generated revenue is separated from total revenue credited and is then divided among labor resource groups. In a basic people services business, this may be no more complicated than distributing revenue evenly against every hour or day worked (an office needs to select one unit of time for productivity computations). In complex service offices with considerable stratification of cost and corresponding revenue, the distribution will need to be at a more granular level of people groupings.

Once revenue per person is established, cost per person and expense per person are correspondingly determined. The choice of people groupings illustrated in this chapter is a compromise between easy revenue distribution and easy cost distribution, with a slight lean toward the cost side. Not by coincidence, the groupings are the same as those used to develop a price.

Computing Revenue Per Person

Firms that bill each person at a separate rate per hour or day have no difficulty in assigning actual invoiced revenue to each person. It is simply an accumulation of all hours/days times rate for that billing month. The only administrative complexity is to adjust the total, if hours were worked, but no revenue was invoiced.

Firms that invoice a blended rate for all people assigned to an engagement, or invoice a fixed amount against an agreed billing schedule have a much tougher challenge when distributing actual invoiced revenue by person or groups of people.

The solutions to this problem can vary from overly simplified to ridiculously complex. It is important to remember a rule taught to all high school science students: The precision of any number in a scientific analysis need be no more precise than the least precise number used in the computation. Therefore, if the cost and expense factors per person that will be compared to the revenue factors are very imprecise, there is no reason to be excruciatingly precise in revenue distributions.

If the firm's contract management system collects hours for all billed and assigned work against engagements (for all people including subcontractors), a reasonable level of detail is available. With this tool, the hours worked by each person on an engagement are divided into the amount invoiced to compute an effective revenue rate per delivered hour for that billing month. The revenue per hour is then accumulated by our groupings for all hours worked. This is illustrated in Figure 8-1, where six consultants, a manager, and two subcontractors are working on three engagements. The engagements each are billed differently.

- Engagement 1: Billed per hour at separate rates for each level of person assigned ($115 for associates, $133 for consultants, $180 for management).

- Engagement 2: Billed at a blended rate for all of $126 per hour.

- Engagement 3: A fixed-price invoiced bimonthly at $140,000.

The analysis shows the number of people assigned by group each month, the number of hours worked on behalf of their engagement, the number of hours billed out of those worked (on hourly engagements), and the revenue distributed to each group. From those data is computed revenue per month and revenue per hour worked (notice that time not billed reduces the overall effective rate per hour). The data is summarized for the quarter on the right and for all engagements at the bottom.

Engagement 1 has been in place for some time and has a number of months to go. Its utilization is fairly constant from month to month. As would be expected, associates perform more rework than consultants. A part-time manager splits billing to this and the other engagements, along with nonbillable marketing and other client relations activities.

Engagement 2 is nearing completion and the negotiations to get acceptance of the work product show in the data for the third month. Delivery has caused a high amount of rework. Engagement 3 is a fairly high-intensity project, with high utilization. Notice that its revenue per person factors are either very high when it invoices or zero when it doesn't.

Looking at the dollars per month column at the far right (under 3-Month Average), you see that the variation in revenue per month for each level is very slight for the two hourly engagements, even though the effective rates per hour vary widely ($20,300 per person at an average of $120 per hour versus $19,300 per person at $115 per hour). Even the fixed-price engagement, with its average of $149 per person, is only slightly higher in revenue per month per person. Given this mix of business, it would be perfectly reasonable to use a simple average of $20,000 per month for consultants and managers when computing revenue per person (contractors would be $24,000 per month).

Figure 8-1 points out a number of things to keep in mind when computing revenue factors.

- **Effect of utilization.** Levels of billed utilization have a much greater effect on revenue per person per month than does rate. This can be seen in Engagement 1 where the effective rate per hour varies between $120 and $167, while the high–rate person with low utilization contributes much the same per month as the low-rate person at high utilization (see associates versus managers).

- **Effect of uneven fixed-price payment schedules.** The fact that no revenue is billed in the second month of Engagement 3 clearly distorts the month-by-month tracking of revenue by person. However, the three-month average provides a fairly clear picture of the overall revenue production for the office and the relative production between the engagements.

- **Five–week months.** The third month in this example has five weeks of labor collection versus four weeks in the first and second months. Per hour contracts will bill more revenue per person per month simply because there is an additional week.

The larger the office, the less the gradation between amounts of revenue per person per month from less experienced to more experienced consultants. This is due to two phenomena—lower level people bill more hours on lower priced engagements, and higher level people bill fewer hours on higher priced engagements. The total three-month average for each level of person at the bottom of Figure 8-1 provides a very accurate base factor for computing resource profitability for this office.

The decision to be granular in distributing revenue per person is one of administrative workload. Figure 8-1 uses data that should be readily available from revenue and resource (utilization) tracking. Figure 8-2 shows how this data can be combined with an income statement spreadsheet to compute revenue productivity for our complex services office. It is an expansion of Figure

6-14, where we looked at the profitability of an office in April. The office was profitable, but was falling behind its revenue plan because of staffing difficulties.

A comparison of the third and fourth quarters dramatizes the effect of utilization. Contractors and borrowed people, who bill to their maximum availability, have very high revenue per month for both quarters. The permanent staff has a 50 percent swing in their revenue productivity due to a comparable 50 percent swing in utilization. We will see later that high utilization also makes the permanent staff a very profitable resource.

As you recall, this office is understaffed against its plan and business demand is strong. Actual revenue per person is running slightly ahead of plan, while revenue itself is falling behind. We would expect to see this trend continue as more and more overtime is used.

Computing Cost and Gross Profit Per Person

Cost per person per month also comes directly from the spreadsheet used to compute the income and expense statement. In Figure 8-3, we have expanded the cost statement part of Figure 6-14 to show revenue per person per month, cost per person per month, gross profit per person per month, and cost per hour.

Again compare the third and fourth quarters. The permanent staff is the most profitable of all resources at high utilization. In fact, the 50 percent improvement in utilization brings a 100 percent improvement in gross profit per person. Contractors and borrowed people are very close in relative profitability. We will see later how risk enters into a choice between these two sources of temporary people.

Notice how little can be concluded from the one month of data (April). No factor is comparable to its corresponding quarterly or annual accumulation. Year-to-date (YTD) data is just starting to be valid for trends. Cost per hour, a key assumption in our pricing, looks to be tracking well for all but managers.

The cost analysis and computation of cost and associated gross profit per person contains a major simplification. It makes managers stand alone as a resource group, rather than attempting to distribute any of their cost to the people and nonlabor costs they manage. It makes managers look like poor profit performers, but it reminds us that all other resources must carry the loss, and it avoids the debate of which resources require the most management.

Computing Expense and Net Profit Per Person

Another trade-off between exquisite accuracy and simplicity must be made when computing total direct expense per person and associated NEBA (net earnings before allocation) per person. Clearly some of the general operating expenses of the office are associated with managing employees, while the remainder is to deliver services and manage the business. In Figure 8-4, total indirect expense has been distributed between labor and nonlabor costs. One-third of administration and other direct expense has been allocated by relative head count to consultants, management, and borrowed people. The remainder of these and all selling expenses have been allocated by relative revenue earned to nonlabor and to each of consultants, management, contractors, and borrowed. Again, managers remain a stand-alone resource that carries expense.

The annual net profit for contractors is better than for borrowed people. The firm will need to reduce its internal salary transfer rate, if it is to encourage offices to borrow more. It would appear that both borrowed and contracted people are more profitable than consultants, until one looks at the effect of just 10 percent increase in utilization. The effect of the 50 percent swing between the third and fourth quarters translates to a 160 percent increase in permanent staff profitability.

The expense distribution method was intended to make the expense per hour fairly consistent across all resources, with a slight emphasis on the burden of employee administration. Going back to the comment regarding the precision of data, it is best to pick a simple allocation that makes sense and stay with it to give a consistent track.

Many field managers distribute management cost and expense similar to the way administrative and other indirect expense is allocated—a percentage to employees, including consultants and borrowed, and the rest to all other sources of revenue. Obviously, management generated revenue then must be distributed and considerable debate is inevitable as to which sources of revenue drag the most management generated revenue (or vice versa). The loss performance by managers makes them visible as a group and supports analysis of the effect of changes in their utilization. The data shows that they are dragging profit this year more than planned, and pricing action may be required.

USING PRODUCTIVITY MEASUREMENTS IN HOURLY/ DAILY RESOURCE DECISIONS

Figures 8-2 through 8-4 confirm our conclusions from Chapter 6 regarding the effect of high demand and a shortage of staff. Revenue rates are up. Cost per person is falling because we are not spending recruiting money. Net per person is down for two reasons: some underlying expenses are higher than expected

FIGURE 8-1
Distributing Revenue Per Person Per Month

Average Revenue Rate Analysis

		Month 1					Month 2					Month 3				3 Month Ave	
	#	Hours	Rev ($000)	$/Mo (000)	$/Hour	#	Hours	Rev ($000)	$/Mo (000)	$/Hour	#	Hours	Rev ($000)	$/Mo (000)	$/Hour	$/Mo (000)	$/Hour
Engagement 1 Total	3.3	580	72.3	$21.7	$124.61	2.3	419	48.2	$20.7	$114.94	2.3	350	41.8	$17.9	$119.29	$20.3	$120.23
Associate Worked	2.0	366		$21.0	$115.00	1.0	187		$17.5	$93.48	1.0	122		$12.4	$101.80	$18.0	$106.65
Billed		366	42.1				152	17.5				108	12.4				
Consultant Worked	1.0	162		$21.5	$133.00	1.0	176		$21.7	$123.18	1.0	201		$24.5	$121.75	$22.6	$125.60
Billed		162	21.5				163	21.7				184	24.5				
Senior Worked	0.0					0.0					0.0						
Billed																	
Manager Worked	0.3	52		$26.2	$166.15	0.3	56		$27.3	$160.71	0.3	27		$14.7	$180.00	$22.7	$166.67
Billed		48	8.6				50	9.0				27	4.9				
Contractor	0.0					0.0					0.0						
Engagement 2 Total	2.3	225	28.4	$12.2	$126.00	3.6	541	64.4	$18.0	$119.01	5.3	1,111	123.9	$23.2	$111.48	$19.3	$115.39
Associate Worked	0.0	0				1.0	138		$13.6	$98.61	2.0	411		$24.4	$118.95	$20.8	$113.84
Billed		0	0.0				108	13.6				388	48.9				
Consultant Worked	1.0	91		$11.5	$126.00	1.0	171		$21.5	$126.00	1.0	292		$23.6	$80.69	$18.9	$102.12
Billed		91	11.5				171	21.5				187	23.6				
Senior Worked	1.0	112		$14.1	$126.00	1.0	153		$19.3	$126.00	1.0	162		$20.4	$126.00	$17.9	$126.00
Billed		112	14.1				153	19.3				162	20.4				
Manager Worked	0.3	22		$8.4	$126.00	0.3	41		$15.7	$126.00	0.3	48		$18.3	$126.00	$14.1	$126.00
Billed		22	2.8				41	5.2				48	6.0				
Contractor	0.0					0.3	38	4.8	$19.2	$126.00	1.0	198	24.9	$24.9	$126.00	$23.8	$126.00

FIGURE 8-1
Distributing Revenue Per Person Per Month (concluded)

Average Revenue Rate Analysis

	Month 1					Month 2					Month 3					3 Month Ave	
	#	Hours	Rev ($000)	$/Mo (000)	$/Hour	#	Hours	Rev ($000)	$/Mo (000)	$/Hour	#	Hours	Rev ($000)	$/Mo (000)	$/Hour	$/Mo (000)	$/Hour
Engagement 3 Total																	
Associate Worked	4.3	635	140.0	$32.3	$220.47	4.3	624	0.0	$0.0	$0.00	3.3	618	140.0	$41.9	$226.54	$23.3	$149.17
Billed	1.0	152	33.5	$33.5	$220.47	1.0	161	0.0	$0.0	$0.00	0.0	0	0.0		$226.54	$16.8	$107.07
Consultant Worked	1.0	148	32.6	$32.6	$220.47	1.0	132	0.0	$0.0	$0.00	1.0	188	42.6	$42.6	$226.54	$25.1	$160.72
Billed																	
Senior Worked	1.0	144	31.7	$31.7	$220.47	1.0	141	0.0	$0.0	$0.00	1.0	192	43.5	$43.5	$226.54	$25.1	$157.74
Billed																	
Manager Worked	0.3	43	9.5	$27.9	$220.47	0.3	42	0.0	$0.0	$0.00	0.3	53	12.0	$35.3	$226.54	$21.1	$155.70
Billed																	
Contractor	1.0	148	32.6	$32.6	$220.47	1.0	148	0.0	$0.0	$0.00	1.0	185	41.9	$41.9	$226.54	$24.8	$154.97
Billed																	
Summary	10.0	1,440	240.6	$24.1	$167.10	10.3	1,584	112.5	$11.0	$71.05	11.0	2,079	305.6	$27.8	$147.00	$21.1	$129.10
Associate	3.0	518	75.6	$25.2	$145.95	3.0	486	31.1	$10.4	$63.97	3.0	533	61.3	$20.4	$115.02	$18.7	$109.30
Consultant	3.0	401	65.6	$21.9	$163.70	3.0	479	43.2	$14.4	$90.24	3.0	681	90.6	$30.2	$133.07	$22.2	$127.80
Senior	2.0	256	45.9	$22.9	$179.14	2.0	294	19.3	$9.6	$65.57	2.0	354	63.9	$32.0	$180.53	$21.5	$142.75
Manager	1.0	117	20.9	$20.9	$178.57	1.0	139	14.2	$14.2	$101.91	1.0	128	22.9	$22.9	$179.02	$19.3	$150.97
Contractor	1.0	148	32.6	$32.6	$220.47	1.3	186	4.8	$3.8	$25.74	2.0	383	66.9	$33.4	$174.56	$24.5	$145.43
Consultants	8.0	1,175	187.1	$23.4	$159.24	8.0	1,259	93.6	$11.7	$74.34	8.0	1,568	215.8	$27.0	$137.65	$20.7	$124.07

FIGURE 8-2
Revenue Per Person Computation

| | | Revenue Productivity (Revenue Per Person) | | | | | | | | | |
| | | Quarter 1 | | Quarter 2 | | Quarter 3 | | Quarter 4 | | Total Year | | April |
		Plan	Actual	Plan	Actual	Plan	Actual	Plan	Actual	Plan	YTD	Actual
Revenue ($000)	Trainee/new trainee	94	94	77		26		54		250	118	23
	Associate	297	279	370		445		629		1,741	391	112
	Consultant/intern	479	454	573		494		654		2,199	611	157
	Senior	150	147	113		190		292		745	196	49
	Consultants	1,019	975	1,132		1,154		1,629		4,935	1,316	342
	Management	142	132	219		213		235		809	195	63
	Contractors	636	637	636		636		636		2,543	833	196
	Borrowed	296	301	296		222		222		1,035	400	99
	TOTAL	2,093	2,045	2,282		2,225		2,722		9,322	2,744	699
Consulting	Labor	430	425	509		507		607		2,053	591	166
	Nonlabor	17	13	20		20		24		82	18	5
	TOTAL	447	438	529		527		631		2,135	609	171
Education	Labor	275	275	297		276		308		1,156	373	98
	Nonlabor	15	16	15		15		15		60	22	5
	TOTAL	290	291	312		291		323		1,216	395	103
Custom development	Labor	1,387	1,347	1,476		1,442		1,808		6,113	1,784	437
	Nonlabor	42	34	44		43		54		183	45	11
	TOTAL	1,429	1,381	1,520		1,485		1,862		6,296	1,829	448
Total Income	Labor	2,092	2,047	2,282		2,225		2,723		9,322	2,748	701
	Nonlabor	74	63	80		78		94		325	84	21
	TOTAL	2,166	2,110	2,362		2,303		2,817		9,647	2,832	722
Revenue/Month	Trainee/new trainee	7,809	7,870	8,545		1,709		4,494		5,212	7,860	7,820
	Associate	15,210	15,491	15,413		15,616		19,063		16,577	15,623	15,964
	Consultant/intern	14,508	14,407	14,688		13,170		18,954		15,273	14,383	14,313
	Senior	16,675	16,389	18,772		15,808		24,371		19,099	16,369	16,308
	Consultants	13,866	13,824	14,516		12,411		17,807		14,688	13,928	14,232
	Management	11,856	11,008	14,569		14,213		15,635		14,185	12,177	15,683
	Contractors	19,266	19,309	19,266		19,266		19,266		19,266	18,933	17,805
	Borrowed	24,648	25,115	24,648		24,648		24,648		24,648	25,028	24,764
	Average	16,038	16,041	16,539		14,834		18,327		16,441	16,097	16,261

FIGURE 8–2
Revenue Per Person Computation (concluded)

Revenue Productivity (Revenue Per Person)

		Quarter 1 Plan	Quarter 1 Actual	Quarter 2 Plan	Quarter 2 Actual	Quarter 3 Plan	Quarter 3 Actual	Quarter 4 Plan	Quarter 4 Actual	Total Year Plan	Total Year YTD	April Actual
Revenue/Hour	Trainee/new trainee	85.03	85.00	84.98		84.89		85.05		85.01	85.00	85.00
	Associate	117.00	118.00	116.99		116.99		117.00		116.99	118.00	118.00
	Consultant/intern	135.02	134.87	135.01		135.01		134.99		135.00	135.09	135.73
	Senior	185.05	186.00	189.94		190.08		190.02		189.00	186.89	189.63
	Consultants	127.49	127.70	127.18		131.73		131.46		129.69	128.12	129.34
	Management	189.95	192.00	205.00		205.00		205.00		202.18	196.00	205.00
	Contractors	117.00	117.00	117.00		117.00		117.00		117.00	117.00	117.00
	Borrowed	158.00	157.96	158.00		158.00		158.00		158.00	158.21	159.00
	Average	130.41	130.49	132.12		133.72		133.56		132.53	131.20	133.34
Hours	Trainee/new trainee	1,102.0	1,111.0	905.0		302.0		634.0		2,943	1,387	276.0
	Associate	2,535.0	2,363.0	3,162.0		3,804.0		5,377.0		14,878	3,310	947.0
	Consultant/intern	3,546.0	3,365.0	4,243.0		3,658.0		4,844.0		16,291	4,525	1,160.0
	Senior	811.0	793.0	593.0		998.0		1,539.0		3,941	1,051	258.0
	Consultants	7,994	7,632	8,903		8,762		12,394		38,053	10,273	2,641
	Management	749.0	688.0	1,066.0		1,040.0		1,144.0		3,999	994	306.0
	Contractors	5,434.0	5,446.0	5,434.0		5,434.0		5,434.0		21,736	7,120	1,674.0
	Borrowed	1,872.0	1,908.0	1,872.0		1,404.0		1,404.0		6,552	2,531	623.0
	TOTAL	16,049	15,674	17,275		16,640		20,376		70,340	20,918	5,244
Average Head Count	Trainee/new trainee	4.0	4.0	3.0		5.0		4.0		4.0	3.8	3.0
	Associate	6.5	6.0	8.0		9.5		11.0		8.8	6.3	7.0
	Consultant/intern	11.0	10.5	13.0		12.5		11.5		12.0	10.6	11.0
	Senior	3.0	3.0	2.0		4.0		4.0		3.3	3.0	3.0
	Consultants	24.5	23.5	26.0		31.0		30.5		28.0	23.6	24.0
	Management	4.0	4.0	5.0		5.0		5.0		4.8	4.0	4.0
	Contractors	11.0	11.0	11.0		11.0		11.0		11.0	11.0	11.0
	Borrowed	4.0	4.0	4.0		3.0		3.0		3.5	4.0	4.0
	TOTAL	43.5	42.5	46.0		50.0		49.5		47.3	42.6	43.0

FIGURE 8-3
Cost and Gross Profit Per Person Computation

		Cost Productivity (Cost & Gross Profit Per Person)										
		Quarter 1		Quarter 2		Quarter 3		Quarter 4		Total Year		April
		Plan	Actual	Plan	Actual	Plan	Actual	Plan	Actual	Plan	YTD	Actual
Total Income	Labor	2,092	2,047	2,282		2,225		2,723		9,322	2,748	701
	Nonlabor	74	63	80		78		94		325	84	21
	TOTAL	2,166	2,110	2,362		2,303		2,817		9,647	2,832	722
Direct Cost	Direct labor	1,392	1,377	1,453		1,451		1,423		5,720	1,781	404
	Direct nonlabor	71	63	76		75		88		310	85	23
	TOTAL	1,464	1,439	1,529		1,527		1,511		6,030	1,866	427
Gross Profit	Margin	702	671	833		777		1,306		3,617	966	296
		32%	32%	35%		34%		46%		37%	34%	41%
Cost ($000)	Trainee/new trainee	88	86	64		91		71		315	103	17
	Associate	157	143	190		202		226		775	187	44
	Consultant/intern	308	292	354		312		285		1,259	374	82
	Senior	108	108	71		133		131		444	139	31
	Consultants	662	630	679		739		713		2,793	803	173
	Management	179	181	222		211		208		820	233	52
	Contractors	353	360	353		353		353		1,413	472	111
	Borrowed	198	205	198		149		149		695	273	67
	TOTAL	1,392	1,377	1,453		1,451		1,423		5,720	1,781	404
Revenue/Month	Trainee/new trainee	7,809	7,870	8,545		1,709		4,494		5,212	7,860	7,820
	Associate	15,210	15,491	15,413		15,616		19,063		16,577	15,623	15,964
	Consultant/intern	14,508	14,407	14,688		13,170		18,954		15,273	14,383	14,313
	Senior	16,675	16,389	18,772		15,808		24,371		19,099	16,369	16,308
	Consultants	13,866	13,824	14,516		12,411		17,807		14,688	13,928	14,232
	Management	11,856	11,008	14,569		14,213		15,635		14,185	12,177	15,683
	Contractors	19,266	19,309	19,266		19,266		19,266		19,266	18,933	17,805
	Borrowed	24,648	25,115	24,648		24,648		24,648		24,648	25,028	24,764
	Average	16,038	16,041	16,539		14,834		18,327		16,441	16,097	16,261

FIGURE 8-3
Cost and Gross Profit Per Person Computation (concluded)

		Cost Productivity (Cost & Gross Profit Per Person)										
		Quarter 1		Quarter 2		Quarter 3		Quarter 4		Total Year		April
		Plan	Actual	Plan	Actual	Plan	Actual	Plan	Actual	Plan	YTD	Actual
Cost/Month	Trainee/new trainee	7,332	7,206	7,165		6,073		5,944		6,560	6,874	5,547
	Associate	8,065	7,948	7,901		7,079		6,854		7,380	7,471	6,244
	Consultant/intern	9,347	9,276	9,071		8,332		8,248		8,745	8,800	7,437
	Senior	11,999	12,045	11,881		11,106		10,928		11,376	11,581	10,189
	Consultants	9,003	8,938	8,707		7,942		7,794		8,311	8,496	7,197
	Management	14,915	15,080	14,805		14,036		13,864		14,378	14,578	13,073
	Contractors	10,703	10,919	10,703		10,703		10,703		10,703	10,723	10,136
	Borrowed	16,540	17,092	16,540		16,540		16,540		16,540	17,035	16,865
	Average	10,669	10,796	10,529		9,675		9,584		10,088	10,443	9,395
Gross Profit/Month	Trainee/new trainee	477	663	1,381		-4,363		-1,451		-1,348	985	2,273
	Associate	7,145	7,542	7,511		8,536		12,209		9,198	8,152	9,719
	Consultant/intern	5,161	5,131	5,617		4,837		10,706		6,529	5,583	6,876
	Senior	4,676	4,344	6,891		4,702		13,443		7,722	4,788	6,119
	Consultants	4,863	4,886	5,809		4,469		10,013		6,376	5,432	7,035
	Management	-3,059	-4,072	-236		177		1,770		-194	-2,401	2,610
	Contractors	8,563	8,390	8,563		8,563		8,563		8,563	8,209	7,669
	Borrowed	8,108	8,023	8,108		8,108		8,108		8,108	7,992	7,899
	Average	5,369	5,245	6,010		5,159		8,743		6,353	5,654	6,866
Cost/Hour	Trainee/new trainee	79.84	77.83	71.25		301.61		112.51		106.99	74.34	60.30
	Associate	62.04	60.55	59.97		53.04		42.07		52.08	56.43	46.16
	Consultant/intern	86.99	86.83	83.38		85.42		58.74		77.30	84.62	77.55
	Senior	133.15	136.70	120.22		133.54		85.21		112.58	132.23	118.48
	Consultants	82.77	82.57	76.29		84.29		57.54		73.39	78.96	68.11
	Management	238.96	263.02	208.32		202.44		181.79		204.94	234.65	170.89
	Contractors	65.00	66.16	65.00		65.00		65.00		65.00	66.27	66.61
	Borrowed	106.03	107.50	106.03		106.03		106.03		106.03	107.69	108.29
	Average	86.76	87.82	84.11		87.21		69.85		81.32	85.55	78.61

FIGURE 8-4
Expense and NEBA Per Person Computation

Expense & Net Profit Productivity (Per Person)

		Quarter 1 Plan	Quarter 1 Actual	Quarter 2 Plan	Quarter 2 Actual	Quarter 3 Plan	Quarter 3 Actual	Quarter 4 Plan	Quarter 4 Actual	Total Year Plan	Total Year YTD	April Actual
Total Income	Labor	2,092	2,047	2,282		2,225		2,723		9,322	2,748	701
	Nonlabor	74	63	80		78		94		325	84	21
	TOTAL	2,166	2,110	2,362		2,303		2,817		9,647	2,832	722
Direct Cost	Direct labor	1,392	1,377	1,453		1,451		1,423		5,720	1,781	404
	Direct nonlabor	71	63	76		75		88		310	85	23
	TOTAL	1,464	1,439	1,529		1,527		1,511		6,030	1,866	427
Indirect Expense	Selling	92	94	98		93		90		373	122	27
	Administration	134	139	141		145		146		566	173	33
	Other indirect	27	29	27		27		27		109	38	9
	TOTAL	253	262	266		266		263		1,048	332	70
Net Earnings (NEBA)		449	408	567		511		1,042		2,569	634	226
	Margin	21%	19%	24%		22%		37%		27%	22%	31%
	Labor	453	414	570		515		1,043		2,582	643	229
	Margin	22%	20%	25%		23%		38%		28%	23%	33%
	Nonlabor	-5	-6	-3		-4		-1		-13	-9	-3
	Margin	-6%	-10%	-4%		-5%		-1%		-4%	-11%	-14%
Expense ($000)	Trainee/new trainee	15	16	12		9		10		46	19	3
	Associate	38	38	46		54		62		200	50	12
	Consultant/intern	62	63	71		63		65		261	80	17
	Senior	19	20	13		23		27		82	25	5
	Consultants	134	137	142		149		164		589	173	37
	Management	20	20	27		27		25		98	27	7
	Contractors	59	63	57		58		47		222	78	15
	Borrowed	34	37	33		25		21		112	46	9
	TOTAL	246	256	259		259		256		1,020	324	68
Gross Profit/Month	Trainee/new trainee	477	663	1,381		-4,363		-1,451		-1,348	985	2,273
	Associate	7,145	7,542	7,511		8,536		12,209		9,198	8,152	9,719
	Consultant/intern	5,161	5,131	5,617		4,837		10,706		6,529	5,583	6,876
	Senior	4,676	4,344	6,891		4,702		13,443		7,722	4,788	6,119

FIGURE 8–4
Expense and NEBA Per Person Computation (concluded)

Expense & Net Profit Productivity (Per Person)

	Quarter 1		Quarter 2		Quarter 3		Quarter 4		Total Year		April
	Plan	Actual	Plan	Actual	Plan	Actual	Plan	Actual	Plan	YTD	Actual
Expense/Month											
Consultants	4,863	4,886	5,809		4,469		10,013		6,376	5,432	7,035
Management	-3,059	-4,072	-236		177		1,770		-194	-2,401	2,610
Contractors	8,563	8,390	8,563		8,563		8,563		8,563	8,209	7,669
Borrowed	8,108	8,023	8,108		8,108		8,108		8,108	7,992	7,899
Average	5,369	5,245	6,010		5,159		8,743		6,353	5,654	6,866
Trainee/new trainee	1,255	1,348	1,279		627		810		952	1,286	1,036
Associate	1,944	2,102	1,897		1,899		1,888		1,903	1,982	1,673
Consultant/intern	1,879	1,995	1,832		1,676		1,880		1,813	1,878	1,544
Senior	2,080	2,191	2,199		1,917		2,280		2,110	2,068	1,699
Consultants	1,819	1,937	1,816		1,606		1,795		1,753	1,835	1,537
Management	1,632	1,658	1,821		1,771		1,634		1,719	1,656	1,651
Contractors	1,795	1,910	1,732		1,763		1,425		1,679	1,780	1,391
Borrowed	2,823	3,054	2,727		2,726		2,301		2,663	2,880	2,360
Average	1,888	2,009	1,876		1,724		1,727		1,800	1,902	1,587
Net Profit/Month											
Trainee/new trainee	-778	-685	101		-4,990		-2,261		-2,300	-300	1,237
Associate	5,201	5,441	5,615		6,637		10,321		7,295	6,170	8,047
Consultant/intern	3,282	3,136	3,785		3,161		8,827		4,715	3,705	5,332
Senior	2,596	2,153	4,692		2,785		11,163		5,613	2,720	4,419
Consultants	3,044	2,949	3,993		2,863		8,218		4,623	3,596	5,498
Management	-4,691	-5,730	-2,057		-1,594		136		-1,912	-4,058	959
Contractors	6,768	6,480	6,831		6,799		7,138		6,884	6,429	6,278
Borrowed	5,285	4,970	5,381		5,382		5,807		5,445	5,112	5,538
Average	3,481	3,236	4,135		3,435		7,016		4,553	3,751	5,279
Expense/Hour											
Trainee/new trainee	13.66	14.56	12.72		31.13		15.33		15.53	13.90	11.26
Associate	14.95	16.01	14.40		14.23		11.59		13.43	14.97	12.36
Consultant/intern	17.48	18.67	16.84		17.18		13.39		16.03	18.06	16.09
Senior	23.09	24.86	22.25		23.05		17.78		20.88	23.61	19.76
Consultants	16.72	17.89	15.91		17.05		13.25		15.48	17.06	14.55
Management	26.14	28.93	25.62		25.55		21.43		24.50	26.66	21.58
Contractors	10.90	11.57	10.52		10.71		8.65		10.19	11.00	9.14
Borrowed	18.10	19.21	17.48		17.48		14.75		17.07	18.21	15.15
Average	15.35	16.34	14.98		15.54		12.59		14.51	15.58	13.28

FIGURE 8-5
Comparing Actual Cost Per Hour to Pricing Assumptions

	Cost Per Hour Versus Pricing			
	Current Pricing Factor	Planned Cost Differential	Actual Cost/Hr	Actual Rev/Hr
Associate	.73	.68	−1.03	+1.01
Consultant	1.00	–	–	–
Senior	1.33	2.15	+1:09	–
Manager	1.66	2.74	+1.10	+1.01

(most notably facilities and computer services); and overall head count is lower, increasing the distribution per person.

We saw an increase in contractors as a possible solution to our revenue problem, and the data shows we can probably remain profitable with contractors, although we will need to track it very closely. Continued high utilization will have the obvious benefit of keeping profits from dipping as much as expected during the third quarter.

These are not startling revelations, but they do provide some additional data to the decision process. An hourly (daily) business needs detailed productivity analysis, when a major plan change is required. Having the data on a quarterly basis, though, can be useful in making other operational decisions that arise.

1. Is the profitability per level of resource consistent with current pricing?
2. If additional people were needed, what is the most profitable choice?
3. Are there any loss leaders among the sources of revenue (i.e., do any revenue sources show increases in revenue and increasing loss)?

The previous illustrations included a computation of revenue and cost per hour, along with revenue and cost per month. Per month productivity is a measure of the relative profitability of the individual. Productivity per hour tells us what our market is bearing, particularly whether we are price competitive.

When we built our plan, we revised our pricing assumptions using cost differentials between our less expensive and more expensive resources. Figure 8-5 shows factors we are using during pricing to discount the labor cost for an associate and add premium for seniors and managers. As can be seen, our cost per hour differentials built into the plan are different, but we have chosen to get a greater return from associates and less from seniors for competitive reasons.

We have built a plan that assumes we will add people, particularly in the lower rate ranks. We are now executing without those people due to staffing problems. Is our pricing still correct?

We see that the first quarter cost and revenue per hour for consultants is very close to plan. For associates, we are running 3 percent less in cost per hour and 1 percent higher in revenue. For seniors, we are seeing revenue productivity as expected, but our costs are up (a cause for alarm, since we are not recovering full cost differential as it is). Managers are costing more, but also returning more.

We might consider raising our rate for associates. The 1 percent means that clients are accepting associates, where we priced higher level people. Demand is high and supply is low, so we are not taking a large risk.

We have already raised senior and manager rates and another might be premature. The cost problem with each might be better addressed with higher utilization. More hours delivered will drive down the cost per hour. If the cost productivity continues to persist through the second quarter, this office may want to again raise its high-end rates.

Choosing Cost Productive Resources

A good use of cost per person in hourly/daily business is in the choice of resources for an existing engagement. The typical situation is a large project that has a predefined rate to be charged and the manager must choose among readily available people for the next person to be assigned. The relative cost per hour among alternatives is a key input to the resource decision.

Choosing a resource against a given revenue rate brings in other factors than pure cost.

- Is there a risk that the individual cannot produce quality intellectual output at the level of other resource choices? Not all people are intellectually equal and some can advance the work faster within the same number of hours.
- Will the individual require more management attention than another choice? The cost per hour of management will increase, if nonbillable time is needed to support this individual.
- Will the person's cost include extra travel or commute?

Figure 8-6 is an example of a quick analysis to choose a person for a 100-hour assignment where the client is paying $133 per hour for the work. The original pricing assumed a consultant level person, but none are immediately available. The client has agreed to a substitute, but expects comparable quality. Each choice of lower level consultant, higher level consultant, contractor, and

FIGURE 8–6
Resource Cost Analysis for an Hourly Assignment

		Cost of Risk			
	Cost/Hour	Work Risk	Mgmt	Travel	Effective Cost/Hour
Consultant	$ 77.30	1.00	1.00	1.00	$ 77.30
Associate	52.08	1.30	1.20	1.00	81.24
Senior	112.58	.75	.90	1.00	75.99
Contractor	65.00	1.10	1.10	1.00	78.65
Borrowed	106.03	.90	.90	1.10	94.47

borrowed person is listed with its relative costs per person from the previous illustrations.

The cost discounts and premiums used in this example are judgments that a manager makes. It is assumed that a specific individual is the subject of each choice. If the senior truly will produce 25 percent more for the 100 hours, that is probably the right choice. It becomes a close call after that, with the contractor having a slight edge.

Looking for Loss Leaders

Identifying loss leaders among resources is a simple by-product of ongoing resource rate analysis. In our analysis, we are getting $48 per hour in gross profit for consultants and seniors through the first quarter. We had expected to see this grow to an average of $52 and $76 per hour, respectively, for the year. Because we cannot hire lower level people, we will be faced a number of times with the decision of whether to use higher rate people to fill assignments at a lower rate to meet client commitments. If by midyear, the gross profit productivity for seniors does not move up toward $60 per hour (our cumulative midyear expectation), we will be well below part of our profit plan.

Loss leaders can occur for other reasons. We may have built a plan and pricing structure with an assumption that we will promote 20 percent of our people through the year. If we exceed that plan, we may be moving our cost per hour up faster than compensating revenue per hour. Revenue per person growth can be delayed by a high concentration of long engagements at old rates.

The business downturn and subsequent recovery in our other profit tracking example can easily be a source of loss leaders. We will put anyone anywhere to get billing during a downturn. When the recovery starts, we need to analyze where we have people stuck in low gross billing and move them out as quickly as we can.

Those who use contractors to supplement their permanent staff are inherently prone to developing low gross per hour situations. Contractor rates change with the market, just as we change our rates. When rates are low, we can take greater risk in using subcontractors. When contractor rates rise, they may no longer be the right choice. We need to avoid locking such an individual into an engagement.

The executive of a purely hourly/daily rate business need not spend much time on productivity analysis. Having the numbers produced automatically in the I & E process makes them available, if needed. The data needs to be reviewed at least once per year to understand the relationships between productivity, revenue stream, utilization, and overall profit for the previous year and to establish planning assumptions for the new year. Beyond that, productivity analysis is a tool to be used when profit is running off track and utilization is not the obvious problem. Most experienced executives can visualize these relationships in their heads as they make decisions. They find themselves regenerating productivity numbers whenever they feel their vision is becoming clouded by reality.

USING PRODUCTIVITY MEASUREMENTS IN FIXED–PRICE RESOURCE DECISIONS

Regular analysis of revenue and cost productivity factors is mandatory when a professional services business contains more than 10 percent fixed-price revenue. Resource decisions and profitability assessment cannot be performed on utilization and profit data alone. As all in the business know, the direct relationship between utilization and profit goes out the window on a fixed-price engagement.

Figure 8-7 shows a project cost curve (also known as the hippopotamus by those who pay for it). It shows the hours of work needed to perform a typical people resource project against time. Superimposed on this chart is another, where the project has gone astray and the project team is obliged to complete the work to a mutually agreed upon level of completeness and quality.

On an hourly/daily rate contract, most of these hours will be paid for by the client and a plot of the revenue stream will have a similar track to the hours (even though agreements may have been reached that some of the overage will be performed pro bono). The billed utilization of the people assigned is a direct measure of the relative profitability of those resources against revenue earned,

FIGURE 8–7
Engagement Work as a Function of Time

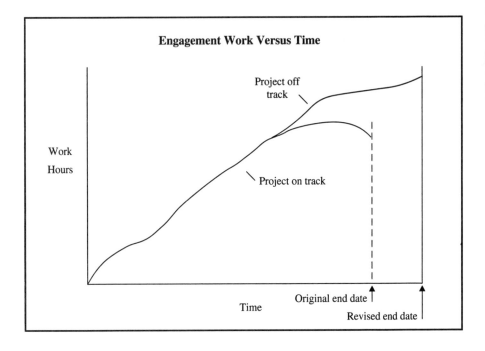

and the difference between billed and assigned hours is a measure of concessions made to the client.

On a fixed-price contract, the revenue stream is often not a function of hours worked. They are payments which are some percentage of the total agreed upon fixed price, scheduled at intervals based on a compromise between cash needs of the firm and the client's demand for demonstrable checkpoints and quality.

Using the example as a fixed price, the firm might have an agreement to bill three times: 25 percent at the end of the first month to confirm and compensate start up; 40 percent at an interim completion point scheduled midway through the effort; and the remainder following completion. When the project comes apart at the midpoint checkpoint, the best the firm may get is their first 25 percent payment, but they may see no further revenue until the revised completion date. At that time, they might recover a small increase in total price as a reward for good change control.

High utilization in the last weeks of this project is not a good deal for the professional services office. Most of the hours past the original end date will not be paid for. The increased hours prior to the original end date will be at an effective revenue rate less than originally planned (effective revenue rate being the original price divided by the originally estimated number of hours). In fact, the higher the utilization on the project, the lower the profit.

Revenue, cost, and expense productivity factors are a key tool in managing this project. The secret to making money in a fixed-price overrun is to use the extra risk and profit that was priced into the original deal to finance the best combination of consultant overtime (cost-free resources), high-priced talent to get the job done right, and low-priced talent to do the bulk work. Computing the new effective revenue rate and knowing the relative cost and expense rates for each kind of talent gives the operational manager for this effort the tools to make correct decisions regarding personnel.

One's first challenge is to choose a consistent technique for computing revenue per hour. A 1,000-hour project to be billed at $200,000 at its completion starts out being an effective revenue rate of $200 per hour. It will not take exactly 1,000 hours to complete—that would be contrived coincidence. Unfortunately, we can't wait until the end to find out what the revenue should have been. We need a mechanism to compute probable revenue rates as the project proceeds as a means to make cost decisions.

There are three methods for computing effective revenue per person per hour for fixed-price engagements.

• **As billed/invoiced.** For any month in which a client is billed, the effective revenue rate will be the hours expended in that month divided into the actual invoice amount. For any other month, the effective revenue rate is $0 per hour. The simplest approach is to equally distribute the dollars to all hours, regardless of level. A slightly more complex approach is to weight the distribution, giving higher rates to higher level people. The as billed method has the advantage of simplicity and is useful when analyzing periods of three months and more. It has the obvious disadvantage of gross inconsistencies in profit measurements from month to month and the inability to plot trends.

This method was used earlier in Figure 8-1 to demonstrate the use of revenue productivity measurements across an entire office. Assuming an office has multiple engagements, there is a high probability that some revenue will be invoiced every month, and that over a quarter, an accurate picture of profitability will appear. The as billed method is, therefore, the simplest for analyzing the entire business base and large groupings of people. On the other hand, it is not very useful in analyzing an individual engagement or an individual person.

• **Preset rate.** At the pricing of the engagement, each type of resource is assigned an effective revenue rate for the hours of estimated work by that level or type of person. This is the effective rate for all hours worked until the accumulated revenue earned reaches the maximum price of the engagement. All hours after that are at $0 per hour until completion of the work or a renegotiation of the agreement to raise the fixed price. In the event of an underrun (fewer hours are used than estimated), the leftover dollars are distributed to the hours worked for that period, similar to the as billed method. This method requires more computation complexity (is very difficult to do by hand), particularly on the day when the maximum price is reached or when a price increase occurs. It does, however, provide a steady revenue stream against cost and expense until the money runs out.

The additional disadvantage of this method is that it does not penalize profitability for bad payment schedule decisions. In the case where the client only pays at the end, it could appear that the office is profitable, when it is not. In the early weeks of a business downturn, cost reduction actions may not get necessary priority, because revenue looks better than it should.

- **Recalculation.** Again, a preset rate is computed from pricing assumptions and is used hour by hour to accumulate revenue earned. At the end of the first measurement period (week or month), the revenue rate is recalculated by dividing the hours estimated to complete into revenue to be earned. Revenue to be earned is computed by dividing each scheduled payment by the number of intervening measurement periods and assigning a revenue earned value to each period. For example, the manager of a five-month project with a $50,000 payment after two months and a remainder payment of $120,000 at completion would expect two $25,000 monthly revenue periods and three $40,000 monthly revenue periods. If at the end of the second month, the estimate to complete is 10 percent higher than the remaining hours in the plan, the revenue rate per hour for the next period goes down by 10 percent. This recalculation will be made again at the end of the next period and the revenue per hour rate will increase or decrease accordingly.

Clearly this is not simple. The recalculation method is very useful in computing individual engagement profitability. It is used by an office where a very large fixed-price deal dominates the financial health of the business. It is used when payment delays occur that change the revenue productivity for the remainder of a year. In the example, a delay of the final payment beyond the end of the year would cause revenue per hour to be calculated as though the effort was a $50,000 effort for the hours to be expended in that year. This might cause the last few weeks to see no effective revenue from this engagement.

Figure 8-8 is a graph of consultant utilization versus revenue productivity for a fixed-price engagement that has a nominal overrun in estimated hours. The upper light dashed line is the overall revenue rate of $165 per hour from pricing. The lower light dashed line is the planned average utilization of 83 per-

FIGURE 8–8
Computing Revenue Productivity for Fixed Price

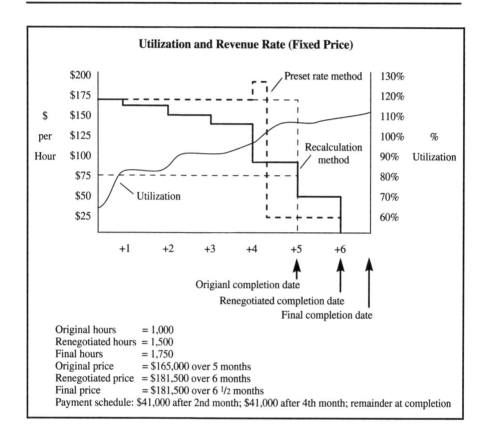

Utilization and Revenue Rate (Fixed Price)

Original hours = 1,000
Renegotiated hours = 1,500
Final hours = 1,750
Original price = $165,000 over 5 months
Renegotiated price = $181,500 over 6 months
Final price = $181,500 over 6 ½ months
Payment schedule: $41,000 after 2nd month; $41,000 after 4th month; remainder at completion

cent. The heavy dotted line is the actual revenue per hour using the preset rate method and the heavy solid line illustrates the recalculation method. The engagement is priced at $165,000 for an estimated 1,000 hours over five months. The payment schedule is 25 percent after the first and third months with the remainder after completion. At the end of the fourth month, an extension of one month and an increase in the fixed price by 10 percent is negotiated, triggered by a revised estimate of 50 percent hours of work. In fact, the effort takes two more weeks beyond that, with a final expenditure of 1,750 hours.

Notice that utilization was under plan for the first month. Unless by some miracle, this project was overestimated, this guaranteed that revenue per person would deteriorate later in the effort. The project manager begins to see the future during the third month and both utilization and recalculated revenue per person show the result (utilization climbs and revenue per person dives).

The recalculation method track tells the story. Each month, the estimate to complete increases, bringing down the remaining revenue per hour. The work is building toward the final actual expenditure of 1,750 hours. The final month (the seventh month) and its 250 hours are at a zero rate, because all revenue was credited to expended hours by the end of the sixth month.

The strange blip in the preset rate track results from the 10 percent price increase coming before the original 1,000 hours are expended at the preset $165 per hour. The rate goes up to $181 per hour for one week and then drops to $18 per hour until the reestimated number of hours runs out.

If priced with sufficient risk added to the expected expense, this project might break even (against a NEBA measurement, not NEBT). Cost was hurt early by poor utilization and later by the addition of extra people. As utilization grew above 100 percent, contractors and borrowed people became more and more expensive (their hours per week billed usually mirror that of consultants on the same project), while consultants decreased in cost per hour. The temptation to overload this effort with cheaper contractors and borrowed people would be a very poor one and a cost per hour analysis at each of the fourth and sixth months would have made that very clear.

This example is intended to stress the need to track both revenue productivity and utilization for fixed-price business. An office executive cannot wait for actual cost and revenue data to make quick resource decisions. Tracking both utilization and revenue productivity against a plan provides tools for guiding these decisions. The potential for profit from high-margin fixed pricing must be matched with the additional management time needed to sort out complex financial signals and make sound decisions.

USING PRODUCTIVITY MEASUREMENTS IN A MIXED PRICING BUSINESS

The percentage mix of per hour/day revenue versus fixed-price revenue will determine which revenue per hour method should be used. If the average quarterly fixed-price revenue is less than 25 percent of overall average revenue, revenue rates can be computed using the as billed method (see Figure 8-1). When the fixed-price revenue comprises a 75 percent and higher portion of the revenue stream, all engagements need to be assessed using the recalculation method and summed together (treat per hour/day as having variable monthly scheduled payments).

This recommendation is based on two premises: the amount of effort needed to be spent on productivity computation grows as the content of fixed-price business grows, while the number of engagements has little to do with the administrative time needed; and the office's approach to clients regarding overruns tends to be the same, whether the business is per hour or fixed price. In other words, a high per hour, low fixed-price content office does not have in place a heavy administrative focus on revenue and cost rates for its engagements. Similarly, its clients are responsible for funding overruns and it performs little pro bono work for its hourly engagements and rarely overruns its small fixed-price deals.

The 75 percent plus fixed-price content office is the opposite. It will have established the administrative resource to keep track of fixed-price revenue crediting and can track its hourly/daily work in the same way. The office probably performs more pro bono work across all its engagements and has adopted a pricing and project management that absorbs the risk.

Not too surprising, the offices with 50–50 revenues from per hour and fixed price find themselves with a foot in both camps. The simplest approach is to let the administrative process use the preset rate method to compute revenue per person. Most contract management systems can compute effective hourly rate, and accumulate actual hours times rate until all expected revenue has been expended. This isn't going to work effectively, if the office performs per hour engagements by giving substantial pro bono hours concessions when overruns occur, wins few price increases for fixed-price overruns, and does not get regularly spaced progress payments for its engagements. Otherwise, the office will have to spend the management time to perform recalculations on each engagement each month.

If starting from below a 25 percent fixed-price mix and growing beyond it, the change from as billed to preset rate method should occur as soon as the revenue mix is consistently approaching the 50–50 mix, and will certainly change if the intent is to be beyond 50–50. Coming down in fixed-price mix requires a change in style to tighter change control and minimal client concessions before switching from the recalculation method. Again, the extra cost of complex analysis (as well as recovery of concessions) needs to be a part of the risk pricing on fixed-price contracts.

USING PRODUCTIVITY MEASUREMENTS FOR SYSTEMS INTEGRATION

In systems integration (and comparable product support and pure education businesses) the mix of labor generated and nonlabor generated revenue allows trade-offs to be made between the relative profitability of the two. This second degree of freedom in negotiating deals often leads to discounting of both components to get the business. The result is very tight margins for both, with the overall profit depending on high volume from the nonlabor components and very careful resource decisions for the labor generated portion.

Keeping measurements for an office's nonlabor business separate from its people business is the key to success. In each of the preceding chapters, we have seen revenue and expense for labor and nonlabor generated income identified as distinct and separate components. By imposing that discipline on financial data recording and compilation, we are now able to weigh their separate effects on profitability for the entire office and, later, for individual engagements.

Going back to the systems integration office example in Chapter 6 (Figures 6-12), we will analyze the profit productivity of both labor and nonlabor to determine whether we are on track to make our NEBA objective for the year. We will be looking at profit and productivity data for our office at the end of the third quarter. Our purpose is to determine whether all components of our business are contributing their share of profit and to take any immediate actions that are needed in the last quarter of the year.

The financial position of the office is displayed in a series of charts, Figures 8-9 through 8-12. Figure 8-9 shows income detail, profit detail for each nonlabor component, a summary of hours, and average head count. Figure 8-10 shows revenue productivity for labor resources and for each nonlabor component. Figure 8-11 contains cost and gross profit productivity for labor. Figure 8-12 is a summary of the expense and net profit productivity for labor.

Our office has had a fairly good year, but not without some difficulty. We had more attrition than planned and have, therefore, hired more than planned. It has been a good year for both consulting and education, which are 22 percent and 19 percent ahead of revenue plan, respectively. This has also helped our average revenue rate, since each of these command our highest rates. Backlog analysis shows that we have enough revenue coverage for the remainder of the year. Normal marketing will build a strong base for the coming year.

We have signed the additional systems integration engagement and will begin work in October. We will now need to staff for that engagement. The client has agreed to a start-up payment of $100,000 in November.

On the negative side, custom development is down, with resources having been shifted to systems integration. This in and of itself was not a problem as long as systems integration revenues stayed strong. Product support is well under plan (60 percent), because our software is not meeting its plan. We have also shifted those resources elsewhere.

Our major problem is that we are one month behind schedule on one of our two systems integration engagements, and we have not received a third quarter labor payment of $133,000 or any of our planned third quarter vendor generated revenue. The overall project will slip by that amount (and maybe more). We have readjusted our effective revenue rate by the recalculation method for September. We will receive one more labor payment this year and can expect all of the planned vendor checkpoints to occur by year end. We will need to carry the recalculated revenue rate through the rest of this year and establish a new rate starting in January.

Later, we will see how the new engagement affects our planning. We will be treating it as a three-month engagement for this year only, using the start-up payment as our only revenue source. The net of the systems integration payment problem will be a continuation of lower revenue productivity through the fourth quarter.

Utilization has not been good. Interns did not become billable as quickly as we planned, but our new trainees are becoming billable faster. Unfortunately, we get less per hour for the trainees. Overall consultant and manager utilization is at 51 percent against a plan of 56 percent.

We are not as profitable as we would like. We are 93 percent against our revenue plan, but we are exactly on our 28 percent gross profit plan. This translates to a 16 percent of NEBA, with a dismal 11 percent in September. If we do not make our revenue plan, we will likely miss our 21 percent NEBA objective by 3 percent.

Part of the problem is our product business. Our nonlabor business is not carrying enough of the indirect expense. The nonlabor business is at 79 percent of its revenue plan and is generating a 10 percent NEBA margin.

Clearly, we need to get more out of our people business in the last quarter. We need to reduce cost per person, increase revenue per person, and increase actual monthly billing to make up for the missed payment and product problem.

Our original plan was to add contractors in anticipation of the additional business in the fourth quarter. As you can see, contractor cost rates have been climbing steadily for the year. Contractors were already expected to be less profitable in the fourth quarter than our people, both permanent staff and borrowed. They will be even more so now.

Our high rate business is up, but we are not getting enough profit from our seniors and managers (see September net profit per person). Their utilization has not been as expected, even though their revenue productivity is up. The plan calls for substantially higher productivity in the last quarter for these resources. We need even higher.

The opportunity to make up both revenue and profit is in the increased demand for consulting and education. We have been focusing our marketing on systems integration. We need to shift to the high rate business. We can also put

FIGURE 8–9
Systems Integration Profit through the Third Quarter

Summary Income & Expense through Third Quarter

		Quarter 1 Plan	Quarter 1 Actual	Quarter 2 Plan	Quarter 2 Actual	Quarter 3 Plan	Quarter 3 Actual	Quarter 4 Plan	Total Year Plan	Total Year YTD	April Actual
Income	Consulting	339	392	334	422	368	454	526	1,567	1,268	159
	%	15.81%	18.40%	14.32%	18.15%	15.34%	19.21%	15.36%	15.21%	18.13%	19.44%
	Education	263	293	259	317	271	332	414	1,207	941	115
	%	12.09%	13.51%	10.94%	13.29%	11.10%	13.67%	12.08%	11.60%	13.11%	13.81%
	Custom development	724	610	777	633	746	647	862	3,109	1,890	219
	%	34.08%	29.10%	33.59%	27.31%	31.31%	27.86%	25.40%	30.44%	27.50%	27.21%
	Product support	377	205	415	253	474	306	534	1,800	764	130
	%	7.15%	4.69%	8.18%	4.79%	8.35%	5.50%	6.89%	7.58%	5.06%	5.84%
	Systems integration	921	1,000	2,105	2,312	1,380	864	1,690	6,097	4,176	293
	%	30.86%	34.31%	32.97%	36.45%	33.91%	33.76%	40.27%	35.17%	36.21%	33.70%
	TOTAL	2,625	2,499	3,889	3,937	3,239	2,602	4,026	13,779	9,039	916
Direct Cost	Labor	2,062	2,048	2,243	2,246	2,310	2,273	3,294	9,909	6,567	783
	%	78.59%	81.92%	57.66%	57.08%	71.29%	87.30%	81.78%	71.90%	74.00%	85.34%
	Nonlabor	563	451	1,646	1,691	929	329	732	3,870	2,471	133
	Travel	136	126	154	144	162	133	255	707	403	43
	Product	237	119	237	158	287	197	312	1,073	474	89
	Vendor	190	205	1,255	1,389	480	0	165	2,090	1,594	0
	Direct labor	1,396	1,404	1,457	1,476	1,649	1,681	1,796	6,298	4,562	568
	Direct nonlabor	464	379	1,276	1,309	741	289	602	3,082	1,977	114
	TOTAL	1,860	1,783	2,733	2,786	2,390	1,970	2,398	9,380	6,539	682
Gross Profit	Margin	766	716	1,156	1,151	849	632	1,628	4,399	2,499	234
	%	29%	29%	30%	29%	26%	24%	40%	32%	28%	26%
Indirect Expense	Selling	130	128	164	170	170	171	169	633	469	55
	Administration	148	159	177	197	188	179	196	708	534	66
	Other indirect	27	27	27	30	27	27	27	109	84	11
	TOTAL	305	314	368	396	385	377	392	1,451	1,087	132

FIGURE 8-9
Systems Integration Profit through the Third Quarter (continued)

Summary Income & Expense through Third Quarter

		Quarter 1 Plan	Quarter 1 Actual	Quarter 2 Plan	Quarter 2 Actual	Quarter 3 Plan	Quarter 3 Actual	Quarter 4 Plan	Quarter 4 Actual	Total Year Plan	Total Year YTD	April Actual
Net Earnings (NEBA)		461	402	788	755	463	256	1,236		2,949	1,412	102
	Margin	18%	16%	20%	19%	14%	10%	31%		21%	16%	11%
Labor		417	378	552	519	371	256	1,167		2,510	1,173	100
	Margin	20%	18%	25%	23%	16%	11%	35%		25%	18%	13%
Nonlabor		44	24	236	236	93	0	69		438	239	3
	Margin	8%	5%	14%	14%	10%	0%	9%		11%		2%
Travel		7	5	11	9	8	5	17		42	20	2
	Margin	5%	4%	7%	6%	5%	4%	7%		6%	5%	4%
Product		8	−11	14	−1	14	−5	25		62	−15	1
	Margin	3%	−9%	6%	−1%	5%	−3%	8%		6%	−3%	1%
Vendor		29	29	211	227	71	0	27		333	234	0
	Margin	15%	14%	17%	16%	15%	0%	17%		16%	15%	0%
Hours												
Trainee/new trainee		1,102.0	1,046.0	905.0	921.0	302.0	772.0	634.0		2,943	2,739	234.0
Associate		2,400.0	2,351.0	3,078.0	3,476.0	3,705.0	3,989.0	5,262.0		14,445	9,816	1,407.0
Consultant/intern		3,546.0	3,434.0	4,243.0	3,995.0	4,095.0	4,237.0	7,808.0		19,692	11,666	1,495.0
Senior		811.0	867.0	593.0	621.0	998.0	1,133.0	1,539.0		3,941	2,621	411.0
Consultants		7,859	7,698	8,819	9,013	9,100	10,131	15,243		41,021	26,842	3,547
Management		749.0	698.0	1,066.0	1,133.0	1,040.0	1,121.0	1,373.0		4,228	2,952	372.0
Contractors		5,434.0	5,519.0	5,434.0	5,152.0	5,434.0	5,498.0	6,422.0		22,724	16,169	1,801.0
Borrowed		1,872.0	1,891.0	1,872.0	1,852.0	1,872.0	1,521.0	1,872.0		7,488	5,264	477.0
TOTAL		15,914	15,806	17,191	17,150	17,446	18,271	24,910		75,461	51,227	6,197
Average Head Count												
Trainee/new trainee		4.0	4.0	3.0	4.0	4.0	5.0	4.0		3.8	4.3	5.0
Associate		6.5	6.5	8.0	8.5	9.5	10.5	11.0		8.8	8.5	11.0
Consultant/intern		11.0	11.0	13.0	12.5	14.5	14.5	19.5		14.5	12.7	14.0
Senior		3.0	3.0	2.0	2.0	4.0	4.0	4.0		3.3	3.0	4.0
Consultants		24.5	24.5	26.0	27.0	32.0	34.0	38.5		30.3	24.5	34.0
Management		4.0	4.0	5.0	5.0	5.0	5.0	6.0		5.0	4.7	5.0
Contractors		11.0	11.0	11.0	10.3	11.0	11.5	13.0		11.5	10.9	12.0
Borrowed		4.0	4.0	4.0	3.7	4.0	3.5	4.0		4.0	3.7	3.0
TOTAL		43.5	43.5	46.0	46.0	52.0	54.0	61.5		50.8	47.8	54.0

FIGURE 8-10
Systems Integration Revenue Productivity

Revenue Productivity Through Third Quarter

	Quarter 1 Plan	Quarter 1 Actual	Quarter 2 Plan	Quarter 2 Actual	Quarter 3 Plan	Quarter 3 Actual	Quarter 4 Plan	Quarter 4 Actual	Total Year Plan	Total Year YTD	April Actual
Revenue ($000)											
Trainee/new trainee	94	89	77	79	26	61	54		250	228	19
Associate	281	274	360	408	433	443	618		1,692	1,125	157
Consultant/intern	479	461	573	536	553	519	1,054		2,658	1,516	185
Senior	138	152	101	112	170	207	262		670	470	77
Consultants	991	975	1,111	1,134	1,182	1,230	1,987		5,271	3,339	437
Management	141	131	200	214	196	205	258		795	550	71
Contractors	636	641	636	599	636	604	751		2,659	1,844	199
Borrowed	296	299	296	300	296	233	296		1,183	832	74
TOTAL	2,063	2,047	2,243	2,247	2,309	2,272	3,293		9,907	6,566	781
Consulting											
Labor	326	377	321	408	354	436	506		1,507	1,213	152
Nonlabor	13	15	13	15	14	17	20		60	47	7
TOTAL	339	392	334	422	368	454	526		1,567	1,268	159
Education											
Labor	250	276	245	299	256	311	398		1,149	877	108
Nonlabor	14	16	14	18	15	21	16		59	54	7
TOTAL	263	293	259	317	271	332	414		1,207	941	115
Custom development											
Labor	703	596	753	614	723	633	836		3,016	1,839	213
Nonlabor	21	14	23	20	22	14	25		91	48	6
TOTAL	724	610	777	633	746	647	862		3,109	1,890	219
Product support											
Labor	148	96	183	108	193	125	227		751	338	46
Nonlabor	230	108	230	145	281	180	307		1,047	434	84
TOTAL	378	204	413	253	474	305	534		1,798	772	130
Systems integration											
Labor	637	702	739	819	783	767	1,326		3,485	2,422	263
Nonlabor	285	298	1,366	1,493	597	97	364		2,613	1,888	29
TOTAL	921	1,000	2,105	2,312	1,380	864	1,690		6,097	4,176	293
Total Income											
Labor	2,062	2,048	2,243	2,246	2,310	2,273	3,294		9,909	6,567	783
Nonlabor	563	451	1,646	1,691	929	329	732		3,870	2,471	133
TOTAL	2,625	2,499	3,889	3,937	3,239	2,602	4,026		13,779	9,038	916

FIGURE 8–10
Systems Integration Revenue Productivity

Revenue Productivity Through Third Quarter

		Quarter 1 Plan	Quarter 1 Actual	Quarter 2 Plan	Quarter 2 Actual	Quarter 3 Plan	Quarter 3 Actual	Quarter 4 Plan	Quarter 4 Actual	Total Year Plan	Total Year YTD	April Actual
Revenue/Month	Trainee/new trainee	7,809	7,380	8,545	6,544	2,136	4,073	4,494		5,559	5,851	3,707
	Associate	14,399	14,055	15,007	15,984	15,210	14,072	18,718		16,116	14,705	14,255
	Consultant/intern	14,508	13,961	14,688	14,303	12,709	11,925	18,018		15,279	13,297	13,237
	Senior	15,323	16,880	16,796	18,594	14,144	17,227	21,805		17,181	17,415	19,158
	Consultants	13,485	13,269	14,240	14,001	12,309	12,057	17,206		14,520	15,144	12,862
	Management	11,731	10,909	13,361	14,272	13,035	13,695	14,338		13,246	13,105	14,103
	Contractors	19,266	19,439	19,266	19,376	19,266	17,508	19,266		19,266	18,742	16,619
	Borrowed	24,648	24,934	24,648	27,058	24,648	22,144	24,648		24,648	24,764	24,747
	Average	15,812	15,685	16,251	16,284	14,800	14,023	17,846		16,268	15,252	14,472
Revenue/Hour	Trainee/new trainee	85.03	84.66	84.98	85.27	84.89	79.15	85.05		85.01	83.31	79.22
	Associate	116.99	116.58	117.02	117.26	117.00	111.12	117.39		117.14	114.60	111.45
	Consultant/intern	135.02	134.16	135.01	134.26	135.00	122.43	135.00		135.00	129.94	123.96
	Senior	170.04	175.22	169.94	179.65	170.07	182.46	170.02		170.03	179.40	186.45
	Consultants	126.12	126.69	125.94	125.82	129.85	121.39	130.38		128.49	124.40	123.29
	Management	187.95	187.55	188.00	188.95	188.00	183.25	187.97		187.98	186.45	189.56
	Contractors	117.00	116.23	117.00	116.21	117.00	109.86	117.00		117.00	114.06	110.73
	Borrowed	158.00	158.23	158.00	162.17	158.00	152.87	158.00		158.00	158.07	155.64
	Average	129.66	129.50	130.45	131.03	132.34	124.34	132.18		131.29	128.17	126.11

FIGURE 8-11
Systems Integration Cost Productivity

| | | Cost Productivity Through Third Quarter | | | | | | | | Total Year | | April |
| | | Quarter 1 | | Quarter 2 | | Quarter 3 | | Quarter 4 | | | | |
		Plan	Actual	Plan	Actual	Plan	Actual	Plan	Actual	Plan	YTD	Actual
Total Income	Labor	2,062	2,048	2,243	2,246	2,310	2,273	3,294		9,909	6,567	783
	Nonlabor	563	451	1,646	1,691	929	329	732		3,870	2,471	133
	TOTAL	2,625	2,499	3,889	3,937	3,239	2,602	4,026		13,779	9,038	916
Direct Cost	Direct labor	1,396	1,404	1,457	1,476	1,649	1,681	1,796		6,298	4,562	568
	Direct nonlabor	464	379	1,276	1,309	741	289	602		3,082	1,977	114
	TOTAL	1,860	1,783	2,733	2,786	2,390	1,970	2,398		9,380	6,539	682
Gross Profit	Margin	766	716	1,156	1,151	849	632	1,628		4,399	2,499	234
		29%	29%	30%	29%	26%	24%	40%		32%	28%	26%
Cost ($000)	Trainee/new trainee	88	87	64	87	104	105	73		329	279	24
	Associate	157	157	190	204	226	253	231		804	614	63
	Consultant/intern	308	307	354	346	396	400	486		1,543	1,053	97
	Senior	108	107	71	71	144	147	133		456	325	40
	Consultants	661	658	679	708	870	906	923		3,132	2,271	223
	Management	179	177	222	227	223	228	252		877	632	64
	Contractors	358	365	358	345	358	374	423		1,495	1,084	123
	Borrowed	198	203	198	197	198	174	198		794	573	54
	TOTAL	1,396	1,402	1,457	1,476	1,649	1,681	1,796		6,298	4,560	463
Revenue/Month	Trainee/new trainee	7,809	7,380	8,545	6,544	2,136	4,073	4,494		5,559	5,851	3,707
	Associate	14,399	14,055	15,007	15,984	15,210	14,072	18,718		16,116	14,705	14,255
	Consultant/intern	14,508	13,961	14,688	14,303	12,709	11,925	18,018		15,279	13,297	13,237
	Senior	15,323	16,880	16,796	18,594	14,144	17,227	21,805		17,181	17,415	19,158
	Consultants	13,485	13,269	14,240	14,001	12,309	12,057	17,206		14,520	15,144	12,862
	Management	11,731	10,909	13,361	14,272	13,035	13,695	14,338		13,246	13,105	14,103
	Contractors	19,266	19,439	19,266	19,376	19,266	17,508	19,266		19,266	18,742	16,619
	Borrowed	24,648	24,934	24,648	27,058	24,648	22,144	24,648		24,648	24,764	24,747
	Average	15,812	15,685	16,251	16,284	14,800	14,023	17,846		16,268	15,252	14,472

FIGURE 8-11
Systems Integration Cost Productivity (concluded)

Cost Productivity Through Third Quarter

		Quarter 1 Plan	Quarter 1 Actual	Quarter 2 Plan	Quarter 2 Actual	Quarter 3 Plan	Quarter 3 Actual	Quarter 4 Plan	Quarter 4 Actual	Total Year Plan	Total Year YTD	April Actual
Cost/Month	Trainee/new trainee	7,323	7,280	7,160	7,212	6,935	7,013	6,093		6,864	7,156	4,733
	Associate	8,057	8,041	7,897	7,991	7,941	8,039	7,003		7,658	8,023	5,749
	Consultant/intern	9,338	9,293	9,067	9,233	9,094	9,206	8,303		8,868	9,240	6,894
	Senior	11,990	11,892	11,877	11,861	11,968	12,228	11,076		11,685	12,034	9,895
	Consultants	8,994	8,950	8,703	8,737	8,783	8,879	7,990		8,558	8,855	6,559
	Management	14,907	14,732	14,800	15,164	14,898	15,197	14,013		14,610	15,052	12,835
	Contractors	10,835	11,055	10,835	11,156	10,835	10,844	10,835		10,835	11,013	10,219
	Borrowed	16,540	16,885	16,540	17,709	16,540	16,537	16,540		16,540	17,048	17,866
	Average	10,697	10,744	10,557	10,699	10,372	10,379	9,735		10,291	10,592	8,582
Gross Profit/Month	Trainee/new trainee	485	100	1,385	-668	-4,798	-2,939	-1,599		-1,304	-1,305	-1,025
	Associate	6,342	6,015	7,110	7,994	7,269	6,033	11,716		8,458	6,682	8,507
	Consultant/intern	5,170	4,668	5,621	5,070	3,614	2,719	9,715		6,410	4,057	6,343
	Senior	3,333	4,988	4,919	6,733	2,176	5,000	10,729		5,497	5,381	9,262
	Consultants	4,491	4,319	5,537	5,263	3,526	3,179	-7,984		5,962	6,289	6,303
	Management	-3,175	-3,823	-1,440	-892	-1,863	-1,502	325		-1,363	-1,947	1,268
	Contractors	8,431	8,384	8,431	8,220	8,431	6,663	8,431		8,431	7,729	6,399
	Borrowed	8,108	8,049	8,108	9,348	8,108	5,608	8,108		8,108	7,715	6,881
	Average	5,115	4,941	5,694	5,585	4,428	3,645	8,111		5,977	4,660	5,890
Cost/Hour	Trainee/new trainee	79.74	83.52	71.21	93.97	344.43	136.26	115.32		111.94	101.90	101.12
	Associate	65.46	66.69	61.57	58.62	61.09	63.48	43.92		55.66	62.53	44.94
	Consultant/intern	86.91	89.31	83.34	86.67	96.61	94.52	62.21		78.36	90.30	84.37
	Senior	133.06	123.44	120.17	114.59	143.90	129.51	86.36		115.63	123.97	96.31
	Consultants	84.11	85.46	76.97	78.52	95.56	89.39	60.54		76.36	84.61	69.77
	Management	238.82	253.27	208.26	200.75	214.87	203.35	183.71		207.33	214.16	172.52
	Contractors	65.80	66.10	65.80	66.91	65.80	68.05	65.80		65.80	67.02	68.09
	Borrowed	106.03	107.15	106.03	106.14	106.03	114.16	106.03		106.03	108.82	112.36
	Average	87.72	88.71	84.75	86.09	94.52	92.02	72.11		83.46	89.01	79.27

FIGURE 8-12

Systems Integration Expense Productivity

Expense & Net Profit Productivity Through Third Quarter

		Quarter 1 Plan	Quarter 1 Actual	Quarter 2 Plan	Quarter 2 Actual	Quarter 3 Plan	Quarter 3 Actual	Quarter 4 Plan	Quarter 4 Actual	Total Year Plan	Total Year YTD	April Actual
Total Income	Labor	2,062	2,048	2,243	2,246	2,310	2,273	3,294		9,909	6,567	783
	Nonlabor	563	451	1,646	1,691	929	329	732		3,870	2,471	133
	TOTAL	2,625	2,499	3,889	3,937	3,239	2,602	4,026		13,779	9,038	916
Direct Cost	Direct labor	1,396	1,404	1,457	1,476	1,649	1,681	1,796		6,298	4,562	568
	Direct nonlabor	464	379	1,276	1,309	741	289	602		3,082	1,977	114
	TOTAL	1,860	1,783	2,733	2,786	2,390	1,970	2,398		9,380	6,539	682
Indirect Expense	Selling	130	128	164	170	170	171	169		633	469	55
	Administration	148	159	177	197	188	179	196		708	534	66
	Other indirect	27	27	27	30	27	27	27		109	84	11
	TOTAL	305	314	368	396	385	377	392		1,451	1,087	132
Net Earnings (NEBA)	Labor	461	402	788	755	463	256	1,236		2,949	1,412	102
	Margin	18%	16%	20%	19%	14%	10%	31%		21%	16%	11%
	Nonlabor	417	378	552	519	371	256	1,167		2,510	1,173	100
	Margin	20%	18%	25%	23%	16%	11%	35%		25%	18%	13%
	Total	44	24	236	236	93	0	69		438	239	3
	Margin	8%	5%	14%	14%	10%	0%	9%		11%	10%	2%
Expense ($000)	Trainee/new trainee	13	14	9	10	6	12	8		36	36	4
	Associate	35	37	37	44	54	67	63		190	149	24
	Consultant/intern	60	63	59	59	71	80	108		298	202	28
	Senior	17	20	10	12	22	30	26		75	62	11
	Consultants	125	134	116	126	154	190	205		599	450	67
	Management	18	19	21	24	25	31	27		92	74	11
	Contractors	67	73	56	56	70	79	66		260	208	26
	Borrowed	35	38	29	31	35	33	29		128	102	11
	Total	246	263	222	237	284	334	327		1,079	834	114
Gross Profit/Month	Trainee/new trainee	485	100	1,385	-668	-4,798	-2,939	-1,599		-1,304	-1,305	-1,025
	Associate	6,342	6,015	7,110	7,994	7,269	6,033	11,716		8,458	6,682	8,507
	Consultant/intern	5,170	4,668	5,621	5,070	3,614	2,719	9,715		6,410	4,057	6,343
	Senior	3,333	4,988	4,919	6,073	2,176	5,000	10,729		5,497	5,381	9,262
	Consultants	4,491	4,319	5,537	5,263	3,526	3,179	-7,984		5,962	6,289	6,303
	Management	-3,175	-3,823	-1,440	-892	-1,863	-1,502	325		-1,363	-1,947	1,268
	Contractors	8,431	8,384	8,431	8,220	8,108	6,663	8,431		8,431	7,729	6,399
	Borrowed	8,108	8,049	8,108	9,348	8,108	5,608	8,108		8,108	7,715	6,881
	Average	5,115	4,941	5,694	5,585	4,428	3,645	8,111		5,977	4,660	5,890

FIGURE 8–12
Systems Integration Expense Productivity (concluded)

Expense & Net Profit Productivity Through Third Quarter

| | | Quarter 1 | | Quarter 2 | | Quarter 3 | | Quarter 4 | | Total Year | | April |
		Plan	Actual	Plan	Actual	Plan	Actual	Plan	Actual	Plan	YTD	Actual
Expense/Month	Trainee/new trainee	1,107	1,151	981	856	431	816	648		757	931	794
	Associate	1,804	1,909	1,554	1,744	1,910	2,126	2,034		1,844	1,943	2,160
	Consultant/intern	1,815	1,898	1,526	1,586	1,636	1,845	1,522		1,601	1,775	2,028
	Senior	1,901	2,230	1,712	1,989	1,793	2,539	2,177		1,924	2,314	2,794
	Consultants	1,707	1,820	1,486	1,557	1,552	1,862	1,627		1,594	1,754	1,979
	Management	1,522	1,552	1,408	1,583	1,672	2,076	1,517		1,530	1,750	2,140
	Contractors	2,036	2,207	1,707	1,822	2,111	2,294	3,686		2,218	2,117	2,152
	Borrowed	2,887	3,144	2,408	2,785	2,944	3,184	2,428		2,667	3,038	3,518
	Average	1,882	2,015	1,610	1,718	1,784	2,059	1,884		1,794	2,129	2,118
Net Profit/Month	Trainee/new trainee	-622	-1,051	404	-1,524	-5,229	-3,755	-2,247		-2,062	-2,237	-1,819
	Associate	4,538	4,106	5,557	6,250	5,359	3,907	9,682		6,614	4,738	6,347
	Consultant/intern	3,354	2,770	4,096	3,484	1,978	875	8,192		4,809	2,282	4,315
	Senior	1,431	2,758	3,207	4,744	383	2,460	8,552		3,573	3,067	6,468
	Consultants	2,784	2,499	4,051	3,706	1,974	1,317	7,589		4,369	4,535	4,324
	Management	-4,697	-5,374	-2,847	-2,474	-3,535	-3,579	-1,192		-2,893	-3,697	-872
	Contractors	6,395	6,176	6,724	6,398	6,320	4,369	4,744		6,212	5,612	4,247
	Borrowed	5,221	4,905	5,700	6,563	5,164	2,424	5,680		5,441	4,678	3,363
	Average	3,233	2,926	4,084	3,867	2,644	1,585	6,226		4,183	2,530	3,772
Expense/Hour	Trainee/new trainee	12.06	13.20	9.76	11.16	21.40	15.85	12.27		12.35	13.26	16.96
	Associate	14.66	15.83	12.12	12.79	14.69	16.79	11.94		13.14	15.14	16.88
	Consultant/intern	16.89	18.24	14.02	14.88	17.38	18.94	13.80		15.15	17.35	24.82
	Senior	21.10	23.15	17.32	19.22	21.56	26.89	16.97		19.04	23.84	27.20
	Consultants	15.97	17.37	13.14	13.99	16.88	18.75	13.42		14.61	16.76	21.05
	Management	24.38	26.68	19.81	20.95	24.11	27.79	19.89		21.71	24.90	28.76
	Contractors	12.37	13.20	10.37	10.93	12.82	14.39	10.33		11.42	12.88	14.34
	Borrowed	18.51	19.95	15.44	16.69	18.87	21.98	15.56		17.09	19.39	22.13
	Average	15.43	16.64	12.93	13.82	16.26	18.26	13.14		14.30	16.27	19.56

at least one marketer on billing and use borrowed people rather than contractors to staff the consulting and education work.

If we rebuild our fourth quarter plan as follows, we can end the year at 100 percent of our revenue plan and our combined labor and nonlabor NEBA objective of 21 percent.

1. Increase manager and senior utilization in the fourth quarter by 7 percent and 17 percent, respectively.

2. Increase consulting and education revenues in the fourth quarter by 48 percent and 28 percent each. This seems optimistic, but each was 23 percent above third quarter objectives. This will increase consultant and manager revenue productivity by $6 per hour each.

3. Reduce the marketing staff by one and increase the consultant staff by two.

Planning is always easier than executing. There are a number of "ifs" that need to come together for our revised fourth quarter to work. It is important to note, however, that we are only risking our revenue plan. All of the actions we are taking will improve profit and our staffing is discretionary.

We are also not operating blindly. We will see the results when we perform this same analysis in early November. We will see the effects of our actions on revenue, utilization, and backlog every week.

Figure 8-13 summarizes the year as we now see it. The labor business will provide nearly 74 percent of our revenue and a 28 percent NEBA. We have built a small cushion into the plan with an overachievement of revenue and profit by 1 percent each. The plan assumes no further slip in systems integration schedules. The key will be our ability to continue to increase consulting and education for the rest of this year.

ENGAGEMENT PROFITABILITY

Another use of revenue and cost per hour data is in the computation of engagement profitability. Theoretically, if each engagement in an office is profitable over its life, the office will be profitable. This, of course, is a long way from the truth. An office with one very profitable deal and 50 percent of its people on the bench is not a happy place. An office where all engagements are doing well, but the administrative and marketing costs are way out of line is bad news.

A better view of the importance of tracking individual engagement profitability is the following.

- An engagement that is currently unprofitable should be assessed for its importance to the office. If considerable, its correction may be the highest priority among management actions.
- An engagement that is very profitable, but has client satisfaction issues is profitable for the wrong reasons and will not stay that way.
- If most engagements are unprofitable, there may be structural issues that are affecting their performance (pricing, project management, skill, morale).

Measuring Project Managers

Another common use of engagement profitability is as a management measurement, often with financial incentives tied in. The project manager of a major engagement may have a series of profit targets to meet for that engagement, with a bonus paid periodically and indexed to how close the engagement is tracking to plan. Consulting services managers may each have a group of engagements, the average profitability of the group determining profit performance evaluation. Managers will likely receive part of their profit compensation from their engagements and part from the overall office success to keep them working as a team.

There is a consideration to be made before assigning profitability targets for project managers. Rarely does the project manager get to decide how an engagement and its contracts are priced. Almost as rare is the project manager's participation in the selection (and cost) of the first members of the team. For these reasons, the project manager ought to be allowed to negotiate the profit track for the engagement.

The profit on an engagement is likely to follow the "S" curve seen in Figure 8-14. The profitability drops rapidly during start up, recovers during midperformance, and drops again as concessions are made to obtain client acceptance. The degree of drop at the end is where most of the profit is won or lost and is the most important financial challenge for the manager. The graph shows two end points for each of the hourly and fixed-price plots. The upper end point for each represents nominal concessions, while the lower illustrates the results of deep concessions.

Since hourly engagements receive revenue as they bill and have a lower effective rate, their accumulated profit is low at the beginning and gradually builds to the end. Fixed-price engagements, on the other hand, incur cost before their first payments. They often start out further negative, but their extra effective rate will cause them to build accumulated profit faster. They can also have a very precipitous profit fall at the end, if priced incorrectly or not managed well.

FIGURE 8-13
Fourth Quarter Systems Integration Income and Expense Forecast

Fourth Quarter Income & Expense Forecast

		Quarter 1		Quarter 2		Quarter 3		Quarter 4		Total Year		Sept.
		Plan	Actual	Plan	Actual	Plan	Actual	Plan	Forecast	Plan	Forecast	Actual
Income	Consulting	339	392	334	422	368	454	526	780	1,567	2,047	159
	%	15.81%	18.40%	14.32%	18.15%	15.34%	19.21%	15.36%	16.18%	15.21%	14.77%	19.44%
	Education	263	293	259	317	271	332	414	529	1,207	1,470	115
	%	12.09%	13.51%	10.94%	13.29%	11.10%	13.67%	12.08%	10.97%	11.60%	10.61%	13.81%
	Custom development	724	610	777	633	746	647	862	976	3,109	1,890	219
	%	34.08%	29.10%	33.59%	27.31%	31.31%	27.86%	25.40%	20.26%	30.44%	20.69%	27.21%
	Product support	377	205	415	253	474	306	534	433	1,800	764	130
	%	7.15%	4.69%	8.18%	4.79%	8.35%	5.50%	6.89%	8.90%	7.58%	8.64%	5.84%
	Systems integration	921	1,000	2,105	2,312	1,380	864	1,690	2,099	6,097	4,176	293
	%	30.86%	34.31%	32.97%	36.45%	33.91%	33.76%	40.27%	43.58%	35.17%	45.29%	33.70%
	TOTAL	2,625	2,499	3,889	3,937	3,239	2,602	4,026	4,816	13,779	13,855	916
Direct Cost	Labor	2,062	2,048	2,243	2,246	2,310	2,273	3,294	3,672	9,909	10,239	783
	%	78.59%	81.92%	57.66%	57.08%	71.29%	87.30%	81.78%	76.24%	71.90%	73.90%	85.34%
	Nonlabor	563	451	1,646	1,691	929	329	732	1,144	3,870	3,616	133
	Travel	136	126	154	144	162	133	255	264	707	668	43
	Product	237	119	237	158	287	197	312	235	1,073	709	89
	Vendor	190	205	1,255	1,389	480	0	165	645	2,090	2,239	0
	Direct labor	1,396	1,404	1,457	1,476	1,649	1,681	1,796	1,890	6,298	6,452	568
	Direct nonlabor	464	379	1,276	1,309	741	289	602	912	3,082	2,889	114
	TOTAL	1,860	1,783	2,733	2,786	2,390	1,970	2,398	2,802	9,380	9,341	682
Gross Profit		766	716	1,156	1,151	849	632	1,628	2,014	4,399	4,514	234
	Margin	29%	29%	30%	29%	26%	24%	40%	42%	32%	33%	26%
Indirect Expense	Selling	130	128	164	170	170	171	169	148	633	616	55
	Administration	148	159	177	197	188	179	196	252	708	787	66
	Other indirect	27	27	27	30	27	27	27	29	109	113	11
	TOTAL	305	314	368	396	385	377	392	429	1,451	1,516	132

FIGURE 8-13
Fourth Quarter Systems Integration Income and Expense Forecast (concluded)

		Fourth Quarter Income & Expense Forecast									
		Quarter 1		Quarter 2		Quarter 3		Quarter 4		Total Year		Sept.
		Plan	Actual	Plan	Actual	Plan	Actual	Plan	Forecast	Plan	Forecast	Actual
Net Earnings (NEBA)		461	402	788	755	463	256	1,236	1,586	2,949	2,998	102
	Margin	18%	16%	20%	19%	14%	10%	31%	33%	21%	22%	11%
Labor		417	378	552	519	371	256	1,167	1,505	2,510	2,278	100
	Margin	20%	18%	25%	23%	16%	11%	35%	41%	25%	28%	13%
Nonlabor		44	24	236	236	93	0	69	147	438	390	3
	Margin	8%	5%	14%	14%	10%	0%	9%	13%	11%	11%	2%
	Travel	7	5	11	9	8	5	17	27	42	43	2
	Margin	5%	4%	7%	6%	5%	4%	7%	10%	6%	6%	4%
	Product	8	-11	14	-1	14	-5	25	44	62	108	1
	Margin	3%	-9%	6%	-1%	5%	-3%	8%	19%	6%	15%	1%
	Vendor	29	29	211	227	71	0	27	125	333	351	0
	Margin	15%	14%	17%	16%	15%	0%	17%	19%	16%	16%	0%
Hours	Trainee/new trainee	1,102.0	1,046.0	905.0	921.0	302.0	772.0	634.0	1,400.0	2,943	4,139	234.0
	Associate	2,400.0	2,351.0	3,078.0	3,476.0	3,705.0	3,989.0	5,262.0	5,440.0	14,445	15,256	1,407.0
	Consultant/intern	3,546.0	3,434.0	4,243.0	3,995.0	4,095.0	4,237.0	7,808.0	9,120.0	19,692	20,786	1,495.0
	Senior	811.0	867.0	593.0	621.0	998.0	1,133.0	1,539.0	2,100.0	3,941	4,721	411.0
	Consultants	7,859	7,698	8,819	9,013	9,100	10,131	15,243	18,060	41,021	44,902	3,547
	Management	749.0	698.0	1,066.0	1,133.0	1,040.0	1,121.0	1,373.0	1,900.0	4,228	4,852	372.0
	Contractors	5,434.0	5,519.0	5,434.0	5,152.0	5,434.0	5,498.0	6,422.0	6,500.0	22,724	22,669	1,801.0
	Borrowed	1,872.0	1,891.0	1,872.0	1,852.0	1,872.0	1,521.0	1,872.0	2,000.0	7,488	7,264	477.0
	TOTAL	15,914	15,806	17,191	17,150	17,446	18,271	24,910	28,460	75,461	51,227	6,197
Average Head Count	Trainee/new trainee	4.0	4.0	3.0	4.0	4.0	5.0	4.0	4.0	4.0	4.3	5.0
	Associate	6.5	6.5	8.0	8.5	9.5	10.5	11.0	11.0	8.8	9.1	11.0
	Consultant/intern	11.0	11.0	13.0	12.5	14.5	14.5	19.5	19.5	14.5	14.4	14.0
	Senior	3.0	3.0	2.0	2.0	4.0	4.0	4.0	5.0	3.3	3.5	4.0
	Consultants	24.5	24.5	26.0	27.0	32.0	34.0	38.5	39.5	30.5	31.3	34.0
	Management	4.0	4.0	5.0	5.0	5.0	5.0	6.0	6.0	5.0	5.0	5.0
	Contractors	11.0	11.0	11.0	10.3	11.0	11.5	13.0	13.0	11.5	11.5	12.0
	Borrowed	4.0	4.0	4.0	3.7	4.0	3.5	4.0	4.0	4.0	3.8	3.0
	TOTAL	43.5	43.5	46.0	46.0	52.0	54.0	61.5	62.5	51.0	51.5	54.0

FIGURE 8-14
Profitability Track for an Engagement

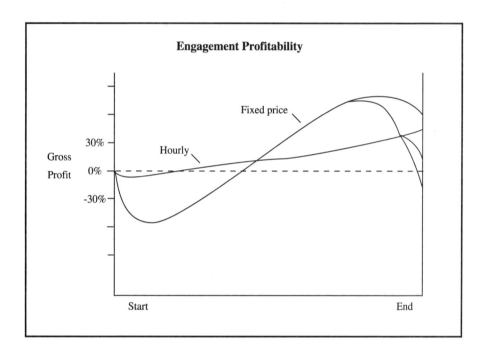

Our project manager should be allowed to establish the accumulated profitability track for the project. This will be done in the first month of the engagement, after the manager has assessed the accuracy of pricing versus client expectations and the cost and quality of initial staffing. Once the track is established, the manager is now measured on the variance against the track and paid periodic bonuses accordingly. Typically, a separate bonus structure is held in reserve to reward managers for their performance during the critical final weeks of an engagement.

Obviously, many per hour engagements are profitable from the outset. Some major engagements take months before a clear financial track can be laid following a very poor piece of deal making. Many of these are never profitable and the manager's assignment is damage control. In all of these cases, though, a realistic profitability track can be negotiated, and measurements made to determine the financial performance of the manager.

Computing Engagement Profitability

The degree of complexity needed to compute engagement profitability follows the same rules as when deciding how detailed one needs to be for the entire office. An engagement made up of a set of per hour contracts with only a small amount of nonlabor generated revenue should be done very simply. A fixed-price engagement will require either the preset rate or recalculation method for distributing revenue. Systems integration will require separation of nonlabor generated revenue and its associated cost.

We will measure the contribution of engagements at only the gross profit level. The exercise to distribute indirect expense across a number of engagements has little reward in affecting management behavior. Only when the entire office is consumed by one or two projects, does this make sense. For these very large engagements, the I & E for the office should be the sum of subsidiary statements for each project.

Figure 8-15 is a statement of gross profit for an engagement for one month. Income is the sum of revenue invoiced for that month for each contract and the revenue credit computed using either the preset rate or recalculation method for fixed-price contracts. Additionally, travel, product, and vendor charges invoiced that month are listed and totaled. An invoice that billed labor and non-labor as a single charge would have to be broken into its separate components using guidelines, such as pricing assumptions. The total labor and nonlabor revenue invoiced in our example is $126,181, while the amount credited is $142,689.

Costs are computed in two ways: an engagement method that uses average cost per person for this office, weighted by whether the people were partially or fully assigned; and the office method which uses the office cost per hour times hours billed (assigned, if fixed price). By the first method, the engagement is protected from any poor utilization across the office that drives cost per hour up. The engagement will pay the price for assigning people and not getting optimum revenue.

By the office method, costs are transferred equally to all engagements. This allows the office to compare engagements to determine which are the better profit producers.

In our example, 12 people are assigned to our engagement. Four are consultants, but only three of a group are assigned full time (one teaches classes two days per week along with a borrowed person). The group of consultant level

FIGURE 8-15
Engagement Gross Profit Statement

Monthly Engagement Profit Statement

Income	Invoiced	Labor Credited	Travel	Product	Nonlabor Vendor	Total
Contract 1	$44,000	$44,000	$7,389	$38,000	$ 83,433	
Contract 2	36,792	36,792				36,792
Contract 3	22,464	22,464				22,464
	$80,792	$103,256	$7,389	$38,000	$38,000	$142,689 ($126,181)

Labor Cost	People	Engagement Method Assgnd	Cost/Mo	Total	Hours	Office Method Cost/Hr	Total
Trainee	1	100%	$ 4,733	$ 4,733	97.0	$101.12	$ 9,809
Associate	2	100%	5,749	11,498	314.0	44.94	14,111
Consultant	4	85%	6,894	23,440	427.0	84.37	21,008
Senior	1	100%	9,895	9,895	122.0	96.31	11,750
Manager	1	25%	12,835	3,209	37.0	172.52	5,520
Contractor	2	100%	10,219	20,438	324.0	67.92	22,006
Borrowed	1	40%	17,866	4,467	48.0	112.36	5,393
				$77,680			$89,597

Nonlabor Cost	Total
Travel	$ 6,281
Product	0
Vendor	28,500
	$34,781

Gross Profit	Labor	Nonlabor	Total
Stand alone	$25,576 25%	$10,608 23%	$36,184 25%
Office	-$8,805 -11%	$10,608 23%	$ 1,803 14%

people delivered 427 hours among them. Since they were presumably available 544 hours during the month, they provided 78 percent utilization while being assigned 85 percent of their time.

Costs for nonlabor components are those actually incurred in that month. They will include any allocations that the office may choose to add.

Gross profit is also expressed in two ways.

- **Stand alone.** This uses the credited income (invoiced, if hourly) against the engagement method cost. This is the profitability of the engagement taken in isolation.

- **Office.** This uses the invoiced income against office method cost. This is the profitability of this engagement compared to all others in the office.

Stand-alone gross profit is used to measure the individual responsible for the engagement. The compensation of project managers would be computed in this way. We have used the September cost rates from the systems integration office. Because utilization has not been good, office cost rates per hour are high. The stand-alone profit for the engagement in September was 25 percent, while the office profit was 14 percent. Presumably, all engagements suffer equally from the high office method costs. This may be the most profitable of the group.

The accumulated profitability is simply the addition of each month's gross profit from the beginning of the engagement. Figure 8-16 shows month by month for both stand-alone and office gross profit. The engagement is six months into a nine-month schedule and has an accumulated stand-alone margin of 19 percent, split 19 percent for labor and 15 percent for nonlabor. To make it interesting, the fixed-price education contract received payment for half of the classes in the first month, with no other payments until completion. The office profit has been very high and has moved downward in its accumulation to 14 percent.

Office Cost Versus Engagement Cost

In the exercise just completed, we made two profit computations—one to focus on the engagement and one to focus on the office. Both are necessary and both are a by-product of normal productivity data management.

Engagement managers have to wear two hats. They have to optimize the financial performance of their engagements and they have to work as a team for the success of the office. Using two profit methods provides support to both roles.

FIGURE 8-16
Monthly Engagement Profit Performance

Engagement Profitability

	Month 1		Month 2		Month 3		Month 4		Month 5		Month 6	
	Month ($000)	Accum ($000)	Month ($000)	Accum ($000)	Month ($000)	Accum ($000)	Month ($000)	Accum ($000)	Month ($000)	Accum ($000)	Month ($000)	Accum ($000)
Stand Alone												
Labor	-1.3	-1.3	4.1	2.8	26.1	28.9	22.4	51.3	22.3	73.6	27.5	101.1
	-4%	-4%	8%	2%	24%	9%	26%	14%	26%	16%	27%	18%
Nonlabor	0.0	0.0	0.9	0.9	5.3	10.6	1.1	11.7	1.1	12.8	10.6	23.4
	0%	0%	15%	8%	22%	12%	15%	13%	15%	13%	23%	15%
TOTAL	-1.3	-1.3	5.0	3.7	31.4	38.1	23.5	61.6	23.4	85.0	38.1	123.1
	-4%	-4%	9%	2%	30%	12%	25%	15%	25%	17%	27%	19%
Office												
Labor	102.5	102.5	5.3	107.8	4.2	112.0	-12.2	99.8	-12.0	87.8	-8.8	79.0
	76%	76%	10%	43%	5%	30%	-14%	19%	-14%	13%	-11%	9%
Nonlabor	0.0	0.0	0.9	0.9	5.3	6.2	1.1	7.3	1.1	8.4	10.6	19.0
	0%	0%	15%	8%	22%	12%	15%	13%	15%	13%	23%	15%
TOTAL	102.5	102.5	6.4	108.9	9.5	118.4	-11.1	107.3	-10.9	96.4	1.8	98.2
	76%	76%	11%	44%	9%	32%	-12%	21%	-12%	14%	14%	14%

Much can be learned by observing the convergence and divergence of stand-alone profit among engagements and their corresponding office profitability. These usually dramatize inherent cost and utilization problems that either show up consistently across all engagements or are unique to one. In our example we can see that cost per hour in the office deteriorated badly during the summer months, against only minor changes in the cost per month. Our engagement has been showing a steady increase in stand-alone profit accumulation, while office profit accumulation has gone down each month.

PLOTTING PRODUCTIVITY DATA

There should be a predictable relationship between revenue per person and utilization of a resource group. In fact, the simple plotting of this relationship on a week-by-week, month-by-month basis is a visible track of profitability when costs and expenses are very nearly constant. Ideally, revenue productivity will follow the same peaks and valleys as utilization, with a slightly faster slope when prices are rising.

Figure 8-17 is an example of simple revenue productivity and utilization plotting. When revenue increases faster or decreases slower than utilization, the resource mix is favoring higher rate people and/or prices are increasing. When utilization increases faster or decreases slower than revenue productivity, the resource mix has been diluted by lower rate people or heavy price discounting is occurring.

The example shows two years of consultant revenue productivity and utilization by quarter. In the first year, rates are increasing in the first half of the year, but remain constant in the second half of the year. For this reason, revenue per person does not dip as rapidly as utilization. Conversely, lower level people are hired in the second half of the first year and revenue productivity does not increase at the same rate as utilization.

In the second year, rates went up again, but all hiring is done in the first two quarters (a mix of both high- and low-rate people). This combination of better rates and more people causes a business boom in the fourth quarter where productivity and utilization are now in balance with each other.

The fourth quarter of the first year and the second quarter of the second year have warning signals. In both of those periods, the office is working harder and getting less. Fourth quarter hiring rarely pays off in revenue, because the next quarter is typically down in utilization. Further hiring in that quarter worsens the effect.

FIGURE 8-17
Plotting Revenue Productivity Against Utilization

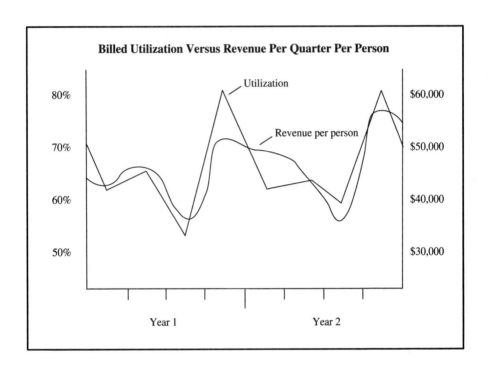

Routinely plotting these and the other productivity factors provides a better means of predicting the longer term effect of hiring and pricing actions. It is one more piece of the complicated puzzle.

MEASURING PRODUCTIVITY

The purpose of this chapter was to give those who are managing fixed-price services and substantial nonlabor revenue generating services a practical set of tools to regularly manage resource productivity. These are managers of large offices with growing complexity. The office must be prepared to pay the price in quality administrative people, disciplined business controls, and the comprehensive business computing tools that provide the financial information we have been discussing. Too often, firms underestimate the cost of growth, forget to price this new cost into major systems integration deals, make cost cutting decisions that deny support to complex engagements and end up delivering poor quality to their clients. Key points to consider from this chapter are:

- Productivity analysis and tracking engagement profitability is the advanced course in how to manage professional services. Most managers will do this no more than once or twice a year, to see whether utilization and profit measurements are working together. Structural issues regarding pricing and business mix can distort the message from simpler measurements. Productivity analysis can be an excellent tool to refine the data and focus on real problems.

- The technique for computing revenue per person on fixed price engagements depends on how the data will be used. Each of the as billed, preset rate, or recalculation methods may be appropriate.

- Cost per person is more than simply the direct cost of the individual. When comparing choices of people sources for an existing engagement, the manager must consider risk, management time, and travel interference.

- Engagement profitability may involve looking at the engagement by itself and also as it compares to others. This requires the use of different cost productivity factors.

All of the techniques just described can be performed locally. The firm that can supplement this local effort with contract management and expense ledger systems that bridge data to local spreadsheets will see the lowest incremental growth in administration expense as the business expands. Alternatively, the firm can choose to keep its business simple and choose growth at more modest rates of 5 percent to 10 percent. But, where would be the fun in that?

Chapter 9

Measurement Roll Up:
A View from the Top

U ntil now, we have been viewing professional services from the perspective of the autonomous field office. In this chapter we will step back and look down on the business from an operating unit perspective. Our purpose is to see how the accumulated measurements of offices roll up into a consolidated measurement for the business and how the top of the business can best influence the measurement process.

We will look at the role of our five measurements in overall pricing policy and the business plan. This will include a general discussion of the planning process and objective setting for professional services. It will demonstrate the advantages gained by the overall business from a disciplined implementation of all five measurement processes at the office level. We will show how a summary of business vital signs, published by headquarters, provides feedback to office executives and builds confidence in the management process.

Expenses incurred by support functions will be discussed, including how these may be distributed as specific or general indirect expense allocations to the local level. We will look at options for measuring profitability of performance and competency centers and the effect these choices have on allocations to field offices.

A major competitive advantage of the large firms is their ability to deliver key people from other locales and to utilize resources elsewhere when temporary downturns occur. We will present methods that encourage this sharing of resources between local offices by equitably adjusting revenue and expense.

TOP DOWN OR BOTTOM UP?

We begin, though, with a discussion of the role of a professional services business headquarters. We go back to the four organization principles introduced at the beginning of the book. Our purpose is to analyze how these are reflected

FIGURE 9-1
Strategic Financial Principles for Professional Services

> **Professional Services
> Financial Strategy**
>
> Revenue growth must be managed
>
> Profitability results from utilization
>
> Cost productivity guides resource selection
>
> Profit is derived bottom up

in responsibilities at the top, while leaving the offices empowered to run their separate businesses. Figure 9-1 restates the four strategic financial principles that support the expansion of a professional services firm.

Managing Top Down

At some point in the life of a business it gets a headquarters. If it was spun off from some other business it starts with one. Most professional services businesses got one when they had too many offices for the original founding entrepreneurs to coordinate without dedicated staff help.

Once a headquarters is in existence it will experience the overwhelming urge to manage the business from the top down. Most businesses need strategic and tactical direction to make their various parts work together. The temptation is to overmanage from the top, when the actions of office executives do not seem to reflect the tactical direction given. The line between strong direction and overmanaging is very fine, but the symptoms are lost clients, throttled quality, and unnecessary expense that results when the direction of the business gets separated from the management of engagements. On the other hand, a professional services business with offices nationally and internationally needs a strong glue to hold it together. The more invisible the glue, the better the network of autonomous offices will function. A well-run headquarters staff can provide solid and unobtrusive support that relieves the offices of many tasks they shouldn't need to perform (to their delight).

Top down management of a professional services business can be a disaster. Beyond establishing strategic direction through an overall business plan, there is little value that those remote from the client can add to the quality delivery of service at a profit. There is a lot that the top of the business can do to interrupt relations between local executives and their ability to make deals.

Services Business Principles

The main purpose of the top of a business is to establish strategic direction and sustain an overall company culture. In creating or maintaining a culture for a firm, four financial principles should be taken into account.
  • **Revenue growth should be managed.** It is very easy to grow in the professional services business. Clients develop confidence in a firm's professionals and invite more and more participation. There is more to growth, though, than simply taking on every need that clients choose to identify. A firm should have a strategic plan for how and in which market segments it chooses to increase its revenues and corresponding profits.

Cost and expense that is anticipated is much easier to control and minimize than that which occurs haphazardly. Growth brings its own cost and expense. Hiring is extremely costly, with out of pocket costs for recruiting, relocation, and training, and the more subtle costs of getting people productive. Retraining of experienced professionals is expensive when new demands by clients cause consultants to be short on skill. Administrative and systems support expenses will quickly get out of hand when the firm takes on engagements that are very different from the previous mix.

Professional services business can most easily afford growth when 80 percent of net new revenue for each office is a continuation of what it knows how to do. This leaves no more than 20 percent from work it has to learn how to do. This keeps the entrepreneurial juices flowing, while putting only nominal strain on the control process. Keep in mind that total growth in revenue for the office ought to be at least 30 percent and climbing.

Mathematicians among you have already figured out that 6 percent annual revenue growth needs to come from new markets, while 24 percent comes from expanding existing markets. Local offices are masters at expanding their existing business; they are often less able to see where new market opportunities might lie. Offices are delighted to take direction on where to go for additional business. They will always listen to advice on what new things to offer to existing clients, what kinds of new clients to approach and which new techniques will impress clients.

Professional services firms should have no difficulty establishing a strategic plan for themselves; they do it for clients all the time (and charge quite a bit for the excellent work they perform). Firms need to make sure they are not shoemaker's children. The professional services industry has now matured to the point that market boundaries are fairly wide and reasonably defined. Assuming the firm wants to consider all levels from basic people services, through complex people services, to labor and nonlabor services, the firm needs to direct upon itself a planning process that segments all of its existing engagements into logical market groupings and then hire a market consultant to prepare a corresponding opportunity segmentation of the total market.

The marketing opportunity analysis that follows will tell the firm where it is growing faster than the competition and why. (Is the firm's strength in its skills, its methods, its reputation, its organization or its price?) A business expansion plan will focus growth in markets that use these strengths to advantage, while addressing marketing, hiring, and training needs for areas in which the firm is lacking.

An important part of the strategic process is communicating both the research and the plan to the office executives. It ensures that those closest to the clients will have the knowledge to use the strengths of the firm to its best advantage. It also alerts the offices to where expansion is planned, so they can best make use of the support that will be offered (and to give vocal feedback on how adequate they think the support will be).

On the other hand, the marketing opportunity analysis will point out where the competition is growing well ahead of the firm. If the firm is truly entrepreneurial in its culture, at least one office has likely tried what the competition is doing. That is the real strength of giving empowerment to office executives. The firm has the wherewithal to determine whether these early ventures represent a path to next year's 6 percent growth from new markets. Headquarters can fund research and development in an area of service that is expanding among competitors and has yet to be tried by an office. It will likely further fund one office through expense recovery to market and perform the service before it attempts mass implementation.

Good communication of new market activities by local offices can blunt the costly effect of haphazard spread of new services. Headquarters can stimulate this communication through councils, newsletters, and task forces. It is also in a position to anoint new work as one chosen for growth.

Finally, the headquarters will likely be the negotiator of alliances between the firm and business partners to marry services with products and other noncompetitive services. The only caution here is to remember the 80–20 rule regarding how offices can best absorb new things. If 6 percent of the growth for the year will come from the firm's first venture into systems integration, this is not the time to jump into a joint venture with another software developer, at least not on a volume basis (there is always one office executive who will be willing to do a pilot).

The top of the business has to work very hard to avoid throttling the aggressiveness of its offices as they continue to deliver what local clients will buy. It needs to avoid too many emphasis bonuses for the favored ventures of headquarters staff. Office executives should give highest priority to their own efforts to find new avenues of business.

The strategic marketing plan is good for about three years (30 percent per year compound growth is not an indicator of quiet stability). In the third year, the firm will have a surprising number of offerings and types of clients that do not fit the market model. Another assessment and corresponding outside analysis is needed to reposition the firm in the marketplace and against its newest competition.

Even though local executives are entrepreneurs, they should welcome pointers to markets and use them wisely. They will readily perform the administrative tasks to record client, engagement, and contract information when the resulting market analysis benefits them directly.

- **Profitability is the result of utilization.** Utilization is more than the tracking of a percentage. Utilization is a culture that comes from the top. The principle here is that 40 hours of every person's week should go toward a profitable use of that person's cost.

Headquarters policy and directives can subvert an office executive's instinctual drive toward optimal utilization. Senior management may set a minimum billable utilization level and measure all office executives on their ability to manage consultants and direct managers at that measurement. As a result, some offices will get less utilization than their business mix allows, while others will try to eke out too much.

There is no right level of billable utilization that applies to all offices. An office with a high concentration of time and materials should get very high utilization. A national measurement would naturally be too low for this mix. An office with a high concentration of fixed price shouldn't be trying to meet a utilization standard.

The focus should be on profit, not on some specific utilization number. Every competent local manager knows that low billed utilization makes achieving profit very tough. Office executives are in the best position to choose the levels that contribute to profit for their business mix.

Headquarters can give the wrong signal when it compensates offices for use of its people in investment activities. Those at the top of the business can see very clearly how wonderful a new service offering will be for future revenue and profit growth. In their enthusiasm, they create a financial reward (either a direct compensation or relief on an existing profit measurement) to encourage offices to train large numbers of people in preparation for a major marketing blitz. It doesn't matter whether this offering is successful or not (some will be, and some won't). The signal from the top is that it is acceptable to forego short-term utilization for long-term growth.

In the professional services business, long-term growth is fueled from short-term utilization. Every action of the firm at all levels must reinforce this. The enthusiastic staff manager at the top should find those specific offices that have potential clients for the offering and have currently high profit. The executives of those offices will probably leap at the chance to try something new. With patience, headquarters will eventually see new services tried across the business, but at a pace that is consistent with the financial capability of each location.

The most significant influence on utilization at the top of the business is in its policy and procedures regarding sharing of people between offices. The major competitive strength of nationwide firms is their ability to supply people to any situation. By encouraging this, the firm is making it very clear that consultants need not, and should not, sit on the bench.

We will be discussing some of the compensation options for cross-territory sharing later. Whichever options are chosen, their purpose should be to reward the office that loans and to avoid punishing consultants who give up personal comfort to make the sacrifice. This is a very positive demonstration of utilization culture. Entrepreneurs also love it, because it creates another way in which they can make deals.

- **Use cost per hour to guide people selection.** Reasons for choosing the person who will perform a service have to do with the best skill, the best leadership, the most poised, and confident, and the most respected by the client. Too often these lead to such obvious choices that the cheapest person within those qualified is overlooked. Actions at the top of the business strongly affect how well local executives can improve cost productivity.

The need here is one of having the proper tools. Any manager who is measured on profit will naturally be cost conscious about people. They represent the single largest cost in the business. That manager may not be able to readily compute the cost per hour of each choice, simply because the information is not available.

Computing cost and gross profit per hour is the most sophisticated business system application in professional services. It combines contract, resource, revenue, and expense management data. It requires all of these systems to provide data at the lowest level. Business computer systems and software applications are very difficult to finance in a professional services business. This is an area where senior management must make tough choices.

Headquarters needs a strategic plan for its business systems just as for its market expansion. This strategy should be based on an enterprise model that fits the process, measurements, direction, and culture of the business. The plan will be most effective, when it builds national systems for billing and expense that interact with simpler local systems for resource, profit, and productivity management.

A large national system of even nominal scope will cost millions to develop and take no less than two years to implement. Local spreadsheet applications can be in place within months. They will require much dual entry of information, if national systems are inadequate. The function of a headquarters systems staff is to administer the communication between the two levels of systems to achieve as much cost per hour computation capability as is affordable.

In addition to providing tools, the top of the business can encourage offices to make good financial choices through the publishing of vital signs. As with the health of a human patient, there is a range of values for measurements that show whether an office is healthy relative to its peers. Cost per consultant and cost per contractor are vital signs that, when compared with a national average, will tell an office executive whether an office is out of tolerance.

A section of this chapter is devoted to a headquarters role in developing and distributing vital signs statistics. As will be seen, cost per person is the most difficult to derive and is the most useful in managing profit.

- **Profit is derived from the bottom up.** There are no inherent barriers to delegating net profit measurements to the office level in the professional services business. Those firms organized as partnerships have demonstrated its practicality and success for years. Those firms that are a corporate hierarchy may not see the light quite so readily.

There is a difference between measuring profit at a low level and empowering office executives to manage profit at their level. First, only measuring on gross profit is not empowerment. By implication, the office executive is not encouraged to control administrative and marketing levels and has little influence regarding equipment and facilities.

At a minimum, empowerment means the office executive has full control to choose the level of all expenses that go into a net earnings before allocation (NEBA) measurement as described in Chapter 6. This includes hiring, pricing, marketing investment, administrative resources, and the relative choices between local and national computer services.

The firm that displays the most confidence in the ability of its local executives to manage net profit is the one that finds ways to distribute most headquarters expense. Overhead expense distribution can be tedious and is always a subject of debate. The more the firm packages its headquarters services, though, the more empowerment it gives in the choosing of the services by the offices.

Ideally, the firm is so structured as to be able to sell services internally, such as personnel, education, computer services, new service offering support, quality assurance, and financial data such as vital signs. These are bought by the offices at the levels chosen by local management and expensed accordingly. The only allocation expense that separates NEBA from net earnings before tax is the recovery of the small amount of nondiscretionary corporate level expense that is left (i.e., executive compensation, internal and external audit, etc.).

Certainly there needs to be a balance between what a local office can use at its discretion and what is expensed to everyone regardless of choice. Local executives will pay for necessities, even their own middle executive, when these allocated expenses are small relative to the expense they can choose, and the benefit of the expense is clear.

The issue here is whether profit is managed upward or downward. The successful professional services businesses are those that make sure the headquarters operation leaves the business of profit making to those who have access to the clients. Satisfying clients is always the essential first step in making profit in professional services.

The Role of Headquarters: Support Your Local Office

First let's look at what the bottom of a professional services organization chart needs from the top. Then we will look at what the top needs to do in implementing overall strategy that sometimes is not viewed as absolutely necessary by local executives.

• **Set employee policy and supervise employee compensation and benefits.** Employee salary and payroll tax law can sap the energy of any organization's managers. The firm that expands to multiple states sees an exponential increase in the variety of payroll and personnel issues. Firms that trade people between offices are particularly vulnerable to employee disquiet, when inconsistent compensation practices become a common topic between consultants.

Providing top down direction of personnel and employee compensation administration is welcomed by office executives as long as it does not dictate how they assign the people and how performance is measured. The best organizational approach is to establish policy and provide payroll and personnel computer services from headquarters, and perform the actual employee administration at the local level. This creates consistency and the added value of full function business computer systems while leaving decisions regarding how much workload, and corresponding expense, is needed to meet the needs of an office's employees. It also puts local employee issues under the management of local executives.

• **Choose line executives.** The number of executives from the office level to the most senior executive will depend on the size and dispersion of the business. Choosing these executives is a well-accepted role of senior management (a democratic vote of the consultants is probably not a practical approach).

The need for middle managers between the office executive and headquarters level executives is a topic of great debate. Clearly, senior executives cannot manage both the strategy and operations of a business without some delegation of their operational responsibilities. Most office executives welcome a second opinion on tough decisions, particularly from a middle executive who can be detached from day-to-day issues and has the experience to truly be helpful.

There is a tendency in large enterprises to overpopulate the middle management ranks. This occurs for a number of both business and personal reasons, not the least of which, is the desire to reward successful office executives with much deserved promotions. The simple test of whether middle executive positions should be created or continued is affordability. Their cost and the cost of their inevitable staff must be allocated to the offices under their management. If these offices are generating enough extra profit to carry the expense of another executive distributed as an allocation, and there is real management work to be delegated, then naming such a position should be considered.

The role of middle executives is to act as an advocate for the offices they represent in the inner circle of the business. Also they choose the office executives. They cannot run the offices. They provide advice and counsel and they conduct at least two business reviews each year, preferably with the office executives as a group (to share problems and solutions).

We will discuss other areas of involvement by middle executives in later sections on quality assurance and financial roll up. Before leaving this subject, though, we should discuss one responsibility that should not be delegated to middle executives: that of high risk and unusually priced offering approval. Most organizations have procedural mechanisms that raise the final offering approval of very unusual offerings outside of the empowerment of the local office executive. Taking these to a higher authority does not prohibit offices from pursuing them, but tests whether the offer can withstand serious scrutiny.

The higher authority for large or high-risk offerings needs to be at the top of the business, where all of these are seen and compared. Middle managers add no value and can slow the process to scrutinize high-risk deals. (We will see that middle executives are tie breakers, though, in disagreements between offices and their corresponding quality assurance support.)

- **Educating professionals.** Nearly 200 hours is the annual average education for consultants and managers. The less experienced receive even more. Class and self-study training has a cost and the time spent away from the client is lost revenue. The obvious benefit is the necessary credentials to command high rates.

It is prohibitive for offices to be the primary source of training offered to its professionals. The consultant's manager plays a key role in seeing that training is effective and that things learned are reinforced by actual work experience. The basic education itself is most cost effective when organized and delivered by a group of training professionals who know the business and can focus on the consistency and student absorption of the subjects taught. This should be administered at a national level.

All consultants need to be trained in the methods of the firm. These are techniques, forms of communication, leadership styles, and business knowledge that characterize the firm's people. The training is usually one or more classes and self-study modules, from basic to advanced, forming a complete series on an area of professionalism. Examples are consulting methods, project management, and effective communication. Very often the office has modules that it must administer in the series, giving local emphasis and using experienced consultants as role models.

The headquarters education function will act as a purchasing agent for external training, particularly in technical subjects offered by manufacturers and developers of technology products. They will also use other professional education firms. To keep expense of education from getting out of hand, the headquarters should only offer mandatory training and facilitate the purchase of all discretionary training from outside.

• **Dissemination of methods and quality assurance.** New and improved methods used by professionals will come to the firm in three ways: individual consultants and local teams of consultants will see the need and begin their practice; other firms or sole practitioners will develop and market them; and headquarters-funded research in centers and other firm units (including offices) will generate them in response to requirements.

Each of these sources is in a continuum of innovation that comes from the fertile minds of professionals. Any firm may choose any of these sources and usually all three at different times. All firms encourage innovation at the client level and are faced with the difficult challenge of recognizing and evaluating local breakthroughs.

Regardless of any other role for headquarters concerning methods, its primary responsibility to the offices is dissemination. Empowerment breeds isolation. An office that can operate completely on its own will do just that. This is all well and good as it regards making deals that get clients, but it has the disadvantage of creating xenophobia (known in the technical world as "not invented here"). This is the propensity of all professionals to be overly proud of the unique tools and techniques they personally bring to engagements and the lack of motivation to look for alternatives.

The offices need a national function to act as a network between peer groups to identify and disseminate methods, and once done, to coordinate the quality assurance of all methods in use. Depending on size and geographic disbursement, a firm may choose a permanent staff, task forces, permanent peer groups, or other combinations to get this done. Local offices generally do not argue the expense, when innovations appear periodically to impress their clients. They also respond positively, when their people are recognized nationally as pioneers. A network for new methods saves consultants from documenting much the same new approach in a number of isolated offices.

Quality assurance is a necessary local function for the review of offerings and ongoing engagements. Most large offices, 60 consultants or more, can even afford a full-time person in this position. The highest and best use of quality assurance is to provide an independent risk assessment of every offer to clients. A small time and materials deal might simply be a scrutiny of the checklist and a couple of key questions to verify that the offer is what it appears to be. A large fixed-price deal might need days of reading and analyzing to form an opinion and to debate whether the engagement can be performed successfully.

The responsibility of quality assurance is to take a position on the offer. If quality assurance and the office executive are in agreement (this may be a negotiated agreement), the offer is made to the client. If there is disagreement, policy will prescribe a remedy. It may be that the office executive wins, regardless. It may be that a middle executive is the point of escalation for disputes and is asked to be Solomon. Some, because they fall into the category of unusual risk, will require senior executive approval once positions are taken by the office executive and quality assurance.

The other role of local quality assurance is to influence consultants and managers during their performance of mainstream firm methods. This usually takes the form of periodic reviews of engagements and critiques of performance quality. Because of this role, quality assurance people are often a built-in network of people for the dissemination of the new and improved methods. Since they act as the local guru for methods, they are the logical people to call consultants together for training in new techniques.

- **Overall tactical direction and support.** Entrepreneurs want freedom to take their businesses in any direction toward opportunity, but will compromise some of that freedom in return for support that makes their job easier (and cheaper). In a national (worldwide) business, common business controls and supporting business systems and procedures are easily justified. They are also welcomed by office executives, when they are recognized as a means to hold down overhead expenses and obtain valuable business information.

The tactical support most needed by professional services offices is in general financial, contract management, client marketing, and general marketing, practices, procedures, and systems. The systems are described in Chapter 2. These should be modern on-line systems with data integrity responsibility in the hands of the local offices.

Regular reporting against the business plan is a constant source of irritation between the top and the bottom of a business. As well it should be. Headquarters generates the plan and passes down individual objectives. Headquarters also expects office executives to report each month on their progress against these measurements. Each office has a slightly different style in managing its own plan, particularly with the advent of personal computing. They are perfectly willing to pass upward monthly reports (with the individual emphasis and interpretation such reports seem to need), but not necessarily in some arbitrary form dictated by headquarters.

Headquarters staff, on the other hand, cannot consolidate 20 to 100 different versions of the same information. Certainly a senior executive needs a consolidation. The top down solution is the issuance of procedures and forms with a do it my way directive to the offices. The offices learn fairly quickly that these forms and procedures are in constant change as senior management wants to focus on varying parts of the business. As a result, offices get rebellious and the quality or timeliness of reporting suffers.

A firm can eliminate the problem with the right business systems. These are ones that capture the overall status of the business through national systems and determine granularity through a roll up of local systems.

Consistency of local systems will be an issue, unless the office executives are rewarded for using standards. Reports on key measurement indicators are a benefit that headquarters can provide. They show how each office is doing against the overall business plan and against each other. Some can be derived from national systems, but most come from the roll up of local financial information (more on this later).

Pricing strategy is welcomed by office executives. This comes in the form of factors to be used to add margin to each category of cost of an engagement and how to further add margin for risk. These are derived from the overall business plan and are inherent in the quotas assigned to the offices. These tell the offices when they are pricing correctly—generating revenue against cost consistent with how profit was derived in computing the business plan.

Ultimately, the price charged a client is a negotiated one. The prudent office executive starts with the price computed from national guidelines and then goes up or down depending on the deal. Competition, other ongoing engagements with the client, unique cost structure of the office and the instincts of the executive about the risks of the deal are all legitimate reasons for pricing differently than a national guideline. Having a guideline, however, allows the local office to be conscious of a point of departure.

There are headquarters functions that are greeted with mixed response from office executives. The issue is usually overhead or investment expenses for these functions that are passed to the offices, where the short-term benefit may not be obvious.

• **Conducting reviews.** Two kinds of reviews should be conducted from headquarters. The first is a senior executive review. The second is a business controls audit. Both are scheduled at least two months in advance with the intent that offices will have time to get their house together.

The senior executive review is a test of the office business plan. It allows a senior executive to hear the office executive's personal views on the health of the office and what is required to run it successfully. The presentation focuses on marketing strategy, market assessment and forecast, current engagements and their issues, personnel plans, position against quotas, and vital signs. It also allows the local executive to show off key people in the office.

A senior executive review is an expensive undertaking for the office. The material is developed well in advance and is rehearsed repeatedly. It is time well spent, though, as it brings a number of festering issues and problems to the surface. The local management and marketing team are forced to take action on each weakness in the office, its business controls, and its engagements.

The quality of this exercise depends heavily on the character of the senior executive. Ideally, the review focuses on the overall health of the office and avoids inconsequential detail.

The headquarters audit is a spot check of an office's files to see that controls are in place and no unpleasantness is found. The auditor randomly chooses engagements and checks to see that all documents are complete and correct. The paper trail leads through contract agreements, labor activity, status reports, invoices, and any other evidence of decisions concerning expense, pricing, and personnel practices.

Again, the headquarters audit is viewed as a major event and significant expense goes into being ready. The fact of the audits is less controversial than their frequency. Auditing every office every year is too often. It says the firm can't trust its office executives and, if so, it has a management quality problem it had better address. Every office should be under the threat of audit every year, and should see an actual audit no less frequently than every three years. Offices that fail an audit should see a follow-up audit within nine months. (A subtle way to create the threat is to declare that a geographical region is to be audited during a certain week, but not name which office in that area until two weeks ahead.)

Protocol demands that the office executive have the ability to answer an audit and to determine the action plan. Audit reports should only focus on serious control issues, rather than provide a laundry list of every weakness.

• **Providing engagement review and counsel.** Offices would prefer to be totally self-sufficient in their negotiations with clients. Unfortunately, the legal and regulatory environment is too much for even the most experienced executives. Some deals and some engagement situations require the intervention and, hopefully, constructive advice and counsel of legal and accounting professionals.

The local executive should believe the help and its corresponding expense is necessary in those situations where the assistance was sought. Office executives chafe when this help arrives as a result of an escalated offering review or is triggered by one of the reviews just described. This is a growing expense for the major firms, particularly those that offer the more complex services or are providing management consulting at very high levels of business or government. These expenses will continue to grow, be passed on to the clients of these firms, and correspondingly be passed on to the customers of client products and services, until the U.S. legal culture is reformed.

- **Investing in new services.** The least acceptable expense at an office level is for staff that research and develop new ways to do business. Offices truly believe that all good opportunities will be raised by clients and effective dissemination of these throughout the business will cover the need to innovate.

What the offices miss in this view is the value of forming alliances with product distributors and other service providers that open up whole new markets or better manage competition. Some ongoing level of overhead is needed to keep the firm in communication with potential business partners. New service development should be zero base budgeted every year (the plan starts with the assumption that no expenditure in this area is needed and the expenditure is added to the plan after a case is made for realistic forecasts of new revenue to recover the expense). How these might be implemented was discussed earlier. Forcing every office to participate, particularly when education expense is involved will not be successful.

The senior executive of a professional services business needs to get the office executives together regularly. It is an opportunity to sell top down services and get feedback on their price performance. It is the best guidance a headquarters can get on what expense will be readily paid as an indirect expense in NEBA and which need to be allocations outside of the NEBA measurement.

COMPARING VITAL SIGNS

A key senior management function in a professional services firm is financial assessment (as it is in any business). In a business where local executives are empowered to make most financial decisions, senior management views many fiefdoms that function independently. Determining whether the overall business is healthy can be a major challenge.

When most offices are making their profit objectives, the overall business is flourishing. Some offices that are making profit can be explained away by local economics. When profit performance is erratic across the business and differences cannot be explained, headquarters can be at a loss to understand where the business is going and what corrective actions to take.

Profit and revenue quotas are the only measurements that can have specific success values. A profit level quota of 28 percent NEBA is very specific. Likewise, revenue at 100 percent is successful. All other measurements are significant only when viewed as trends or as comparisons between offices.

The traditional comparisons in business are from one time period to the next (i.e., month to month and year to year). A valuable comparison in professional services is office to office. Since each office is functioning independently in its unique environment, a comparison of offices provides a distribution of measurement values that points to reasonable ranges of performance that a senior executive can expect. By publishing the results of these measurements for local executives, the offices of the firm can position themselves among their peers and take action when their own measurements are approaching the extremes of tolerances within any one measurement.

Figure 9-2 lists sample vital signs of professional services offices. It provides an example of what a senior executive might publish to assist local executives in positioning themselves among other offices. Figure 9-3 shows corresponding vital signs of an individual office. Notice that vital signs can be very different depending upon the size and business mix of an office.

The vital signs summaries show averages in each key indicator for five sets of offices in the firm. It summarizes all offices, all offices that are meeting profit objectives, all small offices (less than 50 consultants) that are meeting their profit objectives, all large offices (greater than 90 consultants) that are meeting their objectives, and all offices with more than 30 percent revenue from nonlabor sources that are meeting their profit objectives.

The number of different columns should vary depending on how successful the majority of the offices are in making their objectives. In a year of economic downturn, the firm may show all offices in each size and revenue mix, since the number of offices making profit might be statistically insignificant. The firm might show averages for offices with a high mix of consulting versus those with high custom development. The headquarters staff usually has a story to tell with the set that is chosen, and they expect offices with indicators very different from those provided to take action to be more in line with national averages.

In our example at five months into the year, we have provided vital sign indicators in each of the five measurements of professional services.

• **Revenue.** Indicators provided are for revenue billed so far this year against revenue that should have been billed so far (quota) and how much was billed so far at this time last year. Additionally, the percentage of labor revenue out of total revenue is shown to assist offices in judging how they are positioned in their expansion into product and systems integration income. As would be expected the profitable offices are beating revenue expectations, while the average for all offices is slightly under quota. Growth is in the 25 percent range for small offices and offices with significant systems integration growing faster. Our office is under quota, but better than the national average. Our office is also experiencing higher than average growth.

*   **Utilization.** Vital signs are given for consultant and the combination of consultant and manager billed utilization (so far this year and for last month). Assigned utilization is also included (the sum of billed and assigned, not billed, time). Profitable offices are getting over 60 percent billable utilization for consultants and even for the combination of consultants and managers. Smaller offices have a slightly lower utilization because of smaller mass and a higher ratio of managers to nonmanagers. The offices with higher nonlabor mix rely more heavily on revenue (and profit) from products and vendors, and are able to meet profit objectives with lower utilization. Our office is getting respectable billed utilization, but is higher than the average in assigned utilization. This could indicate a larger amount of pro bono work than the national average.

*   **Profit.** Averages are provided for cumulative gross and net margins for the year. The margins are divided into their labor and nonlabor portions, along with the total (net profit margin is for net earnings before allocation, NEBA). Additionally, a vital sign is provided for growth in actual NEBA amount so far this year against NEBA at the same point last year. The profitable offices are all above 33 percent gross and 25 percent net. The offices with systems integration are discounting labor, but in return are getting higher return on nonlabor cost. The small offices have very little nonlabor (mostly extraordinary expense recovery) and are losing money on the component in favor of higher returns on labor. The smaller offices also have a higher percentage of local expense to distribute, so their net is lower. The small offices and the offices with systems integration are seeing the largest growth in net profit. Our office is at 30 percent gross and 20 percent net against quota targets of 32 percent and 23 percent, respectively. The office is healthy in relation to most other offices, but the high amount of pro bono work is hurting.

*   **Backlog.** Indicators are provided for year-end coverage (comparison of accumulated revenue billed plus backlog to be billed this year against total annual revenue quota) and for the ratio of total backlog for this and future years against the amount of revenue billed last month. Most offices have between three and four months of backlog and are covered for over 70 percent of their annual revenue. Large offices that typically have at least one very large engagement and offices with significant nonlabor generated revenue that have two or three large engagements have a correspondingly higher backlog. Our office is in a very comfortable backlog position.

FIGURE 9-2
Vital Signs for Professional Services

Professional Services Vital Signs

		Average All Offices	Average Profitable Offices	Average Small Offices	Average Large Offices	Average Nonlabor Offices
Revenue	Against YTD quota	97.5%	101.3%	106.2%	100.1%	107.5%
	Annual YTD growth	26.2%	31.1%	61.3%	22.4%	32.2%
	Labor component	84.3%	91.5%	98.2%	81.6%	75.3%
Utilization						
Consultants	YTD billed	59.1%	63.3%	61.2%	64.2%	56.5%
	Last month billed	60.2%	64.1%	62.3%	65.1%	57.2%
	YTD assigned	63.4%	65.1%	63.3%	65.4%	68.7%
Consultants & manage	YTD billed	55.7%	61.3%	56.7%	62.1%	55.2%
	Last month billed	56.1%	62.4%	58.3%	62.0%	57.3%
	YTD assigned	57.8%	63.1%	58.9%	63.8%	66.7%
Profit						
Gross margin	Total YTD	27.3%	34.3%	39.1%	32.4%	29.2%
	Labor	33.2%	35.8%	41.2%	34.1%	31.3%
	Nonlabor	1.1%	9.9%	2.4%	10.1%	20.7%
NEBA margin	Total YTD	17.1%	23.7%	28.6%	20.6%	17.2%
	Labor	22.1%	25.4%	30.3%	23.2%	19.3%
	Nonlabor	-2.5%	2.1%	-7.3%	2.2%	11.1%
Annual NEBA growth		26.1%	32.3%	58.2%	22.5%	45.1%
Backlog	Year-end coverage	62.4%	72.6%	69.8%	78.5%	78.6%
	Times current revenue	3.1	3.8	3.4	4.1	5.3
Productivity						
Revenue per year (000)	Consultants	166	173	206	169	166
	Consultants & managers	158	175	202	164	158
	Contractors	226	230	230	227	233
	All labor sources	186	195	207	193	192

FIGURE 9-2
Vital Signs for Professional Services (concluded)

Professional Services Vital Signs	Average All Offices	Average Profitable Offices	Average Small Offices	Average Large Offices	Average Nonlabor Offices
Revenue per hour					
Consultants	128	137	154	129	128
Consultants & managers	152	155	158	152	156
Contractors	115	117	119	116	116
All labor sources	130	138	156	133	131
Cost per year (000)					
Consultants	113	112	118	102	103
Consultants & managers	116	116	121	113	112
Contractors	131	130	130	128	132
All labor sources	127	126	127	125	126
Cost per hour					
Consultants	94	83	84	78	82
Consultants & managers	109	101	93	101	104
Contractors	65	66	69	66	65
All labor sources	96	86	88	85	84
Cost & expense per year					
Consultants	129	127	136	124	122
Consultants & managers	136	135	143	135	130
Contractors	151	151	153	149	156
All labor sources	151	150	149	148	151
Cost & expense per hour					
Consultants	106	97	107	95	95
Consultants & managers	127	121	124	120	120
Contractors	87	86	92	89	77
All labor sources	107	102	106	101	100

FIGURE 9–3
Comparing Individual Office Vital Signs

		Professional Services Vital Signs					
		Average All Offices	Average Profitable Offices	Average Small Offices	Average Large Offices	Average Nonlabor Offices	Our Office
Revenue	Against YTD quota	97.5%	101.3%	106.2%	100.1%	107.5%	98%
	Annual YTD growth	26.2%	31.1%	61.3%	22.4%	32.2%	38%
	Labor component	84.3%	91.5%	98.2%	81.6%	75.3%	87%
Utilization							
Consultants	YTD billed	59.1%	63.3%	61.2%	64.2%	56.5%	62%
	Last month billed	60.2%	64.1%	62.3%	65.1%	57.2%	64%
	YTD assigned	63.4%	65.1%	63.3%	65.4%	68.7%	66%
Consultants & manage	YTD billed	55.7%	61.3%	56.7%	62.1%	55.2%	58%
	Last month billed	56.1%	62.4%	58.3%	62.0%	57.3%	60%
	YTD assigned	57.8%	63.1%	58.9%	63.8%	66.7%	65%
Profit							
Gross Margin	Total YTD	27.3%	34.3%	39.1%	32.4%	29.2%	30%
	Labor	33.2%	35.8%	41.2%	34.1%	31.3%	34%
	Nonlabor	1.1%	9.9%	2.4%	10.1%	20.7%	3%
NEBA margin	Total YTD	17.1%	23.7%	28.6%	20.6%	17.2%	20%
	Labor	22.1%	25.4%	30.3%	23.2%	19.3%	21%
	Nonlabor	-2.5%	2.1%	-7.3%	2.2%	11.1%	-4%
Annual NEBA growth		26.1%	32.3%	58.2%	22.5%	45.1%	37%
Backlog	Year-end coverage	62.4%	72.6%	69.8%	78.5%	78.6%	72%
	Times current revenue	3.1	3.8	3.4	4.1	5.3	3.8
Productivity							
Revenue per year (000)	Consultants	166	173	206	169	166	170
	Consultants & managers	158	175	202	164	158	163
	Contractors	226	230	230	227	233	227
	All labor sources	186	195	207	193	192	191

FIGURE 9-3
Comparing Individual Office Vital Signs (concluded)

Professional Services Vital Signs

		Average All Offices	Average Profitable Offices	Average Small Offices	Average Large Offices	Average Nonlabor Offices	Our Office
Revenue per hour	Consultants	128	137	154	129	128	127
	Consultants & managers	152	155	158	152	156	153
	Contractors	115	117	119	116	116	116
	All labor sources	130	138	156	133	131	132
Cost per year (000)	Consultants	113	112	118	102	103	109
	Consultants & managers	116	116	121	113	112	116
	Contractors	131	130	130	128	132	128
	All labor sources	127	126	122	125	126	121
Cost per hour	Consultants	94	83	84	78	82	87
	Consultants & managers	109	101	93	101	104	104
	Contractors	65	66	69	66	65	65
	All labor sources	96	86	88	85	84	92
Cost & expense per year	Consultants	129	127	136	124	122	131
	Consultants & managers	136	135	143	135	130	138
	Contractors	151	151	153	149	156	152
	All labor sources	151	150	144	148	151	140
Cost & expense per hour	Consultants	106	97	107	95	95	106
	Consultants & managers	127	121	124	120	120	127
	Contractors	87	86	92	89	77	87
	All labor sources	107	102	106	101	100	108

- **Productivity.** The most useful vital signs are for productivity factors. These include revenue, cost, and cost plus expense (annual per person and per hour). They are broken out for consultants, consultants and managers, contractors, and all sources of people (which would include borrowed, too). Higher revenue per year reflects good utilization (with contractors being very heavily utilized) and higher revenue per hour reflects value (price). Small offices perform more consulting and see higher revenue rates (using contractors only for lower value work such as coding). Large offices and systems integration offices do a wider range of work, have a wider range of consultant levels and use contractors in both lower and medium value work. Our sample office has lower than average revenue rates for its permanent staff, although its revenue per person is high due to high utilization.

The cost and expense structure of the offices vary greatly with size and business mix. Small offices have a higher cost per person (higher average salaries) and higher cost plus expense (fewer people over which to spread overhead). Offices with systems integration can spread overhead over large nonlabor components and see lower than average cost plus expense per person per hour. Our office is out of line on cost per hour and cost plus expense per hour. The cost per person also represents a higher than average salary level than more profitable peers.

Distributing vital signs is a valuable service for the offices and it accomplishes some very subtle objectives for senior management. The offices will not travel blind through the year wondering whether their peers see the same trends. Our example office certainly knows that it is incurring rework on its engagements. It may even know that the level is excessive. Not until it can compare itself to its peers, does the effect of the problem become quite so dramatic.

The office is paying more and getting less. Clients are not willing to pay full value for work performed. It may be a serious lack of project management skill. It could be that the people in the office are not getting enough training in new methods and technology. Its people are certainly willing to work and there seems to be sufficient demand. The office is not on the brink of a disaster, but it better take corrective action to improve its revenue rates and reduce its cost rates very quickly.

Good vital signs are a signal from top management. Offices that compare well with those vital signs presented as favorable are on notice to continue to do what they are doing. Offices on the negative side of comparisons are encouraged to address weaknesses. Senior management gets its message out, shows how the national business is performing and avoids public rankings that do little to motivate and often simply embarrass.

Headquarters can vary its message by choosing different groupings of offices and different vital signs. The only caution is that every vital sign chosen is a directive to offices to spend administrative expense to track that statistic.

MOTIVATING OFFICES TO SHARE PEOPLE

A value of size in the professional services business is the ability to share consultants between offices. The demand for any particular consultant is based on the availability of the right work for that individual. Right work is a giddy array of the person's level (and corresponding revenue rate), availability, skill, experience, and need for different experience. When this combination doesn't exist, the assignment is a compromise between what is best for the consultant and the firm. The worst choice, though, is leaving the individual on the bench.

The large firms utilize benched consultants by having them pack a bag and go to where the work is. This sharing of resources strengthens both offices and provides a rich variety of experiences, especially for the young and energetic consultant who has few of the personal complications that restrict out of town assignments.

To implement sharing, firms have had to be very creative in methods to split revenue and profit. On the one hand, firms want to motivate sharing. They need to compensate offices for the better use of resources. At the same time, the firm doesn't want office executives to use sharing as a way to get rid of consultants that should be culled from the business, because they are no longer fully billable. The first priority should be to satisfy the local client market with high-quality people suited to local needs.

Another variable that affects the incentive to share is whether the firm encourages the use of subcontractors as a cost saving alternative to consultants. Compensation for sharing should encourage managers to use firm resources first, before using contractors.

There appear to be three arrangements that typify the incentive to loan and borrow consultants between offices.

1. 50–50 *split of revenue and average cost.* In this approach, the office that receives the revenue from the client credits one-half of the share of revenue attributable to the work of the borrowed consultant to the loaning office. In response, the loaning branch debits one-half of the associated average cost of the consultant for hours (days) that the consultant worked on behalf of the borrowing office. The travel expenses often have a separate arrangement depending on how much compensation is being received from the client for unusual travel expenses. (The client might specifically cover importing a resource from out of town.)

This is a moderately good short-term deal for the loaning office, who would have had all expense and no revenue. The office often rues such a decision when an unexpected full revenue share opportunity for that consultant appears on the horizon. To make sure no other opportunity is available, loaning offices are often slow to provide someone for a long-term assignment under this arrangement. Most offices will have someone on a plane tomorrow for a one-week assignment, under a 50–50 deal.

This is a good deal for the borrowing office only if a subcontractor is not a choice. The cost recovery share paid for the borrowed consultant is usually more than the cost of the subcontractor, but so is the revenue received. Usually, the net profit for the contractor is better. As a result, 50–50 sharing usually requires some form of additional stick and carrot to be effective.

2. *Provider receives revenue and cost.* In this approach, the office that loans the consultant assumes all costs associated with the portion of work performed by the consultant and receives all revenue attributed to that work. Travel expenses can be recovered by the providing office only when the borrowing office has an agreement from the client for such extraordinary expense.

This satisfies most of the loaning office's needs. It gets full return on the resource. Not having its extra travel expenses fully recovered is the only reason this is less profitable than an assignment in a local geography.

Again, the borrowing office has a decision to make between borrowing or using a subcontractor. The borrowing branch does not need to worry about the effect of the borrowed cost share on profit, but likewise gives up the revenue. Usually, this becomes a decision of immediate profit from a contractor versus risk and corresponding cost reduction from using a more qualified consultant. (It requires more time and risk to manage a subcontractor.) If the need for the extra resource is short term with a foreseeable prospect of replacing the extra person with a member of the office staff, a prudent borrower will avoid the risk of a contractor and use a consultant. On the other hand, if this is a long term need, the subcontractor choice usually makes sense.

3. *Revenue and cost to the provider/incentive to the borrower.* In this approach, the revenue and cost belong to the office that loans the consultant, while the borrowing office receives a compensation bonus for its management and marketing team (and possibly consultants) for choosing to borrow versus using a subcontractor. The extra bonus is paid to borrowing office personnel for the revenue attributed to the individual they borrowed. It is over and above the normal compensation to members of the loaning office.

For example, the bonus for revenue in the firm is 2 percent paid to the management and marketing team responsible for the client. This office borrows someone from another office and transfers $30,000 in revenue that the individual earns. The loaning management and marketing team gets the $600 (charged to their direct cost).

The borrowing office team is also paid $600 as a borrowing incentive, but the revenue does not count toward their revenue objective, nor does it count as income against their expenses. The $600 for each team member is, however, a direct cost to their office.

The additional incentive for the borrower tips the scale slightly toward borrowing versus contracting. The negatives to this approach are the increased direct cost and the recordkeeping and additional business controls necessary to ensure that these bonuses are paid correctly. The opportunity for inadvertent error or fraud goes up exponentially when the compensation for revenue generation is based on an amount greater than real revenue itself. The positive (in addition to the personal bonus) is the lower risk of using a borrowed consultant.

The best and easiest to administer method is the 50–50 approach. It works very well for short-term assignments, such as teaching, problem identification and resolution, product installation, and the final tasks to end an engagement. For long-term assignments, experience has shown that some form of an incentive will be necessary to get borrowers to use firm resources over contractors.

Administering Cross-Territory Sharing

Any cross-territory sharing of revenue adds an additional step to the revenue business process. The office that owns the client and which verifies invoice quality has the responsibility for seeing that revenue is transferred to the office that provides the resource and is to share in the revenue. The loaning office has to correspondingly list any shared revenue it expects each week in order to be accurate in its revenue and cost forecast and to follow up when credits are late between offices. Additionally, the loaning office must prepare a cost transfer to the borrowing office commensurate with the deal.

Typically, this step occurs during the weekly trial billing review on Thursday or Friday. If the contract management system and billing systems are smart enough to recognize when a person in one office works on a contract owned by another office, this information and the resulting implied revenue split may be part of the trial reports. In this case, the revenue review step includes verifying that the split is correct. In those cases where no system help is in place, the review will cause a list of expected transfers to be logged for use at period end.

Where the work is per hour or per day, the system generated splits or the manual log can show the revenue attributable to the shared person as time multiplied by rate. Where the work is billed at a fixed price, per client participation, or per charge, the hours of borrowed work must be assessed against the total work performed to determine the revenue attributable to the borrowed person. This can be very elaborate in some offices. In most cases, though, the preset rate method of distributing fixed-price revenue, gives an effective revenue per hour rate that will reasonably compensate the loaning office for a short-term resource (see Chapter 8).

Figure 9-4 shows how revenue sharing complicates revenue forecasting and tracking. The bottom seven engagements, plus education, from the revenue tracking example in Figure 7-8 have been expanded to include revenue sharing. The accuracy of short-term forecasting is severely tested, when offices give away large chunks of revenue. The tracking in Figure 9-4 is essential. In the example, revenue sharing is administered with 100 percent going to the loaning office, except for education which has 50–50 sharing.

In the previous month, the office borrowed people for Xenogamy and Yawls 'R' Boats. They loaned to one or more unnamed engagements listed under resource loan. During the month, the office was a net borrower of resources to its education business (as evidenced by a negative revenue flow). The coming month appears to be much the same.

The office is giving up a net $30,000 or 4 percent of its revenue each month to get the best people to deliver to its clients. This is a small price to pay for the competitive edge this brings. Clients will recognize a firm's ability to continually provide quality people on demand, by responding with more work.

Following invoicing, revenue transfers are inserted to adjust the income credited to each of the offices. This is the data to be used for income and expense and for paying commissions or bonuses. In general, cross-territory adjustments do not appear on billing reports, but appear as items on attainment reports. Figure 9-5 shows an attainment report where cross-territory sharing is occurring. Financial revenue is that invoiced to the client, while net financial revenue is the income to the office after cross-territory adjustments. Total revenue compensation includes an incentive to borrow that is added for Xenogamy and Yawls 'R' Boats.

Notice that one of the Yawls contracts is a fixed-price contract that received no revenue for the month, but for which earned revenue was transferred. It can be very disconcerting for an office to be seeing negative net revenue on attainment reports, and it is often a trigger to negotiate complicated deals to avoid it. Experience tells us to keep it as simple as possible. Presumably the negative accumulation will become very positive when the client is invoiced.

If an incentive for sharing is added, as described earlier in the third option, its bookkeeping must be clearly separate from the revenue amount that is being netted between offices. Firms use distinctive terms to describe these incentives that are computed by a factor times some portion of a revenue stream. The process becomes so clever sometimes that this virtual revenue takes on the ap-

FIGURE 9–4
Revenue Tracking with Revenue Sharing

| | | One Month Revenue Forecast (with Revenue Sharing) | | | | | | | | | | | |
| | | Previous Month | | Week 1 | | Week 2 | | Week 3 | | Week 4 | | Total Month | | Total |
Account	Row	Labor	Nonlabor	Labor	Nonlabor	Labor	Nonlabor	Labor	Nonlabor	Labor	Nonlabor	Labor	Nonlabor	
Sawyer Rafts A4599	Planned share	25,470	32,625	4,000	900	4,000	900	4,000	900	4,000	0	16,000	2,700	18,700
	Actual			3,984	1,102							3,984	1,102	5,086
	Actual share													
Xenogamy Biotechnology B0101	Planned share	133,165	2,895	34,500	1,500	34,500		34,500	1,500	34,500		138,000	3,000	141,000
	Actual			−5,480		−5,480		−5,480		−5,480		−21,920		−21,920
	Actual share			35,687	2,146							35,687	2,146	37,833
				−5,686								−5,686		−5,686
Xenon Natural Gas B1412	Planned Share	−19,454		4,700		4,700		4,700		0		14,100		14,100
	Actual	19,560												
	Actual share			4,722								4,722		4,722
Yam Tubas A1104	Planned share	48,180	0	11,970		8,980		11,970		11,970		44,890		44,890
	Actual share			11,982								11,982		11,982
Yataghan Weapons A3458	Planned share	0	0	0	0	0	0	0	0	0	0	0	0	0
	Actual share			0	0							0	0	0
Yawls 'R' Boats A3891	Planned share	37,655		9,400		9,400		9,400		9,400		37,600		37,600
	Actual			−5,200		−5,200		−9,160		−5,200		−24,760		−24,760
	Actual share			9,523								9,523		9,523
				−4,810								−4,810		−4,810
Education	Planned share	−24,110								44,000		44,000		44,000
	Actual	39,350								−7,040		−7,040		−7,040
	Actual Share			9,300								9,300		9,300
New	Planned share	−3,440								15,535		15,535		15,535
	Actual Share											0		0
Resource loan	Planned share	23,023		5,720		5,720		5,720		5,720		22,880		22,880
	Actual share			6,435								6,435		6,435
TOTAL		793,568	281,130	294,400	4,790	127,880	1,140	126,170	2,640	188,305	4,580	736,755	13,150	749,905
Adjusted		769,587		289,440	4,790	122,920	1,140	117,250	2,640	176,305	4,580	705,915	13,150	719,065
ACTUAL TOTAL		302,514		302,514	5,688	0	0	0	0	0	0	302,514	5,688	308,202
Adjusted		298,454		298,454	5,688	0		0		0		298,454	5,688	304,142

FIGURE 9-5
Attainment Report Containing Cross-Territory Adjustments

Services Attainment Report (with Revenue Sharing)

OFF	TEAM	CLIENT NO	CLIENT	ENGAG NO	CONTR NO	FINANCIAL REVENUE	SHARING ADJUST	NET FINANCIAL REVENUE	YTD NET REVENUE	YTD QUOTA	ATTAIN	INCENTIVE REVENUE	TOTAL REVENUE COMP
ZEN	ZOT	7979008	SAWYER RAFTS	A4599	C2930	$21,867.23		$21,867.23					$21,867.23
					C2957	$3,750.00		$3,750.00					$3,750.00
					C4879	$3,000.00		$3,000.00					$3,000.00
					C9622	$1,700.00		$1,700.00					$1,700.00
		8102885	SURF SAND	A2183	B9899	$338,384.00		$338,384.00					$338,384.00
		9622459	XENOGAMY BIOTECHNOLOGY	B0101	C7649	$136,060.84	($19,454.00)	$116,606.84				$19,454.00	$136,060.84
		9827100	YAWLS 'R' BOATS	A3891	C7428	$37,655.00	($20,150.00)	$17,505.00				$20,150.00	$37,655.00
					C7456	$0.00	($3,960.00)	($3,960.00)				$3,960.00	$0.00
		3124450	CRAZY CRUISES	A0119	A3445	$23,023.00	$0.00	$23,023.00					$23,023.00
						$542,417.07	($20,541.00)	$521,876.07	$931,432.30	$960,000.00	97%	$43,564.00	$565,440.07
ZOO		9412313	VERMIN FOODS	A9908	C0006	$53,633.28		$53,633.28					$53,633.28
		9413002	VULGAR SALES	B0113	C9486	$17,600.00		$17,600.00					$17,600.00
		9544710	WADI POWER	A8888	C7176	$17,610.00		$17,610.00					$17,610.00
		9580202	WAFFLE IRON	B0006	C8420	$48,193.11		$48,193.11					$48,193.11
						$137,036.39	$0.00	$137,036.39	$226,309.54	$200,000.00	113%	$0.00	$137,036.39
EDU			EDUCATION			$39,350.00	($3,440.00)	$35,910.00	$63,234.00	$60,000.00	105%	$3,440.00	$39,350.00
						$718,803.46	($23,981.00)	$694,822.46	$1,220,975.84	$1,220,000.00	100%	$47,004.00	$741,826.46

pearance of actual revenue and finds itself in the income portion of the income and expense statement. When this happens, the business quickly loses sight of the real profit picture of its operations.

ROLL UP: THE VIEW AT THE TOP VERSUS THE VIEW IN THE OFFICE

The reconciliation of income and expense between the overall business and the aggregate books of the local offices is a major source of conflict in a large professional services firm. It is fraught with so many annoyances and so much administrative wrangling that many firms resort to top down management as the simpler and less contentious solution. The cost of reconciliation is obvious in the time and aggravation spent on phone calls, faxes, computer messages, and meetings to negotiate discrepancies. The benefit of better profitability that comes with local empowerment is less obvious and often ignored.

The process that creates the conflict is roll up. At some regular day following the end of each accounting period, the offices send their final income and expense to headquarters to be aggregated and compared to the overall income and expense that is reported from the firm's general ledger system. If the totals match, there is no conflict. They rarely match.

The reconciliation is made difficult by five accounting activities that can be performed differently between headquarters and the offices.

• **Expense and invoice adjustments.** Last minute errors in expense transactions and billing are discovered by the local office and action is taken. These may be recognized by the national system or they may not, depending upon whether the adjustment was entered before the cutoff. The adjustment is always recorded in the local system awaiting confirmation of its acceptance by the national system.

In the meantime, the headquarters financial staff can make adjustments after the cutoff and before closing of the month's books. These may not be reflected in the local books. Again, all parties will eventually have common data, but not until the national system's monthly cycle is run and its statements are distributed.

• **Cross-territory revenue transfers.** These are all negotiated between offices, and headquarters does not see them until the end of the period. Only the most sophisticated contract management systems will accommodate them automatically. Inevitably, the amounts recorded by loaners and borrowers will differ and headquarters must act as the third party to get revenue sharing to balance.

• **Expense accruals.** In firms that have large nonlabor costs, the offices will try to time product and vendor cost to coincide with the corresponding revenue. The expense is either accrued, if the office has not been officially charged, or carried over, if the charge is early in relation to revenue. Again, only very sophisticated national expense systems will support this, and the office books that contain these accruals may not balance to headquarters.

• **Disputed cost transfers.** Debit transactions between offices and between the offices of the firm and its parent often need correction. The errors may not be discovered until a month or so after the event and the correction may require another month or so to be negotiated. Often the correction is in dispute. In any case, the office will usually make the correction to its income and expense (based upon how they see the dispute being resolved) and the national system will still contain the amount in error. (If these are recorded as expense accruals, this situation combines with the one above.)

• **Changes in expense distribution.** Very often, expenses that are distributed to the offices are changed and not all offices hear (or are listening). As a result, the expense is recorded incorrectly in the local record. Even when the correct rate is used, the expense distribution can be computed or entered in error (this can occur in either set of books).

Time is the enemy of those who are responsible for reconciling headquarters and local office income and expense. If the offices are allowed to wait until after the national system reports are distributed and then an additional week or so for them to revise their local records, much of the conflict between headquarters and the offices would evaporate. The offices could use the national system as a reconciliation base and use a simple accrual process to reflect any deviation, thus reporting a truer profit position. Detailed reconciliation would still be required, but the majority would be between offices (with headquarters acting as intermediary).

Unfortunately, the senior executive can rarely wait three to four weeks to hear a true financial position. Secondly, the offices need to pay themselves for their success through the previous month, either through accruals against year-end bonuses or actual payments. These costs need to be made based on the true financial position, and since the payments may be significant, they themselves affect the financial position of the office.

Firms that recognize the value of office autonomy and empowerment have a three-step roll up process that is not perfect, but can meet most of the information needs at the top of the business.

• Each office uses the same spreadsheet to compute income and expense, as well as each of the vital signs currently used to assess the business. These spreadsheets are sent electronically to headquarters for consolidation within two days after national invoicing and expenses cutoff. The consolidation produces a "flash" position for each office and the overall business that is subject to later reconciliation.

- By mid-month, another unreconciliated position is prepared from the national systems, but it is not broken out by office.
- By month end (just prior to the next invoicing and expense closing), the offices will electronically send a revised spreadsheet that balances to the national systems. Depending on policy, the offices may also provide a revised position that incorporates accruals.

The senior executive gets three financial position reports. They will be different, and headquarters staff learns to predict the final result from the characteristics in the first two. By using a common spreadsheet, vital signs will be an automatic by-product of the final consolidation. These can be summarized and published fairly easily, giving the offices the benefit of national comparison data within no more than six weeks after it was originally reported.

Headquarters will need to review the profit compensation computed in the reconciled spreadsheet of each office. This is a natural step to take, since these will need to be entered in the national system (usually bonuses of this type are estimated by headquarters and then adjusted in the next month's books for the actual amount paid). The audit protects against fraud and it is an opportunity to review how each of the offices administers compensation policy.

The information available to senior management on the inherent financial health of the business improves dramatically when headquarters has visibility into office income and expense. Offices with a high concentrations of a particular business mix can be segregated and their cost and expense productivity can be analyzed against averages. Offices that specialize in industries can be compared with each other to see whether they are pricing consistently. Revenue and cost performance of selected offices can be analyzed as new offerings are introduced, to see the effect on profitability. This information can be used to modify the introduction of other offerings or to accelerate expansion in new markets.

Lest we forget, the purpose of the headquarters of a professional services firm is to serve its offices. Gathering information for the sole purpose of second guessing how well offices are being managed and then charging that expense back to the offices is wrong. Using the information to improve overall business productivity and to accelerate growth and expansion is an expense no one will dispute.

A VIEW FROM THE TOP

This chapter focused on the measurements of a professional services business looking down from the top. It dealt with the problem of overmanagement: taking the tactical operation of an office away from its executive. When a local executive takes actions that are dictated from the top, the office will not do the natural things to maximize placement of resources, satisfy clients, manage for follow-on, and the other instinctual strategies that make professional services successful.

Other key points from this chapter are:

- Professional services marketing and development strategy can be managed from the top down, as long as financial success is from the bottom up.
- Compliance reviews and new methods development are headquarters functions that can disrupt the freedom of office executives to manage financial success. The enlightened firm is the one that can perform and fund these activities as a benefit to its offices.
- The dissemination of financial vital signs is a very valuable national service. It will buy considerable adherence to standards and cooperation among offices.
- Sharing of resources across offices is a major competitive strength of the major firms.

It is right and proper that senior executives should replace office executives who do not perform as they would expect or choose. Senior executives have the same threat to their position. While office executives are in place, though, the office is theirs to run and the only measurement of consequence is net profit. All others are indicators of business direction and health and should be treated as such at headquarters.

It follows then that the role of headquarters is to provide support that helps offices make profit. Some of this is in direct services. Much is in information about the business that helps local executives see where they fit among their peers. The best is sage advice on actions they can take to fix problems or expand. The entrepreneurs at the bottom will follow the entrepreneur at the top, if there is freedom to do so.

Chapter 10

Managing the Services Office: Are You Ready?

I n this chapter we will review the organization of a professional services office and the training and experience you need to manage one. The chapter will view a typical professional services office from two perspectives. The first focuses on skills needed to effectively manage a complex professional services business, including references to other sources on these skills. The second section of the chapter describes the typical functions performed within a professional services office. For each function we will examine mission and responsibilities, personal characteristics and qualifications of staff, and ways to motivate performance.

Professional services remains an entrepreneurial business, and its managers must display high energy and be prepared to take risks. Change is continuous and no two days are alike. On bad days it seems that the only part of an engagement agreement that a client understands is the termination clause.

The professional services business is not, however, for those who want to work in an unbridled world with no constraints. It requires careful strategic and tactical planning with solid business controls and a sense of when the business is off plan. The successful executive knows the value of every resource (people, subcontractors, vendors), the potential sales and revenue from every client, and all market sources of needed new clients. Attention must be given equally to cultivating client relationships and to monitoring the quality of services delivered.

CHARACTERISTICS OF THE SERVICES MANAGER

The ideal professional services manager should have knowledge and experience in the skills listed in Figure 10-1.

Typically, a firm will look to candidates who have at least two of these four areas of qualification in assigning new first line managers. Obviously, the indi-

FIGURE 10-1
The Skills of a Professional Services Office Executive

Professional Services Management Skills
People
Consulting methods
Marketing
Business management

vidual with the broadest set of these skills has the highest probability of climbing the management ladder.

People Management

New managers in professional services quickly learn that managing consultants is very different from managing other white-collar employees. Part of this is due to the nature of the job, part to the type of person who makes a successful consultant, and most to the fact that these individuals are not only people, they are inventory.

One of the intellectually joyful exercises in the professional services industry is to define the term *consultant*. The debate tends to focus on credentials and methods. Does the individual have sufficient education? Does the individual have a sufficient resume? Does the individual use academically acceptable methods of analysis? Has the individual been certified by a recognized institution or association?

To the person assigned to manage these folks, these questions are moot. A consultant is someone for whom a client pays money for delivery of intellectual results. Typically, consultants are willing and able to do the following.

- Demonstrate experience and education in a set of management and/or technical skills that are recognized as valuable by a set of clients.

- Act as self-starters and function well in an environment of little or conflicting direction.

- Are aggressive in asserting themselves in situations where their leadership is required, but stop, think, and get advice before they charge off into the unknown.

- Readily accept the disciplines of project management, when the client situation demands careful planning, tracking, and reporting.
- Demonstrate quick learning.
- Have communication skills that are sufficient for effective teaching and can be improved as the level of their influence within a client expands.
- Are willing to go where the work is and manage the compromise between a personal life and a life on the road.
- Have relationship skills that allow them to be the person each client needs in appearance and demeanor.

A good consultant is one who can read a manual or guideline on a weekend and show up Monday morning at the client location, with the client convinced that this was the right person for the job. Clearly, these are not ordinary people. They do not require management to get the job done. They need management support.

Before we go on to discussing what skills and experience are needed to effectively manage consultants, we need to touch on the other unique characteristic of consultants—consultants are inventory.

Every business has some form of inventory from which it generates income. Most are physical such as merchandise, products, material, and property. Some are less tangible, but no less inventory, such as deposits, portfolios, beds, and seats. In the professional services business it is people.

There are a lot of people inventory businesses, but most do not involve the low supply and high ongoing investment of professionals in the professional services business. This resource costs a lot, whether it is bringing in income or not, and is in great demand by the competition by the very nature of its capability to bring in revenue.

Consultants will deteriorate in value, if not provided with consistent training. Consultants will leave, if not provided with challenging work. Consultants on the bench (i.e., available but not assigned to an income generating activity) become even more costly individuals, because their dissatisfaction grabs more and more management attention. The short-term business need to maintain high utilization of consultants and the long-term desire to nurture the good employee challenges the people skills of a professional services manager.

To manage consultants, a manager needs to hone the following skills.

- Practice strong "Y" leadership, encouraging people to take initiative in directing their work efforts. Consultants shouldn't require supervision.
- Visibly act as an advocate of the consultant during consultant/client differences of opinion. If one determines that consultants are out of

line, get agreement off line as to the position to be taken with the client.

- Be up front and consistent regarding perceived interference in employees' personal lives through overtime, travel, and temporary assignments. Consultants may not like the pressures of utilization, but there is no use sugar-coating it.
- Be generous in education and make professional development planning and execution a part of a consultant's performance objectives.
- Be prepared to listen at any hour of the day or night. Consultants should be willing to use their managers as a sounding board for their ideas and concerns first, before the client.

People management has to be the number one management skill in a people inventory business. One of the advantages of coming up through a major company is the management development offered, especially by those companies such as IBM that stress strong people management. One should read all that's available on the principles and practices of situational leadership, listening, managing by objectives, and managing professional excellence.

Consulting Service Delivery and Methods

Consultants must know the methods that make a firm successful in its marketplace. The development of knowledge in these methods and underlying technology should be part of consultant performance objectives and be measured accordingly. Consultants who contribute to advancement in the methodologies of the firm are inherently the most valued employees. Those who can't learn these practices are encouraged to seek other employment.

The long-term success of the firm depends on its ability to expand the reputation of its methods. This is particularly true as competition sees the light and adopts alternative methods that also impress clients. An essential part of the successful application of methodology is a comprehensive education program for the firm's consultants. This program should start with an orientation class for all new personnel and be followed with annual education milestones that advance the level of a consultant's knowledge and ability to deliver quality and to provide leadership.

The following is an example of an education series for consultants leading to management.

1. All consultants attend a one-week orientation upon joining the firm. This class teaches the fundamentals of the consulting business, an overview of the key methods in each service offered, how the business

is marketed, how consultants are measured and rewarded, and the principles of the firm's relationships with its clients.

2. All consultants are required to take a multicourse self-study series on basic leadership and consulting methods within the first four months of joining the firm.

3. All consultants attend a one-week class on the same methods within the first six months which provides role playing situations between consultant and client.

4. All consultants spend 15 to 25 days per year in technology and methods update training, both self-study and classroom (or satellite).

5. Twenty percent of the consultants are enrolled in an advanced training series that focuses on methods of leadership and project management. The series is combined classroom education and internship, supervised by a mentor, where graduation is expected within two years.

6. All new managers attend a business management and people management class. Additionally, all managers attend annual management update training.

A number of excellent books have been written on the subject of consulting methods and techniques. One of note is *Consulting to Management* by Larry E. Greiner and Robert O. Metzger. Although Greiner and Metzger describe consulting practice in the pre-systems integration era, the basics are still the same.[1] *The Handbook of Management Consulting Services* contains an excellent set of method checklists in its appendix.

There is much debate as to whether a field executive of a professional services firm needs to be competent in the methods of the consulting business. Many managers are required to market their own services at a premium rate to clients. When they do, it often diverts their attention from the marketing and business management necessary to keep the office in business and to make a profit.

Of the four skill areas discussed in this chapter, the knowledge and demonstrable experience in the methods of the consulting practice ranks as the number two skill for first line managers and the number four skill for a professional services executive. The first line manager must back up consultants in the day-to-day delivery of service. First line managers evaluate the effectiveness of methodologies and make tough calls when quality is in question.

---

[1] Larry E. Greiner and Robert O. Metzger, *Consulting to Management* (Englewood Cliffs, NJ: Prentice-Hall, Inc., 1983).

Office executives must be conversant with the methods at a level equal to corresponding client executives. An executive must be able to compare the firm's strengths to those of the competition and to market realistic expectations to clients. The field office executive must do the right job of marketing, managing the business, and managing the people, before trying to be the top consultant, too.

Marketing

The key element in the long-term success of professional services is a strong, carefully staffed marketing. Over half of an office executive's time should be spent directly and indirectly in marketing. Some firms can sustain themselves on reputation alone. Few, however, can achieve long-term growth without effective marketing.

One of the ironies of the business is that consultants are good communicators and most often good presenters, but not necessarily good salespeople. A consultant is conservative by nature. Consultants often believe they are skirting the edge of integrity when asked to convince a client that its money will be well spent or that an engagement will have a predictable and sure conclusion.

The successful manager of professional services is one that can effectively market and can choose effective marketers. A solid selling track record is likely a significant credential in qualifying for a field executive position. Using that knowledge and experience to manage a marketing strategy and the resulting marketing program is the number two skill needed by a professional services field executive.

There are excellent sources available to broaden one's vision regarding marketing of professional services in general and consulting in particular. Most are written with the independent consultant in mind, but the four listed below were written to address the marketing needs of an established practice with existing personnel and client base.

Philip Kotler and Paul N. Bloom, *Marketing Professional Services* (Englewood Cliffs, NJ: Prentice-Hall, 1984).

Howard L. Shenson, *Shenson On Consulting* (New York, NY: John Wiley & Sons, 1990).

Richard A. Connor and Jeffrey P. Davidson, *Marketing Your Consulting and Professional Services* (New York, NY: John Wiley & Sons, 1985).

Edward W. Wheatley, *Marketing Professional Services* (Englewood Cliffs, NJ: Prentice-Hall, 1983).

The subject of marketing is well covered in these books and others that they reference. A successful professional services office must have a strong marketing program. The fundamental fact of this business, like all others is nothing happens until the sale is made.

Business Management

The key element to sustained profit production by a professional services firm is the consistent profit of its separate offices. The key element in the success of a field executive is the ability to make profit annually, regardless of whether it was a growth year, a year of retrenching, or a year of hanging in there. The successful managers of the past were allowed to start a limited business and grow it; then they learned the intricacies of managing increased complexity. The new manager of today is thrust into a very complex business on day one.

Making profit in any business is knowing the knobs to turn to maximize earnings on income in a changing business environment. The preceding chapters examined each measurement of the professional services business. They are reasonably straightforward and do not require advanced degrees in accountancy, mathematics, or rocket science. There is some prerequisite knowledge that any new manager in today's business world should acquire before arriving at this point in his or her career.

1. Understand financial statements, particularly income and expense (profit and loss) and cash flow. Knowledge of balance sheets is useful, but professional services is not an asset-based business, so the balance sheet is not very complex.

2. Understand budgeting and expense accounting, including the principles (and practical use) of charts of accounts and general ledgers.

3. Understand the fundamental accounting processes of accounts receivable and accounts payable.

4. Understand payroll and personnel systems, and be conversant in federal and state practices regarding salary and benefits and the taxing thereof.

The first three items of knowledge can be picked up in a number of ways, not the least of which is through college business courses. One of the ways to become a quick study in budgeting and accounts is to manage one's personal finances using any of a number of accounting packages available for the home computer and small business user. Local bookstores have a number of volumes on basic accounting and basic business management that can be placed by your pillow for light, sleep-inducing reading.

The office executive spends every day in business management. If the office is well organized, information systems are effective, and the office can afford a knowledgeable administrative staff to condense the vital signs of the office into quickly absorbable reports, executives can use their time to plan rather than execute. As might be suspected, the talents of the manager are severely tested when these elements are all over the floor. At that point, prioritization of where to focus attention becomes critical. Thus was the purpose of this book.

STRUCTURE OF A PROFESSIONAL SERVICES OFFICE

Certainly, there is a wide variety of organization charts to describe the thousands of offices that make up the major professional services firms. Within these structures, though, are functions that are commonly found in various degrees in all offices. These are consulting services, marketing, and administration. These functions tend to be organizationally separate because the staffs are very different. In the following discussion, we will describe characteristics that set these functions apart. These characteristics include:

- **Mission** assigned to the function and its role in overall office objectives.
- **Personal characteristics** of the staff and management of the function. These include typical personal goals, individual motivation, personality traits, and personal needs.
- **Incentives and recognition** that are needed to obtain quality personnel who will perform to their best.
- **Education and experience** that are typical qualifications looked for in choosing staff for the function.
- **Subfunctions** that describe common work assignments.

The book is not so bold as to suggest an optimal organization chart for a professional services office. A strength of the entrepreneurial spirit that spawned the rapid growth in the industry has been the tendency to allow local management to organize themselves as best fits the needs of their clients, their geography, their local economy, and their cost structure.

We would suggest, though, that the three functions described on the following pages must exist in some form. The descriptions of mission, people, and departmentalization are helpful in establishing common ground between the hypothetical office and the infinite variety facing a new manager who assumes responsibility for a real office.

FIGURE 10–2
Organization Chart for a Large Services Office

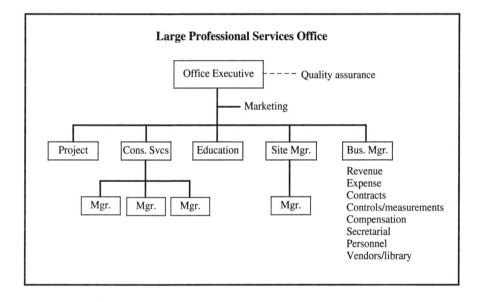

Figure 10-2 is a hypothetical organization for a large professional services office. It has a wide mix of both large and small engagements at a remote site.

Consulting Services

The mission of the consulting services function is to deliver service to the client. This involves profitably utilizing the consultant personnel of the office. By virtue of its ownership of the consultants, this function carries responsibility for delivery of the intellectual products associated with consultant services (i.e., documents and software) and for the management of vendors that deliver subcontracted labor and products.

At least 90 percent of the employees of the office fall under this mission. There is very likely a two-tiered management structure with consultants divided between first line managers, who report to a middle manager. Often the person at either the first or second level is a project manager assigned to a single client. Managers receive bonuses for generating revenue and profit, and often for meeting utilization targets.

The managers under consulting services are usually assigned two separate responsibilities: the people management of specific employees and the contract/engagement management of specific clients. Conflicts occur in the relationship between employee and manager as consultants are moved from one client engagement to another. The new client may be the responsibility of a different manager. This may require that the employee be transferred to another manager sooner than planned. Otherwise the employee will effectively report to two managers—one for personnel purposes and the other for work performance. Except for large, long-term projects, a majority of the consultants that report to a manager may not be assigned to clients managed by that manager.

A number of organization options are employed to relieve this conflict, including reduction in client responsibility for primarily people managers, the use of account managers, the use of project or engagement leaders, and consultant pools. Before discussing these, though, let us look at the criteria that are used to group consultants into first line departments (usually 9 to 15 employees).

- **Geography** is usually the first criterion for grouping consultants when the office covers multiple communities. In the case of a suboffice, geography is often the only criterion. When the office is the single location in a metroplex, geography is usually a very low priority criterion.

- Long-term assignment to a **client/engagement** is usually the first criterion for grouping consultants within an office or suboffice. As just pointed out, this creates the opportunity to match managers and employees with common client responsibilities. Long term in this context is through a reasonable employee performance evaluation period, which is a year or more for most companies. Since the average contract length for consulting is typically four to eight months, this criterion can only be used where the engagement is a multiyear project or a series of follow-on contracts utilizing some of the same consultants on each.

- Mixing or isolating **experience levels** is a criterion for grouping consultants. Levels are mixed when there is a high degree of interaction and interdependency among a group of consultants. The mixing allows development of leaders and support to the growth of lesser experienced personnel. Levels are isolated when inexperienced people are pooled into internship (apprentice) programs and/or experienced people perform as independent consultants and interact only when new methods are created, developed, and debated.

• Mixing or isolating **skills** is another strong criterion in grouping consultants. The mixing of skills tends to broaden the skills of each member of the group as they are teamed in various interchange activities (client contracts, marketing support, internal technical, and process reviews). The isolation of skills tends to deepen the skill of each member of the group as they reinforce each other. Isolation allows managers to utilize their own strengths on behalf of the group and provide development impetus through personal leadership.

An office reorganization twice a year is not unusual. No matter what combination of these criteria is used to group consultants, the dynamics of the professional services business causes single criterion alignments to become obsolete very quickly and multicriteria alignments to lose the rationale that guided them.

The company's employee culture regarding change will determine whether six-month reorganizations are a positive or negative motivation. If change embraced by the employees and multiple managers over a two-year period is not viewed as damaging to one's career, the business is free to choose mix options that simply balance the workload of the management staff. If change and multiple managers is historically a demotivator, then isolation options tend to be used to create stability.

Where isolation of skills, levels, and geography can never be matched to clients and projects, a common organization choice is consultant pools. These are large departments under a manager who has no responsibility other than the people management of a group of consultants. The grouping can be any combination of the four listed, but the manager is particularly skilled in the development and recognition of professional employees. Often the client responsibilities are assigned to account or project leaders who report to another manager, and who each have a matrix management relationship with the consultants currently assigned to their clients.

There is no right or wrong set of options for managing consultants. The easiest to accommodate is the balanced approach where each manager has a mix of professional skills and levels and, additionally, has two or more client relationships to manage. The benefit of this flexibility provides that:

• Managers are rarely assigned more than 10 employees, and can focus on each as individuals.

• All managers are tuned to the needs of clients and can react quickly when an issue is the competence or demeanor of a consultant.

- Managers are better able to take a balanced position with the client. The balanced manager finds middle ground between giving money away and defending the consultant when performance is in question.
- Managers are forced to participate in the marketing process through their client responsibility, and, thus grow in their business skills.
- Balanced resources create equality among managers for revenue potential with resulting motivation through competition.
- The broader the responsibility of a manager, the more likely that manager will be to delegate a variety of activities to key leaders. These leaders can then develop into more effective management candidates.

To support 30 percent growth, professional services needs a reliable source of new first line consultant managers. In choosing organization options the firm and its offices must be sure to focus on management qualification and development as a key objective.

Marketing

The organizational challenge facing the marketing function is not one of managers and grouping, but one of recruiting and motivation. A professional services marketing force is usually very small relative to the size of the consultant force. Large-scale marketing is rarely affordable within the profit structure of the consulting business. For this reason, marketing is staffed completely by the management of the office or in combination with a small, but very qualified set of people.

Qualifications for marketers of professional services is dictated by the type of work associated with consulting sales activities.

- **Responding to referrals.** The most common source of business for an established professional services office is referrals from current or past clients. If all goes according to plan, the most common referral is for new and additional work at clients where existing work is in progress. These referrals tend to be well structured and require very little analysis before a qualified proposition can be returned.

Referrals from one client on behalf of another require qualification to determine whether the client has the willingness to pay what the firm perceives the work will require. Professional services qualification involves analysis and negotiation to match an offer of services to the expectation and funding of the client.

- **Following up marketing leads.** Leads to new client business are generated in professional services through traditional direct marketing and advertising, a firm's relationship with the marketing arm of its parent business, or relationships with manufacturing and development partners. In any case, the marketing leads usually require significant investigation and selling before a qualified offer can be made. (The two exceptions to this are packaged installation or support services that surround such products as software and education service offerings.)

- **Writing proposals.** All professional services offers should be made via a written communication that establishes an expectation of work product, time frame, completion criteria, and charges. At one time, a letter was sufficient for most time and materials and daily rate services. In this litigious era of American business, a complex contract and attached proposal has become the common vehicle for agreement between consultant and client.

Marketing to governments is the ultimate in proposal generation. With commercial clients, the give and take of the qualification process guides the client toward a decision between competitive services. With governments, the proposal may represent the only comprehensive communication with the client.

Proposals are written to convince the reader that the submitting firm is the only one that understands the need (and is, therefore, the only firm credentialed to fill the need). Proposals contain descriptions of services in order to limit what the client can expect (to guide any legal disputes in the future). As a result, effective proposal writing approaches an art form, that achieves an abstract balance between a positive willingness to achieve great things and an ominous litany of future dangers.

- **Estimating.** Every professional services offering is measured by the number of professional hours needed to meet the client's expectation. These hours are translated to dollars through pricing. In general, pricing is a closely guarded process, but the estimates of the hours needed and the forecasting of how that will translate to cost is a major challenge of professional services marketing.

The process of estimating has not changed much over the last few centuries. It involves establishing a starting point through a set of assumptions, describing the end product that will satisfy the client's expectation, listing the steps to get there, and estimating the resources needed for each step. The challenge facing most professional services marketers is that the end product is most often an abstract concept of improving a client's business process and many of the steps require invention.

The solution to this dilemma is a carefully crafted series of checkpoints designed to take the agreement between the consultant and the client back to the negotiating table each time the consultant is in a position to make a definitive estimate of the next series of steps. The responsibility of marketing is to create a long-term strategy for a relationship that is conservative enough to set the client's expectation of a practical cost and a schedule that allows trade-offs during the renegotiations, but not so high that the client goes some place else.

These marketing activities are shared by all members of the office, including marketers, consultants, managers, office executives, and administration. The coordination and management is most often in the hands of one or more dedicated marketing representatives or account executives. If the group is large (more than four), they might report to a marketing manager, who deals with the people issues and manages territory and compensation negotiations.

In a business where 80 percent of the new opportunities come from referrals and the remainder from marketing leads generated through a business alliance or national advertising, the office executive plus one experienced marketer can support 50 consultants. In an environment where referrals are less than 50 percent of the opportunities, the ratio of dedicated marketing people to dedicated consultants is likely to be 1 to 10.

Marketing personnel and management usually have an array of incentives and an intellectually absorbing incentive formula. Incentives can be generated through quotas for revenue, sales backlog, profit, new accounts, growth, number of prospects, number of offerings, and ratios of offerings to sales. A good simple approach is to pay commissions on revenue and net backlog attainment and handle the rest through performance bonuses.

An effective professional services marketer needs four key skills.

• A professional services marketer needs to have **moves** that include a high energy personality, a positive approach to any set of problems, the ability to handle failure, and a quickness of intellect during negotiations. Professional services marketers spend most of their time turning around negative situations. Very often the first draft of a proposal does not meet the preconceived expectations of a client. Those that supply marketing leads never seem satisfied that marketing is addressing their deal quickly enough. Good marketers are able to convince antagonists that the firm can offer the best alternative among many to meet everyone's overall objectives.

• A professional services marketer needs to be an effective **project manager.** The length of time from first call to signed agreement for professional services is usually weeks. If the effort requires a formal proposal, it is often months (and, unfortunately, years). A typical marketer often has five or six of these going concurrently. The secret to success is solid management of each as projects in and of themselves. Marketers that manage well can multitask their own time effectively (thus maintaining a high close to opportunity ratio), use other office resources effectively (thus speeding offers to clients at minimum expense), and demonstrate the professional leadership of the firm to clients and other marketing organizations.

- A professional services marketer needs to be an effective **communicator** to groups both large and small. The talent to create presentations and be effective in a small meeting room is very different from that needed for a classroom. Since marketers often do not control the client account, they have little control over audience or facility. They must be able to adjust to any environment.

In addition, professional services marketers must present abstract concepts. Describing how a business process can be improved requires pictures and graphs. Lots of people and machines can produce the art. The challenge is in formulating the few key concepts that sell the firm's understanding of and correctly sized approach to the abstract problem at hand.

- A professional services marketer must be an effective **writer.** A marketer can't agonize over a one-page letter for an hour or so. A 20-page proposal has to be drafted in a few hours, not days. The first draft must be in readable form quickly, so the rest of the group involved in the marketing effort see the standards and guidelines for the document.

Where to obtain people with these needed talents has been a hotly debated topic for years. Ideally, an office would have a supply of experienced consultants with excellent project leadership background and great moves. Unfortunately, not enough consultants have these credentials. Even those that are good on their feet and have the energy needed for marketing are often intimidated by the perceived risks of the job.

On the other hand, a successful salesperson from another business may not be equally successful marketing professional services. Most salespeople are successful in selling things. These things might be very complex and require significant communication skill and technical understanding in order to sell their value to a customer. Professional services is not a thing. The marketer must be able to grasp the abstracts of an intellectual process and sell its need, features, and benefits to a client.

The best long-term approach to developing professional services marketing personnel is to require that all consultants participate in marketing as a development responsibility. This is a challenge to those charged with managing utilization, but the investment of time pays off in a number of ways. The value is realized by the business and the consulting professionals as follows.

- Consultants who demonstrate the personality characteristics needed for successful marketing (moves), can be given low probability deals to test their willingness to take risk and accept failure.

- Project leadership and project management education program investment provides equal benefit to consultants and potential marketing people.

- Consultants learn the selling process and become more sensitive to the difficulties of marketing people who create structure in the face of unknowns. The result is a higher level of cooperation between consulting and marketing.

- Estimating becomes a partnership activity between marketing and consulting, with both adding value to the process.

The second choice to developing marketing people from within is to hire fully qualified salespeople from outside the office. Their background must show that they can sell the abstract. A clue might be previous experience in selling software that improves communication throughout a business enterprise, but cannot be justified by a specific displacement and avoidance of people. To be successful, the person had to create a mental image of the improvements in business performance that result when barriers to communication are removed.

Business Management

The business management functions of the professional services office most likely reports to a business controls manager. The title may be business manager, office manager, administration manager, accounting manager, and so on, but the functions are pretty much the same.

- **Revenue processing:** Recording of labor and direct expense recovery against client engagements and the timely billing, invoicing, and accounts receivable processing of client accounts.

- **Expense processing:** Paying of bills (including compensation) and tracking of outstanding expense. This function manages expense allocation across accounts and units of the local office. This function may manage purchasing, accounts payable, payroll, and bank reconciliation.

- **Contract management:** Maintaining client historical data, current contract and correspondence files and status of work, billings, and backlog on behalf of each client.

- **Business controls:** Ensuring that the basic business processes of billing, cost control, compensation, and contract management are executed efficiently and are audit ready (i.e., would pass an internal audit, if normal advance warning were provided).

- **Measurements and compensation:** Establishing quotas and the monthly preparation of revenue and profit reports. This function includes review of the general ledger and the computation of incentive payments for each of consultants, managers, and marketing personnel.

- **Administration and secretarial:** Performing correspondence, document, and filing services for the office. This function also includes providing for adequate services, equipment, and facilities for the office.

- **Personnel records:** Preparing and maintaining personnel records, ensuring readiness for state and federal personnel audits.

The ratio of business controls personnel to consultants depends heavily on the quality and functions of the business systems available to the office. If contract management, billing, invoicing, expense control, general ledger, payroll, personnel, purchasing, and utilization are all automated (and work in a reasonably user friendly manner), the ratio can be 10 consultants to 1 business controls person for an office of 20 or more people. An office heavily involved in systems integration will need additional personnel for such functions as vendor relations and purchase control. The minimum for any office is two administrators.

Business administration managers should be on straight salary. Some firms pay business managers a bonus for attainment against profit. This often creates more intra-office contention than it is worth.

This book has focused in detail on these functions and how they are performed. There has been a constant emphasis on quality. That quality starts with the type of people recruited in the business controls function. The staff must be lean and mean in order to keep the overhead expense at a minimum. They should be well paid to attract people who are willing to multitask. They should demonstrate a willingness to absorb change, to allow shifting work in various proportions as the business volumes change.

Other Staff Functions

The broader the service line offered by the professional services office, the more likely that specific functions will become isolated into separate staff positions or even departments. Some examples that lend themselves to organizational isolation are the following.

- **Quality assurance.** Every successful professional services business has a formal quality assurance process. The tasks are either shared among all managers, isolated within a separate staff, or a combination of staff and line. The key areas of focus are:

- Review and analysis of service offerings to assess the risk of performance against client expectation. This includes analysis of estimates, review of baseline documents, and assessment of contractual agreements.

- Audits of client work in process to assess quality of work plans and client satisfaction. This often includes a review of the leadership methods and practices of the consultant team to ensure that quality assurance practices are in place and effective.

- Analysis of deliverables to clients against consultant standards and commitments, and in terms of client expectation.

The business case for quality assurance resource is the reduction of costly rework that is the inevitable result of poor quality. The most important expenditure of the resource is before an offer is made and early in the engagement. The cost of remedial actions caused by quality assurance is less at the beginning.

It is unlikely that a full-time quality assurance position can be affordable with less than 50 consultants. Until that level, the position may be filled by the management staff or provided as a regional service across a number of offices.

- **Education offering coordination.** Most often, education offerings are an ancillary service line for a consulting office. They are easy to sell compared to complex consultant service offerings and are often a first offering to a new client to build credibility. In many cases education offerings are advertised through mass marketing, separate from the mainstream marketing functions of the office.

Where the office has dedicated instructors within its consultant staff, the education group is likely to be one of the consultant first line departments. In the case where instructors are assigned for one-half to two-day periods to teach a particular class or session in addition to their normal consulting assignments, a coordinator may be named to manage the calendar and logistics of client classes. The size of the revenue stream will determine whether a full-time staff coordinator is justified. Given that the margins for education are typically three times those of daily rate consulting, the business case for a coordinator is how much more revenue can be generated.

- **Library and distribution.** If the basis for the major revenue opportunities in the office is in support of publication and/or software, the office most likely has a coordination function that synchronizes distribution of products and materials with corresponding consultant scheduling. In many cases materials are hand carried by the consultant (i.e., class handouts, installation software), and must be stocked locally. Most consulting offices have a library facility and a large library operation often requires its own staff. The business case is the reduction in cost to the stocking operation with dedicated support.

- **Subcontractor and vendor coordination.** In an office where subcontractors represent less than 50 percent of the consulting resources, it is likely that the first line consultant managers are responsible for the acquisition and technical coordination of the subcontractors for their respective accounts. As that percentage grows, and, as the amount of systems integration grows in the office, a staff coordinator for vendor relations becomes a necessary evil. The business case is similar to the traditional one for purchasing departments. You can make better deals when you centralize the knowledge of competing suppliers. The down side to be avoided is when subcontractors do not perform, due to misunderstandings with the consultant manager to whom they were assigned.

ARE YOU READY?

The purpose of this chapter was to introduce the reader to the basic functions and management demands of a professional services office. Each subject is a book's worth of material in and of itself. Some key highlights from this chapter are:

- The professional services office executive needs to be a people manager first. Having taken care of the people, the executive can focus on consulting delivery, marketing, and business management. Of the skills, business management is the one most managers are least prepared in.
- The easiest office to manage is one where the people can accommodate organization change. This allows the consultants to be grouped as best suits the responsibility of managers, and marketing can be performed by those best suited.
- A professional services office can afford only a few very good people in administration.

People who aspire to services management need to assess their readiness to assume any of these positions and then take steps to build knowledge and experience through a number of sources. Hopefully, those who are ready to be professional services executives (or already are) have read the rest of this book. If not, now would be a very good time to do so.

Chapter 11

Getting Started: "Now for My First Trick..."

T his last chapter focuses on how a manager in a professional services firm should approach a new office executive assignment. The chapter provides a checklist of common-sense actions that should help reduce the guesswork during this significant moment in your career. It addresses two important topics:

- How does a newly assigned manager order priorities, particularly during the first few weeks of the job?

- In what order should the business management techniques of this book be implemented?

This chapter will consider three cases. In the first, the manager is starting an assignment in a professional services office which has an existing base of people and engagements. The focus of the newly assigned executive is on assessing the health of the business. The other two cases are variations on the first. In the second case the manager is entering a business that is just getting started. The office has no existing engagements and no permanent people. In the third case, the manager is stepping into a complex office that has very large engagements that dominate the financial health of the office.

In all three cases, choosing a personal role is a key consideration. New managers cannot treat every demand for their attention equally, even though the engagements, clients, people, and finances of an office all seem to beg for highest priority.

We will explore the inherent conflict between changing the direction of the business or maintaining status quo. Managing this conflict is the secret to success as a professional services entrepreneur.

STEPPING IN AS SERVICES OFFICE EXECUTIVE

There are a series of logical steps to follow when you begin an assignment as executive of a professional services office. The sequence of these steps reflects the basic operating strategies of the business. They begin with assessing how people are placed, whether clients are satisfied, and which of the current engagements will bring continuing business. An understanding of the engagement base and people resources of the office leads you to an assessment of financial health. Throughout, you will be testing the effectiveness of your managers and your marketing program.

Before we explore these steps in greater detail, we should confront the most difficult part of any new executive assignment—balancing your priorities to those of the people who put you in the assignment. In an ideal world, the priorities of the office and those of senior management should be the same. As you know, you may find yourself at odds with those above when faced with the realities of managing your own business. Common sense calls for gathering information on how you and your office are perceived before getting too deeply embroiled.

Your office will be ranked objectively and subjectively in the minds of higher executives. Your office is known for how it satisfies its clients, relates to its business partners, its rate of growth, its profitability, and the popularity of your predecessor. You have been chosen to keep it going or make it better. Your challenge is to juggle the direct orders you receive with the realities you face in the first few months of your assignment.

Before starting the assignment, there are three questions you should ask any higher executive. The answers will help you to understand your new environment.

1. *Why was I chosen?* Each executive to whom this is addressed will give an assessment of your strengths, their perception of the strengths and weaknesses of your new office, and their opinion of your predecessor. The executive expects you will add value and believes you can make a difference. Knowing how you have been matched to your office can be very useful later in demonstrating how you have applied your strengths.

2. *Why did my predecessor leave?* Your predecessor left voluntarily or involuntarily and this executive may or may not have precipitated it. The answer to this question allows you to judge your latitude for making changes. Little change may be eventually needed, but much might be expected (or much needed and little expected). Inevitably, the actions you take may be exactly those of a predecessor who was viewed with disfavor and exactly opposite of one viewed favorably. You will need to know how strong a case to build for your actions.

3. *How long can I run on my own, before you reel me in?* This question tests your empowerment as an entrepreneur. Presumably you have at least one year and, ideally, two years to prove your leadership. This is your opportunity to negotiate an agreement on how success will be judged. You should also ask, "Why would you reel me in?"

You should have performance objectives for revenue, backlog, profitability, people management, and business control. You need to probe for any additional hidden agenda. The amount of time you are given and the measures used to demonstrate initial success, tell you much about the pressures on your own manager. Your challenge is to negotiate a performance measurement that allows both parties to demonstrate improvement in the business and gives you freedom as a manager.

There are two other important sources of information when stepping into the executive leadership of an office. One is from a peer and the other is your predecessor. It is simply foolish not to avail yourself of both of these.

Your peer should be someone, who knows both you and the office you will be managing, and is also an office executive. Ideally, it is an executive of another office in your geographic area for whom you have worked. This person can give you a more objective comparison of your strengths and the office's weaknesses. Peers bias their view to their relationship with your predecessor and how they believe senior management judges their own success. You will need to understand their bias and take it into account.

Your peer is the best source of pitfalls in the measurement process and what internal issues will most occupy your attention. Your peer can relate how he or she spent the first few weeks in their assignment and what they would do differently. This discussion is a valuable source of how your priorities as an office executive may not balance to those of the executives above you.

A visit with your predecessor is always a revelation. You should plan to meet twice: once before or as the assignment starts, and again, two months later.

Your predecessor knows the people in the office. In the professional services business, all information about people is valuable and your predecessor's successes and failures were directly a result of the consultants, managers, subcontractors, and other vendors within the resources of this office.

Your interview with your predecessor can be as far ranging as he or she is willing to pursue, but at a minimum should focus on the following.

• **An opinion on each person that is a resource to the office.** This should start with the managers and marketing staff (if they are separate individuals), then continue to the consultants and any borrowed people. Finally, your predecessor should be asked for an opinion on current contractors and vendors.

The information you want most is strengths, weaknesses, and personal career desires. Assuming the firm has formal employee performance and career development practices, where the written evaluations and plans for the individual can be learned, the importance of this interview is to learn what may not be written about their value as a billable resource. Often, opinion of value and the written information about development and performance are at odds with each other.

The opinion of your predecessor will be weighed later with that of your staff and, finally, with your own.

• **An opinion regarding the health of each current engagement.** Your predecessor knows something about every engagement. You want his or her assessment of client satisfaction, quality of performance, appropriateness of method and technology, effectiveness of leadership, and probability of follow-on which will again be biased. Use this information as a starting point for the information gathering and assessment we will discuss next. After all, every opinion you will get is biased. In this case, you are interviewing someone who can make comparisons among all engagements in the office.

• **History on the clients and sources of marketing leads that got away.** Those you meet as you step into the leadership of an office have a very short memory. The current demands of clients and the known prospects for new clients dominate your staff's attention. They have no reason to reflect on (nor in many cases were they even aware of) clients and engagements from the past. Your predecessor is an excellent source of this important knowledge.

Inevitably, history becomes the present. At some point in your first few months, you will encounter a need to know how this office related to a previous client, business partner, or vendor. Any information you have will make you smarter and more effective. Your predecessor is possibly the only source of much of the history you will need.

Assessing Your Engagements: The First Month

The first priority of the new executive is to understand the engagements that currently occupy the resources of the office. Your first week will be spent meeting with the key leadership in your office and you should ask each to schedule a review of their engagements for you as quickly as is practical. You should set them at ease and assure them that your purpose is to become prepared to meet clients. In fact, you will also be using these reviews as a device to:

• Begin to assess performance quality across the office.

• Assess the effect of past financial practices.

• Understand current demand for people.

• Observe the leaders of the office in action.

Regardless of your style, the reviews of each engagement ought to be conducted in a formal meeting setting. Each engagement leader (project manager, project leader, or lead consultant) should be provided with an outline of items to present and given one to three weeks in which to get prepared. Small time and materials engagements may only need one week, while major projects might need three.

You should make it clear that the purpose is to educate the new manager, not to make judgments about the engagements. They should know that you plan to meet all of the office's key client executives and will need to be armed with a solid understanding of the client's expectation toward each engagement. Your staff may see your hidden agenda, but by portraying a friendly and relaxed demeanor, you should be able to dispel the fear that the review is an inquisition.

Figure 11-1 is a useful checklist for an engagement review. Not all of the material is necessarily gathered and presented by the engagement leader. The manager on your staff with account responsibility has a role to play. So also do those with marketing and business controls responsibility. The best approach is for the engagement leader to present all but the items noted and then call on each of the support staff to make their comments. The business controls person should have a one-page briefing chart with the items listed under measurement status.

The review checklist is in three sections.

• **Project recap.** The engagement leader will summarize the work in terms of what the firm was asked to do, the original and current estimates of the effort, how the effort is being conducted, the responsibilities of all parties (including vendors and the client), tools, methods and techniques being utilized (and their effectiveness), and an assessment of the resources in use and planned. The account manager should be asked to comment, when the engagement leader concludes his or her assessment of resources.

• **Client status.** The engagement leader should describe the client organization, where the effort fits in the client organization, what is expected of the firm, how the results will benefit the client, key decisions that the client has already made and how the client's expectation is being managed. This section will also cover how risk was assessed, how risk is being managed, what changes have been identified (and their disposition), and which opportunities for additional business have the highest potential. The marketing and management staff should be called upon to comment on actions being taken regarding managing risk and pursuing opportunity.

• **Measurement status.** The engagement leader should describe the staffing (including vendors). Your business controls staff leader should then summarize

FIGURE 11-1
Engagement Review Checklist

Engagement Review Agenda

Project Recap
- General engagement description
  - Project title, business type, type of service, amount
  - Contract and project history
- Deliverables, work products, major milestones
- Status review
  - Original estimates
  - Status to date
  - Estimates to complete
- Project organization
- Project plans and methods
  - Techniques being used
  - Assessment

Client Summary
- Client organization
  - Decision makers
  - Responsibilities and interfaces
  - Significance of engagement and its benefits
  - Key decisions to date
- Client expectation
  - Firm's responsibility
  - Expected methods and approach
  - Expected completion criteria
- Environment
  - Facilities, equipment, services
  - What is needed
- Risk assessment
  - Original key assumptions and risk assessment
  - Current issues
- Recap of change activity
  - Changes to date
  - Cumulative impact
- Client satisfaction
  - Major areas of satisfaction
  - Major dissatisfaction

Measurement Status
- Pricing assumptions
- Income and invoicing history
- Cost history
- Utilization history
- Profitability projection
- Financial exposures

income history, cost history, utilization percentages for the assigned staff, and an assessment of profitability.

An engagement review should require at least an hour. There should be enough questions and discussion for you to get a good view of how the staff interacts. You should learn enough about the engagement to avoid making imprudent commitments when meeting the client.

Obviously, major engagements might require several hours. A conscious effort should be made to keep the material presented at summary levels and leave time to discuss issues, exposures, and opportunities. You do not want to appear ready to assume any management responsibility for engagements, unless asked specifically to do so by your staff.

The number of people in attendance can vary. Since one of your hidden agendas is to observe your staff in action, the more members of the engagement team and from the supporting staff in the office that attend, the more interaction you will observe. By the same token, you are taking people off billing to conduct the review and you do not want to appear to waste revenue time. You might choose to defer staff issues to a separate recap meeting after you have released the engagement people.

The manager of the engagement leader (assuming it is someone other than yourself) is in the most difficult position. A new manager has arrived and wants to look over his or her shoulder. When you meet with each of these individuals privately during your first week to introduce the subject of the review and the schedule you would suggest, give them a chance to voice their concerns. You ought to be prepared to compromise on scheduling and to allow each of your managers to play whatever role they would choose for themselves to support their people and protect their turf.

Inevitably, some of the items on your checklist will not be readily available. Beware of making premature judgments. If all engagements lack the information, you may later determine that your business is simple and low risk, with little need for much project management and business control. Engagements that seem in better control than others, may conceal major client issues that will reveal themselves later. You need to encourage your people to continue their good work and react only to those needs that they expressly direct to you. You still have many weeks before you have enough information to judge the quality of your organization.

You will want to schedule four other activities during the first month of your assignment to occur concurrently with engagement reviews.

1. *Business status review.* Hopefully, you will have at least one month of grace before you are required to make a forecast (six months would be nice). If you inherit someone who coordinates data gathering for measurements, the individual will be most anxious to brief you on the last forecast and to build an

immediate partnership for the next forecast. If your office has no such person, you will need to meet each member of your administrative staff to learn his or her relative role and responsibility in compiling measurement data.

Execute the first month's measurement process in a manner that is familiar to your staff. Start with a review of the previous month's business status, become clear as to what each person (including yourself) is expected to do and when, create a personal calendar of the events (that you can privately check off), and proceed to the next monthly checkpoint.

Since your administrative people are control and process oriented, they will be the most resistant to change. You can begin to make changes when you understand why they are comfortable with the current process and you can sell how the change reduces their personal discomfort and improves the overall business. You pay them to defend their controls and should be comforted when they resist encroachment. The earlier you get started in understanding how they serve you, the sooner you will be able to exert your own influence over controlling your business.

2. *Marketing process review.* You are the top marketer in your office. The process depends on your effectiveness in that role. If your predecessor has been gone for some time, marketing momentum may be at a stand still.

The only marketing you can do in the first month is on a crisis basis. You will be asked to make resource allocation decisions that are escalated to your level, including meeting with clients and business partners that want answers and offers more quickly than your staff can provide. You will be asked to approve offerings and must decide how much trust to put in your staff.

By the end of the second week, your marketing staff (one or all) should be prepared to give you a briefing on the marketing process and the status of the current marketing program. The material in Chapter 7 should set an expectation for what you should hear. You are particularly interested in knowing the next action and who will take that action for each active prospect.

You need to try to give yourself until the end of the second month before you begin to spend the normal 40 percent to 50 percent of your time in marketing. Your staff will need you sooner and you must walk a line between seeming reluctant to be their marketing leader and showing a willingness to take full responsibility immediately. The longer the marketing program has needed you, the tougher this role becomes. Your challenge is to buy yourself some time to get through the other steps, while picking and choosing those marketing activities that absolutely require your participation.

3. *Basic business process assessment.* One of the first actions you will take as the new executive is to correct fundamental quality exposures. The engagement reviews are your first step toward identifying quality issues surrounding client performance. A review of the billing, labor collection, and expense pro-

cesses is your first step toward assessing exposures in invoicing, people management, and cost control.

The first month is for discovery, not action. If, however, you discover quality and control problems in any of these three areas, they will become high priorities in your second and third months. You discover whether you have control issues in two ways—by simply observing the process and by listening for symptoms.

You should ask your administrative staff to show you how they perform the invoicing, labor claiming, and expense control described in Chapters 4 through 6. Key steps to examine are: invoice line item audit; follow-up on missing or incorrect labor sheets; and key expense line item audit. Each of these needs a reasonably disciplined set of predecessor steps, in order to be executable themselves. Each is very time consuming when quality is low. They are your simplest points at which to test overall quality.

While reviewing engagements, meeting your staff, and, later, meeting your clients, you will be given additional clues to control problems. The most common is that invoices and status reports do not agree (assuming your staff prepares status reports, which might lead you to ask other penetrating questions). Another clue is that consultants are too busy to report their time and travel.

Again, the first month is discovery, not change. You have yet to hear from your clients and their perceptions of your quality should carry significant weight in later decisions to inject change.

4. *Reading employee files.* In the first month, you will begin meeting each of your people personally. By the end of the second month, you should have met everyone in your office. Use the first few weeks to quietly read their employee files. Your purpose is to learn at least one key strength and one important career aspiration about each person. Your professionals are self-motivated people and it is very helpful to know their personal priorities when you see them in action. They also consider themselves to be very valuable (as evidenced by the fact that clients pay for their minds), and will be disappointed if they find you have not taken the time to learn the basic facts about them in their official files.

The best time is early in the morning or after hours in the evening, when few members of the staff are coming in and out of your office (nothing is more disconcerting than to surprise the new boss reading your employee file). Provide your secretary (or personnel coordinator) with instructions to deliver groups of files to you in an envelop.

Hopefully, you can read each of the files before meeting the individuals themselves. As you know, employee files are the ultimate in government officialdom. They contain bare, incontrovertible facts. Beware of making value judgments. By the same token, the file information can help you to avoid misjudging a strong member of your staff, simply because your first meeting was on one of his or her bad days.

By the end of the first month, you will be part of the process and no longer its observer. You will be approving offerings, taking escalations on disputes over people assignments, calling on angry clients, and hopefully, attending bi-weekly (or weekly) marketing and management reviews. These steps are designed to let you see across your domain, before you step into the trees and lose sight of the forest.

Meeting Clients and the People: The Second Month

Starting immediately in your second month, you should call on every client. You have three visits to make for every engagement.

- **Sponsoring client executive(s).** This individual is the top executive in the portion of the client enterprise affected by the engagement. Ideally, it is the top executive of the enterprise, itself. More often it is two or three key executives that have funded the effort and will be jointly responsible to own and use the results.

- **Client project manager.** The client has delegated responsibility to a person who is the point of contact for your engagement leadership. Protocol and common sense demands that you visit this person, concurrent with any visit to sponsoring executives.

- **Your team and its leader.** You should have already met your engagement leader. This is your opportunity to meet all of the team members, including contractors and borrowed people. You can now also see their actual work environment. Do they have individual work areas? Must they contend with noise and mess? Are they isolated from their client counterparts? These are issues you should have heard by now.

Protocol also demands that you visit the team before meeting with the client. You have placed your trust in the person who leads this engagement. That trust includes managing all communication between the firm and the client. Your leader should be briefed on the objectives of each of your client meetings and, where possible, be invited to attend. There should be nothing you would discuss with the client that you could not discuss in front of your leader. Only when the client insists on a private call should you go alone.

Figure 11-2 is a checklist of questions to ask your client. One is more appropriate to the client's project manager and is so marked with an asterisk. Notice that some of the questions put your engagement leader on the spot and you should be sure to discuss those together before the client meeting. Your leader may persuade you to avoid confrontation, although you may be simply postponing the inevitable.

FIGURE 11–2
Client Meeting Checklist

> **Client Meeting Checklist**
>
> –Why have you asked us to perform this work?
>
> –What will be your next action after we complete?
>
> –When do you understand we will complete?
>
> –What will you have when we complete?
>
> *What is your view of the work we most recently completed?
>
> –How would you rate our leadership?
>
> –What are our three top strengths?
>
> –What is our major weakness?
>
> –What would you have us do to improve the engagement?

The objective of every client meeting should be an action to improve the engagement and an opportunity for more work. You should be able to schedule another specific meeting for each, making it clear to the client who on your staff will represent the firm at that meeting. Obviously, you should only name yourself, when no other choice is satisfactory.

You may step into or precipitate a client crisis. There should be no delay in addressing the issues raised, particularly those of a top executive. Be prepared to clear everything else from your personal schedule, since you may be involved in problem determination and resolution. You will not and should not delegate the return meeting with the client to another on your staff, even if you are simply the messenger from the office. The client is testing to see if the top person from the firm cares enough to respond personally.

The engagement reviews will have prepared you for which client visits are the most likely to need your personal follow-up. Common sense suggests to schedule them early and to space them out. The difficulty of getting time on a client executive's calendar demands planning these visits well in advance and making sure that a crisis at one does not encroach on another. You should not attempt to meet more than three new clients a week.

As you meet your clients, you will be meeting your people. Take them to lunch in groups or individually. Try to have a moment of face to face conversation with each one. In the coming weeks, you will hear positive and negative judgments about these people, as you and your staff review assignments and utilization. It becomes difficult to picture the person, separately from their inventory characteristics of skill, resume, and billed versus assigned utilization. This is your opportunity to compare them to the impression built in your conversations with their immediate manager and your predecessor, as well as, the cold facts of their file. These people are your product and all confident business people need to understand their product.

The potential down side to all this exposure to clients and your people is the spotlight you turn on yourself. They will expect you to be knowledgeable in the methods of your business and will be disappointed, when you fail to exhibit the moves of a top consultant and the sensitivity of a good people manager.

Fixing Only Those Things That Are Broken: The First Six Months

By the beginning of the third month you should decide whether you need to make immediate improvements in business administration. You certainly do not want to fix things that are not broken. Have you received two fairly accurate revenue positions? Have you been able to forecast one month's revenue with reasonable accuracy? Do you know the assignments of all members of the staff? Do you know the billed and assigned utilization of each of your resources last month and so far this year? Will you see a fairly accurate expense statement for the first two months within the next two weeks? Did your discussions with clients focus on their problems, not yours?

If all of these answers were yes, then you have few serious control issues. "Fairly accurate" can be broadly interpreted, but you need to weigh the cost of disrupting the efficiency and confidence of your administrative staff against how much benefit you might receive from "complete accuracy" (a sometimes elusive quality in business controls).

The following list is a recap of the most basic business control needs of the professional services business from the preceding chapters. Some form of each of these controls must be in place, and you should take action if they are not. The first list will be followed by a second list of practices that are strongly recommended, but are not critical. The second list contains the practices that improve your knowledge of your business and aid in planning and forecasting. A later section in this chapter expands this recap further to include the added controls of nonlabor services.

Minimum business controls include the following.

- **Engagement file:** The central repository of information describing the office's relationship with its clients. The minimum file contains formal communication such as letters, agreements, delivered work products, status reports, invoices, and internal documentation of verbal communication.

- **Daily or hourly labor recording and data collection:** A weekly (no less frequently than monthly) record of hours or days by all billable people. At a minimum, the data collected must contain time spent billing and, additionally, time assigned, not billed. Only slightly above the minimum level of recording is the collection of time spent in education, administration, and support to the office. The data collection process must be able to report utilization by individual and by groups of people types (each level of consultant, managers, contractors, etc.) at least monthly.

- **Billing and invoice audit:** In addition to preparing invoices and reporting of billing to the financial reporting process, your staff should be comparing each line of billing data with its labor record or engagement agreement source for accuracy.

- **Assignment calendar and review:** The updating of the master calendar of all current and planned assignments for people who are billable and the communication of the information to those committing resources. The communication is best accomplished through a meeting of all parties (at least a conference call) to resolve conflicting needs.

- **Expense audit:** The comparison of all nonrecurring expenses charged to the office against a source document for the expense (invoice, travel expense sheet, internal debit memo, purchase order, etc.). The audit is to ensure accuracy of payment to employees and suppliers and to prevent fraud. A slightly higher than minimum requirement is to audit recurring expenses, such as payroll, rents, and allocations, on a quarterly basis to test the accuracy of those computer systems.

- **Income and expense spreadsheet:** The summary of all revenue, cost, and expense onto a monthly spreadsheet to compute local profit. The summary should separate labor and nonlabor revenue, direct labor cost, direct nonlabor cost, selling expense, administrative expense, and other indirect expense. The profit computations should be for both gross and local net profit.

- **Backlog reporting and analysis:** A list of remaining revenue from current engagements. The analysis determines short-term revenue demand and points to engagements that are about to lose funding.

- **Commissions and bonus audit:** Each commission and bonus payment should be compared with its billing or profit line item source. This is a protection against fraud.
- **Marketing activity review:** A list of potential new engagements and current actions to gain client funding and agreement to proceed. The review must include all with marketing responsibility (at least by conference call) to avoid embarrassing overlap and ensure that the highest priority opportunities are being pursued.
- **Regular engagement status reviews, status reports, and change control:** In addition to quality delivery of the firm's leadership, business, and technology improvement methods, the adherence to a disciplined communication process within engagements.

Recommended management practices for effective planning and forecasting include the following.

- **Comprehensive labor reporting.** This is the distribution of a 2,080-hour year, plus overtime, for every billable person to at least high-level components of billing, assigned, personal, education, administration, marketing, office support, and travel. Further distinctions between nondiscretionary and discretionary personal time (holidays and vacations versus personal business and illness), proposal development versus general marketing, and classroom versus self-study education will be helpful in forecasting people availability.
- **Computation of simple revenue and cost productivity.** This is a bimonthly computation of average revenue per month, revenue per hour, cost per month, and cost per hour for consultants and managers as a group and for contractors (along with an average for all resources). Having these numbers at your fingertips is a great time saver, if you need to rebuild the business plan or restructure pricing. If the office is very profitable, the need for this data will not be critical until October and November business planning. If you have determined profit to be a serious problem and, particularly, if you suspect pricing is a cause, you should begin to gather all the productivity data that your income and expense and utilization processes can bring together.
- **Outstanding expense log.** This is a record of all discretionary expense commitments, particularly those to internal suppliers and external vendors. As discussed previously, it is used to match major revenue and major costs in order to eliminate distortions in profit that can occur, when the two are not synchronized. The expense control log is also an excellent tool for expense audit. If there is any suspicion that profit-

ability problems are masked by expense timing, the expense control log should be in place for at least three months before trying to fix the problem through changes to pricing assumptions.

The toughest issue you will face in modifying business controls is workload. Ineffective controls create work for administration, managers, and you. Adding new controls creates more work before they take effect. Beware of doing too much of the additional administration yourself.

By the third month you should be spending more than 50 percent of your time marketing. Your highest priority after assessing engagement quality is addressing marketing quality. Whereas you can delegate the follow-up of engagement exposures to your managers, in most firms you are the top marketer and will have primary responsibility for marketing problems. This is not a good time to get yourself bogged down in administrative detail.

The one task that many office executives choose for themselves, with good success, is the structuring and execution of resource and financial spreadsheets. One reason is that it can be done away from the office, where you can focus on a single subject. Working with summary level spreadsheets gives office executives a perspective of all parts of the business. You can stay above the detail, but you are required to understand and question how each financial and utilization component of the business comes together.

The mechanics of maintaining your own spreadsheets are as follows.

- Your administrative staff delivers regular utilization reports to you, similar to those contained in Figures 5-7 and 5-8.

- Your administrative staff delivers monthly revenue and expense data to you, summarized at the line item level depicted throughout Chapter 6.

- You structure spreadsheets that are illustrated in each of the tracking sections of Chapters 5 and 6, and again illustrated in Chapter 8.

If the information you need for spreadsheets is not readily available, your request alone begins to change your administrative process. You may need to be patient and allow the actions just described to be successful, before pressuring your staff to deliver what you need. Assuming you start your staff to correcting problems in the basic list by the third month, you can reasonably expect to have information for your spreadsheets by the eighth month. Obviously, with an office that is under control at the outset, you can build your spreadsheets as soon as your own time allows.

By the end of the first six months, the office's problems are your problems. In a professional services business, where changes can be implemented quickly, the honeymoon for the new executive is very short. At this point you can choose to throw caution to the winds and proceed to make whatever changes you believe necessary.

Building the Plan

Much of this book is devoted to strategic and tactical planning. In the second half of your first year and at least once every year thereafter, you will build your plan. You should start with strategies and end with a specific income and expense forecast that is both makeable and challenging.

As we have discussed, your strategies will address expansion rate, the markets that you choose, and your people management policies. These will lead you to specific planning assumptions for business (revenue) mix, revenue growth, resource mix, utilization, and pricing. As we have seen, the process is iterative and rarely does the first utilization plan lead to an acceptable profit plan.

You will use backlog analysis as a source of revenue potential and current business mix. You will talk to peers to see what offerings are generating increased demand. You and your marketers will survey the sources of your marketing leads to determine their view of future demand. When you are finished, the office will be on the path you set for it.

Seldom can you delegate the planning exercise to a key lieutenant (or colonel, depending on how you view your own rank). This is where you should plan to have your own spreadsheets. Spreadsheet tools are very easy to use and usually inertia is your worst inhibitor. By doing your own computations (and iterations), you will best understand the interrelationships among business mix, resource mix, pricing assumptions, and real costs that should be instinctual to an entrepreneur in the professional services business. You certainly don't have time to run these numbers when you are face to face with a key client executive, who wants to negotiate your rate.

If you are totally inexperienced in spreadsheets, lay out what you need and ask a member of your staff to build templates. These are spreadsheets that contain your calculations, but to which you enter the information. More than likely you have someone who sells that skill within your consulting staff. Once you start working with existing spreadsheets, your own confidence will improve very rapidly.

Use the examples in this book if they fit. The accounting guidelines of your firm and the resource mix in your office may be very different than those portrayed. The relationships among hours planned and worked, revenue forecasted and invoiced and expense expected and incurred should be similar to those illustrated. The material in the book will help you to decide how extensively you want to track your data.

STEPPING INTO A FRESH TERRITORY

Only two priorities dominate the attention of an executive starting up in a new territory—finding clients ready to pay and getting people that clients will pay for. Business controls have little need for attention. Success, though, in the two priorities will change them very quickly. Our discussion will address when and where to begin your focus on basic business management.

Getting Started in a New Territory

Your first task is to cultivate your firm's established sources of clients within the boundaries of the territory to which you have been assigned. These can be the account managers of your firm's parent (accounting services practice, computer products marketing, aerospace manufacturing, etc.), the local management of an intercompany alliance (a product distributor for whom you supply client services), or a targeted client set that receives specific benefits from the unique methods and skills of your firm. With the first two sources, your starting point is with your local business partners, rather than a list of clients on whom you can start making marketing calls.

You will probably be 100 percent of your marketing resource. Typically a new territory is a first venture for a firm in a geography, the expansion of a firm's general services from a base of one unique client project or the introduction of an entirely different set of offerings in an existing geography. The simple business principle in all three cases is to get one client that will fund at least one consultant, which starts a revenue stream that funds getting the next client and so on. Until that first engagement starts to bill, you are pure expense (which is anathema to whatever firm organization is providing the seed money).

Your first few weeks will be a blitz of marketing calls on your client sources. Your marketing will focus on the benefits your consultants will provide to your alliance partners, while further providing value to your joint client. The strongest marketing tool you will use is references to client situations similar to theirs, where both the client and the partner speak gloriously of your services and their worth.

By the end of the first month you should be making actual client calls. The first call is usually to present credentials, to encourage the client to check your references and to ask for a problem to solve. By the second or third call, you will face two key inhibitors to making this deal.

- The client requires you to perform pre-offering work for which you neither have the time, nor are qualified.

- The client will not make the deal until you can show them the lead consultant that you expect to assign.

Until this point, you have been your major expense. The ante now goes much higher. The success of your next actions will likely determine the profit performance of your new business for the remainder of the current year. You have the following judgments to make.

- Is this a fully qualified client?

- Is the client definitely ready and able to buy, if you offer the right person to perform the detailed pre-offering work and, in the process, demonstrate their personal value?

If the answer to the first question is yes and the engagement is less than three months, you will want to borrow an experienced consultant from another office and get this work started as quickly as possible. If the answer to the first question is positive, but not a definite yes, and/or the engagement is longer than three months, you will be likely to use temporary help to complete the offer. The client will need to understand that the consultant they see is an example of the knowledge and experience available from the firm. You will then need to recruit the permanent staff member.

If the answer to the first question is negative, you should lower your responsiveness to this client and move on. If you are successful elsewhere in raising engagement funding needed to start a staff, you may choose to return.

The best of all possible worlds is to start your new territory with a short engagement, staffed by a borrowed resource and a long engagement, staffed by a newly hired or permanently transferred person. The revenue from the first engagement will offset your expense and the revenue from the second will offset the cost of acquiring the staff and allow you to get some administrative assistance. Multiples of short (with borrowed) and long (with permanent) staffing will accelerate the growth of your venture.

You probably are not living in the best of all possible worlds. As just illustrated, the first rule is: only incur consultant cost on behalf of first clients that are nearly certain to buy. Building an offer can take a day or weeks and it is all cost. You will be able to afford the less immediately qualified opportunities once you have consultants that can spend a little nonbilling time to gather the qualifying information.

The second rule is: incur cost only in people resources that your client will buy at first sight. Borrowing proven people is your strongest choice and how the major firms are able to open new territories very aggressively. Exquisitely careful hiring is your only other choice.

Controlling a New Business

Certainly business administration is not a priority in the first few months of opening an office. Your most time consuming administrative duties will be related to payroll for yourself and each person that is added to the permanent staff. Hopefully, your firm administers payroll at headquarters.

You should start your client and engagement filing immediately. Use simple paper collection of everything about each client you discover, including your notes. If you use a daily notebook, you might start separate client pages from the back forward to reduce the amount of transcribing needed for the client or engagement file.

Record labor time from the very first week (starting with your own). Even if no billable time occurs until weeks into the life of this new office, the discipline gets established and the historical data will be available when you need it. Your staff will already be recording their time, when you pass that point where you need utilization tracking. No change in behavior need be forced upon them at a time when you will least want false starts.

You can perform invoice auditing yourself. You should get at least a temporary secretary as quickly as money allows. Your secretary can process income and expense, while you perform the audits or vice versa. Be sure to plan for your education and your secretary's education on your firm's business computer systems. You do not have time to create duplicate computer function. On the other hand, you should start fairly quickly to develop spreadsheets that are not provided by your firm.

Obviously, a new professional services territory executive performs a number of administrative tasks that someone setting up a new product marketing office would not. The profit expectations of the firm will dictate how much cash advance you have before the business must be self-supporting. It is very likely you will use your advance to pay consultants, not administrators. Once you have four people billing at better than 50 percent utilization, you should be able to afford a permanent business controls person.

STEPPING INTO A LARGE PROJECTS OFFICE

There are three additional priorities that the new executive faces, when assuming responsibility for an office that contains one or more very large engagements. They are:

- Assessing the decision support structure that surrounds the project managers.

- Meeting key vendors that supply subcontractors, products, and other services.

- Measuring the underlying productivity of the office and assessing the relative impact of the large project business on short-term staffing and current pricing.

In an office dominated by one or two very large projects, the office may be organized to provide optimum support to the projects or to the remaining smaller engagements, but rarely both. The people management and administrative needs of each are very different. The projects have working managers with fewer directly reporting employees than general consulting and education, where managers may only bill 30 percent to 50 percent of their time. Projects have people who perform project control duties that are billed to the client and reduce the administrative support that a comparable set of smaller engagements would require. On the other hand, large projects require quality assurance support for project reviews and major change assessment that is not needed on smaller engagements and is most likely not billed to the client.

You need to decide whether your office organization and administrative support is in balance. If the projects are a fairly recent evolution, there may be considerable duplication of effort. Consultants assigned to a project, but still receiving employee management from the office may have conflicting performance objectives or other signs of over-management that will waste management time and energy (and not help the consultant's energy much either). The office administrative people may be performing revenue, utilization, and expense control tasks that fully duplicate those of the project control staff.

You may have the opposite problems. In an office that has been the home of very large projects for some time, the general consulting business may get very little support. Worse, the smaller engagements may be subjected to highly rigorous labor hour recording and project task management that is characteristic of a project, but is overkill for hourly assistance to a client.

The clues you receive to these problems during your first two months of reviewing engagements and meeting people are fuel to the changes you will make by the sixth month. You probably need an organization realignment. The organization you inherit evolved as a preservation of whichever size of engagements came earliest and an accommodation of the other. Whatever is in place fit the role that your predecessor chose to play nurturing one or the other. You need to choose your role and organize the rest of the office accordingly.

Beware of acting precipitously. Your most important role will be to support your project managers. They have the most difficult jobs in your office and, as we will see, your financial success is intimately connected to their engagement success. Until you have personally observed many weeks of activities and decisions to the contrary, you must assume that they are in control and should receive strong sustenance.

You should plan to meet the executives of your key vendors during your second month. It is just one more reason why you need to manage your involvement in marketing during the first two months. You will meet your vendors as their client, and you should expect them to ask you the same questions that you ask your client (Figure 11-2). As a courtesy and to add value in an important relationship to the success of your office, you should be prepared with the answers. Figure 11-3 is a checklist of information you should have received before meeting with a subcontractor firm. Notice that you are acting as a conduit to your managers, rather than assuming a tactical role regarding any existing performance issues. As a client executive, though, you want to demonstrate an understanding of the business between the two firms and your willingness to be open and available to your counterpart.

You should invite all key managers in your office that deal with this vendor (hopefully, no more than two). They should be prepared to offer examples of performance that support positive and negative feedback provided during the meeting. The vendor should see that you, the new client executive, continue to delegate authority to your managers.

The price you pay for assuming responsibility for an office with very large projects (and correspondingly large revenue and profit bonuses for its executive) is that you leap into the advanced arena of professional services financial analysis. The list of controls and information gathering that needs to be assessed during the first two months and fixed during the third and fourth month contains some additional items.

• **Revenue should be segmented** at least by labor and nonlabor, between large project and the aggregate of small engagements. The small engagement revenue should be broken out by groupings that separate profit and growth parameters (consulting versus education).

• **Nonlabor revenue and expense matching** needs to be well controlled using an expense control log and further invoice line item auditing. The relative roles of office administration and project control staff must be balanced to ensure completeness, but to avoid duplication.

• **Backlog analysis should be performed at least bimonthly,** particularly as a large project approaches a major checkpoint. Changes in the estimate of hours needed or payments scheduled in the current year on one large project can greatly affect the revenue coverage for the office. Regular backlog analysis is the best protection against surprises.

• **Revenue, cost, and expense productivity analysis** is needed to ensure that the utilization and pricing assumptions for the office are in balance between the large projects and the aggregate of smaller engagements. In an office where

FIGURE 11-3
Checklist for Meeting with a Subcontractor Executive

Subcontractor Vendor Checklist

•Be able to identify their top performer in each of their rate categories.
–What the individual contributes
–Why the person is a top performer

•Be ready to discuss how many hours of work are remaining and the probability for additional work.

•Be prepared to request follow-up actions to address performance issues.
–Facts that support the concern
–Who represents you on your staff
–When you expect a resolution

•Be prepared to answer these questions.
–How you rate their leadership
–Your view of their top strength
–Your view of their weakness
–Where they can improve

---

one project accounts for 40 percent of the monthly revenue, its gross and net profit per person are dominant factors in office productivity. If they are low (which they often are), the remaining business of the office needs to bring in premium margins to make overall profit objectives. If your staff shows you productivity factor analysis, similar to that illustrated in Chapter 8, you can be comforted that there is good work in place. You will then need to determine whether the pricing assumptions you inherited are adequate to balance the profitability between your large and small engagements.

Believable productivity factors are a combination of a comprehensive labor recording process and locally reported cost and expense data. This means you should see hours recorded for all people, including contractors and your managers. It implies that cost and expense reporting is broken down to your individual office level and at the line item detail described in this book. Your toughest challenge may be to implement data collection and information management practices that have simply never been considered by your predecessors.

• **Engagement profitability measurements** should be in effect for your large engagements. This implies that cost productivity computations are in place as described above and that the projects are computing earned revenue (as you recall this is easy for hourly billed revenue, but is more time consuming and complex for fixed price). On projects of one year or more, a quarterly profitability assessment is sufficient.

You are looking for the relative profitability between your engagements and the weight any one project's profitability has on the overall office. You may have inherited a large project engagement that cannot be profitable and contributes half of the office revenue, while your office is expected to make money. Your job at the end of your first six months will be damage control for the large engagement and a serious confrontation with those who put you in your assignment. Well-developed financial data on both the engagement and the overall office will be essential to resetting the expectation of those above you.

In contrast to someone who starts a new territory, the executive who steps into the large projects office has administrative people in place, who are knowledgeable of the firm's procedures, systems, and practices. They may resist change, so you will need to be patient. You need to avoid diverting their attention from basic business controls. Again, as recommended, you may choose to perform the spreadsheet work to generate productivity data yourself, using information you request from your staff. Your first profitability exercise may be to analyze the affordability of more administrative staff.

Finally, beware of taking over the office's largest engagement. Naming yourself as acting project executive, while recruiting a replacement for one you have chosen to displace, will seem to be a politically correct move. You cannot do both jobs, so you will do at least one badly. Make sure you have a replacement, before you intentionally lose the current one.

"NOW FOR MY FIRST TRICK..."

The purpose of this book was to give the current and future executives of professional services firms a start on the subject of business management. The subject is one that often eludes you in the training and experience that precedes promotion to the executive ranks. Although the bulk of the book has been on processes, measurements, reports, and numbers, there have been three themes that have permeated the book and bear repeating at its end. These are:

- Managing a large professional services office is a great job, be it law, architecture, engineering, consulting, or systems integration. It has all the risk, authority, and empowerment that an entrepreneur could want.

- The least encumbered entrepreneur is one who practices the layers of control illustrated in this book against the levels of diversity and complexity of the business. The secret is enough discipline to have the information that allows you to manage using your instinct.

- Growth is exciting and most of us cannot resist the temptation. Choose growth wisely. Growing without diversity will be slower, but can be very profitable. Growing with diversity will be rapid, but will be profitable only when business management is given its due attention.

Your first office executive assignment will be a high point in your career, regardless of what else you accomplish. It may be the most personal authority you will ever have, short of the top job in a company. You need to approach it with enthusiasm, high energy, and confidence. Once there, you need to exercise patience, common sense, and a willingness to trust your instincts. Above all, you need to retain the two most important attributes that got you there—a willingness to act decisively and an innate sense of humor.

Index